CHRISTIANITY
and
AMERICAN CULTURE TODAY

Essays in Honor of
Richard D. Land

Edited by
Melton B. Winstead

CHRISTIANITY
and
AMERICAN CULTURE TODAY

Essays in Honor of
Richard D. Land

Edited by
Melton B. Winstead

Bennington, VT

Christianity and American Culture Today
Essays in Honor of Richard D. Land
Copyright © 2022 by Melton B. Winstead

Published by Northeastern Baptist Press
      Post Office Box 4600
      Bennington, VT 05201

All rights reserved. No part of this book may be reproduced in any form without prior permission from Northeastern Baptist Press, except as provided for by USA copyright law.

Scripture quotations taken from the New American Standard Bible® (NASB), Copyright © 1960, 1962, 1963, 1968, 1971, 1972, 1973, 1975, 1977, 1995 by The Lockman Foundation. Used by permission. www.Lockman.org.

The Holy Bible, English Standard Version® (ESV®) Copyright © 2001 by Crossway, a publishing ministry of Good News Publishers. All rights reserved.

Scripture quotations marked (NLT) are taken from the Holy Bible, New Living Translation, copyright © 1996, 2004, 2007, 2013, 2015 by Tyndale House Foundation. Used by permission of Tyndale House Publishers, Inc., Carol Stream, Illinois 60188. All rights reserved.

Scripture quotations marked CSB have been taken from the Christian Standard Bible®, Copyright © 2017 by Holman Bible Publishers. Used by permission. Christian Standard Bible® and CSB® are federally registered trademarks of Holman Bible Publishers.

Scripture taken from the New King James Version®. Copyright © 1982 by Thomas Nelson. Used by permission. All rights reserved.

Permission is granted for reprinting: Brown, Michael, *A Stealth Agenda*. The reprint is adapted for inclusion and used by permission in *Christianity and American Culture Today: Essays in Honor of Richard D. Land*. Edited by Melton B. Winstead. Published by Northeastern Baptist Press, 2022.

Cover design by Leason Stiles and Allie August

Hardcover ISBN: 978-1-953331-10-6

To Richard D. Land, as a thank-you for decades of biblical guidance for Baptists and for all Christians and for an example of courageously defending the faith in the public square.

Dr. Richard Land served for a quarter of a century (1988-2013) as President of the Ethics & Religious Liberty Commission (ERLC) of the Southern Baptist Convention. Prior to that he served as Vice-President for Academic Affairs and Professor of Systematic Theology at Criswell College in Dallas, TX. From 2013-2021 Dr. Land served as President of Southern Evangelical Seminary (SES) in Charlotte, NC. Dr. Land was honored with the title President Emeritus by both the ERLC and SES upon his retirement from those institutions.

Dr. Land, a graduate of Princeton University (A.B. magna cum laude), Oxford University (D. Phil.) and New Orleans Baptist Theological Seminary (Th.M.), has pastored or interim pastored 21 Baptist churches and delivered approximately 6,000 sermons since he answered God's call to ministry at age 16. He currently serves as Executive Editor of the Christian Post and hosts a daily weekday radio program called "Bringing Every Thought Captive."

Dr. Land and his wife have been married 51 years. They have 3 children, Jennifer, Richard Jr., and Rachel. Dr. Land is a native Houstonian and 6th generation Texan. The Lands reside in Franklin, TN.

TABLE OF CONTENTS

List of Contributors   i

Introduction   vii

Chapter 1
A Christian's Stewardship Responsibility toward Government   1
Tony Perkins and Kenyn Cureton

Chapter 2
Christians and Public Policy: Why We Engage   23
Barrett Duke

Chapter 3
Citizen Christians Revisited   51
Mark H. Ballard

Chapter 4
Christians' Involvement in Politics/Government   73
J. Gerald Harris

Chapter 5
The Impact of Preaching on the American Revolution   93
Jimmy Draper

Chapter 6
Mammas, Don't Let Your Babies Grow up to be Ethicists, Unless ...   115
Mark Coppenger

Chapter 7
Understanding the Difference Between Religious Liberty   139
and Religious Autonomy
Daniel R. Heimbach

Chapter 8
A Stealth Agenda   161
Michael Brown

Chapter 9
A Life for Life: Dr. Richard Land's Legacy of Defending   197
Pre-Born Persons
Sharayah Colter

Chapter 10
Christian Leadership in The Public Square   225
Janice Shaw Crouse and Gilbert L. Crouse

Chapter 11
An Understanding of Evangelical Christian Support for Israel   253
James Showers and Christopher J. Katulka

Chapter 12
Against the Tide: The Role of Distinctive Identity   277
in the Great Commission
Charles S. (Chuck) Kelley

Chapter 13
A Rudder for a Historian and Ethicist: 299
The Avocation of Evangelist
Paige Patterson

Chapter 14
Social Justice in Light of Scripture   317
Ronnie W. Rogers

Chapter 15
The Relevance of the Bible to   357
21st Century American Christianity
Mel Winstead

List of Contributors

Mark H. Ballard is the Founding President of Northeastern Baptist College, Northeastern Baptist Press, a member of the Steering Council of the Conservative Baptist Network and a past member of the SBC Executive Committee and LifeWay Christian Resources. He has started and pastored churches in Texas, North Carolina, Florida, Virginia, New Hampshire, and New York and regularly speaks at Bible conferences, revivals, and special events around the country. He enjoys the full support of his lifelong partner, friend, and wife Cindy, along with their son Benjamin.

Michael L. Brown is the founder and president of AskDrBrown Ministries and of FIRE School of Ministry, and host of the daily, nationally syndicated talk radio show, *The Line of Fire*. He also hosts TV shows on GOD TV, METV (in Israel and the Middle East), and NRBTV. He became a believer in Jesus in 1971 as a sixteen-year-old, heroin-shooting, LSD-using, Jewish, rock drummer. Since then, he has preached throughout America and around the world, bringing a message of repentance, revival, reformation, and cultural revolution. He holds a Ph.D. in Near Eastern Languages and Literatures from New York University.

Sharayah Colter is a journalist and founder of Colter & Co., a communications firm serving businesses and non-profit clients in the U.S. and abroad. An advocate for pro-life legislation and Christian influence in American public policy, Sharayah serves on the steering council of the Conservative

Contributors

Baptist Network and as editor of Conservative Baptist Network Press. Having worked in newsrooms around the nation and publishing with a wide range of media outlets, Sharayah has experience in in-depth investigative reporting and has covered a broad spectrum of issues and breaking news including presidential elections, the ongoing American border crisis, and biblical theology, among many others. Find Sharayah online at sharayah.org.

Mark Coppenger is Retired Professor of Christian Philosophy and Ethics at Southern Baptist Theological Seminary. Drawing on decades of college and seminary teaching, pastoring, and military service, he continues to write, edit, teach, preach, and speak in a variety of contexts. He and his wife Sharon have done volunteer mission work on five continents and are gratefully engaged with their three children (all involved in some form of ministry) and ten grandchildren.

Janice Shaw Crouse and Gilbert L. Crouse live in the DC area and are involved in cultural issues that affect families —Janice writes/speaks on policy and political issues; Gil writes issue briefs/speaks on data trends. They also speak at universities and national/international conferences. They are parents of two adult children and have 7 grandchildren.

Kenyn Cureton serves as the Vice President for Christian Resources with a mission of equipping Christians to become spiritually active, governance engaged conservatives (i.e., SAGECONS). Previously, Dr. Cureton served as a pastor for twenty years, most recently at First Baptist Church in Lebanon, Tennessee. While there, he authored Lost Episodes in American History, a pilot video curriculum intended to teach citizens about America's Christian heritage. Dr. Cureton also was co-creator of the iVoteValues Voter Impact Toolkit for the SBC, Focus on the Family and Family Research Council, which equips churches to conduct a Christian Citizenship Sunday and a non-partisan voter registration drive. Dr. Cureton holds a bachelor's degree in Religion from Carson Newman College and a Master of Divinity (MDiv) and Doctor of Philosophy (PhD) from Southwestern Baptist Theological Seminary. He has done additional study at the University of Texas at Arlington and completed his doctoral dissertation while at the University of Lund, Sweden. Dr. Cureton and his wife, Pat, have two married children.

Jimmy Draper was a Southern Baptist pastor for 35 years, the son and grandson of Southern Baptist pastors. He and his wife of 65 years reside in Colleyville, TX where he continues to preach and mentor pastors across the country. He is the author of 32 books and has had ministry opportunities in 36 countries around the world.

Barrett Duke is the Executive Director-Treasurer of the Montana Southern Baptist Convention. Prior to serving the Southern Baptist churches of Montana, Dr. Duke spent 20 years at the Ethics & Religious Commission with Dr. Richard Land, serving most of those years in Washington, DC as Vice President for Public Policy and Research and Director of the ERLC's Research Institute. He has spoken and written extensively on public policy issues to help Christians understand the Bible's teachings on the great moral and cultural questions of the day. He and his wife Denise have three grown children and live in Billings, MT where they serve in their local church and travel regularly across the state of Montana to minister to pastors and their wives.

J. Gerald Harris was a pastor for 41 years before becoming the editor of The Christian Index, the Baptist publication for the state of Georgia where he served for almost 16 years. Harris has written five books and currently preaches and writes for Love Lifted Me Higher Ministries (www.loveliftedmehigher.org).

Daniel Heimbach serves on the faculty of Southeastern Baptist Theological Seminary as Senior Research Professor of Christian Ethics. He is a scholar, writer, and social critic who works at the interface between Christian moral witness and secular culture and has written or contributed to over nineteen books and more than sixty articles and reviews. He advised Dr.

Contributors

Land as a research fellow for the SBC Ethics & Religious Liberty Commission and founded the Christian Ethics section of the Evangelical Theological Society.

Chris Katulka is host and Bible teacher for The Friends of Israel Today weekend radio program and assistant director of North American Ministries for The Friends of Israel Gospel Ministry, a worldwide Christian organization headquartered in Deptford, NJ. He recently was the featured teacher in the six-part Common Thread DVD and regularly speaks in churches, at conferences, and at schools. Chris writes the editorial and author's articles for *Israel My Glory* magazine. He earned a ThM from Dallas Theological Seminary.

Chuck Kelley was the 8th President of New Orleans Baptist Theological Seminary, serving from 1996 to 2019. He continues to serve at NOBTS as President Emeritus and Distinguished Research Professor of Evangelism. He is founder and director of Innovative Evangelism as well as an itinerant preacher and evangelist. He has written numerous books including *The Dilemma of Decline: Southern Baptists Face a New Reality*, *Fuel the Fire: Lessons from the History of Southern Baptist Evangelism*, and The Baptist Faith and Message (written with Richard Land and Al Mohler).

Paige Patterson, following forty-two years of presiding over three colleges and seminaries, serves as president of The Sandy Creek Foundation in retirement, traveling and preaching especially in seminaries and Bible schools overseas. He lives with his wife of fifty-eight years, Dorothy, in Parker, TX.

Tony Perkins, who is an ordained minister, remains active in Christian ministries and frequently fills pulpits across the country. He is a board member of Caring to Love Ministries, one of Louisiana's largest pregnancy resource centers. Tony is the immediate past president of the Council for National Policy. An effective communicator, Tony is the host of a daily, nationally syndicated radio show, Washington Watch with Tony Perkins. He frequently appears as a guest on national news programs and talk shows. Tony holds a Bachelor of Science degree from Liberty University, a Master of Public Administration degree from Louisiana State University and was awarded an honorary Doctor of Divinity from Liberty University. He and his wife Lawana have been married since 1986 and have five children.

Ronnie W. Rogers is pastor of Trinity Baptist Church, Norman, Oklahoma. He has a BA in biblical studies and an MS in counseling. He has presented at the Oxford Round Table and authored seven books. He served as president of the Arkansas Baptist State Convention, chairman of the Board of Trustees of Midwestern Baptist Theological Seminary, and chairman of the Nominating Committee of the Southern Baptist Convention. He interacts with current events at www.ronniewrogers.com.

Jim Showers is executive director and president of The Friends of Israel Gospel Ministry, a worldwide Christian organization headquartered in Deptford, NJ. Dr. Showers speaks at conferences, churches, and schools nationwide, is a frequent participant in events supporting Israel, and is a strong advocate of the country's growing Jewish-Christian alliance. Jim authors "Inside View," a regular column featured in The Friends of Israel magazine *Israel My Glory*.

Mel Winstead teaches Biblical Studies at Southern Evangelical Seminary and pastors a small church in Marshville, NC. He and his wife and two daughters reside in Marshville, NC. Winstead's PhD in Biblical Studies is from Southeastern Baptist Theological Seminary. In addition to teaching and pastoral duties, Dr. Winstead speaks at apologetics conferences, leads local summer mission trips, and periodically helps with North Carolina Baptist Men's Disaster Relief (recovery and rebuild).

Introduction

What this book will do for you is inform, equip, and inspire you to a greater understanding of the relevance of biblical Christian faith. The chapters will enlighten you as to the scriptural command and necessity of Christians being involved in the politics of the nation of which they are a part and educate you as to what the hot-button issues are in ethics and morality in America today. Additionally, these pages will equip you to be able to knowledgeably, calmly, and kindly discuss these issues with your friends and coworkers. These chapters will also inspire you to practice discernment (to obey the scriptural command in 1 Thess 5:21 to "examine everything carefully"), concern yourself with the culture at large, and pray for the spiritual health of our neighbors and our nation. Finally, these chapters are here in honor of, and as a thank-you to, Richard D. Land for his dedication as a Christian leader, preacher, and defender of the faith for the last several decades.

Many of the contributors to this volume offered memoirs and accolades to Richard Land at the beginning of their chapter. Some authors applied their knowledge of Dr. Land's expertise in the area in which they wrote. For example, Jim Showers wrote on Evangelical Support of Israel, knowing of Dr. Land's support of Israel and the homeland for the Jews; Sharayah Colter wrote on the pro-life movement, knowing of Land's fight against the horror of abortion in America; Daniel Heimbach wrote on the topic of religious liberty, knowing of Land's fight to preserve that blessing in America; Ronnie Rogers wrote on Critical Race Theory, knowing of Land's lifelong fight against real racism; and Paige Patterson wrote about being a historian, ethicist, politician, and evangelist, realizing Land's enormous contributions in these areas.

The other chapter topics, in no particular order, include: The Crouses' covering Christian leadership which Land has modeled over the years; Mark Coppenger covers Christian ethics; Michael Brown covers the stealth agenda of the homosexual movement; Mel Winstead offers the relevance of the Bible to the topics of abortion, homosexuality, and social justice, knowing Land has worked to right these wrongs for years; Chuck Kelley covers the topic of what it means to be a Southern Baptist, a topic always close to Land's heart; Mark Ballard reviews the book *Citizen Christians* that Land co-edited some years ago and notices its continual relevance; Barrett Duke, Tony Perkins, Jimmy Draper, and Gerald Harris each tackle the issue of Christians and politics, each from a different angle (if I was not previously convinced of the biblical directive for Christians to get involved in the nations they find themselves in, I would definitely be convinced after reading these chapters).

And so, this book is dedicated to Richard D. Land on the occasion of his 75th birthday. Dr. Land currently lives in Tennessee, recently retiring as president of Southern Evangelical Seminary in Charlotte, NC. Dr. Land has led the way in defending and explaining the Bible and its application to Christian values to the public and to public policy for the last several decades.

Richard Land served as the President of the Ethics & Religious Liberty Commission of the Southern Baptist Convention for a quarter of a century (1988-2013). He appeared on *Meet the Press, Face the Nation,* and *The O'Reilly Factor* numerous times, as well as ABC, NBC, CBS, and Fox News in addition to being interviewed by PBS and CNN many times. A prolific author, debater, and preacher, he has deftly applied the truths of the Bible to a myriad of ethical, political, and moral issues of our great nation. His has been a truly prophetic voice in a wasteland of sentimentalism and relativism.

After deciding to honor Dr. Land for his lifelong and unique Christian service, I thought is best to ask for essays from other conservative Christian leaders. Some I had in mind already, some couldn't oblige at the time because of other writing deadlines, and others were recommended to me by Dr. Land's wife, Becky. She heartily helped me by giving me names of people she knew would be a part of the project and by securing the contacts for several of the writers.

Richard Land has helped Christians and Baptists specifically to develop a biblical perspective on the issues covered herein. Hopefully, that task will continue in these pages.

Chapter 1

A Christian's Stewardship Responsibility toward Government

Tony Perkins
Kenyn Cureton

Dr. Land,

In America's decades long cultural conflict, our movement has been blessed to have you as an articulate ally and field general. God gifted you with the mind of a scholar, enabling you to stand toe to toe with any among the intellectual elite in making a compelling case for the biblical worldview. At the same time, God gifted you with the heart of a pastor, enabling you to communicate God's word clearly and powerfully to people in the pews. You have been a favorite as a speaker for our Watchmen network of pastors and as a guest on Washington Watch radio. I count it an honor to lock arms with you in the ongoing battle for the soul of America.

* * *

What is a Christian's stewardship responsibility when it comes to government? That question continues to be the source of intense debate among various faith communities. Yet the Bible provides the answer. God established three institutions: the family, the church, and the civil government. The Apostle Paul states in Rom 13:1: "Let every person be subject to the governing authorities. For there is no authority except from God, and those that exist have been instituted by God."[1] Then Paul enumerates several

---

1   While there may be references to Scripture in this chapter, any actual citations are from the ESV, unless otherwise noted.

responsibilities (vv. 2-7). In his first letter, Peter does the same (2:13-17). Indeed, Jesus Himself speaks of our obligation to civil government (Matt 22:21). Therefore, Christians have a stewardship responsibility regarding the divinely ordained institution of government, which is a part of our biblical worldview as believers.

What is a worldview? A worldview is the "big picture"—the basic set of presuppositions, beliefs, convictions from which we look at and make sense of the world. Think of it like a pair of tinted sunglasses that color how the world looks to you. For example, if you look at the value of human life through biblical glasses tinted with the belief that we are the unique creation of a loving God, you will arrive at one view of abortion. However, if your glasses are tinted with the belief that man simply evolved because of chance, and we are therefore no different than the animals, you may arrive at another view of abortion. Your worldview matters!

What is a biblical worldview? At the core of genuine Christianity is a personal relationship with Jesus as Savior and Lord. What the Lord Jesus expects of His followers is articulated in the Bible. Those biblical teachings should determine the way we see and understand all reality. So, a biblical worldview is a set of presuppositions, beliefs, and convictions defined by Scripture and shaped by our relationship with Christ.

While a bare majority of Americans (51%) claim to have a biblical worldview, unfortunately only 6% of Americans do. This according to a recent national survey of over 2,000 adults conducted by the Cultural Research Center, which is led by George Barna, Senior Research Fellow with Family Research Council's Center for Biblical Worldview.[2] While good news was difficult to find in the survey, here was one bright spot: Among the seven out of ten adults who believe that God does (or might) exist, fully 78% say that God cares "a lot" about what they believe and do in relation to every dimension of society. That finding lines up with biblical truth. In-

---

[2] "American Worldview Inventory 2021 Release #1: America's Dominant Worldview Syncretism," accessed May 26, 2021, https://www.arizonachristian.edu/wp-content/uploads/2021/05/CRC_AWVI2021_Release01_Digital_01_20210413.pdf?bcs-agent-scanner=b27763e2-1804-f644-9301-bbb50f377bce.

deed, Jesus made it abundantly clear that His followers are to influence and impact the entire earth and the whole world.

Influence and Impact as Salt and Light

One of the clearest examples of Jesus commanding His followers to influence the world is in Matt 5:13-16. There Jesus uses two metaphors, parables in miniature that are so basic, so fundamental to life to describe the very essence of what we are to do and to be as His followers in relation to every dimension of society. We are to influence and impact all of it as the "Salt" and the "Light."

Salt

Jesus declared: "You are the salt of the earth, but if salt has lost its taste, how shall its saltiness be restored? It is no longer good for anything except to be thrown out and trampled under people's feet" (Matt 5:13).

Salt is essential to life

Without salt, the fluids in our body could not be kept in proper balance. Consequently, pure salt was a valuable commodity in the ancient world. In the Greek world slaves were bought with salt, and in the Roman world soldiers were paid with salt. We even get our English word "salary" from the Latin *salarium*,[3] meaning salt. If you have ever wondered where the phrase: "He is not worth his salt" came from, now you know. There is an abundance of salt in the world. The oceans contain 1/4 pound of salt for every gallon of water. If that salt were not present, the oceans would become a rotten cesspool. The Greek writer Homer referred to it as "that divine salt," meaning that salt was as essential to maintaining physical life as the divine is for the spiritual life. Salt is essential. When Jesus called us salt

---

3 Walter W. Skeat, *A Concise Etymological Dictionary of the English Language* (New York: Perigee Books, 1980), 460.

(and light), He meant this: "You are indispensable for what I want to do in your world."

Not only is salt indispensable. Its vital function is only performed when it is made available – when it is "sacrificed." Salt does what it does in the dissolving; it does what it does by giving of itself. Only when it is dissolved does it perform its function and make an impact. Salt exercises its influence by the sacrifice of itself. We will make an impact on our community and the culture, on education and government, etc. only to the extent that we make ourselves available and give ourselves to be used of God.

Salt penetrates

Take a pinch of salt, sprinkle it in a glass of water, and it will penetrate and permeate the entire glass. Unfortunately, since many have erected that "wall of separation" between the sacred and the secular, many come to church on Sunday and think that is the end of their responsibility. However, Jesus didn't call us to be the salt of the Sunday School or the salt of the church sanctuary. Jesus called us to be the salt of the earth! As the salt of the earth, we must penetrate and permeate all of it: our neighborhood, our community, our culture, or our society—every human institution and endeavor, including government.

Salt promotes flavor

As salt lends flavor to food, the Christian is to lend flavor to life. From the world's perspective, Christianity takes out all the flavor of life. We do not need to be the bland leading the bland. Jesus was not that way at all. Jesus Himself said, "I came that they may have life and have it abundantly" (John 10:10b). He was so magnetic and winsome that the common people flocked to hear Him. As Jesus brought out the full flavor of life for those around Him, so should we as His disciples in every sphere of society.

Salt preserves

Salt holds in check the corruption and retards the rot. Jesus lived in a day before refrigeration and freezers, so salt was the only element readily available that prevented food from going bad. Salt preserves from contamination, salt delays decay. As followers of Christ, we must therefore act as a preservative influence, to stem the tide of corruption, to stand against impurity, to defeat the decay, to retard the rottenness of this world. That preservative and preventative influence needs to be brought to bear on entertainment, education, business ethics, the media, politics, the arts – in every level and area of life. Jesus is saying in verse 13 that our righteous presence is essential to prevent decay and rottenness in our world. We have much work to do in America!

Salt purifies

Salt has a medicinal quality to it. Yet while it heals, it hurts. Have you ever gotten salt into a cut or wound? It stings and burns, doesn't it? When the truth of God's word is rubbed into the open wounds of a sinful society, a corrupt culture, a government with gangrene, it will sting and hurt before it can heal. The salty prophet Elijah was certainly an irritation to the wicked political leader King Ahab (1 Kings 18:17-18). When we function as salt, our very presence will irritate people who are of the world. Jesus said: "If you belonged to the world, it would love you as its own. As it is, you do not belong to the world, but I have chosen you out of the world. That is why the world hates you" (John 15:18-19). Salt irritates. It burns even as it purifies and brings healing.

Salt also becomes polluted (v 13b)

Did salt ever lose its saltiness? Yes. In the ancient world salt was often collected in an impure state with other chemicals. As it was subjected to moisture or heat, a reaction would take place that would alter the chemical make-up of the salt so that it was no longer salt! It was salt that had "lost its taste." What is Jesus saying? Salt-less salt represents our loss of influence by accommodating to the ways of the world, the corruption of the culture, and the sins of society.

Someone has said: "I looked for the church – and found it in the world. I looked for the world and found it in the church." That's more truth than poetry. However, Jesus said we are to be in the world but not of the world (John 17). We are to penetrate the culture, but not to partake of it. We are to engage the culture, not entertain it. We are to challenge and change the culture, not compromise with it. The judgment Jesus pronounced here is startling. Jesus said: "It is no longer good for anything except to be thrown out and trampled under people's feet." Salt that lost its saltiness was worthless. When salt loses its salinity, it is irreversible. There is no remedy. There is only one recourse: Throw it out!

We spend a fair amount of time casting blame for the moral mess in which we find ourselves in America. Talk radio is a daily torrent of the blame game. Some say: "It's Hollywood and the social media giants promoting ungodly lifestyles." Others say: "It's the LGBTQ activists tag-teaming with educators, promoting their radical agenda." Others say: "It's the abortion advocates and their paid politicians promoting the murdering of innocents." Still others say: "It's the cultural Marxists together with renegade judges disrespecting and even removing our First Amendment freedoms." Others say: "It is the social media giants, spreading lies and propaganda." Certainly, they are all doing their part, but do you know what the biggest problem is in America? Where a large part of the blame lies? As much as any other group, the blame for the moral crisis in America needs to be laid at the feet of salt-less saints. Their salt has lost its savor in a culture that is rotting and a world that is headed for hell!

God help us to take up the challenge Jesus gave us to be salt. Not just the salt of the Sunday School or the salt of the church sanctuary, but the salt of the earth. Salt that penetrates and permeates all areas of life. Salt that preserves society from judgment by retarding the rot of sin. Salt that prophetically irritates and burns but, in the end, brings healing. If there was ever a day, if there was ever a time for us to function as the salt of the earth to make an impact on our world, now is the day, now is the time!

Light

Then Jesus offers the second of this twin illustration of our influence in every dimension of society, including culture and government: "You are the light of the world. A city set on a hill cannot be hidden. Nor do people light a lamp and put it under a basket, but on a stand, and it gives light to all in the house. In the same way, let your light shine before others, so that they may see your good works and give glory to your Father who is in heaven" (Matt 5:14-16).

Light is also the essence of what we are to do and to be as Christ-followers in the world around us. The Bible tells us plainly not only that God is love but also that God is light (1 John 1:5; 4:16). Jesus said of Himself: "I am the light of the world. Whoever follows me will not walk in darkness but will have the light of life." (John 8:12). Light reveals, light exposes, light illumines, light guides, light warms, light penetrates and conquers the darkness.

Light is essential to life

The light of the sun powers the food chain. It is essential to the process of photosynthesis that enables plants to grow which in turn become our food and food for the animals we use for food. Life cannot exist without light. Again, this points out how indispensable our influence is in the world. Scientifically speaking, light is energy, and energy is the ability to do work. When the light of Jesus Christ shines, things begin to happen. Sin is exposed. The way of salvation is revealed. Truth is proclaimed. Life is transformed. Light has a tremendous influence, but there are two areas for further explanation.

Light reveals

John described Jesus as "The true light, which gives light to everyone, was coming into the world" (John 1:9). Jesus is the great revealer of truth because He is Truth (John 14:6). Light brings revelation: sometimes negative (exposing sin), sometimes positive (revealing truth). God's word is a flaming torch of divine revelation. The psalmist said: "Your word is a lamp to my feet and a light to my path" (Ps 119:105).

Yet our generation stumbles in the darkness asking with Pilate: "What is truth?" Our generation is "always learning and never able to arrive at a knowledge of the truth" (2 Tim 3:7), so much so that the vast majority of Americans now believe Satan's lie: "There is no such thing as absolute truth." In other words: "Truth for you may not be truth for me; truth is in the eye of the beholder." Or in the words of the popular meme: "Live your truth" as if each person can define it for themselves. This confusion about truth is nothing new. The church father Augustine wrote:

> Why does truth call forth hatred? Why is Your servant treated as an enemy by those to whom he preaches the truth, if happiness is love, which is simply joy in truth? Simply because truth is loved in such a way that those who love some other thing want it to be the truth, and precisely because they do not wish to be deceived, are unwilling to be convinced that they are deceived. Thus, they hate the truth for the sake of that other thing which they love because they take it for truth. They love the truth when it enlightens them, they hate truth when it accuses them. Because they do not wish to be deceived and do wish to deceive, they love truth when it reveals itself, and hate it when it reveals them.[4]

Chuck Colson brilliantly related the quest for truth back to the Christian worldview:

> Genuine Christianity is a way of seeing and comprehending all reality. It is a worldview. The scriptural basis for this understanding is in the creation account, where God spoke everything into being out of nothing (see Gen 1 and John 1:3). Everything that exists came into being at his command and is therefore subject to him, finding its purpose and meaning in him. The implication is that in every topic we investigate, from ethics to economy, to ecology, the truth is found only in relationship to God and his revelation.... In every area of life, genuine knowledge means discerning the laws and ordinances by which God has structured creation, and then allowing those laws to shape the way we should live. As the church fathers used to say, all truth is God's truth.[5]

---

4   Augustine, *Confessions*, trans. Frank Sheed (Indianapolis: Hackett, 1993), 191.

5   Chuck Colson and Nancy Pearcey, *How Now Shall We Live?* (Wheaton, IL: Tyndale, 1999), 15.

In our day, people need to understand that truth is not what one says it is, truth is not what one thinks it is, truth is what God's word says it is. Jesus prayed to the Father: "Your word is truth." (John 17:17). God's word has the answer to every moral crisis we face as a nation. Do you want to know the truth about abortion? The Bible says that God hates the shedding of innocent blood (Prov 6:17). Do you want to know the truth about LGBTQ behavior? The Bible says it is among the list of sins under the judgment of God (Lev 18:22; Rom 1:18-32). Do you want to know the truth about why our education system is failing and why we have kids killing kids and babies having babies? We've kicked the Light of the world out of the classroom. Ps 119:130 says: "The unfolding of your words gives light!" We must become defenders and revealers of the truth. We are to be that light that shines on the path that leads up and out of the darkness and the deception of sin.

Light overcomes

John 1:5 speaks of Christ and says: "The light shineth in the darkness, and the darkness comprehended it not" (KJV). Some understood the light, and some did not. Why? Choice. However, the KJV does not completely do John 1:5 justice. A better rendering is "The light shines in the darkness, and the darkness has not overcome it" (ESV). The NLT has "could not extinguish it." The darkness could not put it out. All the darkness of this world and of hell itself could not and cannot put out the light of Jesus Christ!

You are the light

Being light is our responsibility as Christ-followers. Jesus said: "I am the light of the world" (John 8:12), and then He passed the torch to the Church and said: "You are the light of the world" (Matt 5:14-16). It is a fundamental principle that we must impact our world as Jesus did and be lights in the darkness. Translated from the original text, v 14 reads: "You and you alone are the light of the world." God instructs us to shine His light in this sin darkened world. We can't pass the buck. It is our exclusive responsibility. If we don't shine, who is going to? It is our duty, our privilege, our exclusive responsibility.

It is also an inclusive responsibility. This verse can read: "You, all of you, are the light of the world." There are no pinch hitters, no hired guns in the kingdom of God. Nobody can do it for you. You, every one of you, are the light of the world. I have a sphere of influence you could never have. You have a sphere of influence that I could never have. So, the responsibility to reach people living in and practicing darkness rests squarely upon each of us and all of us. Now we realize this may be intimidating, but God gives all of us certain talents and abilities according to His divine purpose for our lives. You may not have the passion of a Luther, the brilliance of a Calvin, the eloquence of a Spurgeon, the faith of a Mueller, the zeal of a Moody, or the renown of a Billy Graham – but you can shine where God has placed you. While our abilities and circumstances may all be different, as Jesus communicated in the parable of the minas in Luke 19, we've all been given the same opportunity to faithfully serve.

One might say, "Well I'm not much, I can't speak well, I can't sing, I don't have a lot of money, I'm not all that smart or gifted." It does not matter – just let your light shine! Remember, it is not your light, it is His light anyway! God has calibrated your watts. So, whether you are a candle glowing softly in a home or a laser beam that can cut the gates of Hell off at the hinge, turn on the light! He has given you unique talents and abilities that He expects for you to use to bring Him glory.

Several years ago, Chuck Colson told a story about Ron Greer, an ex-offender who once hated all white people, but was radically saved and is now a pastor in Madison, Wisconsin:

> Greer was dismissed from his regular job at a fire department for passing out Christian tracts describing homosexuality as a sin. Madison's homosexual activists were enraged and stormed into Greer's church, disrupting the service, throwing condoms at the altar, and shouting obscenities. Ron Greer responded by graciously inviting them to join in the worship service. Later, when the press asked how he had kept his cool, he smiled and said: "I have no more reason to be angry with them than I would with a blind man who stepped on my foot." Precisely. Most of those who object to Christianity are simply spiritually blind and our job is to lovingly bring them into the light.[6]

---

6   Colson and Pearcey, *How Now Shall We Live?*, 32-33.

A Christian's Stewardship Responsibility toward Government

Light of the world

Don't miss *where* Jesus wants us to make an impact as light. It is the world. One of our greatest obstacles in the contemporary church is that the greatest concentration of salt and light is in the church building from nine until noon on Sunday morning. I say again, Jesus didn't call us to be the salt of the Sunday School and the light of the church, but the salt of the earth and the light of the world. The "world" means out in the businesses, the classrooms, the halls of government, the school boards, the neighborhoods, and communities—that is where we retard the rot and dispel the darkness. So, we need to understand that the church is not primarily the place of ministry, it is the base of ministry.

Even as Jesus spoke these words, 100 miles to the south near the Dead Sea was the Qumran Community, which produced the Dead Sea Scrolls that were discovered back in 1948. The Qumran Community was made up of men and women who had left Jerusalem and retreated to the desert near the Dead Sea. They said: "We're going to save Jerusalem by getting out of Jerusalem and starting a commune out here in the desert." One of their teachers even wrote a book called the "Sons of Light" about a battle between the sons of light and the sons of darkness.[7] Jesus may well have had these folks in the back of His mind when He spoke these words, for you see it is not by removing ourselves from the world that we can retard the rot and dispel the darkness—it is the very opposite. Our Lord said: "You are to go back to the very world I called you out of and there you are to be salt and light."

Certainly, these are dark days in America. The Bible says that "men loved the darkness instead of light because their deeds were evil" (John 3:19). The forces of darkness have succeeded in bringing down the light of truth and reason found in God's word and have plunged our nation into a moral gloom. Arnold J. Toynbee, in his multi-volume *Study of History*, concluded that the average civilization was 200 years old when it collapsed. He clearly demonstrated that out of the previous 21 civilizations that 19 of them were destroyed from within – by atheism, anarchy, materialism, socialism, immorality, etc. America is nearly 250 years old, and it may be that the

---

7   Theodor H. Gaster, ed., *The Dead Sea Scriptures in English Translation with Introduction and Notes* (New York: Anchor Press, 1976), 399-423.

closing chapters of this once great nation are being written today because they are being dominated by the prince of darkness and because there is an appalling absence of light. The sun seems to be setting on America.

Unfortunately, many Christians are getting used to the dark. There is a slow, subtle, sinister brainwashing process going on whereby we are gradually being desensitized to the dimming conditions of our culture. Little by little, sin has been made to appear less sinful. No more black and white, just a dingy shade of gray.

There can be no fellowship between light and darkness. There can be no agreement between good and evil. When the world wants you to "Coexist" as the bumper sticker suggests, what they want you to do is crucify your conscience and compromise with evil. In this dark day, it is time to take a stand. Stop cursing the darkness and turn on the light! Stop whining and start shining!

Light is not to be hidden

We are to impact our world like light, but too many Christians suffer from *photophobia* – they are afraid to shine. They are so fearful of being offensive that they are no longer effective in making an impact in the culture and on our government. So, they would rather grieve the Holy Spirit than grieve the godless. In fact, many have chosen to become "Undercover Christians" and "Secret Saints." Yet Jesus did not allow that option, commanding: "What I tell you in the dark, say in the light, and what you hear whispered, proclaim on the housetops" (Matt 10:27). Indeed, notice His similar statement in Matt 5:15: "Nor do people light a lamp and put it under a basket, but on a stand, and it gives light to all in the house."

Palestinian houses usually had only one window, about 18 inches square, if it had one at all. The lamp was a clay boat filled with oil with a floating wick, usually held up by a branch. The bowl spoken of here is an earthenware grain measure. The point is simple: You would not light a lamp just to put it under a clay jar – you don't obscure the light if you want to see. That is silly, it is absurd, it is senseless. Neither does it make sense to say in your heart: "I belong to Jesus, the Light of the world, and I know He wants me to be a light in my world," and then to deny it by your words and deeds. When we were saved, we were saved to shine! Christ loved us so much that He was unashamed to die naked and nailed to a cross before a mocking world. He didn't keep His love for us a secret. He let it shine for all the world to see.

We are not to keep our love for Him a secret. Jesus said: "Whoever acknowledges me before men, I will also acknowledge him before my Father. But whoever disowns me before men, I will disown him before my Father in heaven" (Matt 10:32-33). Do people know that you are a follower of Christ or are you hiding your light under a bowl? He wasn't ashamed to die for us; can we continue to be ashamed to live for Him? No. Let your light shine!

Back in verse 14, He says: "A city set on a hill cannot be hidden." What we are and who we are is ultimately self-evident. It is an eternal principle that the essence of what and who we are will eventually come out. It has been said that "What you are screams so loudly that I cannot hear what you say." Our Lord seated on a hill overlooking the Sea of Galilee probably pointed over at the hilltop city of Safed that had a beautiful, white-washed wall that was visible for miles around. And the point He's making is this: "If you are light, you will shine." So don't cower in the darkness – turn on the light!

How do we turn on the light?

In Matt 5:16, the text literally reads, "Let your light shine in their very faces." Now this is not talking about a kind of Academy Award religion, putting on a show to be seen of men. That is not what Jesus had in mind. Notice He says: "Let your light shine." That involves surrender. Let it happen. When you get right with God by repentance and faith in Jesus Christ, and when Jesus becomes your Lord, and when you are filled with the controlling influence of the Holy Spirit, you don't have to make yourself shine, you will shine. You don't have to force it, fake it, or manufacture it, just let it happen. If you force it, it will cause a glare and not a glow. Be like Moses who went up on the mountain and met with God, day after day. So much so that the glory of God was reflected in his face, and when he came down the people were terrified. However, he was oblivious to the shine (Ex 34:29). He didn't force it, fake it, or manufacture it. He just let it happen. Spend time with the eternal Light and you will shine too.

Then notice in verse 16: "Let your light shine...so that they may see your good works and give glory to your Father who is in heaven. The word translated as "good" means winsome, attractive, deeds of such pristine moral and spiritual beauty that all who see them will be compelled to give glory to God. I think our Lord had the kind of life He described in the Beatitudes. The kind of life He described in the rest of the Sermon on the Mount. The kind of life He Himself lived. It was a life of winsome, attractive, beautiful deeds that compelled people to give glory to God. They were drawn to the Light.

Turning on the light in our world requires a similar approach. We need to be able to communicate biblical truth in terms that the secular person can understand. We need to get a handle on the spiritual beliefs or lack thereof and show how God's word provides a superior worldview and way of life. And as much as we enjoy Christian fellowship, we cannot win the lost until we get out among them. We need to form intentional relationships with unbelievers for the purpose of bringing them to Jesus Christ. Do you know some people who are unsaved or unchurched? Love them enough to pray for them, invite them to dinner, take them a dessert, drive them to the doctor, keep their kids, pick up their mail, mow their lawn when they are on vacation, etc. Then strike up a conversation about spiritual matters and let your light shine! Jesus rubbed shoulders with sinners, and we need to do the same because He is our example in these matters. He was a beacon of light to those who were stumbling in darkness and now He has passed the torch to you. You are the light of your workplace, your classroom, your neighborhood, your city council, your state and national government. You are the light of this world.

Again, light doesn't stop at the doors of our home. It shines brightly in the neighborhood. Light doesn't stop at the doors of education. It shines brightly at school board meetings. Light doesn't stop at the doors of the city municipal building. It shines brightly at the city council meetings. Light doesn't stop at the doors of the state or U.S. Capitol buildings. It shines brightly in the offices of elected officials and in the halls of government. We can't simply sit in our holy huddles and curse the darkness. We must turn on the light! We must stop whining and start shining! Let your light so shine before others so that they see your good works and praise your Father in Heaven until the light of the glory of the Lord covers the earth as the waters cover the sea!

Salt and Light—Together

Christians must function both as salt and light if we would exert the influence and make the impact Jesus intended. Dr. Richard Land offers a brilliant summary of how and why salt and light must work together:

> The idea that there are two Gospels, a social Gospel and a spiritual Gospel, was hatched in the pits of hell. There is only one Gospel, and it is a whole Gospel for whole people. It is a denial of the Gospel for Christians to seek to feed the hungry and not tell people about the bread of life. It is a denial of the Gospel to seek to house the homeless and not tell them that in our father's house are many mansions. It dishonors the incarnation of our Savior to talk about the bread of life and heaven and be insensitive to the fact that our hearers are hungry and homeless and thirsty. Jesus has commanded Christians to be both salt and light. Salt is defensive in that it stops the decay and the degradation. Light is offensive: it dispels the darkness and illuminates the path. There are limitations to what the law can do. You can't legislate revival or reformation. However, if revival and reformation occur, they will be reflected in legislation and society's values. The salt of the law can change actions, but it's only the light of the Gospel that can change attitudes. The salt of the law can change behaviors, but only the light of the Gospel can change beliefs. The salt of the law can change habits, but only the light of the Gospel can change hearts.
>
> Here is the way it's supposed to work. We as Christians share our faith and, when people come to know Jesus as Savior, their worldviews should change. When those with biblically informed worldviews reach critical mass, they then can begin to influence legislation. That's not called a theocracy, that's called the demo-

cratic process. It's the way slavery was eventually abolished. It's the way racial segregation was banished from the law. And it's the way Christians can restore once again to America a biblically based legal system that protects all human life from conception to natural death and everywhere in between.[8]

Being salt and light is not an "either/or" but a "both/and" proposition. If we exercise our influence in the proper balance, we can have enormous influence and make a tremendous impact for the kingdom of God.

Christian Citizenship

We have examined our impact as salt and light, but are there some specific responsibilities that Christians have as citizens of America? Jesus Himself gave us guidance. In Matt 22:15-21, the religious leaders were trying to trap Jesus on the issue of paying taxes, but Jesus turned the tables on them. He asked them for a coin, and then asked whose portrait and inscription was stamped on it. They replied: "Caesar's." Jesus responded: "Give to Caesar what is Caesar's and to God what is God's" (v. 21). His point? All citizens—including His followers—are obligated to support their government. As a matter of fact, He had even sent Peter fishing to hook the one fish that had the very coin in its mouth to pay the tax for Peter and Himself (Matt 17:24-27)!

Obviously, we are not citizens living under a Roman regime, yet the principles of stewardship and obligation apply. Americans are blessed to have, as Abraham Lincoln put it, a "government of the people, by the people, and for the people."[9] Ever noticed that the original parchment of the Constitution begins "We the People" in big, bold letters? Our form of government requires

---

8 Richard Land, *For Faith & Family* (Nashville: B&H Publishing, 2002), 195-196.

9 Abraham Lincoln, "Address at Gettysburg," delivered on November 19, 1863, as found in *The Collected Works of Abraham Lincoln,* edited by Roy P. Basler (Rutgers University Press, 1953), 7:22.

A Christian's Stewardship Responsibility toward Government

our active involvement. In fact, Maryland delegate James McHenry tells of an encounter Ben Franklin had with a Mrs. Powell, as the Constitutional Convention ended in 1787. "Well Doctor what have we got, a Republic or a monarchy?" she asked the oldest of the Founding Fathers. You can almost see the twinkle in his eye, as he peered over his spectacles and quipped: "A Republic, if you can keep it."[10] Wise old Ben Franklin knew that Republics were not easy to keep. Consequently, our Republic was designed for participants not spectators.

How can we "give to Caesar what is Caesar's" and fulfill our stewardship responsibility as Christians who are citizens in America today? There are numerous applications, but we will focus on a few things that every Christian ought to give our government. Here are some specific responsibilities:

Prayer

Paul instructed: "First of all, then, I urge that supplications, prayers, intercessions, and thanksgivings be made for all people, for kings and all who are in high positions, that we may lead a peaceful and quiet life, godly and dignified in every way. This is good, and it is pleasing in the sight of God our Savior, who desires all people to be saved and to come to the knowledge of the truth." (1Tim 2:1-4). We are to pray for our president, our congressmen, our judges, our governors, our mayors, our councilmen, our law enforcement officials, etc.—for all who have a place of authority. We don't pray that they would continue in their wickedness, but we do pray that God would give them wisdom—the wisdom to lead our nation according to Judeo-Christian principles rooted in biblical authority. Above all we pray that they would come to Christ, become His followers, and be saved (v 4). It is only through a relationship with Jesus as Lord that they will lead in such a way that we as believers can live "peaceful and quiet lives in all godliness and holiness" (v 2).

---

10 Max Farrand, ed., *The Records of the Federal Convention of 1787*, 3 vols., (New Haven, CT: Yale University Press, 1911), 3:85.

Respect

Peter instructed: "Be subject for the Lord's sake to every human institution, whether it be to the emperor as supreme, or to governors as sent by him to punish those who do evil and to praise those who do good. For this is the will of God, that by doing good you should put to silence the ignorance of foolish people. Live as people who are free, not using your freedom as a cover-up for evil, but living as servants of God. Honor everyone. Love the brotherhood. Fear God. Honor the emperor." (1 Peter 2:13-17). The Greek word for "submit" means to fall in rank under an authority. Government exists to keep order, and we must submit to the rule of law. Peter says that the authorities are commissioned to punish wrongdoers and commend the do-gooders (v 14; cf. Rom 13:2-5). Then Peter says that we are to show these authorities honor or respect (v 17).

Sometimes respecting our government is a challenging task. However, if we think it is bad in our day, just think about who was in charge when Peter wrote this: Nero. Ever noticed that we name our sons Peter but our dogs Nero? Nero wasn't exactly an altar boy. In fact, Nero was a brutal, wicked ruler who was likely responsible for the deaths of both Peter and Paul. Yet, God's word says that we are to respect the governmental authority, for if we rebel against it, we are in fact rebelling against the God who ordained it (Rom 13:1-2). We may not have much respect for the man of the office, but we must respect the office of the man.

Protest

The right to peacefully protest is enshrined in the Bill of Rights: "The right of the people peaceably to assemble, and to petition the government for a redress of grievances." When the government commands what God condemns, *then* we are obligated to disobey. For example, when Pharaoh commanded that all the male Hebrew babies were to be put to death at the moment of birth, the midwives responded with civil disobedience, and God blessed them for it (Ex 2:15-21). When the King Darius made a law against praying to anyone but himself, Daniel responded with civil disobedience, and God blessed him by delivering him from the lions (Dan 6:1-23). When the Christians in Asia Minor were commanded to burn a pinch of incense and swear: "Caesar is Lord," they refused, threw their incense to the ground in defiance and declared: Christ is Lord!" Jesus commended them for their civil disobedience (Rev 2:8-10; 2:13). Finally, the same Peter who wrote that we should submit to the government's authority and respect the king is the same Peter who boldly told the religious rulers of his day who ordered him to stop preaching Jesus: "We must obey God rather than men" (Acts 5:29).

Consequently, there is a time for peaceful protest and even civil disobedience. However, the latter should come only as a last resort, after all other solutions have been tried and all other avenues exhausted, especially in America, which was founded upon Judeo-Christian principles and biblical laws. However, if the government commands what God condemns, then we are obligated to disobey.

Payment of Taxes

Paul spoke of the government's responsibility to punish evildoers and instructed: "This is why you pay taxes, for the authorities are God's servants, who give their full time to governing" (Rom 13:6). Be honest. This one hurts, especially when tax time arrives. However, when Jesus was asked about paying taxes, He commanded that we are to give to Caesar what is Caesar's" (Matt 22:21), and He also led by example (Matt 17:24-27).

Admittedly, there is a lot of waste and questionable spending, especially by the current regime in Washington. Like the Titanic, we have hit an iceberg, we are taking on water, we are still afloat, so some people are still having fun throwing snowballs on the deck, but we are about to drown under a sea of debt and rising taxes unless drastic measures are taken, and the first one is to stop the spending and borrowing against our children's future. The Bible says: "Let no debt remain outstanding…" (Rom 13:8), but we are amassing debt at an unsustainable rate.

Now we know what you are thinking, you've complained but the politicians aren't listening, they don't care, and they are going to do it anyway. But the great thing about America is that if our elected leaders won't change their political and policy positions to line up with the constitution, then we, the people, can change their geographical positions by voting them out of office and sending them home.

Participation

In America, we have a representative form of government, but we are a part of it. Again, this form of government is intended as a "government of the people, by the people, and for the people." Therefore, if we do not actively participate, then we are not fulfilling the totality of Jesus' command to "render to Caesar" (Matt 22:21). God expects us to get involved. After all, if Christians retreat from this arena, then we have allowed Satan to prevail in the very place where Jesus commanded us to make an impact as salt and light.

There are many ways we can participate in our government, such as helping with a voter registration drive, commenting on legislation and public policy, speaking out on moral and social issues on social media, holding public office, volunteering for the election commission, etc. Perhaps the most basic form of participation is voting—selecting our government. Exodus 18:21 says: "But *select* capable men from all the people—men who fear God, trustworthy men who hate dishonest gain—and appoint them as officials . . . ."

Voting is a simple act with a significant impact. When we vote, we help determine who will lead our nation, make our laws, and protect our freedoms. Founding father Samuel Adams said: "Let each citizen remember at the moment he is offering his vote ... that he is executing one of the most solemn trusts in human society for which he is accountable to God and his country."[11] Here are three practical actions steps on voting:

Register to Vote

Telling citizens of a democracy to register to vote should go without saying, but one can't vote unless he or she is registered. And there are still many eligible Americans who are not even registered to vote. Some might

---

[11] Harry Alonzo Cushing, ed. *The Writings of Samuel Adams* (New York: G.P. Putnam's Sons, 1907), 4:256 (originally in the *Boston Gazette* on April 16, 1781).

A Christian's Stewardship Responsibility toward Government

say: "What's the difference, my one vote doesn't really count." Yes, it does! There are numerous examples where a handful of votes or even one vote made the difference. First you need to register, and it is so easy to do. Step one: Register to Vote.

Register a Friend

Take your friend a Voter Registration Form and help them fill it out and send it in. Point your friends to our FRCAction.org website to start the process. There they can fill out their form online, print it, and mail it in or take it to their election commission office. Help organize a Voter Registration Drive at your church, your school, place of business, etc. – just be sure to get permission. Step Two: Register a Friend.

Vote Your Biblical Values

Make the commitment to vote in the upcoming primary and in the general election. Here is an old proverb that is still true today: "Bad politicians are elected by good people who don't vote." Indeed Prov 29:2 declares: "When the godly are in authority, the people rejoice. But when the wicked are in power, they groan." And if we don't vote, we have no right to groan. So, voter apathy is indefensible, especially among Christians, who have been commanded by Christ to penetrate and influence our culture as salt and light (Matt 5:13-16) and participate in government as engaged citizens (Matt 22:21). So, Christians must vote!

Voting is a vital part of our stewardship responsibility. Yet voting for voting's sake is not enough. We need to take it one step further and *vote our biblical values*. Think about this: Every candidate has his or her own set of values and positions on important issues, issues to which the Bible has principles that have specific application for believers. It is critical that we discover where a candidate stands on the issues and how their values line up with biblical principles. Shouldn't we vote for candidates who share our values? John Jay, our nation's first Supreme Court chief justice and one of the three authors of the Federalist Papers explaining our U.S. Constitution, said: "Providence has given to our people the choice of their rulers, and it is the duty, as well as the privilege and interest of our Christian nation . . . to select and prefer Christians for their rulers."[12]

Unfortunately, many Christians don't even consider biblical values when voting, often choosing candidates whose positions on moral issues are at odds with their own beliefs, convictions, and values, not to mention biblical principles. That's tragic because remember the Lord Jesus expects us to influence and impact, to permeate and penetrate "the earth" and "the world" as the salt and light, which would necessarily include the democratic process. We need to become informed on the issues, study the party platform statements, know what the candidates stand for and how they vote on issues we care about, read what they say about the issues, check out their websites, find out who are their enemies and who are their friends, then weigh the candidates' values against biblical values, and prayerfully consider voting for the ones who are the best match. The closer we get to election time, FRCAction.org will be a great place to start.

One caution: Don't align yourself too closely with a political party or a politician. That is unwise because we need to be free to call all political parties and politicians to repentance when they step outside of biblical morality and principle. Founding father Benjamin Rush is quoted as saying: "I have been alternately called an Aristocrat and a Democrat. I am neither. I am a Christocrat."[13] As Dr. Richard Land often says: "Our loyalty needs to be first, last, and always with the Lord Jesus Christ." So, look for statesmen to support, not mere politicians. Politicians think about the next election; statesmen think about the next generation. Strongly consider voting for candidates who most closely align with biblical principles, who believe like you do. Don't just vote to be voting—vote your biblical values!

Imagine the impact Christians could have on the direction of our government, the character of its leadership, and the moral health of our nation if we simply applied our biblical worldview and biblical principles to every aspect of our lives—including our participation in government. Under God, we could literally see America transformed. May God make it so!

---

12 Henry P. Johnston, ed., *The Correspondence and Public Papers of John Jay* (New York: G.P. Putnam's Sons, 1890), 4:365.

13 David Ramsay, *An Eulogium upon Benjamin Rush, M.D.* (Philadelphia: Bradford and Inskeep, 1813), 103.

Chapter 2

Christians and Public Policy: Why We Engage

Barrett Duke

I first met Dr. Land in 1978 when I was a student at the Criswell Center for Biblical Studies in Dallas, TX. At that point, I had only been a Christian for about two years. Learning Systematic Theology and Christian Ethics from Dr. Land was my first real exposure to the intellectual side of evangelical Christianity. To my delight, I discovered that it was quite robust. Being tested on everything, including the footnotes in my assigned textbooks, was challenging, but it helped equip me for the next 40+ years of ministry. I can say without hesitation that my years of study with Dr. Land are largely responsible for the opportunities I have had since then to serve the Lord and Southern Baptists. I couldn't have written the chapter I provided for this volume if it hadn't been for Richard Land's years of faithful tutelage, friendship, and trust.

Richard and I served side-by-side at the Christian Life Commission, now the ERLC, for nearly twenty years. I have developed a deep respect and appreciation for his intellect, his courage, his heart, and his joyful optimism in the Lord. I'm grateful that he poured so much of his life into me and worked with me as a colleague for all those years. We don't have another Richard Land on the horizon. I thank the Lord for him and look forward to his continued service to the Lord's people. I am sure there is more to come, and it will be good. God bless you, my friend.

★ ★ ★

So, you take a frog and put him in a pot of water and then slowly turn up the heat. According to legend, you can boil the frog without him even knowing what is going on. It's remarkable that you can do this. At least in the frog's case, he has an excuse. God made him the way he is. His body takes on the temperature of his surroundings. There's nothing he can do about it. But if you take that same frog (before you boil him of course) and drop him in a pot of scalding water, he is aware enough to know that's not good for him, and he'll try to jump out. Even a frog knows he's in hot water when he's dropped in it.

George Barna used the frog in hot water imagery as a metaphor to illustrate the current threat of American culture to the church. In his 1990 book *The Frog in the Kettle*,[1] he described the ways in which the church was endangered by incremental changes in culture that could lead to its increasing lack of relevance and effectiveness. He warned that the church was being slowly cooked and needed to wake up to what was happening.

To some degree, no pun intended, Christians have probably always been like frogs in the kettle. The kettle is human culture. We swim around in that culture like everyone else. At times, the culture gets the best of us. We all know of Christians and churches that have succumbed to popular culture or that have remained so stuck in the past that they cannot even relate to the current culture. In both cases, the church is no longer able to bring God's worldview into the present culture effectively.

For decades, Christian ethicists have used the five-fold model developed by H. Richard Niebuhr to describe the different ways people relate to culture. In his 1951 book *Christ and Culture*, Niebuhr described the positions Christians take relative to culture. He named those positions: Christ against Culture, Christ of Culture, Christ above Culture, Christ and Culture in Paradox, and Christ the Transformer of Culture.[2] Niebuhr sought to explain these various attitudes of Christians toward culture by appealing to Bible passages that support them. He even named significant Christians in history who have represented them. While somewhat simplistic in its characterizations of Christian attitudes to culture, his work remains helpful because it gives Christians an opportunity to reflect on how we each relate our Christian faith to culture.

---

[1] George Barna, *The Frog in the Kettle: What Christians Need to Know about Life in the Year 2000* (Ventura, CA: Regal Books, 1990).

[2] H. Richard Niebuhr, *Christ and Culture* (San Francisco: Harper & Row Publishers, 1951). See pages 39-44 for a succinct explanation of the unique characteristics Niebuhr associates with the five types.

Christians and Public Policy: Why We Engage

A little more than a decade ago, D. A. Carson provided a needed critique of Niebuhr's approach. In his work *Christ and Culture Revisited* he says, "choosing one of Niebuhr's models is an exercise in reductionism."[3] He spends much of his time discrediting Niebuhr's categories by appealing to biblical passages the categories don't take into consideration. Carson wants his readers to understand that the Bible's guidance on life in this world is a much more complex thing than Niebuhr's categories suggest. To be fair to Niebuhr, he was not unaware of the problem posed by his method. In several places, he also briefly discussed the problems inherent in some of the categories he pushed people into. He even agreed with Carson that "no one person or group ever conforms completely to a type."[4]

This is an important corrective. Very few people, if any, fit neatly into any of Niebuhr's categories. There are points at which almost all of us step outside of our box and into one of the others. It is true that Christianity can be countercultural, but it isn't as though we operate completely in a bubble, either. We are part of human culture. We enjoy some aspects while we are repulsed by others. So, for example, sometimes we take the Christ against Culture stance, as in our opposition to abortion on demand. While, at other times, we sound like the Christ of Culture adherents when we often uncritically embrace popular fashion trends.[5]

---

3 D. A. Carson, *Christ and Culture Revisited* (Grand Rapids, MI: William B. Eerdmans Publishing Company, 2008), 145.

4 Niebuhr, *Christ and Culture,* 43-44. Craig Carter has reacted more strongly against Niebuhr's typology. He rejects Niebuhr's approach because it presupposes that Christendom is the norm behind any Christian attitude toward culture. He accuses Niebuhr of creating a "false dichotomy" between accepting Christendom or being out of step with it in some way (Craig Carter, *Rethinking Christ and Culture: A Post Christendom Perspective* (Grand Rapids, MI: Brazos Press, 2006), 25). Carter is right that Niebuhr viewed Christianity and the world through a different lens than exists today, but in his effort to create a new taxonomy of Christian attitudes to culture, he falls into the same trap. Only his trap is to divide people into groups of pacifists and non-pacifists. In the end, no one fits into his types completely any more than they fit comfortably into Niebuhr's.

5 I use a sports example to try to help people understand the differences between Niebuhr's types. The Christ against Culture person: I love God, and I

No matter how comfortable we might feel in this world, we must remember that this isn't our home. In fact, this environment is always going to be somewhat hostile to us. Jesus told His disciples that He was sending them out like sheep among wolves. He warned them that the world would hate them because they represented God's judgment on the world for its sin (Matt 24:9).[6] And we have the added problem that we have a spiritual enemy who seeks to destroy us as well (1 Pet 5:8). And he will use every means at his disposal to accomplish that.

We can't allow ourselves to get too comfortable here, but we can't just shut ourselves off from the world, either. The same Jesus who said the world would hate us also called us the salt of the earth and the light of the world (Matt 5:13-16) and told us to love our neighbors as ourselves (Matt 22:39). These passages hardly suppose that Jesus believed that human culture was beyond help. It sounds much more like a transforming relationship.

Clearly, there are different ways to think about our relationship to culture and what we think the Lord wants to accomplish here through His church. Niebuhr's types help us, at the very least, to reflect on how we each initially think about our place in this world. Most of us probably do have a consistent, initial, knee-jerk, first-blush response to things we encounter in the culture. Is our primary inclination to our surroundings one of opposition, indifference, acceptance, or something else? If we can do that much self-reflection, it can help us begin to see ourselves as separate from culture and yet at the same time part of it. Once we've done that, we can begin to think about our role here. Stott wrestled with the extremes in evangelical-

---

think the New York Yankees are the worst thing that ever happened to Major League baseball. The Christ of Culture person: I love God, and I think the New York Yankees are the best thing that ever happened to baseball. The Christ above Culture person: I love God, and the New York Yankees are fun to watch. The Christ and Culture in Paradox person: I love God, and it's a shame that the New York Yankees treat the rest of Major League baseball like its own personal farm team. The Christ the Transformer of Culture person: I love God, and I'm going to do what I can to stop the New York Yankees from using the rest of the MLB as its own personal farm team.

6   While there may be references to Scripture in this chapter, any actual citations are from the NASB, unless otherwise noted.

ism that sought either to remake all human culture or give up on it as a lost cause. The balance is found in 1 Thess 1:9-10. Stott focused on the two words "working" and "waiting" in that passage and concluded: "The need to wait for Christ from heaven will rescue us from the presumption which thinks we can do everything; the need to work for Christ on earth will rescue us from the pessimism which thinks we can do nothing."[7]

As I think about the Christian's role in culture, the starting point for me is Matt 5:13-16. This passage reveals the complexity of living in culture that Carson attempts to get at in his book. In this passage, Jesus calls His disciples "the salt of the earth" and "the light of the world." While we certainly can interpret these metaphors spiritually and associate them with our call to change people's lives through evangelism, Jesus' use of the word "world" preserved for us in the Greek as *kosmos* tells us He had more in mind. I. Howard Marshall notes that the Greek word *kosmos* used in this passage doesn't refer simply to the created universe inhabited by man. He says, "it is much more human society itself as it stands over against God."[8] In other words, Marshall understands that Jesus is calling His disciples, the church, to be the light of fallen human culture. Understood this way, we can see that God intends Christians to engage human culture as salt and light. Matthew 5:13-16 compels me to understand that Christ expects His people to be both positive and negative agents toward human culture, depending on the issue. Sometimes, we preserve. Other times, we expose. The Southern Baptist Convention's statement of faith, the *Baptist Faith & Message*, shares this understanding. Its section "The Christian and the Social Order" states:

> All Christians are under obligation to seek to make the will of Christ supreme in our own lives and in human society. Means and methods used for the improvement of society and the establishment of righteousness among men can be truly and permanently helpful only

---

7   John Stott, *Decisive Issues Facing Christians Today* (Old Tappan, NJ: Fleming H. Revell Company, 1990), 43.

8   I. Howard Marshall, "Culture in the New Testament," in *Gospel and Culture*, eds. John Stott and Robert Coote (Pasadena, CA: William Carey Library, 1979), 39.

when they are rooted in the regeneration of the individual by the saving grace of God in Jesus Christ. In the spirit of Christ, Christians should oppose racism, every form of greed, selfishness, and vice, and all forms of sexual immorality, including adultery, homosexuality, and pornography. We should work to provide for the orphaned, the needy, the abused, the aged, the helpless, and the sick. We should speak on behalf of the unborn and contend for the sanctity of all human life from conception to natural death. Every Christian should seek to bring industry, government, and society as a whole under the sway of the principles of righteousness, truth, and brotherly love. In order to promote these ends Christians should be ready to work with all men of good will in any good cause, always being careful to act in the spirit of love without compromising their loyalty to Christ and His truth.[9]

Human culture is a complex, constantly changing product of the interplay of personal, collective, private, and public activities. As the *Baptist Faith & Message* makes clear, Christians must seek to influence every aspect of human culture in appropriate ways to fulfill our roles here on earth as Christ's ambassadors.

One method at our disposal to engage culture is public policy advocacy. Public policy affects every life and practically every part of life. Issues like abortion, marriage, religious liberty, human flourishing, and end-of-life decisions are affected by our nation's policies. We cannot fully represent the gospel of our Lord and His intention to make the will of God supreme on earth as it is in heaven without involving ourselves in our nation's policies.

The reasons for this engagement in so many areas of national life are many as well. It can be helpful to understand why we engage. We aren't simply being busybodies when we get involved in public policy advocacy. I have listed below what I believe are six motivations for Christian engagement in public policy. We engage:

---

9 *The Baptist Faith & Message* (Nashville: Lifeway Christian Resources, 2000), 19.

1. for self-defense,
2. for the sake of others,
3. for moral reasons,
4. for stewardship reasons,
5. for citizenship reasons,
6. to deflect the judgment of God.

We are guided by Scripture in each of these motivations. In what follows, we see an application of Scripture to these motivations, provide some examples of why we engage, and explain why engagement matters. After considering the following explanations, each Christian should consider his/her own role in the life of our nation.

ENGAGING PUBLIC POLICY AS SELF-DEFENSE

Given the condition of our culture today, a posture of self-defense makes sense. Much of society is growing increasingly hostile to the Christian message and more resistant to the biblical worldview. This hostility has now come to the point that some are attempting to force Christians to violate their biblically informed convictions to accommodate and even affirm unbiblical values and worldviews.

This shouldn't surprise any serious Christian. Jesus warned His disciples that the world would hate them (John 15:18). Jesus also told them why this would be the case. In commenting to His at-that-time unbelieving family members, He said the world hated Him because He testified "that its deeds are evil" (John 7:7). This testimony to the world's fallen nature continues through Jesus' disciples. The Spirit who resides in us continues to convict the world of "sin and righteousness and judgment" (John 16:8). Through our words, deeds, and faithful presence, we remind a lost world of a holy God and His call to righteousness and repentance.

At times, this hostility toward Christians is a natural result of an interest in silencing our witness because of its offense. The Apostle Paul noted the effect the gospel would have on those without Christ (2 Cor 2:14-16).

People do not like being told they are sinners. They want to be affirmed. But the gospel of Jesus must first expose the problem of human sin before it can apply the remedy of forgiveness through faith in Jesus.

Examples of resistance to gospel witness are numerous. People in the workplace have lost their jobs because they have shared their faith or their biblically informed views with others in the workplace. Children are being discouraged from sharing their faith with their classmates because it has been labeled as bullying. Most people are familiar with the unjust firing of Kelvin Cochran, the decorated Atlanta Fire Chief, who was fired because he wrote a book in which he expressed support for the Bible's teaching that sexual activity is to be between a man and a woman within the marriage relationship.[10] In other circles, Christians are being threatened with the loss of their livelihoods if they refuse to endorse unbiblical views. Sexual Orientation and Gender Identity (SOGI) laws are being used to punish Christians who provide services for weddings, like florists, bakers, and photographers, if they refuse to use their creative capacities to help celebrate same-sex weddings.

At other times, Christians must defend themselves in the public arena from those who do not understand or adequately appreciate our faith-informed values. This is nothing new, of course. Peter noted that Christians in his day were maligned for their lifestyle choices as well (1 Peter 4:3-6). Some people just don't understand how we can believe some of the things we believe, or they consider our positions to be simply in error. The ongoing effort by the U.S. Department of Health and Human Services (HHS) to force religious employers to provide contraceptives, sterilization, and abortion-causing drugs and devices in their employees' insurance plans is a good example of this failure to appreciate the depth of pro-life convictions held by many Christians. Many of us who are pro-life take our faith-informed belief about the sanctity of every human life very seriously. We cannot imagine assisting in the destruction of an innocent human life. We certainly can't imagine being forced by government to do this.

We resist this effort by HHS for numerous reasons. For one, we resist it because we refuse to facilitate the destruction of an innocent human be-

---

10 Kelvin Cochran, *Facing the Fire: The Faith that Brought "America's Fire Chief" through the Flames of Persecution* (Washington, D.C.: Salem Books, 2021).

ing. For another, we resist because we do not believe that government has the authority to dictate when our faith is valid and when it is not when it comes to something as important as human life. Not only is this an attack on our pro-life convictions, but it is also an attack on our religious freedom. The offense is contraception and/or abortion. The issue is religious freedom—the freedom to live out our faith in our daily lives.

Additionally, challenges to Christians come from those who are in rebellion against God's design for humanity. Paul described such people, which before our salvation included us, as "alienated and hostile in mind" (Col 1:21). Perhaps no issue reveals the threat to Christian faith posed by this rebellion more than the current efforts to undermine the biblical teaching about human sexuality. Scripture is clear that God created humans as man and woman (Gen 1:27). Yet, today, there are those who argue that gender and sex are not even linked. Today, some claim that there are dozens of genders, and that gender itself is fluid. At this time, Christian hospitals are being sued because they refuse to perform hysterectomies on perfectly healthy women because they want to become men.[11]

Understandably, we cannot allow institutions to force Christians to comply with unbiblical policies. We should come to the aid of those who seek to live out their biblically informed values and to express those values through their livelihood. Christians have not sought out these and other conflicts. They are being forced on us for the reasons I have stated and for other reasons as well, no doubt. To simply stand aside and capitulate is to risk sending the message that there really aren't any absolutes to which God holds all men (especially those of the household of faith) accountable. That is simply not the case. God expects His people to call sin what it is, and He expects us to stand for His truth in the world and in our own lives, in private and in public. We must defend the faithful who are being pressured to conform to worldly standards with every appropriate spiritual, legal, moral, and intellectual tool at our disposal in a loving but resolute manner. Turn-

---

11 Wesley J. Smith, "Another Catholic Hospital Sued for Refusing Transgender Hysterectomy," National Review Online, July 20, 2020, https://www.nationalreview.com/corner/another-catholic-hospital-sued-for-refusing-transgender-hysterectomy/.

ing the cheek has its place, as Jesus made clear, but not when the things of God are at stake. The early church understood the difference as well. They would not obey men at the expense of their obedience to God (Acts 5:29). We must not either.

Engaging Public Policy for the Sake of Others

Public policy engagement by the Christian community is also about helping others. The Gospel of Matthew records a pertinent question from one of the religious leaders of Jesus' day. The man asked Jesus which is the greatest commandment (Matt 22:36-40). Jesus responded that the command to love the Lord was the greatest. But then, just to make sure this man didn't think his vertical relationship with God was all that mattered, He expanded on His answer and said the second commandment was "like" the first: to "love your neighbor as yourself."

And, of course, we all know Jesus' answer to another religious leader who tried to get out of the implications of that second commandment. This leader asked Jesus to tell him who qualified as his neighbor. Jesus answered with the story of the Good Samaritan (Luke 10:25-37). By this story, Jesus made it clear that everyone is our neighbor. In fact, Jesus turned the tables on this man and told him that he should see himself as neighbor to everyone else (see v. 36). In other words, he had a responsibility to look out for others, as a good neighbor should.

Loving one's neighbor is an indispensable part of the Christian life. We love our neighbors by looking out for them and helping them. Stott called such political advocacy "love seeking justice for the oppressed."[12] For example, many Christians are involved in anti-sex trafficking efforts. We believe

---

12 Stott asked the question: "Would [first century Christians] have been politically active if they had had both the opportunity to be and the likelihood of success?" His reply: "I believe they would. For without appropriate political action some social needs simply cannot be met" (John Stott, *Decisive Issues Facing Christians Today*, 58).

sex trafficking is the modern-day slave trade. What is done to young girls and boys by other humans in these situations is barbaric and inhuman. It is only right that we would call on our government to do all it can to find those involved in sex slavery and prosecute them to the fullest extent allowed by law. This isn't a church protection effort. It's a humanitarian effort.

Our concern for our neighbors also leads us to attempt to prevent the sale of aborted baby parts. Today, there is a lucrative trade in freshly harvested fetal tissue.[13] The battle against so-called therapeutic cloning continues, as well. In this practice, a human embryo is created and then destroyed by removing its stem cells to be used in stem cell therapy. The practice destroys a human being in his or her earliest stage of development. Such barbarism should be banned, for it violates the commandment not to murder (Ex 20:13).

Immigration reform is another example of loving our neighbors. Our guidance for this posture comes not only from the command to love our neighbor but also from God's instructions to His people Israel. In the book of Leviticus, God commanded Israel to love the foreigner who lived among them "as yourself" (Lev 19:33-34). Jesus, as well, talked about the stranger. He said that how we treat the stranger is a direct reflection on how we treat Jesus Himself (Matt 25:31-46).

When we look at the undocumented immigrants in our nation, we see a majority who are law-abiding, hard-working people with good values, notwithstanding their presence here illegally, of course. Most of these immigrants are actively engaged in providing for themselves and their families. Our country is at a point where it must do something about their presence. It is neither humanitarian nor practical to attempt to deport these 11 million souls. Our nation should enact a system that assures us we will not be in this situation again, but it should also give those undocumented immigrants who are currently here and who qualify the opportunity to join fully in the life of our nation. This is the loving response to people who

---

13 Alison Durkee, "Biden Administration Overturns Trump-Era Ban on Fetal Tissue Research," *Forbes*, April 16, 2021, https://www.forbes.com/sites/alisondurkee/2021/04/16/biden-administration-overturns-trump-era-ban-on-fetal-tissue-research/?sh=75a8645f6003.

were allowed by our country's lax immigration practices to make lives and form families here.[14]

Loving one's neighbor also leads us to seek to protect the unborn. We do not see this as a "war on women," but rather as an effort to save innocent human lives. We recognize that women bear much of the responsibility for the care and rearing of children. We understand that too many men have failed women miserably in fulfilling their obligations to them and their children. We recognize that some women do not feel they are ready to have children. Yet, we cannot simply turn our heads away and accept the killing of millions of innocent humans in their mothers' wombs for such elective reasons as these.

Our faith, as well as common sense and science, convince us that this presence in the mother's womb is a person. Under the inspiration of the Holy Spirit, King David wrote a magnificent expression of God's involvement in the development of the unborn (Ps 139:13-16). These unborn humans deserve a chance to live. The loving response to this unborn person is for his or her mother to bring her baby to term if possible. If she still cannot or does not want to keep her baby after giving birth, then she can give him or her up for adoption. To help women with challenging pregnancies, Christians support public policy that provides alternatives for women dealing with an unplanned or challenging pregnancy. We are also actively working to improve adoption laws that make it easier for people to adopt.

Space prevents me from discussing the many other ways we express our love for our neighbors, from advocating for religious freedom for peo-

---

14 The Southern Baptist Convention has passed resolutions calling for humane treatment of undocumented immigrants that include a call to find a way that honors the nation's laws while allowing them to remain in the United States legally. See the 2018 Resolution "On Immigration" as the latest example of this call. It includes this language: "We desire to see immigration reform include an emphasis on securing our borders and providing a pathway to legal status with appropriate restitutionary measures, maintaining the priority of family unity, resulting in an efficient immigration system that honors the value and dignity of those seeking a better life for themselves and their families." "On Immigration," accessed May 31, 2021, https://www.sbc.net/resource-library/resolutions/on-immigration/.

ple of all faiths and no faith, to meeting human needs during catastrophes, to end-of-life care, and a myriad other things. We do this, not because we are commanded by God to love, though we are, but because loving others is the natural outgrowth of our relationship with God. At times, our love is not welcomed. We understand that and are grieved. At other times, our love is embraced. We cherish that. But most of all we are disciples of Jesus Christ, bringing the message and values of His Kingdom into our world. It is a matter of remaining faithful to our God and to our neighbors.

ENGAGING PUBLIC POLICY FOR MORALITY

Another strong motivating factor for Christian engagement is that we know that moral absolutes exist. Universal standards of right and wrong exist. We believe that God has revealed Himself as a moral being and that He has a moral ideal for humanity. In the words of Carl F. H. Henry, "The same God who created the universe sets the moral standard."[15] His guidance to Israel reveals that sin is not only our failure to place our faith in Him, though that is the ultimate act of rebellion. It is also sin to rebel against God's moral standard.

Sin is not only a spiritual matter. It is also a behavioral matter. God holds people accountable for how they behave. Sodom and Gomorrah could serve as exhibit A. The biblical text says the Lord was headed to Sodom to witness for Himself what the people of that city "have done" (Gen 18:21). The account that follows describes a situation of moral decadence. The Lord responded by destroying the city. This was a judgment meted out against a people who were not in any special covenant relationship with Him. They were simply a community of people living according to their own moral standards. That did not excuse them from God's judgment. He has a moral code by which He wants all humans to live. Clearly, He holds those in relationship with Him to a higher expectation of moral rectitude, but He holds all humanity to a moral code.

---

15 Carl F. H. Henry, *Christian Personal Ethics* (Grand Rapids, MI: Baker Book House, 1977), 195.

Our engagement does not stop at our recognition of the existence of universal moral standards. We also have much more personal motivations to engage in public policy for moral reasons. For one, we believe that a people's morality reflects their perception of themselves. We believe there is such a thing as human dignity and that our culture should honor and lift up the best of what it means to be human, not celebrate the depth of human depravity or accommodate every possible so-called morality.

This isn't only a matter of personal dignity and self-respect. It is also a matter of respect for God. The Bible asserts that humans are created in the image of the God of the universe (Gen 1:26-27). That image is supposed to mean something to humanity. Being created in God's image should motivate humans to seek to live in such a way that they honor the God whose image they bear. Christian bioethicist Nigel Cameron argues that the fact of humanity's creation in the image of God is "the fundamental ground of human dignity."[16] We believe that those who live contrary to God's moral standards grieve the God whose image they bear and exercise gross neglect of their special status as the only created beings in all of creation to bear the *imago dei*.

Yet there is more. We believe that those who fail to live according to God's moral standards bring harm to themselves. Solomon, whose own life reveals what happens when one strays from God's moral standards, asks rhetorically, "Can a man take fire in his bosom and his clothes not be burned?" (Prov 6:27). No, he cannot. The lifestyle choices people make affect their lives and futures – for good or for bad. And these choices affect others' lives as well.

Therefore we engage in efforts to rid communities of harmful behaviors. We seek to eliminate gambling, for example, because we know that it

---

16 Cameron seeks to rest the entire Christian enterprise to protect humanity from a bleak future of scientific abuse on this very truth. He says, "While not addressing every problem in contemporary bioethics debate, its radical assertion of the unity and common dignity of the human race in the Maker's image establishes a framework of understanding within which many questions are immediately resolved, and those that remain unclear may be addressed." Nigel M. de S. Cameron, "The Sanctity of Life in the Twenty-first Century: An Agenda for Homo sapiens in the Image of God," in *Toward an Evangelical Public Policy*, eds. Ronald D. Sider and Diane Knippers (Grand Rapids, MI: Baker Books, 2005), 215.

impoverishes millions. It isn't only the gambler who is hurt by this behavior. Families are devastated. Children go hungry. Some turn to crime to support gambling addiction and to recover losses. All of society is affected.

We also seek to eliminate pornography because of its destructive effects on people. In addition to its affront to human dignity, it also destroys those caught up in it. It is not a victimless activity. Those who create pornographic material often turn to drugs and alcohol to numb them from the reality of what they are doing. Those who view pornography are deeply affected by it; many are unable to have healthy, satisfying relationships with members of the opposite sex. Some become so addicted that they seek to act out ever more aggressive sexual desires. Pornography is known to coarsen men's attitudes toward women and is usually implicated in sexual assault.

The issue of morality ultimately comes down to values. One's concepts of right and wrong are shaped largely by what that person values. If we value people because they are created in the image of God, we will seek to treat them with more respect. That belief, among others, convinces us that it is wrong to engage in activities that demean people, as, for example, pornography does. The apostle Paul told the Christians in Philippi, "Whatever is true, whatever is honorable, whatever is right, whatever is pure, whatever is lovely, whatever is of good repute, if there is any excellence and if anything worthy of praise, dwell on these things" (Phil 4:8). Paul knew that action is preceded by thought. He knew that if the Philippians valued those things characterized by these attributes, they would be better Christians. The same holds true for the broader society. The values a society embraces influence how it behaves.

We know that everyone doesn't have to live or think exactly as we do. We must leave adequate room for different choices. We also know that we can't make people moral simply by passing laws. But we do believe in the didactic nature of laws and codes. While laws and codes cannot change the heart, they can teach a people what society values and can encourage behavior that upholds those values. Therefore Christians must also support laws and policies that honor biblical values. Essentially, laws and policies teach generations the boundaries for moral lives. At the very least, laws and codes can help to restrain immoral behavior and its impact on those who want to engage in it and everyone else around them.

Our engagement for moral reasons embraces everyone. All humans have a sin nature, including those in Christ. This sin nature can lead us all down its immoral trajectory if left to its own inclination. Most Christians know that we have a long way to go in our own lives. We understand the principle of the speck and the log (Matt 7:1-5). We need to spend more time cleaning up our own backyards than looking over the fence at others' backyards. But, while we engage in our own personal moral and spiritual formation, we believe we must also help our fellow citizens understand and live in accordance with God's universal moral standards. The book of Proverbs tells us (and then repeats itself for emphasis): "There is a way which seems right to a man, but its end is the way of death" (Prov 14:12; 16:25).

Guided by God's indwelling Spirit, our understanding of what it means to be spiritual salt and light compels us to engage culture with God's guiding and preserving morality. Carl F. H. Henry stood firmly on this ground. In explaining the important role the church plays in revealing God's moral law to a lost world, he states "the believing church has a globe-girdling mission to an unbelieving world. Rather than being a mere derivative from or intensification of a universal ethical impulse, Christian ethics made the church the light of a dark world and the salt of a putrefying earth."[17] Morality matters.

ENGAGING PUBLIC POLICY AS STEWARDS

Christians engage public policy as stewards. Wayne Grudem describes the Christian's responsibility to engage in the national public life as a stewardship. He writes, "I believe that every Christian citizen who lives in a democracy has at the very least a minimal obligation to be well-informed and to vote for candidates and policies that are most consistent with biblical principles."[18] A steward is a person who has been entrusted to care for something

---

17 C. F. H. Henry, *Christian Personal Ethics*, 203.

18 Wayne Grudem, *Politics According to the Bible: A Comprehensive Resource for Understanding Modern Political Issues in Light of Scripture* (Grand Rapids, MI: Zondervan Academic, 2010), 74. Grudem attaches much of this stewardship to the

Christians and Public Policy: Why We Engage

by its owner. Jesus spoke clearly about Christian stewardship (e.g., Matt 25:14-30). This stewardship encompasses a broad scope. It begins with the stewardship of God's revealed truth—the Bible. We recognize that the Bible is God's inerrant word. Among other things, it communicates His moral will for all humanity, not only the church. It isn't as though there is one moral truth for Christians and another for everyone else. God has a right way for all humans. The closer all of us come to that right way, the better off we are in our lives and at every level of human interaction.

Without God's revealed moral truth, humans would be left on their own to discern the best way to live. They would be like a person who is trying to reassemble a complicated machine without the instructions. Anyone who has tried such a thing knows they usually end up with a few parts left over. Some of those excess parts turn out to be important once you try to start the machine. We cannot expect sinful, fallen people to make laws that will honor God's moral law. Stott argues that we shouldn't be surprised if fallen humans create a declining culture. They do not have God's presence within to guide them. It is the Christian's responsibility to bring God's salt and light into the world. He says, "If therefore darkness and rottenness abound, it is our fault, and we must accept the blame."[19] It is a tribute to the perfection of God that fallen people still have enough of the law written on their hearts that they understand as much as they do about what makes for a moral society (Rom 2:14-15). But fallen people, left on their own, are not capable of discerning the full extent of God's moral law (Jer 17:9).[20]

Three areas, by way of example, in which we exercise this stewardship in public policy are government, creation care, and the family. Our

---

legacy of sacrifice and service of previous generations, but he also makes the argument that Christians like all citizens in a democracy have a "responsibility before God to know what God expects of civil government and what kind of moral and legal standards he wants government to follow." (62).

19 John Stott, *Decisive Issues Facing Christians Today*, 67.

20 Henry sums it up well, "The whole content of the moral law was not inwardly communicated even before the Fall. Rather, the moral law was dependent upon supernatural revelation for a decisive content." C. F. H. Henry, *Christian Personal Ethics*, 242.

stewardship toward government derives from our understanding that God instituted government and charged it with a purpose. In Rom 13:1-7 the Apostle Paul says God designed government to reward good and to punish evil. With this understanding, we seek to do such things as overturn abortion-on-demand as a violation of the sanctity of human life. We support efforts to bypass Internet firewalls set up by totalitarian governments that prevent their citizens from obtaining and sharing information, including the gospel. We support efforts to end religious persecution, which is an inappropriate intrusion by government into matters of faith. We advocate for greater freedom in such countries as North Korea out of our understanding that these governments have exceeded their authority by their brutal treatment of their citizens.

When government no longer serves God's purposes, it is no longer fulfilling its purpose. The fathers of our nation argued that was the case with the king of England when they began their great rebellion. They argued he was no longer rewarding good and punishing evil. The Declaration of Independence is essentially their argument that the king had forfeited his right to govern the colonies because of his abusive policies. They were backed by much of the colonial church in this assertion. Of course, disobedience and revolt are not early options. Scripture is clear that we must respect the governing authorities (1 Pet 2:13-17). We must exercise our stewardship of government with great humility and care, knowing that we, too, are still prone to sin and error.

Creation requires the exercise of our stewardship as well. As creation fulfills its purpose, it glorifies God. God put Adam and Eve in the Garden to tend it. It was their responsibility to help the Garden fulfill its purpose. While creation itself has been subjected to the decay of sin in this present age (Rom 8:18-22), it still glorifies God (Ps 19:1-6). Even in its state of subjection, creation can be helped to bring greater glory to God. In fact, one can argue that because of its subjection to decay, creation is in greater need of human care to help it fulfill its purpose. Consequently, we are right to insist that humans not wantonly destroy the environment. Further, it is appropriate to seek to pass laws to prevent cruelty to animals for sport (e.g., dog fights) and other activities that senselessly destroy creation.

Christians and Public Policy: Why We Engage

Here again, however, there is room for caution. While we are creation's stewards, creation is not our master (Ps 8:1-9). We live in a symbiotic relationship with all of creation. Each needs the other to fulfill its purposes. But while humans are part of creation, they are also separate from the rest of creation. We are differentiated from creation by kind, not degree (Gen 1:26-28). As a result, when we consider proposed environmental policies, we ask what is best for creation, but especially for humanity. This understanding that our stewardship of creation must prioritize human needs should be a crucial consideration when we talk about things like reducing greenhouse gas emissions. Many of the proposals will have devastating impacts on humans, especially the poor. Policies that prevent people in third world countries from obtaining abundant, inexpensive energy trap them in lives of poverty, with all its attendant problems. They also make life more difficult for the poor in developed countries by driving up the prices of food, clothing, and other necessities as higher energy costs in production are passed along.

A third area in which Christians exercise stewardship is toward the family. We learn from Genesis chapter two that God instituted the family. It is not a human invention. Consequently, we feel a sense of responsibility to advance policies that strengthen the family. The Bible makes it clear that the family, rooted in the marriage of one man and one woman in covenant commitment to each other, is the lynchpin of society, not the individual. As the family prospers, people and society prosper.

Richard Land summed up the importance of the family very well: Families are "mini-communities of interdependent people who learn roles and behaviors and acquire expectations and obligations that take on life-and-death importance. Our family determines who we are and how we enter the world, and it is our first and last line of defense against the threats and dangers of the world. It is also our primary learning laboratory for how to go out into the world on our own and succeed in it."[21] Policies that weaken the family as God designed it to function weaken society. We consider it our responsibility to support programs that promote responsible fatherhood. We advocate for policies that send couples to counseling rather than divorce

---

21 Richard Land, *Imagine! A God-blessed America: How It Could Happen and What It Would Look Like* (Nashville: Broadman and Holman, Publishers, 2005), 101.

court. We support programs that help single-parent households to be able to flourish, without creating long-term dependency.

God is concerned about every aspect of human life. Because of this, Christian stewardship embraces all human culture. We must exercise this stewardship to be faithful to our God. We recognize, though, that God has still given humans the freedom to make many personal decisions about their lives. We must balance human freedom and human responsibility as we seek to be good stewards of God's design for His creation, especially for humanity, and all for God's glory.[22]

ENGAGING PUBLIC POLICY AS CITIZENS

Our role as citizens is another driving factor in our public policy engagement as Christians. Augustine of Hippo argued effectively that Christians possess dual citizenship, a heavenly and an earthly. While the Christian's principal citizenship lies with the kingdom of heaven (Phil 3:20), he also has responsibilities toward his earthly citizenship. This earthly citizenship compels him to seek the well-being of his earthly kingdom or nation.

Some Christians believe they have limited obligations toward their earthly citizenship. They do not believe Christians should be involved in earthly political activities, for example. John MacArthur, for one, argues that using temporal methods to promote legislative and judicial change "is not our calling."[23] Without question, our first allegiance must be to the kingdom of our Lord (Matt 6:33). But Scripture requires significant Christian engagement in the political life of earthly kingdoms, as well. The prophet Jeremiah instructed the Jews who had been taken into captivity to Babylon to "seek the welfare of the city" (Jer 29:7). Jesus declared that the Jews of His day were to

---

22 Grudem disagrees with MacArthur's opposition to the whole enterprise of the church's involvement in public policy. He ties that involvement directly to Matt 5:16, as well as Eph 2:10. These are "good works," and Christians are obeying God by doing them. Wayne Grudem, *Politics According to the Bible*, 51.

23 John MacArthur, *Why Government Can't Save You: An Alternative to Political Activism* (Nashville: Thomas Nelson, 2000), 15.

"render to Caesar the things that are Caesar's, and to God the things that are God's" (Mark 12:17). The Apostle Peter connects the dots for us when he says, "Submit yourselves for the Lord's sake to every human institution, whether to a king as the one in authority, or to governors" (1 Pet 2:13-14). Grudem agrees. He ties the church's efforts to affect society through public policy advocacy to Matt 5:16 and Eph 2:10. It is an appropriate "good work."[24]

In the United States, engagement in the political sphere is part of rendering to Caesar and submitting to every human institution. In fact, in a representative democracy like ours, citizen engagement is not only expected but necessary.[25] The laws and policies of the land are determined by the people, usually through their elected officials, in such a system. Whether or not those laws and policies are God-honoring depends largely on who shows up to vote. Who better to help a nation choose the right leaders and enact the right laws and policies than those who accept God's revealed moral truth?[26]

Several particulars are required of a Christian to exercise this responsibility rightly. First, the Christian must be intimately aware of the teaching of Scripture regarding morality. As I noted earlier, God has one set of moral values for all of humanity. He expects humans to live by those values. Grudem

---

24 Grudem argues that Christians are obeying God by doing these good works. Wayne Grudem, *Politics According to the Bible*, 51. I agree. Millions of lives have been made better and been protected because Christians have decided that public policy is an appropriate venue for Christian engagement.

25 In his introduction to the "Church and State" volume of the Southern Baptist Theological Seminary's journal, journal editor Stephen Wellum makes this very point, "As citizens of the state, especially democratic governments, we have a privilege and responsibility to participate in the political process and express our views as Christians." Stephen Wellum, "Editorial: Reflecting on Our Christian Responsibility to the State," in "Church and State," *The Southern Baptist Journal of Theology*, 11, no. 4 (Winter 2007): 3.

26 This is a foundational point in Chuck Colson's "three compelling reasons" Christians must be involved in politics and government. His three reasons: 1. They have the same civic duties as all citizens. 2. As citizens of the Kingdom of God, they "are to bring God's standards of righteousness and justice to bear on the kingdoms of this world." 3. They have "an obligation to bring transcendent moral values into the public debate." Charles Colson, *God and Government* (Grand Rapids, MI: Zondervan Publishing House, 2007), 314-315.

comments that the moral standards that God reveals in the Bible "are the moral standards by which the one true God, the Creator and Lord of the entire universe, will hold every single person accountable at the last judgment."[27] The Christian must vote and influence public policy in such a way that God's moral values are reflected in secular policies. Nothing less than eternal judgment for the "things done in the body" (2 Cor 5:10) is at stake.

Some argue that to do such a thing injects religion into the secular sphere. They assert that even the Christian must maintain a secular mind-set when influencing public policy. They are mistaken in this assertion in many ways. For one thing, one's view of right and wrong is not religion. One's view may be informed by his or her religion, but the view is different from the faith that informs it. A Christian is not injecting religion into politics by advocating for his or her faith-informed policy positions.

Advocacy for the sanctity of human life is a good example of this fact. Some avowed atheists share a commitment to protecting unborn human life in the same way that pro-life Christians do. Their reasons for holding the same position regarding human life differ at certain important levels, but the resulting policy position is the same. Clearly, the view that all human life should be held inviolable is not a uniquely religious belief.

Additionally, there is no requirement that people leave their personal values systems at the door when they enter the voting booth or seek to influence policies. On the contrary, it is expected that people would choose according to their values. They are choosing the people and policies that will create an environment in which they must live. For instance, a person who believes that personal property is an important aspect of human flourishing shouldn't be expected to vote for someone or support polices that advocate nationalizing all property.

Caution is also in order at this point, however. The Christian—or a person of any faith for that matter—must make sure he or she is supporting laws and policies that are universal in their application. Some expressions of Christianity have unique requirements that apply to their adherents, not to all people. For example, some require strict dietary measures of their adherents. This requirement is not binding on all people. It would be inappro-

---

27 Grudem, *Politics According to the Bible*, 118.

priate, therefore, to advocate for laws that require everyone to follow those dietary measures.

A second requirement of Christians who choose to exercise their citizenship responsibilities is that they stay aware of the issues. It is not possible to engage only during an election and be effective in guiding a nation toward God's moral truth. The responsible Christian citizen must make awareness of current events part of his or her life. For example, how else would a person know whether he should support or oppose something like embryonic stem cell research? There are many good resources to help provide the knowledge base that makes for responsible citizen participation. Christians have a responsibility to be well-informed before they take positions on issues that affect the lives of others.

Third, but certainly not last, every responsible Christian citizen must be a person of prayer. Ultimately, prayer is the Christian's most powerful citizenship tool. The book of Proverbs tells us the heart of the king is in the hand of God (Prov 21:1). Paul urged prayers for the governing authorities of his day (1 Tim 2:1-2). God can work through any problem confronting a nation. First and foremost, then, Christians must present the needs of their nation to God.

The citizen Christian is an indispensable member of national life. Jesus knew what He was saying when He called His disciples the salt of the earth and the light of the world (Matt 5:13-14). By God's Spirit and His inerrant word, the Christian can adequately discern the moral law of God. If we take His moral values into the public square and the voting booth, we will be doing society a great service. God's way is the best way for all people to live. Exercising our citizenship responsibly enables us to help all our fellow citizens experience the best of what God's creation has to offer.

Engaging Public Policy to Avert God's Judgment

Christian engagement in public policy is an act of compassion and mercy toward others. God judges people and nations for their sin. God destroyed Sodom and Gomorrah because of their sin. Through His prophets, He pronounced judgment on many nations for their sinful behavior (Jer 46:1-51:64; Nahum). In telling Abraham that He would give the land of Canaan to his descendants, God said He would do this when the iniquity of the Amorite was "complete" (Gen 15:1-21).

Fortunately for all of us, God judges as a last resort. The book of Jonah describes God's desire to stave off His judgment. He sent Jonah to preach a message of impending judgment (Jon 1:1-2). Jonah understood that this call included the possibility of repentance and the avoidance of God's judgment. He deliberately resisted God's call because he wanted God to judge the city (Jon 4:1-2). While the text does not tell us that the people embraced the totality of the faith of Israel, it does say that the people "believed in God" (Jon 3:5) and "turned from their wicked way" (Jon 3:10). God's response was mercy. He "relented" of the calamity He had declared He would bring on them (Jon 3:5-10).

Genesis 6 tells us the judgment of God can fall on a people for its utterly wicked thoughts (Gen 6:5), but there is a stronger connection between wicked behavior and judgment. God's judgment is certain to fall when the sinfulness of the human heart acts itself out and becomes unbearable to Him. Jude declares the judgment of God fell on the "ungodly" for all their ungodly deeds and words spoken against God (Jude 14-15). Even in Genesis 6, while the emphasis is placed on the evil "thoughts" of the heart, we are told that God "saw that the wickedness of man was great" (Gen 6:5) and "the earth [was] filled with violence" (Gen 6:13).

We should be grateful that God is slow to send judgment. But clearly, His patience has limits. One reason Christians oppose the abortion culture in our nation, for example, is because we cannot imagine that God can sit back idly while our fellow citizens kill nearly a million babies in their mother's wombs every year. People were aghast a decade ago at the revelations of Kermit Gosnell's horrific atrocities against newborn babies, and rightly so, but understand, such things are legal right now if they are inflicted in the womb. God must be horrified by such violence to innocent human life. His judgment on this nation for such barbarism is certain.

Christians and Public Policy: Why We Engage

God's judgment may not take the form of immediate, cataclysmic action, however. His judgment can come in the gradual removal of His protective hand and occur over long periods of time. God is all that stands between humanity and chaos (2 Thess 2:6-9). The world is immersed in sin (Rom 8:19-23). The Apostle John tells us this world is currently the domain of the evil one (1 John 5:19). Satan hates all humans and relishes any opportunity to deface what God loves (John 8:44; 1 Pet 5:8). The only thing preventing him from carrying out the destruction he seems to desire is God Himself. Satan acts within the space granted to him by God (Job 1:12). God's judgment might be just a matter of granting Satan more freedom to destroy. It might be just a matter of giving human sinfulness more reign.

In Amos 4, God describes how He increased His judgment on the people to get them to turn back to Him. He describes how He took them through increasingly devastating periods, from hunger to plague to calamity, to persuade them to return to Him. All of that failing, there was only one last thing. He says, "Prepare to meet your God" (Amos 4:12). God was slowly turning up the heat to get Israel's attention, but to no avail.

As Christians engage public policy, they can have a hand in helping to avert the judgment of God. Moral laws and policies can restrict the outward expression of the worst of what lies in the human heart. The surest way to avert judgment is to win the lost to Christ and make disciples. A converted heart submitted to Christ's Lordship is always the best means to moral behavior. But absent a nation of such people, laws and policies that restrain sinful human tendencies can also avert God's judgment. They may also train a people to act differently. As I said earlier, it is possible for God to judge a people simply because their hearts are thoroughly wicked, but the biblical testimony bears greater witness to His judgment on a people when the wickedness within is acted upon.

Christians should do all they can to seek the well-being of their fellow citizens. Averting God's judgment is one sure way to do this. And make no mistake, if we avert the judgment of God on the nation, we also make life easier on those living their lives in faithful obedience to Christ. The righteous people and the unrighteous in any nation suffer when God sends His judgment.

Conclusion

By now, it is obvious that the frog in the kettle analogy is applicable to Christians. Christians are like that frog because we are in this world, which in many ways is hostile to us. We are like that frog because we are human, and we naturally want to find a way to adjust to our surroundings. So today, we have Christians accommodating culture in many ways to get along or to minimize its resistance to us. We are like that frog because if the heat is turned up too fast, we also recognize that we are in trouble and we try to get out. We are like that frog because if the heat is slowly turned up on us, we often don't recognize what is happening until it is too late.

There are also ways in which we are not like that frog. We are not helpless. We can influence how hot the water gets by getting involved in activities that influence the culture. We can also recognize when the water is getting hot, even slowly, and we can protect ourselves from it. We can simply refuse to let the culture influence how we live. We are also not like that frog because we are not only self-interested. We can choose to stay in the heat to help our fellow citizens as they slowly cook in a culture run amok with human sinfulness.[28] Furthermore, we are not being helplessly heated. No one can turn up the heat on us without permission—God's permission. If God is permitting the heat, He has reason. It is the church's job to respond to that heat according to God's will.

Understand, this is not a call to Christian Reconstructionism or the exercise of raw power to coerce behaviors by others. The work of the church is not done best by a government that it controls, nor can its gospel work be achieved with the government's sword. Nevertheless, there is a legitimate space in government and public policy that is appropriate for

---

[28] Perhaps this is the point at which we can say in response to Carl F. H. Henry's early concern about fundamentalism's influence on evangelicalism that humanitarianism has not evaporated from Christianity. See Carl F. H. Henry, *The Uneasy Conscience of Modern Fundamentalism* (1947; repr., Grand Rapids, MI: Eerdmans, 2003), 11. We are now likely in the space about which J. Budziszewski has critiqued evangelicalism for being devoid of an adequate doctrine of politics. See J. Budziszewski, *Evangelicals in the Public Square* (Grand Rapids, MI: Baker Academic, 2006), 26.

Christians and Public Policy: Why We Engage

Christian involvement as citizens of this worldly kingdom and the salt and light of human culture.

In his essential work, *The Naked Public Square*, Neuhaus has cogently argued that if Christians abandon the public policy debate and take the truth of God's moral law with them, some other value system will be "bootlegged" into the abandoned space, or, in his term, "the naked public square," in order to give legitimacy to the laws being proposed.[29] In other words, if we who have the truth of God's word to help society understand right from wrong refuse to bring God's truth to bear on the laws being enforced or proposed, others will fill that vacuum with some other system of absolutes on which to ground laws. Society can either be guided by truth or by error, but it will be guided. We must make sure God's truth continues to speak. We have just explained six reasons why this is necessary.

The Southern Baptist Convention's statement of faith, the *Baptist Faith & Message*, is especially helpful as we consider our lives in the kettle of human culture: "Every Christian should seek to bring industry, government, and society under the sway of righteousness, truth, and brotherly love."[30] We are in the kettle, but we don't have to be thermometers. We can, and should be, thermostats. May God help us to be so.

---

[29] Richard John Neuhaus, *The Naked Public Square*, 2nd ed. (Grand Rapids, MI: William B. Eerdmans Publishing Company, 1984), 80. In a nutshell, "In a democratic society, state and society must draw from the same well" (82).

[30] *The Baptist Faith & Message*, 19.

Chapter 3
Citizen Christians Revisited

Mark H. Ballard

Ophir James Ballard raised his nine children to love God, His Word, and the United States of America. He and his wife Velma taught their five girls and four boys that every person who turns from sin and trusts Jesus to be his or her Lord and Savior holds a citizenship in two countries. First, every true believer is a citizen of Heaven. Secondly, every true believer has the responsibility to be a good citizen of his/her country. Those believers living in the United States enjoy the blessings, the rights, and the responsibilities of exercising those rights and responsibilities under God.

Ophir not only taught his children that believers are citizens of heaven,[1] he also taught them that believers are citizens of an earthly nation. He often reminded his family that Jesus said, "Render therefore to Caesar the things that are Caesar's, and to God the things that are God's."[2] Based on Jesus' words, as well as texts such as Rom 13:1-7, 1 Pet 1:13-17, and the apostles' example in Acts, Ophir J. Ballard taught his children that Jesus expects His followers to be good citizens.

No Christian leader in the last 50 years embodies the concept of being a Citizen Christian more than Richard Land. From the first time this writer enjoyed the privilege of meeting Dr. Land at Criswell College in the 1980s,

---

1 Phil 3:20. Scripture references in this chapter are from the NKJV.
2 Matt 22:21.

to the present day, it has been my privilege to observe in him, the embodiment of the principles taught in my home. Richard Land has influenced countless believers to embrace their role as Citizen Christians through his writing, teaching, preaching, and through his example throughout the last several decades. The principles embodied in books like *Citizen Christians, Homeland Security, The Divided States of America,* and *Imagine! A God Blessed America* call on all believers to recognize the rights and responsibilities of being a citizen of two countries. Land's leadership and influence among Baptists, the Evangelical world, and within our nation has long been recognized.[3] His influence continues to be felt today through his recent service as the President of Southern Evangelical Seminary.

While serving as the President of the Christian Life Commission and the Ethics and Religious Liberty Commission of the Southern Baptist Convention, Land produced several resources to aid one in exercising their rights and responsibilities of dual citizenship. This chapter will revisit one of those resources, *Citizen Christians*. Published in 1994, the book presented essays edited by Land. Land not only conceived and edited the project, but also contributed his own chapter to the work.

The present chapter asks and answers two questions. Is the concept of being a *Citizen Christian* biblical? Are the concepts related to being a *Citizen Christian*, as described in various chapters of the book, relevant today? This chapter will summarize the book *Citizen Christian*, examine three chapters of the book, and answer both questions in the affirmative.

CITIZEN CHRISTIANS: A SUMMARY

Richard Land presided over the Christian Life Commission's 25th Annual Seminar in Washington, D.C. in March of 1992. The theme of the seminar

---

3   In addition to all the ways Dr. Land has influenced Southern Baptists through the years, his influence has been recognized across the evangelical world. Dr. Land received the *Philip E. Johnson Award for Liberty and Truth* from Biola University in 2010, and The Champions of Justice Award from the National Hispanic Christian Leadership Conference (also known as The Hispanic Evangelical Association) in 2012.

focused on aspects of living as a Citizen Christian. Following the meeting, the Christian Life Commission and Broadman Press determined to address the topics further in book form. Richard Land and Louis Moore edited the volume which included twelve essays written by eleven recognized leaders on the topic of *The Rights and Responsibilities of Dual Citizenship*.

In the preface Land writes, "We are citizens of two realms—the earthly and spiritual. Such dual citizenship includes rights and responsibilities in both spheres."[4] Land desires to set the tone for the book by helping the readers to understand that the believer's priority is God. Yet, this does not negate the responsibility of believers to support the government, unless the government requires something that conflicts with the Lord's commands. Land contends that the title of the book was chosen carefully to emphasize this priority. "Grammatically, Christian is our subject, our basis. Citizen is our adjective: it modifies and explains further who we are. Our citizenship modifies our Christianity. It is certainly not the other way around. We are not citizens first, and then Christians."[5] Having set the tone of the work right up front, Land explained the origin of the work.

Following a brief introduction by Land and Moore, the book is divided into four sections. Section one titled, "What Does It Mean to Be a Citizen Christian?" contains three chapters. Richard Land's first chapter argues that *Citizen Christians Have Rights Too*. In chapter 2, Morris Chapman urges Christians to *Kneel Down and Be Counted*. In chapter 3, Edwin Young, then serving as the Southern Baptist Convention's President, draws on the Book of Nehemiah to suggest that Christians must *Rebuild the Walls in America Today*.

The second section of the book boasts only two chapters under the heading, "Defining Separation of Church and State." Lynn R. Buzzard discusses the *Separation of Church, State, and Religious Liberty*. Respected theologian Carl F. H. Henry revisited an earlier work under the chapter title, *The Uneasy Conscience of Modern Fundamentalism: 45 Years Later*.

---

4   Richard D. Land and Louis A. Moore. *Citizen Christians: The Rights and Responsibilities of Dual Citizenship* (Nashville: Broadman & Holman Publishers, 1994), v.

5   Ibid.

The third section, consisting of four chapters, examines "Issues Looming on the Horizon." Carl F. H. Henry offers a second chapter titled, *Religious Liberty as a Cause Celebre*. Roy T. Edgemon offered encouragement that Citizen Christians should focus on *Reacting to the Needs of the Nation*. Syndicated columnist and talk radio personality, Cal Thomas asks, *Whose Church Is It Anyway?* In this chapter Thomas argues that all believers are equally called of God into Christian service. Some are called to be pastors or missionaries, but Thomas is called to serve Christ in the world of the media. William Bennett rounds out this section of the book by considering what to do *When Culture Degenerates*.

The final three chapters are grouped together under the heading, "Practical Application." Beverley LaHaye examines *How Christians Make an Impact on Their Government*, offering several practical suggestions. H. Robert Showers draws on Scripture and his personal experience to explain *How Christians Can Make a Difference Within the Government*. Jay Strack closes out the book by discussing *How Christians Can Have an Impact by Volunteering*.

While every chapter provides significant insight into the concept of being a Citizen Christian, this essay will focus on evaluating three chapters. Land's chapter titled, "Citizen Christians Have Rights Too" will be considered first. Lynn Butler's chapter on the "Separation of Church, State, and Religious Liberty" will then be discussed. From the final section of the book on practical application, Rob Showers' chapter on "How Christians Can Make a Difference from Within the Government" will be examined.

CITIZEN CHRISTIANS, AN EXAMINATION OF THREE KEY CHAPTERS

In examining the three chosen chapters of *Citizen Christians*, we will begin by giving an overview of the content and argument of the chapter. We will then offer a brief critique of the chapter under consideration. We begin with the first chapter of book.

Citizen Christians Have Rights Too
by Richard D. Land

Overview

Land begins this chapter reminding the reader of the purpose of the book as noted in the preface. He again argues that believers have both rights and responsibilities in both the spiritual as well as the physical world. Further, he sets the tone of his chapter by suggesting that the rights and responsibilities in both realms call believers to make a difference in our nation. He states, "Our involvement, our attempts to make a difference are because we are Christians and because we have responsibilities both in the realm of the nation and in the realm of our Lord's Kingdom."[6] Drawing on Phil 3:20, Ex 20:1-5, Luke 20:25, and Rom 13:1-7, Land argues that as a citizen of heaven the believer's first responsibility is to obey God. However, the believer is under Jesus' direct command not only to pay taxes, but to be good citizens for the sake of maintaining a good conscience before God. The only exception to the believer's responsibility to support the government is if doing so would require one to be disloyal to God.

Having set the tone for the book in general and for his chapter in particular, Land divides the balance of his chapter into five subtopics. First, he considers Jesus' command to be "salt" and "light." Referring to the Sermon on the Mount, Land reminds the readers that Jesus Himself commanded His followers to be the "salt of the earth" and the "light of the world." Land writes, "This means that Christians as citizens are to be in active engagement with the world, preserving as salt and illuminating as light."[7] Land then connects this biblical concept specifically to Baptist tradition by quoting from the *Baptist Faith and Message* of the Southern Baptist Convention. Land states, "When we bring our religious and moral convictions into the public marketplace of ideas and involve ourselves in the social and political arena, we are standing solidly within the best of our traditions as Americans and as Baptists."[8] Land concludes this section of his chapter by suggesting that in the last decade

---

6 Land, *Citizen Christians,* 6.
7 Ibid., 7.
8 Ibid.

of the twentieth century some people seemed to imply that Christians were somehow disqualified from speaking into the issues of the day.

When discussing Christian involvement in the social and political realms of our nation today many have suggested, "you cannot legislate morality." In the second section of his chapter Land confronts this claim head on. The section title says it all, *Yes, We Can Legislate Morality*. He began this section by demonstrating the reality that all governments legislate morality. "Laws against murder, laws against theft, and laws against rape are the legislation of morality."[9] Land then discusses Romans 13, the most extensive passage in the New Testament on the believer's responsibility to government. In his discussion, he demonstrates the responsibility that one has to government. He concludes this section of the chapter by showing some of the evidence of Christian involvement in the affairs of government throughout the history of the United States.

The longest section of Land's chapter argues that *Christians Have Rights and Responsibilities in Society*. He begins by considering Roger Williams who is credited for his emphasis on the separation of church and state. Land demonstrates the reality that even for Williams this did not mean that one should check their faith at the door when engaged in public debate. Williams dealt with one of the most complicated moral issues of his day—the mistreatment of Native Americans.

Land then refers to Jesus' statement, "You will know the truth and the truth will make you free."[10] Land argues that it is not enough for a believer to discover the truth, he/she must also share the truth with the world. He further emphasizes this reality by reminding believers that Peter called them to always be ready to provide a reason for the hope they have in this life.[11]

In the fourth section of his chapter, Land reminds his readers that believers should not debate whether their responsibility is to be a witness to the Gospel or to be "salt and light." Land argues that it has always been and continues to be the responsibility of all believers both to share the Gospel and be salt and light within the nation. He states, "It denies the incarnation

---

9 Land, *Citizen Christians*, 8.

10 John 8:32.

11 Land, *Citizen Christians*, 9.

to preach the gospel of light without also being the salt that preserves and the light that penetrates the darkness."[12] With this, Land moves to his final section which only contains one paragraph and serves as the conclusion to his chapter. Quoting William Bennett and John Killinger, Land argues that believers must tell the whole truth, be engaged in society by being "salt and light," but also remember that it is only the Gospel that will ultimately change the human heart.

Critique

Land's chapter draws on Scripture, Baptist doctrine, and history, to attempt to prove his thesis that Christians have rights and responsibilities both as citizens of heaven and citizens of the United States of America. His Scripture references are accurate and are used appropriately considering the context of each text used. His representation of Baptist history and doctrine correspond to the Baptist Faith and Message and Baptist historical facts. His references to American history, as exampled in the inclusion of Roger Williams, furthers his argument well.

Land's writing style is appropriate, understandable, and communicates a much-needed message for Christians. This chapter serves as an entry guide into the topic of being a Citizen Christian. Every Baptist and every Evangelical believer should read and learn from Land's chapter in this book.

Separation of Church, State, And Religious Liberty
by Lynn R. Buzzard

Overview

Lynn Buzzard identifies the purpose of his chapter in the opening paragraph. He states, "The phrase *separation of church and state* has become for many people the premier slogan with which all constitutional questions are addressed and disposed. I want to examine the adequacy of that image in terms of both its strengths and liabilities, and particularly in the context of Baptist theological commitments and our Baptist experience."[13] Buzzard

---

12 Land, *Citizen Christians*, 10.
13 Ibid., 32.

fulfills his purpose by setting the context of the discussion, pointing out three strengths of the phrase, and then demonstrating the problems associated with the phrase as it is used today.

The author begins by demonstrating that the issue of church/state relations is not simply a United States concern. At the time the chapter was written, the former Soviet Union states were struggling over the relationship between these two institutions ordained by God. On the heels of introducing the reader to the Russian dilemma, Buzzard writes, "Amid all of these cultural and worldwide concerns and changes swirling around us, the phrase *the wall of separation* has become a pivotal point of discussion."[14]

While this phrase does not appear in the US Constitution, it is often invoked to end discussion when someone speaks to an issue from a spiritual/moral/religious perspective. Whether this word picture is utilized or whether the slogan, *separation of church and state* is utilized, the effect is often the same. The word picture and the slogan are most often invoked to shut out religious opinion in today's world.

Having set the context of the debate, Buzzard turns his attention to noting three positive usages of the slogan. The phrase serves as a helpful tool when a government adopts a particular religion and either prioritizes that religion or excludes other religions. This has been particularly important to Baptists throughout their history. History is replete with examples of Baptists being a dissenter group and thus facing persecution. Buzzard also provides more recent examples from the 1990s. As the former Soviet Union country of Georgia was transitioning into a free society, the nation struggled over prioritizing the Orthodox Church over Baptist and other religious groups.[15] Understanding a separation between the role of church and state could serve to help a nation avoid the establishment of a particular faith while excluding the free exercise of other religious groups.

Buzzard argues that the slogan, *separation of church and state,* has a second area of helpful usage. The author notes the problems related to a political usage of religion. As an example of his concern he states, "For instance, politicians seeking office often court members of the Evangelical communi-

---

14 Land, *Citizen Christians*, 33.
15 Ibid., 34.

ty, promising allegiance. This is a fraud. It is a misuse of religion."[16] In this case, the author sees value in using the slogan to expose the political misuse of religious speech.

Excessive government regulation to limit religious exercise serves as a third concern of the author. Buzzard demonstrates that while a government may not overtly persecute a religious group, it can hinder the free exercise of a religious group through regulation in the name of a compelling "public interest." He writes, "The state which is out to do us 'good' is the most dangerous state."[17] In the name of the compelling public interest, a government entity may subtly hinder the free exercise of one's deeply held religious beliefs. Buzzard accurately notes, "Most of the questions in the constitutional area today are not 'Establishment Clause' cases about how much the government can side with the Christians but really crucial questions about what limits exist against government intrusion, regulation, and management of Christians, their ministries, and their witness."[18] If this statement was true in 1994, it certainly is the case in 2022.

Over the last 15 months, we have witnessed extensive government intrusion into the free exercise of religion around the world and within the borders of the United States. During the COVID-19 Pandemic, nearly all States in the US attempted to restrict religious activity in various ways. Among the more extreme examples, California restricted churches from singing when they gathered for worship.[19] However, even greater concerns surfaced after Joe Biden took office as President of the United States in January of 2021.

In the first five months of 2021, numerous attempts have begun to hinder the free exercise of religion. For time and space, we will only mention three. In February, an assembly member introduced California Bill *AB655*, the so-called "California Law Enforcement Accountability Act."

---

16 Land, *Citizen Christians*, 35.
17 Ibid., 35.
18 Ibid., 35.
19 "California Bans Singing in Church: Just One of Many Outrageous Acts of Discrimination," accessed May 28, 2021, https://firstliberty.org/news/california-bans-singing-in-church/.

The bill, if passed, could keep a person who believes abortion or homosexuality to be sin from serving as a police officer in the state.[20]

In March, a group of students identifying as members of the LGBTQ+ community filed a lawsuit asking a federal judge to overturn the "Religious Exemption" clause of Title IX, which exempts Christian Colleges from being required to affirm unbiblical lifestyles.[21] On May 19th a federal judge ruled that the Biden Administration can force Christian colleges to change housing policies relating to the LGBTQ+ community.[22] It is unlikely that Buzzard could have envisioned the extent to which his concern in 1994 has proven true in the last 15 months. However, his concerns over government hindrance of the free exercise of religion through regulation were indeed valid.

After noting the possible usefulness of the slogan "separation of church and state," Buzzard began to expose problems with the way the slogan is typically applied these days. He began by pointing to the Supreme Court's decision in *Employment Department v. Smith*, which he argues created a

---

20 "California Bill Could Ban Christians Who Oppose Abortion, Same-Sex Marriage from Serving as Police," accessed May 28, 2021, https://www.christianheadlines.com/contributors/michael-foust/california-bill-could-ban-christians-who-oppose-abortion-same-sex-marriage-from-serving-as-police.html?utm_source=ChristianHeadlines%20Daily&utm_campaign=Christian%20Headlines%20Daily%20-%20ChristianHeadlines.com&utm_medium=email&utm_content=4536049&recip=542205729.

21 "LGBT Students Ask Court to Overturn the Government's 'Religious Exemption' for Christian School," accessed May 28, 2021, https://www.christianheadlines.com/contributors/michael-foust/lgbt-students-ask-court-to-overturn-the-govts-religious-exemption-for-christian-schools.html?utm_source=ChristianHeadlines%20Daily&utm_campaign=Christian%20Headlines%20Daily%20-%20ChristianHeadlines.com&utm_medium=email&utm_content=4568662&recip=542205729.

22 "Judge Says Biden Admin. Can Force Christian Colleges to Change LGBT Policies," accessed May 28, 2021, https://www.christianheadlines.com/contributors/michael-foust/judge-says-biden-admin-can-force-christian-colleges-to-change-lgbt-policies.html?utm_source=ChristianHeadlines%20Daily&utm_campaign=Christian%20Headlines%20Daily%20-%20ChristianHeadlines.com&utm_medium=email&utm_content=4806433&recip=542205729.

constitutional crisis.[23] Prior to this case, "a compelling interest" had to be demonstrated before a "sincerely held religious belief" could be infringed upon. However, this decision removed that standard. This action almost completely removed the government's obligation to protect the Free Exercise clause of the first amendment.

Having begun to demonstrate how the slogan "separation of church and state" was being applied to hinder the free exercise of religion, Buzzard reminded his readers that neither the slogan nor the mantra *wall of separation*, were in fact in the constitution. He then declared, "Many of us believe the form of separation of church and state now advocated by many who use that phrase was clearly never intended by the framers of the Constitution. In fact, I believe that anyone who suggests that is either ignorant or dishonest."[24] Buzzard then dedicates the next section of his chapter to demonstrate that the framers of the US Constitution neither attempted, nor desired, to hinder the free exercise of religion in the public square.

Buzzard argues that the separation idea sets up an impossible division of the religious and the secular. He writes, "There is no such thing as a neutral environment."[25] Indeed, public square involvement requires one to draw on the roots of their moral, spiritual, and religious values to engage an issue at hand. The author notes that if a public discussion is held on policies concerning resource allocation, bioethics, family values, human life, or a host of other concerns the body politic draws on whatever informs their value system.[26] To illustrate the problem, Buzzard draws attention to the country of Georgia, the Soviets, the US public school system, and the unintentional actions of Baptists which have contributed to the problem.

As Buzzard moves to the conclusion of his chapter he asks, "What Should be the Baptist Response?"[27] In response to his question, the author offers four encouragements. He begins by suggesting that when we engage the topic, we need to realize that we are not dealing with the same

---

23 Land, *Citizen Christians*, 35-36.
24 Ibid., 37.
25 Ibid., 39.
26 Ibid., 38-39.
27 Ibid., 43.

issues as our forebearers dealt with at the time of our nation's founding, or even the issues of the 1940s and 1950s. Therefore, he suggests we need to find new images and models of discussing the issues of today. Further, he reminds the readers that in doing so, Baptists must not simply rely on current laws, or even the Constitution. We must look to God's Word to be our guide.

Building on his first suggestion, Buzzard argues that Baptists need to have a serious biblical discussion about jurisprudence and the state. The author warns that the discussion must be biblical in nature, not simply a discussion based on quoting federal court rulings. He writes, "For us, ultimately, the framers of public life are not Jefferson and Madison—not even Scalia and Rehnquist or Bork and Thomas. The framers of an understanding of the public sphere also include our biblical traditions, our Lord, the apostles, and the New Testament."[28] Indeed, for the believer, the Bible is the final source of authority not only for faith but also for our practice in living out life in every realm, whether public or private.

Buzzard's third suggestion for a Baptist response is "to reject openly and candidly the notion that absolutes and moral values must be held privately but not discussed publicly."[29] One's moral values, whatever they are based on, guide one's private and public actions. One cannot truly divorce his/her secular activities from his/her deeply held beliefs. We must not pretend otherwise. We should boldly acknowledge the biblical basis of our values and act accordingly within the public square.

The author's final suggestion relates to maintaining a prophetic stance. He writes, "We have to recover our prophetic stance, and then we have to refuse to be co-opted."[30] In other words, we must speak the truth, in love, but without compromise in order to gain a "seat at someone's table." Recognizing the human temptation to be liked, Buzzard concludes the chapter by reminding his readers of the example of Ezekiel who was told he would not be successful in turning the tide in ancient Israel, yet he was to faithfully proclaim the truth. As the author indicates by the title

---

28 Land, *Citizen Christians*, 43.
29 Ibid., 44.
30 Ibid.

of this final section, we cannot take this stance in our own strength, "We Need God's Help in This."[31]

Critique

Buzzard's chapter in *Citizen Christians* offers a much-needed encouragement for the Evangelical world. When he wrote this chapter, the religious liberty long enjoyed in the United States faced early threats under the guise of the slogan, *the separation of church and state* and the mantra, *wall of separation*. He effectively sets the issue in context, discusses the potential positive uses of the slogan, and demonstrates the dangers faced because of it.

The present writer only struggled with one area of the chapter. Buzzard offered three potential positive uses of the term on pages 34-35. It seems the second may not have been clearly developed. This author shares the concern that some politicians use religious language to court evangelical support "only to divorce themselves from their promises after the election."[32] However, to suggest that this may somehow be a place where there should be a clearer separation between church and state, misses the mark. The issue is not that church and state should be separated, but that politicians should not separate themselves from their campaign promises. Believers should be weary of a candidate's promises, but this is not really a separation of church and state issue. In fact, Buzzard demonstrates that it is indeed impossible for one to remove religious value statements from public policy discussions.[33]

At the time of publication, the chapter presented a much-needed word for Baptists and evangelicals in general. The chapter is even more needed today. Buzzard's work should be read, considered, and applied by every true believer in Jesus.

---

31 Land, *Citizen Christians*, 44.
32 Ibid., 35.
33 Ibid., 38-39.

Mark H. Ballard

How Christians Can Make a Difference from Within the Government
by H. Robert Showers, Jr.

Overview

In the late 1980s Robert (Rob) Showers moved to Washington D. C. to serve as "the Special Assistant to the Attorney General, heading up the Criminal Justice area."[34] In the introduction to his chapter, the author describes his desires to make a difference in government. Upon arrival in D. C., he sought what could be done to make a difference in the nation's capital, or for that matter, in any sphere of government. Showers notes two basic approaches.

The first is the typical approach taken by most. In analyzing the two approaches, one must consider the motive, the method, and then the goal. Showers indicates that by motive, the focus of the first approach is on gaining "power, prestige and position because that is how you are going to get something done."[35] He describes this approach's method as using one's brain to get what you want. This use of the brain includes deceptive and manipulative tactics to achieve one's desires. Showers describes the goal in the first approach is about personal gain, and rising in the ranks, to "make a difference."

The author then describes a second approach to making a difference based on 2 Cor 5:17. He writes, "As I became a new creature in Christ, I learned I must make a difference for God and His kingdom, not for myself to get my position and power. This method must be according to His Word—truthfulness, straightforwardness, humility, meekness. And the goal must be for God's purpose and His glory."[36] The author argues that by following this method one can become an impact player, serving God and making a difference in government.

Based on his personal experience of serving God in our nation's capital, Showers sets forth four crucial principles that will enable a Citizen

---

34 Land, *Citizen Christians,* 122.
35 Ibid.
36 Ibid.

Christian to make a difference in government. The first principle that the author reveals as crucial is *humility*. He describes how the Lord used James 4:6-10 and 1 Peter 5:5-6 to teach him that humility is key. Coupled with these verses, Showers reveals that a friend taught him that he could get more done, if he were willing to give others the credit. The author describes how he learned to make a difference by prayer, fasting, and giving others credit for the victory. He also describes how the Lord used that process to make a difference on the Attorney General's Commission on Pornography.[37] Humility may be the opposite of the methods utilized by most people serving in government, but it is a crucial trait for a Citizen Christian to make a difference.

Showers' second key principle declares, "Obey God, Not People." In this section of the chapter, the author describes the challenge to obey God and His Word. Using the analogy of opening a gate of obedience to God, Showers suggests five gates the believer must open to obedience if he/she is to make a difference. First, the author encourages readers to open the "ear gate" by learning to listen to God's Word and Spirit.[38] Second, opening the "heart gate" to obedience is accomplished through developing an attitude of gratitude.[39] Third, the "mind gate" must be opened to obedience by becoming teachable. Fourth, the "soul gate" is opened by returning to the first principle—humility. Fifth, the "body gate" must be kept holy by obeying God's Word. This is the area Showers focused on through his work in the Justice Department as he dealt with drugs, pornography, and sexual abuse.[40]

A Citizen Christian can make a difference in government by walking in humility and obeying God rather than people. However, a third principle must also be followed for one to remain consistent. One must not only obey God, rather than people, the believer must also seek to *please God and not people*. Based on 1 Thess 2:4, Showers calls his readers to reject being people pleasers and seek to please God above all else. The author reminds the reader that there is only one way to please God—faith.

---

37 Land, *Citizen Christians*, 123.
38 Ibid., 124.
39 Ibid., 125.
40 Ibid.

Showers calls his readers to trust God in the face of the impossible. The author describes how the Lord used him and others to make a difference in North Carolina, South Carolina, and twenty-four other states. Ultimately, this led to Showers being able to draft *The Child Enforcement Act of 1988*, despite the objections of many people. Despite all odds, "the bill passed on the last day, the last hour, and the last minute" of 1988.[41]

As Showers' chapter ends, he reveals the fourth and final principle necessary for a Citizen Christian to make a difference. *One must have an eternal purpose.* To make this point the author draws from a story from the Lincoln/Douglas debate. After Douglas eloquently argued that the slaveholders must have the right to choose whether to keep slaves nearly convinced the crowd, Lincoln spoke one simple sentence that won the day. "You never have the right to be able to choose wrong."[42] Showers reminds his readers that while many may claim various rights to do wrong, "We have to stand in the gap."[43] Citizen Christians can make a difference in government by *walking in humility, obeying God, pleasing God, and living with an eternal purpose.*

Critique

Drawing on Scripture and his personal experience of serving in the federal government, H. Robert Showers demonstrates that a Citizen Christian can indeed make a difference within government. The testimony of his personal transformation as a new creature, rejecting the typical approach of Washington D. C., and adopting four guiding principles was a powerful testimony. The four principles were not only a guide for Showers but should guide every Citizen Christian who desires to make a difference within government. The chapter may have been even more effective with a few adjustments in the formatting of the headings. However, the point of the chapter was not only needed in 1994 but is a needed word for believers today. We can make a difference as a citizen of this nation if we will live our lives by prioritizing our heavenly citizenship, while not neglecting our civic duties on earth.

---

41 Land, *Citizen Christians,* 125.
42 Ibid., 127.
43 Ibid.

CITIZEN CHRISTIANS: BIBLICAL & RELEVANT

Having summarized the book *Citizen Christians* and examined three sample chapters of the book in more detail, it is now time to ask the two crucial questions posed at the beginning of this chapter. Is the concept of being a *Citizen Christian* biblical? Are the concepts related to being a *Citizen Christian* as described in various chapters of the book relevant today?

The Concept of Being a Citizen Christian

Land set the tone for the book by describing the concept intended by those who contributed to the work. He argued that a true believer in Jesus has both rights and responsibilities as dual citizens of heaven and of the nation in which he/she is a citizen. While the believer's first loyalty is to God, the Lord expects one to be a good citizen of the country in which the believer resides. Thus, a believer who is a citizen of the United States is expected to be a good citizen of both heaven and the United States. The question that arises is whether this concept of dual citizenship is biblical. We need to ask if Land's concept of rights and responsibilities in both realms is indeed valid. If so, then the implication is that a believer who is an American should not only be a good citizen of heaven, but also a good citizen of the United States. This requires engagement in the affairs of the nation.

To answer this first question, one needs to look no further than 1 Peter 2:13-17:

> Therefore, submit yourselves to every ordinance of man for the Lord's sake, whether to the king as supreme, or to governors, as to those who are sent by him for the punishment of evildoers and *for the* praise of those who do good. For this is the will of God, that by doing good you may put to silence the ignorance of foolish men—as free, yet not using liberty as a cloak for vice, but as bondservants of God. Honor all *people.* Love the brotherhood. Fear God. Honor the king.

This text reveals three crucial truths that when understood will enable us to answer the question before us with a resounding 'yes.'

God Expects Believers to Submit to the Laws of the Government

The text notes that we are to submit ourselves to the government's laws because of the Lord. In other words, by obeying the laws of our government, we are obeying God. The text also instructs the reader that submission to government is necessary because of the Lord's sending. Notice, the kings and governors are *sent* by God for "the punishment of evil doers and for the praise of those who do good." Here Peter repeats Paul's admonition in Romans. "Let every soul be subject to the governing authorities. For there is no authority except from God, and the authorities that exist are appointed by God." (Rom 13:1) Peter provides the reader with a third reason to submit to the laws of the government—"For this is the will of God."

God Expects Believers to Engage Government, As Citizens of the United States

One does not have to search hard to find believers who are ready to obey the speed limit, building codes, etc. At the same time many are unwilling to engage the governing authorities by voting in elections, participating in (or even discussing) political affairs, or running for public office. However, one should note a key word in the above text of Scripture. "Submit yourselves to *every* ordinance of man."

As a citizen of the United States, one is subject to many laws. There are local laws, state, laws, and federal laws, all of which must be obeyed, according to this text. The supreme law of the land in the United States is the Constitution. This crucial document reveals that this country uniquely established a government where its citizens were both needed and expected to be engaged. In the closing words of Abraham Lincoln's Gettysburg Address, he describes the United States as a "government of the people, by the people, and for the people."[44] Therefore, for us to submit to "every

---

44 "The Gettysburg Address," accessed March 10, 2021, https://rmc.library.cornell.edu/gettysburg/good_cause/transcript.htm.

ordinance of man" we must be engaged as citizens, utilizing our rights and responsibilities as citizens of this nation for God's glory.

God Expects Believers to Engage Government,
According to His Priorities

Before Peter leaves the topic at hand, he wants his readers to understand that they are not merely to engage their government, but they are to do so while considering God's priorities. Notice, while believers are to "honor all people, love the brotherhood, and honor the king"; we are also to "fear God." In other words, as Land points out in his book *Citizen Christians*, believers are to prioritize their relationship to God recognizing that their first citizenship is in heaven. As we "fear God" we will then obey all the ordinances of man, including the constitutional right and responsibility to engage in government.

Conclusion to Question One

The concept of being a *Citizen Christian* is clearly biblical. In fact, according to 1 Peter 2:13-17, if one is truly a citizen of heaven and lives in the United States, he or she is under obligation to be engaged in voting, discussing, acting on political issues, and for some, running for public office. Furthermore, one's engagement of government must be guided by God's priorities. Thus, if one is a believer and a United States citizen, and if that person refuses to engage government, he/she is not only failing to fulfill the rights and responsibilities of United States citizenship but is also failing to fulfill the rights and responsibilities of his/her heavenly citizenship.

THE RELEVANCE OF THE CHAPTERS FOR TODAY

Land and his co-contributors wrote *Citizen Christians* in the early 1990s. While this chapter has demonstrated that the overall concept of being a *Citizen Christian* is a biblical idea, there remains one significant question. Do the chapters of this book remain relevant in 2021? To that question, we now turn our attention.

Every chapter of *Citizen Christians* proved helpful to this reader. However, to remain within the scope of this essay, only three chapters were examined in detail. We have already observed that Richard Land's chapter, *Citizen Christians Have Rights Too*, presents the biblical concept that true believers have a right and a responsibility to be engaged in the government of the United States. The question of relevance is answered simply by acknowledging that the concept is biblical. If being a Citizen Christian is biblical, then it is relevant. Not only was Land's chapter relevant in the early 1990s, but it is just as relevant today.

The relevance of Lynn Buzzard's chapter titled, the *Separation of Church, State, and Religious Liberty*, to believers living in 1994 is certain. The principles discussed in this crucial chapter are as relevant, if not more so, today. In our examination of the chapter, we noted several concerns in Buzzard's day. However, we also noted several religious liberty issues currently in the news. Similarly, the same principles that enabled Rob Showers to make a difference within government in the 1990s also prove relevant for today. Therefore, we can conclude that the book *Citizen Christians* is not only *biblical*, but it also remains *relevant*.

Conclusion

This chapter began by recounting the fact that the present author was brought up in a home that believed, taught, and lived out the idea that all true believers are Citizen Christians. The author then suggested that Richard Land, in whose honor this chapter was written, embodies the very principles taught in the Ballard home. Following these introductory comments, the author stated his purpose—to ask, and answer, two questions. Is the concept of being a *Citizen Christian* biblical? Are the concepts related to being *Citizen Christians* as described in various chapters of the book still relevant today?

The chapter accomplished its purpose by summarizing the book, examining three chapters of the book, and answering both questions in the affirmative. Having demonstrated the overarching principle and the sample chapters are biblical and remain relevant, this writer invites the reader to revisit *Citizen Christians*. Read it, contemplate its wisdom, and let the words of this small book empower you to once again engage the culture in which we live. We owe an eternal debt of gratitude to Dr. Richard Land, not only for this book, but for a lifetime of demonstrating through his teaching, preaching, writing, and living what it means to be a *Citizen Christian*.

Chapter 4

Christians' Involvement in Politics and Government

J. Gerald Harris

Richard Land became a part of my life in the early 1980s when I became a trustee at Criswell College in Dallas, TX, where he first taught as a professor of theology and church history, before becoming the College's vice-president of Academic Affairs. I was inspired by his effective and courageous leadership as the president of the Ethics & Religious Liberty Commission and even more recently as the president of Southern Evangelical Seminary. Through his syndicated radio program, frequent television appearances, and role as executive editor of The Christian Post, he has become one of America's most effective spokesmen on several political, social, moral, and ethical concerns. It was no surprise to me when Time Magazine selected Dr. Land as one of "The Twenty-Five Most Influential Evangelicals in America."[1]

When he was providing leadership at Criswell College, he often served churches across the convention as their interim pastor. When he was the interim pastor of First Baptist Church in Irving, Texas, he invited me to preach a revival meeting in the church. In the succeeding years we would see each other at the annual sessions of the Southern Baptist Convention, and I was grateful that he always had time to stop and visit for a few minutes. We had dinner together at the Peachtree Plaza Hotel in Atlanta when the Convention met there in 1995. For me it was a memorable experience.

Dr. Land always gave me a sense of worth, causing me to recall Ralph Waldo Emerson's statement, "A great man is always willing to be little."[2] *I*

---

1 "Richard Land," accessed February 05, 2021, https://ideas.time.com/contributor/richard-land-2/.

2 https://www.goodreads.com/quotes/243242-a-great-man-is-always-

consider Richard Land a great man and only heaven will properly reveal the extensive impact of his life and ministry. Therefore, I am honored to write one of the chapters for this Festschrift in his honor on the occasion of his 75th birthday. Happy birthday, Dr. Land and thank you for your far-reaching, impactful, and Spirit-directed ministry.

* * *

The United States of America was established on a firm and unwavering belief in Almighty God. In the hearts of the Pilgrims, in the words of men like George Washington and Benjamin Franklin, in our Declaration of Independence, in the pledge of allegiance to our flag, in our congress and in our courtrooms, in our national anthem and on our money, there is evidence that this country was founded and has been perpetuated by Christian principles. George Washington himself said, "It is the duty of all nations to acknowledge the providence of Almighty God, to obey His will, to be grateful for His benefits, and humbly to implore His protection and favors."[3] Therefore, if we are to preserve the rich and blessed heritage that has been entrusted to us Christian citizens, we must be involved in the political process in this beloved country. If we fail to assert ourselves into the affairs of our government, the United States will become another statistic in the long list of nations that have squandered away their blessings and responsibilities and degenerated into obscurity.

THE PROBLEM OF COMPARTMENTALIZATION

Christians must be involved in politics and government because one's Christian faith cannot be compartmentalized. If they dare to permit their

---

willing-to-be-little#:~:text=Quote%20by%20Ralph%20Waldo%20Emerson,always%20willing%20to%20be%20little.%E2%80%9D, accessed February 05, 2021.

3 "America Acknowledges God," accessed February 05, 2021, http://morallaw.org/resources/america-acknowledges-god/#:~:text=On%20October%203%2C%201789%2C%20one%20week%20after%20Congress,form%20of%20government%20for%20their%20safety%20and%20happiness.

government to function without the spiritual influence of those who are committed to Christ, they do so at their own peril. To allocate one's faith to Sundays only, to some edifice of worship or certain limited aspects of life is to trivialize and limit one's religion. When Jesus interceded for His followers as their great High Priest in John 17, He prayed to the Father, "I have given them Your word; and the world has hated them because they are not of the world, just as I am not of the world. I do not pray that You take them out of the world, but that You should keep them from the evil one. They are not of the world, just as I am not of the world" (John 17:14-16).[4] Billy Graham explained, "Christians are like the gulf stream, which is in the ocean and yet not part of it. This mysterious current defies the mighty Atlantic, ignores its tides, and flows steadily upon its course. Its color is different, being a different blue. Its temperature is different, being warmer. Its direction is different, being from the south. It is in the ocean, and yet it is not part of it."[5]

God has left us in the world so that we might permeate this planet with our influence. We are to be a positive, godly influence on those in spiritual darkness. We are to live in such a way that those outside the faith see our good deeds and our manner of life and know that there is something "different" about us. So, we are not supposed to compartmentalize or pigeon-hole our lives to some restricted segment of our society, but permeate, penetrate, infiltrate every corner of this world and every facet of our culture with the spirit of Christ and the truth of His Word.

A compartmentalized faith becomes like an addendum to a book, a postscript to a letter, or a codicil to a will. It is like a side street rather than a major highway, a strip mall rather than a downtown shopping district, a pinch hitter rather than a starter in the line-up, the appetizer rather than the main course, and a backyard football game rather than the Super Bowl. When professing Christians fail to integrate their faith into the whole of their lives and do not boldly live out their beliefs in terms of politics, ed-

---

[4] While there may be references to Scripture in this chapter, any actual citations are from the KJV, unless otherwise noted.

[5] "Billy Graham: In the World, Not of It," accessed February 05, 2021, https://decisionmagazine.com/in-world-not-of-it/.

ucation, commerce, and entertainment, the church loses it influence and becomes nothing more than an irrelevant sideshow rather than a transformative agent in society.

Unfortunately, the world has begun to recognize Christianity as just one element of society among many. We are tolerated and occasionally defended, just like other components in our culture, but not really taken very seriously. Sadly, Christianity has for the most part acclimated to the culture rather than successfully called the culture to acclimate to Christ.

Jesus gave us two metaphors – salt and light – that teach us that Christianity is designed not to just be a minor part of the society, but the defining part. Salt permeates! It flavors! It arrests corruption. Similarly, Christianity should influence everything it touches, correct errant philosophies, promote a healthy and moral government, and arrest the decay of a society that is tending toward corruption.

Similarly, light has a permeating influence. It drives out darkness completely. In a very dark room, a small candle will give an individual enough light to see. The good thing about light is that it affects everything within its domain. A light does not touch part of the room. It drives out darkness totally from its sphere of influence. Light and darkness are totally incompatible. Where one exists, the other is driven away. Wherever truth is, deceit and dishonesty must excuse themselves. Wherever Christians are, society should be better.

Martin Luther, the 16th century Augustinian monk, said that the Christian was worthless until he could vibrantly live a profane life (in Latin "profane life" means "life outside the temple"). Luther not only brought clarity to the Gospel message, but he also catapulted believers beyond the stained-glass walls of the church. Exhorting them to be salt and light in places where they might be skewered and lampooned.

George McLeod commented,

> I am trying to recover the claim that Jesus Christ was not crucified in a cathedral, between two candles, but on a cross between two thieves, and that on the town garbage heap; at a crossroad of politics so cosmopolitan that they had to write His title in Hebrew and in

Latin and in Greek. . . .. and at the kind of place where cynics talk smut, and thieves curse, and soldiers gamble. Because that is where He died, and that is what He died about. And that is where Christ's own ought to be, and that is what church people ought to be about. That is where the church must be and that is what churchmanship should be about.[6]

True spirituality is incredibly practical, robust, and workable, no matter where you dwell or what you do. If your Christianity is not viable and stout in the most difficult of cultures, like the political arena, then it isn't made of the same stuff that characterized the believers of the early church. To help you take your Christianity out of the Christian ghetto where the secularists would love to have you remain, here is a simple prescription: Stop compartmentalizing Christianity and love God with all your heart, all your mind, all your soul, all the time, and in every place.

THE OPPORTUNITY TO PARTNER WITH GOD

Occasionally, we look at what is happening in our government and conclude that Satan must have established the government to create turmoil and confusion among people. In the second temptation of Jesus in the wilderness, Satan took the Son of God up on a high mountain and showed Him all the kingdoms of this world and said, "All this authority I will give You, and their glory; for this has been delivered to me, and I will give it to whomever I wish" (Luke 4:6). Does that mean that Satan has established earthly kingdoms (governments) and rules over them?

First, it is important to understand that when reading a narrative passage quoting Satan, one should keep in mind what else the Bible says about him. In John 8:44 Jesus is speaking of the devil and states, "(He) has nothing to do with the truth, because there is no truth in him. When he lies, he speaks out of his own character, for he is a liar and the father of lies." (ESV). Satan did

---

6 George Macleod, accessed February 05, 2021, https://www.goodreads.com/quotes/1468095-i-simply-argue-that-the-cross-be-raised-again-at.

not create government and God did not hand government over to the devil as much as the devil would like to think that. Second, it is true that God, in His sovereignty, considered it wise, as part of His curse on the world after the Edenic sins, to give Satan a significant measure of power in this world.

Many Christians have hesitated to get involved in governmental affairs because they perceive politics as corrupt or even antithetical to Christianity. However, if that point of view were applied to everything that is thought to be crooked or unethical, Christians would have to isolate themselves from the world and lead a monastic life.

Christians must understand that God created three institutions: the home, government, and the church. The home was established by God in the Garden of Eden when Adam and Eve were joined together. He knew that "it (was) not good for man to be alone," so He caused a deep sleep to fall on Adam whereupon He took one of his ribs and made a woman. Jehovah God brought Adam and Eve together and it is clearly stated, "Therefore a man shall leave his father and mother and be joined to his wife, and they shall become one flesh" (Gen 2:24). Even after that first couple fell into sin, God continued His plan for families, and even spoke prophetically of the salvation that would come through the seed of the woman (Gen 3:15).

The church was established by God with Jesus as the cornerstone and the apostles as the foundation. In Ephesians 2:20 the Apostle Paul describes the church as being "built on the foundation of the apostles and prophets, Jesus Christ Himself being the chief cornerstone." The visible church was revealed in Acts 2, when a mighty rushing wind and a transforming fire formed the apostles and disciples into a visible community and empowered them to proclaim the Gospel of Jesus Christ.

God established the civil government shortly after Noah and his family exited the ark following the great flood described in Genesis 7. In Gen 9:6 God spoke to Noah and his three sons and said, "Whoever sheds man's blood, by man his blood shall be shed; for in the image of God He made man." In this sentence God gives to man both the right and the responsibility to put murderers to death. Dr. Ronald Youngblood, professor of Old Testament at Bethel Theological Seminary, writes,

Christians' Involvement in Politics and Government

The reason is (obvious): God has made man in his own image, and therefore the murderer, in taking the life of a man, displays contempt for God as well. This principle has important implications for the function of the state in capital punishment. Civil government, as instituted by God, involves the power of life and death. It is not the mindless blood revenge of a murdered man's relatives but the orderly processes of civil law that should be the deciding factor in cases of capital offenses. In this respect, government is God's gracious provision for the preservation of human life in a fallen world.[7]

Henry M. Morris, a Christian apologist, scientist, and young earth creationist, explained that the biblical record shows that the primary purpose of government initially was the protection of its citizens beginning with the protection of the foundational right to life as a gift from God. He explained, "It is clear, of course, that the authority for capital punishment also implies the authority to establish laws governing those human activities and personal relationships which if unregulated could soon lead to murder (e.g., robbery, adultery, usurpation of property boundaries). Thus, this simple instruction to Noah is the fundamental basis for all human legal and governmental institutions."[8]

The point is this: if God established three institutions for the good of mankind, Christians should be eager and willing to cooperate with God and zealously engage in supporting those institutions. Most Christians very likely find it much easier to invest in the home and the church rather than the government, because the political arena seems to be so beleaguered by partisanship, selfish agendas, reckless spending, conflicting ideologies, unpleasant rancor, and general hopelessness. Ernest Benn, British publisher and political publicist, summarized politics by saying, "Politics is the art of

---

[7] Ronald F. Youngblood, *The Book of Genesis: An Introductory Commentary* (Grand Rapids, MI: Baker Book House, 1991), 120.

[8] Henry M. Morris, *The Genesis Record, A Scientific and Devotional Commentary on the Book of Beginnings* (Grand Rapids, MI, Baker Books, 1976), 225.

looking for trouble, finding it everywhere, diagnosing it incorrectly and applying the wrong remedies."[9]

Jesus lived under the ruthless regime of an oppressive imperial dictatorship and had absolutely no opportunity to participate in governmental affairs, no chance to influence those in charge and no opportunity to cast a ballot in an election. And yet, when He was accosted by hostile inquirers who wanted to trap Him into taking a risky and dangerous stand on whether Jews should pay taxes to the Roman Empire, He declared, "Render to Caesar the things that are Caesar's, and to God the things that are God's" (Mark 12:17). If Jesus could be that positive about an inimical and hostile government, it is certain that we should look beyond the faults and flaws of our current political situation and find out what we can do to make what God established more effective and more pleasing in His sight. Plato, the Athenian philosopher stated almost 2500 years ago, "One of the penalties for refusing to participate in politics is that you end up being governed by your inferiors."[10]

God Almighty established the institution of government generally; and history indicates that God was exceedingly instrumental in establishing the United States of America. Obviously, there are those who want to rewrite history and denigrate any thought of our forefathers being led by the Spirit of God in founding this country, but the facts are incontrovertible. While not all the founding fathers were men of faith, historical records clearly reveal that almost all of them had a biblical perspective on governing. Patrick Henry, Governor of Virginia, stated, "It cannot be emphasized too clearly and too often that this nation was founded, not by religionists, but by Christians, not on religion, but on the Gospel of Jesus Christ."[11]

John Jay, first Chief Justice of the Supreme Court, declared, "Providence has given to our people the choice of their rulers, and it is the duty,

---

9 "Brainy Quote," accessed February 05, 2021, https://www.brainyquote.com/authors/ernest-benn-quotes.

10 "Brainy Quote," accessed February 05, 2021, https://www.brainyquote.com/quotes/plato_101112.

11 Richard G. Lee, ed. *The American Patriot's Bible* (Nashville: Thomas Nelson, 2009), 1-12.

and well as the privilege and interest of our Christian nation, to select and prefer Christians for their rulers."[12] Charles Carroll, signer of the Declaration of Independence, declared, "Without morals a republic cannot subsist any length of time; they therefore who are decrying the Christian religion, whose morality is so sublime and pure . . . are undermining the solid foundation of morals, the best security for the duration of free governments."[13]

In founding this nation our forefathers admittedly pledged to each other their lives, fortunes, and sacred honor. If we are to remain a free republic and "one nation under God" we must partner with our Heavenly Father and be willing to pay the price to keep it that way.

It's Time to Pray

When the Apostle Paul wrote to Timothy he instructed, "Therefore, I exhort first of all that supplications, prayers, intercessions, and giving of thanks be made for all men, for kings and all who are in authority, that we may lead a quiet and peaceable life in all godliness and reverence" (1 Tim 2:1-2). Could it be that many Christians are no longer praying for our public servants because we have lost confidence in the sovereignty of God and think governmental leaders are beyond the effective reach of prayer? Have we become so absorbed with the cynicism of the times that we have become convinced that all office holders have thrown their hats in the ring to slide their hands down someone else's pocket?

When we listen to all the negative campaign ads and observe all the mudslinging we begin to wonder if the only choice we have at the voting machine is between the devil and a witch or the lesser of two evils. Over the past 20 years I have spent a lot of time both in Washington and Atlanta reporting on both state and national political leaders and I have discovered that there are a significant number of honest, faithful, dedicated public servants, and we must not judge all those in politics by those who are bad apples.

---

12 "Founding Father Quote," accessed February 05, 2021, https://www.foundingfatherquotes.com/quote/675.
13 Lee, *The American Patriot's Bible,* 1-12.

Since we are commanded to pray for those who are in authority over us, it is important for you to know exactly who those people are. Pray for the United States President and Vice President by name. God may not expect you to pray for the senators from Main to California and from Minnesota to Louisiana, but He very likely expects you to pray for the two senators from your state. Similarly, God may not expect you to pray for all the congressional representatives from the 27 districts in New York or the 53 representatives from California, but it is important for you to know the name of the individual who represents your district in the U. S. House of Representatives and pray for him or her. If we cannot name those who are in authority, we have never prayed for them.

If you are systematic, try following the model below:

Sunday – pray for the U. S. president and vice president
Monday – pray for your governor and lieutenant governor
Tuesday – pray for your state's two senators
Wednesday – pray for your district's congressman
Thursday – pray for your state senator
Friday – pray for your state representative
Saturday – pray for your mayor and city council

When you begin to really pray for the men and women who represent you in government you will soon discover that it is not enough to say, "Lord, bless all the political leaders" any more than it is to say, "Lord, bless all the missionaries, whoever they are, wherever they serve and whatever they are doing." That kind of praying is ineffectual; and it is so general that you would never know if God ever answered that kind of prayer.

Efficacious praying demands intellectual praying. When praying for your leaders you must learn their values, understand something about their personal characters, find out how they are voting on issues, and then pray pointedly and specifically for those who represent you. When you pray with understanding the results can be phenomenal. After months of faithful, fervent, focused prayer you may very likely begin to see that God has been answering your prayers for some of those people and their demeanor, their views, and their votes reflect that God is at work in their lives and they need to be re-elected. Conversely, you may get weary that God is not working in the lives of others who hold a political office and as your knowledge grows about their leadership, you will conclude that they ought not to be in office any longer unless things change, and that they should be replaced.

It Is Time to Stand Up

Prayer should never include a "let God do it" attitude. Prayer and faith without works are dead. Once we have met God at the throne of grace and made our requests known to Him, we must voice our concerns and take our stand for truth and righteousness. Dr. Jeff Myers in his article titled, "Politics: Should Christians Get Involved?" reminds us that while Romans 13 stresses the importance of obeying governmental leaders, we also express our obedience to God by exercising our rights and privileges as citizens. Myers writes,

> A democratic republic such as we have in America is perhaps the most difficult form of government to maintain. As Benjamin Franklin emerged from a meeting of the Constitutional Convention, a woman asked him, 'Mr. Franklin, what sort of government have you given us?' Franklin replied, 'A republic, madam, if you can keep it.' Franklin and the other founding fathers understood the peril of apathy. If citizens don't get involved, elected representatives quickly begin to express their own interests or the interests of those who are willing to pay them money and attention. Apathy and greed soon give way to corruption and injustice which gives way to tyranny and misery.[14]

---

14 Jeff Myers, "Politics: Should Christians Get Involved?," accessed February 05, 2021, https://www.crosswalk.com/family/homeschool/politics-should-christians-get-involved-1128040.html.

The Bible states, "When the righteous are in authority, the people rejoice, but when a wicked man rules, the people groan" (Prov 29:2). In our day it is not just a matter of bad people being in politics, but good people not willing to get involved. In fact, to not be political is to be political. If God ordained human government, then told His people to stay out, who does that leave to run it? Christians must get involved to preserve this democratic republic of ours. Who is in a better position to help us return to the moorings of our founding fathers and comprehend the standard of righteousness than those who are committed to the sacred Scriptures and who know "the Power that hath made and preserved us a nation?"[15]

Can we turn this nation back to the principles inculcated in the hearts and minds of our founders and in the documents they authored? There are political pundits and governmental experts who contend that we have gone too far to the left and past the point of no return. Perhaps we have listened to them so often and so long that we have just about abandoned all hope – or if we have hope, it is the hope of the postponement of what we consider to be the inevitable.

Alexander Tyler, a Scottish history professor at the University of Edinburgh, made the following statement about the fall of the Athenian Republic over 2000 years ago:

> A democracy is always temporary in nature; it simply cannot exist as a permanent form of government. A democracy will continue to exist up until the time that voters discover they can vote themselves generous gifts from the public treasury. From that moment on, the majority always votes for the candidates who promise the most benefits from the public treasury, with the result that every democracy will finally collapse due to loose fiscal policy, which is always followed by a dictatorship.[16]

---

15 Francis Scott Key, Star Spangled Banner, 1814.
16 "A Democracy Will Only Last Until . . .," accessed February 05, 2021, http://www.lsconservative.com/a-democracy-will-only-last-until/.

If one adds current political trends to Tyler's analysis of a democracy the future looks exceedingly dim, but while I am a realist, I prefer to take an optimistic approach at this point. Negativity never accomplished anything but sorrow, depression, and regression. Thomas Edison was credited with the invention of the electric light bulb, but his creation was met with skepticism and ridicule. "Henry Morton of the Stevens Institute of Technology predicted the invention would be a conspicuous failure and a British parliamentary committee, apparently determined to keep Old Blighty in the dark ages concluded the light bulb was good enough for our transatlantic friends, but unworthy of the attention of practical or scientific men."[17]

When Orville and Wilbur Wright made their historic flight at Kitty Hawk, NC, on December 17, 1903, many of their acquaintances refused to discuss it, because "it was embarrassing to discuss anything so preposterous. . ... One reason nearly everyone in the United States was disinclined to swallow the reports about flying with a machine heavier than air was that important scientists had already explained in the public prints why the thing was impossible. . . (and) why should the public be fooled by silly stories about two obscure bicycle repairmen who hadn't even been to college?" The Wright brothers' father, a Bishop in the Church of the Brethren, had argued from his pulpit years earlier that air flight was (1) impossible, and (2) contrary to the will of God.[18]

Scientists and preachers can often be wrong in their assessments and predictions, but we know that God is sovereign and powerful; and with Him all things are possible – even the restoration of a nation. Why? If God can redeem human life and if God can revive a church, He can retrieve a whole nation.

---

17 Accessed February 05, 2021, https://theculturetrip.com/north-america/usa/articles/10-inventions-no-one-thought-would-be-a-success.

18 Accessed February 05, 2021, https://www.wright-brothers.org/History_Wing/Aviations_Attic/They_Wouldnt_Believe/They_Wouldnt_Believe_the_Wrights_Had_Flown.htm.

J. Gerald Harris

Practical Suggestions

Vote!

Christians must register to vote and cast their ballots in every election. I remember the first time I was privileged to vote. One had to be 21 years old at the time to cast a ballot in a national election. The year was 1964. Lyndon Johnson was the incumbent Democratic Presidential candidate and Barry Goldwater was the Republican candidate for president. As a North Carolinian I grew up in a democratic home. One evidence of that is that my brother's name is Truman. He was named after the 33rd president of the United States. I am not sure why I broke the family tradition, but I knew that I liked Goldwater's conservative views on small government, free enterprise, and a strong national defense. Voting then was a great privilege and my appreciation regarding the right to vote has only grown through the years. It is difficult to believe that I have now voted in 15 different presidential elections.

When it comes to being a Christian advocate of good governmental policies and motivating people to vote, Richard Land is a champion. In 2004 Dr. Land was the featured speaker at the Georgia Right to Life Rally. He stood on the steps of the State Capitol and boldly declared, "A woman's womb is the most dangerous place that has ever existed in the United States of America." I was the editor of *The Christian Index* at the time and wrote the story on Dr. Land's message. The weather was cold, but to an enthusiastic crowd Land thundered, "You can't relegate God Almighty to any human construction, especially a political party, but I will tell you God is pro-life."[19] Later that same year the president of the ERLC brought the agency's iVoteValues Mobile Voter Registration Rig and Information Center to Atlanta and I was privileged to write another story in *The Christian Index* on his initiative to register voters and underscore the importance of voting one's values.

Whether Christians vote in local, state, or national elections, they should make sure they have all the information necessary in order to make

---

19 "Marchers Walk the Talk of Pro-Life," accessed February 05, 2021, https://georgiabulletin.org/news/2004/01/marchers-walk-talk-pro-life/.

wise decisions. In many cases they must vote on the platform rather than the personality. All politicians have flaws like other people, but if they embrace truly Christian values, we should not let their pride, arrogance, or bluster cause us to vote for someone who may be charming and charismatic but opposed to the ideals and principles we hold dear. Colin Powell commented, "As I have done in every election since I started voting so many years ago, I always like to take my time and examine the two candidates, see not only two candidates but the policies they will bring in, the people they will bring in, who they might appoint to the Supreme Court, and look at the whole range of issues before making a decision."[20]

Proclaim!

The hour is too late, and the crisis is too great for Christians to be silent. Evangelist Steve Hale in his book *Storm Warnings: America's Race to a Day of Reckoning,* writes,

> Stay out of politics, just preach the Gospel. This is the mantra of many well-meaning laymen and preachers alike. It sounds so 'right on' and no doubt would elicit loud 'amens' in conference gatherings but preaching the whole counsel of God does not exclude what the Bible teaches about the Christian's involvement in civil government or political activism. While the road to redemption does not travel through Washington, D. C., and while Jesus did not come to restore old creatures through government reform, but to make new creatures through the transforming power of the Gospel, this does not negate the responsibility for the believer's political involvement, nor does it nullify evangelical preachers from addressing the relevant moral issues of our day that may contain political overtones.[21]

---

20 "Brainy Quote," accessed February 05, 2021, https://www.brainyquote.com/quotes/colin_powell_891500?src=t_voting.

21 Steve Hale, *Storm Warnings! America's Race to a Day of Reckoning* (Jasper, GA: Riverstone Group Publishing, 2017), 390.

Hale continued, "A failure to hold the government or the legislative branch accountable for their unbiblical actions by refusing to preach such from the pulpit due to the pressures of political correctness leaves the impression that we are adhering to the separation of church and state, when, in fact, our Founding Fathers did just the opposite."[22] The Word of God provides multiple examples of God's representatives confronting political leaders: Moses warned Pharaoh, Elijah confronted Ahab, Nathan counseled David, Daniel spoke to Nebuchadnezzar and had a significant influence on the government of Babylon. Christians must say to the government, "Whatever is morally wrong is not politically right." As long as the government legalizes killing babies, normalizes sexual perversion, compromises the sanctity of marriage, passes laws that desecrate the Lord's Day, pushes God out of our educational system, and makes decisions that open the door to socialism, we must not be silent.[23] Adrian Rogers said, "Be civil, but don't be silent."[24]

Evangelize!

As we have already stated, some think politics is corrupt to the core and that political involvement is incongruous for those who are serious about their walk with Christ. That is a view that conforms to what Wayne Grudem calls the "Do Evangelism, Not Politics" approach to civic engagement. However, I believe that the more effective we are in evangelizing our society, the more support we will get for our Christian values. So, we evangelize not only to save souls, but to save society.

Adrian Rogers stated,

> Our goal must be to change public opinion. The only way we'll change it is through the living, powerful Word of God. We must get the Gospel out into the public square. We're not going to out-argue

---

22 Hale, *Storm Warnings!*, 390.
23 Ibid.
24 "Did God Tell us to Stay Out of Politics?," accessed February 05, 2021, https://www.lwf.org/articles/did-god-tell-us-to-stay-out-of-politics-article.

the lost. They are blind, they don't see it. The Bible says, 'But the natural man does not receive the things of the Spirit of God, for they are foolishness to him; nor can he know them, because they are spiritually discerned' (1 Cor 2:14). The natural man must come to know Jesus. We're to persuade people, winning them back one at a time, bringing them to Christ.[25]

In the 1970s, the church I served in as pastor had a bus ministry. It was a ministry that required a lot of work and expense. We had to buy old school buses and maintain them, find qualified drivers, establish a children's church, and often buy clothes for the children that were impoverished. We initiated the ministry to reach underprivileged children in mobile home parks and some of the government projects in the area. We eventually acquired ten buses and maintained 8 bus routes that required Saturday visits to all the children we were trying to reach. Some of the bus captains took the entire day to visit the children on their route. On Sundays some of the captains drove over fifty miles to complete their routes beginning early on Sunday morning to pick up their riders and getting home after two o'clock in the afternoon once they returned all their children to their homes.

Some in the church opposed the ministry because many of the children did not look like the children of our church members. The economic level of those we were reaching was far below the economic level of our congregation. The bus ministry introduced ethnic diversity into our church; and at times the emergency financial needs of the bus ministry preempted purchasing some of the "nicer" things that would have added beauty to our facilities or enhanced some social function that was in no way essential to carrying out the Great Commission. Occasionally a member would complain about the bus ministry, but after time they began to see how the children's lives were being transformed. Some of the children persuaded their parents to ride the buses as well and when the parents began to trust Christ and demonstrate thanksgiving for the welcome and love they felt from many of the members, the acceptance of the ministry began

---

25 "Did God Tell us to Stay Out of Politics?"

to soar. We witnessed the salvation of a few children that spiraled into the salvation of entire families in those mobile home parks and government housing projects. The transformation was incredible.

So, we need to reach the lost for the sake of their souls, but we also need to reach them for the sake of society. If we have not noticed, our society needs Jesus. As the percentage of lost people increases, they have increasing influence. Lost people seldom care about the sanctity of life, so the number of abortions escalates. Lost people are less interested in truth and more interested in tolerance. Lost people are more likely to conform to the culture than transform the culture. Lost people are less likely to be tied to traditional values and biblical morality, so we have the rise of secularism and hedonism. Therefore, every time an individual truly embraces the Christ of Calvary, we move an inch closer to a society that more nearly reflects a biblical worldview.

Volunteer!

Too few Christians get involved in the political process from the beginning. Call the party of your choice – the county headquarters – and ask if there is some way you can help. You will be surprised and pleased with how fast they will welcome your help and support. If Christians were involved in party politics, there would be an opportunity for the brightest, strongest, and most politically attractive individuals to be considered for public office, but if believers remain outside the framework of party politics the best and most qualified people will never be considered for office. Consequently, they will have to go to the polls to vote for the candidates who in our opinion will do the least amount of damage to our republic.

There is also a need to get involved at the level where the candidates are selected and work for people who are worthy of support, individuals who have the right views, the right character, the right values whether they are running for the school board, the U. S. Senate or for the presidency. It has been said by campaign strategists that in a successful election the victory is due to three things: the ability and appeal of the candidate (25 percent), the issues (25 percent), and the organization (50). Most organizations are made up primarily of volunteers. Rasmus Nielsen, in his book *Ground Wars*, contends that political campaigns today are won by the strategic deployment of teams of staffers and volunteers who work the phones and canvass block by block, house by house, and voter by voter.[26]

Some elections in US history have been incredibly close. In 2000, George Bush squeezed by Al Gore in Florida by a certified count of 537 votes. In a New Hampshire Senate race in 1974 Louis Wyman won over John Durkin by a two-vote margin. In a 1910 contest for the congressional district in Buffalo, New York, Charles B. Smith snuck by incumbent De Alva S. Alexander by one vote, 20,685 to 20,684.[27] In essence, if the losing candidates had secured a few more volunteers to work in their office, licking postage stamps, going door to door, making phone calls, and doing those little things that make up a volunteer organization those few votes might have gone the other way.

Focus!

There are some issues that absolutely require our focus and attention. First, we must plead with every Christian to stand up for religious liberty. Dr. Land has stated, "To help preserve the First Amendment for all Americans, we have the right to the free exercise of our faith without the interference of the government. We agree with that as Baptists. We believe that people have the freedom to worship and to express their faith and to have houses of worship in the places where they live."[28] Many have given their lives because they believed religious liberty was worth the supreme sacrifice. Dare we sit idly by and watch as our "right to freedom of religion . . . (and) the

---

26 Rasmus Kleis Nielsen, *Ground Wars: Personalized Communication in Political Campaigns* (Princeton, NJ: Princeton University Press, 2012), 166.

27 "11 Elections Decided by One Vote (or Fewer)," accessed February 05, 2021, https://www.mentalfloss.com/article/59873/10-elections-decided-one-vote-or-less.

28 "20 Quotes from Baptists on Religious Liberty," accessed February 05, 2021, https://erlc.com/resource-library/articles/20-quotes-from-baptists-on-religious-liberty/.

free exercise of religion" is systematically and deliberately removed from our society? We must not!

Christians must do everything they can to reverse the Roe v. Wade decision of the Supreme Court and speak out loudly for those who cannot speak for themselves. What the culture calls a woman's choice, the Bible calls murder. God plainly says in Prov 6:16-17 that one of the things that God hates is "hands that shed innocent blood." Scientists are practically unanimous in their conviction that life begins with conception. Abortion has become the "Great American Holocaust." Christians must never allow their passion to fight for life from conception to natural death flag or abate.

Despite Supreme Court decisions, Christians must continue to contend for God's design for the sanctity of marriage. The Democratic Party Platform endorsed the 2015 Supreme Court ruling that "LGBT people, like other Americans, have the right to marry the person they love."[29] The Republican Party Platform condemned the Supreme Court decision that removed the ability of Congress and the people to define marriage as the union of one man and one woman. It is a Christian's responsibility to oppose any decision that overrules God's design for marriage.

Christians should also boldly stand against racism, simply because those who have been reconciled to God should also be reconciled to one another. The issue of poverty in America should also be addressed as well as the issues of law and order, support of Israel and Jerusalem, the persecution of Christians, human rights, terrorism, national defense, and the selection of judges. We must never doubt the social relevance of the Gospel in our nation and in our world. We must always be prepared "to engage the public square by applying the fundamentals of our faith to the full range of issues to which the government speaks, including government and politics."[30]

---

29 "LGBTQ Community," accessed February 10, 2021, https://democrats.org/who-we-are/who-we-serve/lgbtq-community/. See also https://billygraham.org/story/2016-party-platforms/.

30 David Closson, "Biblical Principles for Political Engagement," accessed February 10, 2021, https://downloads.frc.org/EF/EF19G02.pdf.

Chapter 5

The Impact of Preaching on the American Revolution

Jimmy Draper

Richard Land and I grew up in Houston, TX in the middle of the 20th century, though we did not meet there. It was in the early 1970s when we actually met. Carol Ann and I immediately became friends with both Richard and Becky. We served alongside of them in Nashville when I was president of the Sunday School Board, and he was president of the Ethics and Religious Liberty Commission. We watched their children grow up and have travelled with them many times going to Baptist World Alliance meetings throughout the world. Without a doubt, he is one of the most knowledgeable men in Southern Baptist Life and has been a capable and effective voice for the Southern Baptist Convention in the cultural and political arena. I trust him completely and have always valued his counsel both culturally and theologically. Carol Ann and I both cherish their friendship and partnership in ministry. I pray that these pages will be a fitting tribute to one of God's choicest servants!

* * *

Background to the Revolution

The most unexpected and unlikely event in modern history was the establishment of the United States of America. Its founding developed with the convergence of massive cultural developments that created the perfect storm for the American Revolution. The 17th and 18th centuries were the hinges that swung the world from the Middle Ages to modern times. Phenomenal social, civil, and religious events were occurring around the world and especially in Britain and the American colonies.

By the late 16th century, the political and religious philosophy of the "Divine Right of Kings" was widely accepted and was one of those cultural movements. It had gradually developed in the later part of antiquity and was a strong influence in the world. The belief that kings were ordained by God was used to justify the absolute authority of the king in all matters. That philosophy ended in Britain with the "Whig revolution" in 1685-89. It appears that King George III was using Parliament to regain some of the power lost in that 17th century Revolution. In the Declaratory Act, 1766, the British parliament claimed that it "had hath and of a right to have, full power and authority to make laws and statutes of sufficient force and validity to bind the colonies and people of America…in all cases whatever." [1]

Samuel Stillman, pastor of the First Baptist Church in Boston, in an Election Sermon vigorously opposed this Act of the British Parliament as an arbitrary concept of a by-gone age: "The time has been when the divine right of kings sounded from the pulpit and the press; and when the sacred name of religion was brought in to sanctify the most horrid systems of despotism and cruelty. But, blessed be God, we live in a more happy era, in which the great principles of liberty are better understood. With us, it is a first and fundamental principle, that God made all men equal." [2]

The world was about to see something unthinkable happen that was beyond the comprehension of the times – a free people in a free land, choosing their own form of government based upon the will of the people, resulting in a new nation. Additionally, that government was based on the clear guidance of the Bible for its laws, processes, and principles.

The Age of Enlightenment was an intellectual and philosophical movement that swept across Europe and beyond during the 17th and 18th centuries. It included an emphasis on the pursuit of happiness, sovereignty of reason and the evidence of the senses as the primary sources of knowl-

---

[1] "Declaratory Act," accessed February 10, 2021, https://en.wikipedia.org/wiki/Declaratory_Act.

[2] Frank Moore, *Patriot Preachers of the American Revolution*, (Coppell, TX, 1860), 2.

edge. It transformed how one could receive knowledge and presented germinal ideas of liberty, toleration, constitutional government, and proper relationship between civil and religious institutions. This movement prepared the world for the political and cultural disputes of the 18th and 19th centuries as many intellectual concepts found their source in this period.

The two Great Awakenings was another major influence that emerged in colonial times. Religious beliefs were diverse in the colonies including Congregational, Quakers, Dutch Reformed, Anglican, Presbyterian, Lutheran, and Baptist churches.

The stirrings of the First Great Awakening impacted the colonies from 1730 and into the 1760s. The Awakening was triggered by a remarkable revival in Northampton, Massachusetts in 1734-35 under the leadership of Congregational minister Jonathan Edwards. Following a sermon by Edwards on 'Justification by Faith Alone,' the community erupted in signs of spiritual fervor with a significant response from the young people. This enthusiasm spread to twenty-five communities in western Massachusetts and central Connecticut until waning in 1737.[3]

Another primary catalyst for the First Great Awakening was George Whitfield. He first arrived in America in 1738 in the colony of Georgia. "For 34 years, he travelled throughout the American Colonies and Europe, preaching some 1,800 times, and drawing huge crowds in churches, streets and open fields. Amazingly, an estimated 80% of all Americans heard him preach... Whitfield maintained a grueling travel and speaking schedule in countless locations across the nation...As a result, thousands converted to Christianity, and churches were filled."[4] Whitfield was tireless in his efforts to preach at every opportunity and his preaching greatly affected both Britain and the American colonies. His ministry shook two continents for Christ.

Revivals occurred throughout the colonies with great emphasis on prayer, Scripture reading, and a renewed focus on a converted church

---

3 "First Great Awakening," accessed February 10, 2021, https://en.wikipedia.org/wiki/First_Great_Awakening.

4 David Barton, *The American Story, The Beginnings* (Aledo, TX: WallBuilder Press, 2020), 99, 101.

membership. Revivals continued to spread across the colonies in the 1750s and 1760s. The revival theology focused on three things. First was conviction of sin, which prepared individuals to receive salvation. Second was conversion,[5] which was viewed as an instantaneous, supernatural work of the Holy Spirit bringing the convicted sinner into salvation. This always involved repentance, saving faith, love for God, and obedience to God. Third was consolation which was the assurance of salvation.

We must never forget that the remarkable moments in the founding of our nation was in the context of a vital and resurgent spiritual awakening that called for repentance and faith. That spiritual awakening nurtured the independent spirit of the colonies and ultimately led them to resist tyranny and a corrupt religious system and to live as sincere believers in Jesus Christ as they became responsible citizens of the new nation.

This Awakening led to remarkable changes in how the colonists understood God, themselves, and the world around them. It was in those years that the movement to abolish slavery was begun. Both white and black converts regularly appeared in churches and white preachers and congregations began to welcome African Americans into their churches. Barton states that, "Originally, American colonies had indentured servants, but no slaves. At that time, an indenture was similar to arranging a loan."[6] Slavery did not become legal until 1654 when an African American man, Anthony Johnson,[7] who had become a prosperous landowner, began employing indentured servants. It seems that Anthony Johnson's was the first case of legal slavery in the United States.[8] The court granted Johnson ownership of a Mr. Casor. Johnson used Casor to work his tobacco farm. The New York Times 1619 Project and many academics assert that slavery in the American

---

5 "Revivalism," accessed February 10, 2021, https://www.britannica.com/topic/revivalism-Christianity.

6 Barton, *The American Story,* 285.

7 "History of Slavery in America," accessed February 10, 2021, https://www.ocf.berkeley.edu/~arihuang/academic/abg/slavery/history.html.

8 "The Horrible Fate of John Casor, the First Man to be Declared Slave for Life in America," accessed February 10, 2021, https://www.smithsonianmag.com/smart-news/horrible-fate-john-casor-180962352/.

colonies began in 1619, but this is almost certainly incorrect. In 1619 British privateers captured a Portuguese slave trading ship and brought the slaves to sell in Jamestown, but instead of remaining slaves they became indentured servants. After serving several years, they were given their freedom and awarded land."[9]

Slavery was practiced throughout the known world in these years. Britain was a major leader in slave trade as it was a very prosperous endeavor. When some of the colonies passed anti-slavery laws in 1773, King George III vetoed those laws. Within two decades of King George's veto, William Wilberforce began his efforts to abolish slavery in Parliament in Britain. He began his efforts in 1780, presenting many bills into Parliament to accomplish that goal, but none was passed until three days before his death in 1833. [10]

The 1691 Election Sermon of James Dana was entitled "The African Slave Trade." [11] Dana did a masterful job in presenting the historical record of the slave trade and concluded with a call to banish slavery. The seeds of abolition of slavery were now woven into the fabric of colonial culture.

Samuel Stillman, a native of Philadelphia, was extremely popular for fifty-two years in Colonial America and in the beginning years of our Republic. In 1788 he delivered a powerful message in his Election Sermon: "In order to complete a system of government, and to be consistent with ourselves, it appears to me that we ought to banish from among us that cruel practice, which has long prevailed, of reducing to a state of slavery for life the freeborn Africans…To reconcile this nefarious traffic with reason, humanity, religion, or the principles of a free government, in my view, requires an uncommon address." [12]

The seeds of the abolition of slavery, while in its infancy conceptionally, was active in the colonial period and ultimately led to the Civil War

---

9 "The Horrible Fate of John Casor."

10 "William Wilberforce," accessed February 10, 2021, https://www.britannica.com/biography/William-Wilberforce.

11 Ellis Sandoz, *Political Sermons of the American Founding Era, 1730-1805*, vol. 2 (Indianapolis: *Liberty Fund*, 1998), 1031.

12 Moore, *Patriot Preachers of the American Revolution*, (Coppell, TX, 1860), 18-19.

in the 1860s. Evangelicals led the abolitionist movement before the Revolutionary War and were the most active in the efforts to abolish the slave trade and slavery itself.[13]

The religious fervor that broke out in the First Great Awakening waned during the period of the founding of the United States, but its influence soon broke out again in a Second Great Awakening shortly after the adoption of the United States Constitution. Religious passion stirred again as camp meetings and revivals began in Kentucky and Tennessee around 1790 and into the early 1800s. The Awakening helped to give guidance and encouragement to the fledgling nation and the uncertainties that were before its citizens.

The French and Indian War, 1754-63 was also a key to what was happening in the colonies. The War pitted the colonies of British America against those of French America. Each side was supported by military units from Britain and France and by native Indian allies. At the start of the war, the French colonies had a population of roughly 60,000 settlers compared with 2 million in the British colonies. The outnumbered French army turned to the Indians for support.

This war, known as the Seven Years War in Europe, nearly doubled Britain's national debt. The incredible debt they amassed became the most critical challenge that influenced Britain's relationship with the colonies. This was stated emphatically by John Rodgers in his Election Day sermon following the end of the Revolutionary War. "There is one circumstance that has had no small influence on the speedy accomplishment of this happy event, that must not be omitted! I mean the impoverished state of Britain, as a nation, notwithstanding her great resources, and the princely wealth of many of her subjects. Moore wrote that, "Had it not been for this enormous, and this accumulating debt, which shook their national credit, they would not have so readily listened to terms of pacification with us, much less would they have given us the advantageous and honorable terms we have obtained." [14]

---

13 "Abolitionist Movement," accessed February 10, 2021, https://www.history.com/topics/black-history/abolitionist-movement,

14 Moore, *Patriot Preachers*, 16.

The Impact of Preaching on The American Revolution

PREACHING AND THE REVOLUTION

All these significant movements created the ripe environment for Colonial America as it searched for religious and civil freedoms. All else had failed and the last resort available to the colonists seemed to be independence.

The main motivation of the American Revolution was the matter of religious freedom. The abuses and hypocrisy of the religious leaders in the official church in Britain was a great disillusionment to the colonists. They came to America to get away from the lack of religious integrity and freedom in Britain, and the moral and ethical failure of Britain's religious leaders.

Of those religious leaders it was said, "The very men who were appointed the guardians and conservators of the rights of the people, have dismembered the empire; and by repeated acts of injustice and oppression, have forced from the bosom of their parent country, millions of Americans, who might have been drawn by a hair, but were not to be driven by all the thunder of Britain." [15]

There were several hundred Puritan preachers in Britain and almost a third of them came with the colonists to settle in America. The preachers were among the best educated and most knowledgeable of the people and the most powerful, and direct method of communication was the pulpit. "In early times, when learning was almost exclusively with the clergy, they, by this monopoly, held almost the whole power of church and state." [16] Thus, preaching became the centerpiece in the life of colonial America.

Preachers were called upon by the civil authorities often and on almost all festive occasions and these sermons were generally political and were heard in virtually every public celebration. The sermons on Election Day began around 1634. They were sermons that applied Biblical principles to the challenges facing the colonies. Those sermons formed the basis for the laws and polity of colonial life and the founding documents of the United States. The Election Day preachers were zealous supporters of colonial independence and

---

15 Moore, *Patriot Preachers*, 5.

16 John Wingate Thornton, *The Pulpit of the American Revolution* (Boston: Gould and Lincoln, 1860), X.

strongly supported the move to separate from Britain. Barton notes, "As Alice Baldwin documented, such sermons were indispensable in shaping America's unique view of civil and religious liberty: 'There is not a right asserted in the Declaration of Independence which had not been discussed by the New England clergy before 1763'. She further noted, 'The Constitutional Convention and the written Constitution were the children of the pulpit.'"[17]

Election Day sermons involved the citizens and the newly elected officials gathering at the church or town hall after an election to hear a message on the responsibility of representatives to lead justly and with integrity for the good of the people and the citizens' responsibilities to those who were elected. The passion of these preachers challenged the colonists to obedience to God's law, and affirmed the cause of independence, launching them into the Revolutionary War. These Election Day sermons were printed so that every preacher had a copy, each of the elected officials received copies and one for the preachers in the area. Frequently these messages were distributed throughout the colonies. Sandoz explains, "Of the several vehicles for expounding political theology available to American ministers, the most venerable were the election sermons preached for 256 years in Massachusetts and 156 years in Connecticut…These were sermons preached annually to the Governor and legislature after the election of officers." [18]

The many occasions provided for the preachers of colonial America gave ample opportunity for them to exhibit their passion for independence and for a new government for the colonies. Their boldness in dealing with current events in the light of God's Word was largely responsible for the mobilizing of the people for the conflict ahead.

The strong support given to the case of independence by the clergy was based upon their understanding of Scripture. Jonathan Mayhew, speaking of the duty of citizens as found in 1 Peter 2:13-14, said, "There is one very important and interesting point which remains to be inquired into, namely, the extent of that subjection to the higher powers which is here enjoined as a duty upon all Christians." [19] He left no doubt about his

---

17 Barton, *The American Story*, 109.
18 Sandoz, *Political Sermons*, xx.
19 Thornton, *The Pulpit of the Revolution*, 62.

conclusion. "The reason of the thing itself would have obliged us to limit the expression 'every ordinance of man' to such human ordinance and commands as are not inconsistent with the ordinances and commands of God, the Supreme Lawgiver, or with any other higher antecedent obligations." [20]

The preachers were consistent and clear in their view that the Scriptures supported the efforts of independence. They strongly believed that the British Parliament, the king, and religious leaders did not lead in a way that resulted in the good of the people.

Those chosen to preach the sermons declared the biblical perspective on the fight for independence. They took current events in the struggle with Britain and revealed political goals and events considering the teachings of Scripture. Thornton noted the source for these preachers, "It is the voice of the Fathers of the Republic. They invoked God in their civil assemblies, called upon their chosen teachers of religion for counsel from the Bible, and recognized its precepts as the law of their public conduct."[21] The significant energy the colonists had for independence came largely from the passion of those preachers.

The importance of these sermons in expressing the sentiment of the colonists cannot be overestimated. Contained in these remarkable messages is the guidance of biblical faith in determining the fundamental questions of human existence. The messages always included the belief that Civil Government was founded by God for the purpose of maintaining order in society and to promote good for the people. Citizens were urged to live with honesty and to be advocates for virtue, to oppose evil, and support those elected as a Christian duty. They developed a political theology based upon the Bible and believed that religious truth and political liberty are vitally connected.

These Election Day sermons always described the kind of nation that receives the blessings of God's approval. They always warned of the sin and reproach that comes when God's laws are violated. Ever present was the expectation that the new nation should follow biblical truth and the principles of Christianity. The Bible was revered as being the Word of God and always the guide for personal and collective behavior. This was further

---

20 Thornton, *The Pulpit of the Revolution*, 67.
21 Ibid., iii.

illustrated by the selection of ministers at key points in the process of the colonies becoming the United States of America.

Barton writes,

> In 1662, at the earnest solicitation of the General Court and of the ministry, Mr. Simon Bradstreet and Rev John Norton went to England, as colonial agents, to secure the charter against their ancient foes, who had distinguished their restoration to power by the cruel Act of Uniformity; and twenty-five years later, in a most important crisis, we find Massachusetts again represented by a clergy man, the Rev Dr. Increase Mather, who procured the provincial charter of 1694. The clergy were generally consulted by the civil authorities, and not infrequently the suggestions from the pulpit, on election days and other special occasions, were enacted into laws. The statute-book, the reflex of the age, shows this influence. The State was developed out of the Church.[22]

Nathaniel Whitaker in his 1677 Election Sermon summed up the message of those who preached Election Sermons. Delivered nearly one hundred years before the Revolutionary War, it shows how long the resentment toward Britain had been simmering. Moore comments,

> We may deduce the following doctrinal observations: 1) That the cause of liberty is the cause of God and truth. 2) That to take arms and repel force by force, when our liberties are invaded, is well-pleasing to God. 3) That it is lawful to levy war against those who oppose us, even when they are not in arms against us! 4) That indolence and backwardness in taking arms, and exerting ourselves in the service of our country, when called thereto by the public voice, to recover and secure our freedom, is a heinous sin in the sight of God. 5) That God requires a people, struggling for their liberties to treat such of the

---

[22] Thornton, *The Pulpit of the Revolution*, xxii-xxiii.

community who will not join them, as open enemies, and to reject them as unworthy the privileges which others enjoy.[23]

Revolution

This spirit of independence continued to build until King George III and the British Parliament adopted a series of Acts for taxing the American colonies. From 1763 to 1776, Parliament, King George III, royal Governors, and colonists aggressively disputed over trade restrictions, representation, and taxation. Up until that point, the relationship between Britain and the American colonies had been more congenial and less threatening.

British troops were stationed in Massachusetts Bay beginning in 1768 to support British officials and enforce Parliamentary legislation. Those Acts ordered by Parliament and approved by King George III drove matters to the breaking point. These Acts included the Sugar and Currency Acts in 1764 which dealt with taxing sugar and molasses on non-British sources and the regulation of paper currencies issued by the colonies. The year 1765 saw the Quartering Act and Stamp Act passed by the British Parliament. One required the colonies to provide barracks & supplies to British troops and the other required the use of stamped paper produced in London for printing purposes. The Declaratory Tax in 1766 was the most despised of all. In that bill Parliament declared that it could make laws that forced compliance by the colonies "in all cases whatever." The Townshends Acts in 1767-68 was a series of at least five Acts on goods imported to American Colonies.

In 1769, a resolution was passed in the Virginia House of Burgess condemning Britain's actions. In that same year conflict between the colonists and British troops in New York intensified. Soldiers surrounded by a hostile crowd fired shots killing three and wounding two others.

On March 5, 1770, the Boston Massacre occurred when a British soldier struck a young man in the head with his rifle for insulting a British offi-

---

23 Moore, *Patriot Preachers*, 7.

cer. Colonists rushed to his aid, tempers flared, and insults abounded. Soldiers were attacked and when one soldier fired, others fired killing three people and wounded eight others, two of whom later died of their wounds. [24] This chaotic event greatly increased the support for the American Revolution.

Samuel Adams, known as the Father of the American Revolution, believed King George III and the British Parliament had violated the rights of the colonists and that the conflict was not just political and economic but spiritual. Barton explains, "Adams understood that a knowledge of their rights in each of these three areas must be known and appreciated. To help achieve this unity of ideas and principles, Adams proposed that Committees of Correspondence be established in every colony. Each would set up communication with the others, reporting to the rest what was occurring in their state…Many responded enthusiastically to Adam's proposal." [25]

Adams launched his plan and personally wrote the first communication. In that circular letter, he gave the clear Biblical basis for all their endeavors and challenged all the colonists "to study the institutes of the great Law Giver and Head of the Christian Church, which are to be found clearly written and promulgated in the New Testament."[26]

The British Parliament passed the Tea Act on May 10, 1773, which reduced the tax on imported British tea giving British merchants unfair advantage over the colonies in selling American tea. On the evening of Dec. 16, 1773, a group of men, many of whom were disguised as Mohawk warriors, silently boarded three ships in Boston Harbor and over a period of three hours, dumped 342 chests of tea into the water. The weight of tea in those chests was 92,000 pounds, worth $1.8 million dollars of 2021 currency. That event became known as The Boston Tea Party.[27]

Another ship of tea ran aground at Cape Cod on December 10, 1773. Word came that the fifty-one chests of tea on that ship were stored in the

---

24 Barton, *The American Story,* 129-130.

25 Ibid., 132.

26 Ibid.

27 "Boston Tea Party," accessed February 10, 2021, https://en.wikipedia.org/wiki/Boston_Tea_Party.

barracks on Boston's Castle Island. On March 7, 1774, men, dressed as Mohawk warriors again broke into the barracks. Several of the chests were burned, but it is not known for certain what happened to the other forty-nine chests of tea.[28]

The Coercive Acts, which severely punished Boston colonists for their opposition, was enacted by British Parliament in 1774. The second Quartering Act passed which allowed British troops to occupy any dwelling in the colonies.

On May 10, 1774, British troops began to fortify Boston and seized ammunitions belonging to the colony of Massachusetts Bay. A militia known as the Minutemen was formed by the colonists and stood ready to fight.

The First Continental Congress was called into session on September 5, 1774. Of the thirteen colonies, only Georgia was not present for that Congress. Jacob Duché, an Episcopalian clergyman was asked to open the Congress with prayer. "Rather than solely following the traditional Anglican formality of reading from the Book of Common Prayer, he launched into an unforeseen, passionate, and spontaneous prayer, surprising everyone present. He also spent time reading Psalm 35.

What was the impact? According to John Adams:

> I never saw a greater effect upon an audience. It seemed as if Heaven had ordained that Psalm to be read on that morning. After this, Mr. Duché, unexpected to everybody, struck out into an extemporary prayer which filled the bosom of every man present. I must confess I never heard a better prayer...with such fervor, such ardor, such earnestness, and pathos, and in language so elegant and sublime, for America, for the Congress, for the province of Massachusetts Bay, and especially the town of Boston. It has had an excellent effect upon everybody here.
>
> Several delegates likewise commented favorably on Duché's remarkable prayer, including Samuel Adams...Silas Deane reported that the prayer not only was 'worth riding one hundred mile [sic] to hear' (about 3 days in the saddle) but that it was so powerful even

---

28 "Boston Tea Party."

the stern Quakers (a group frequently harassed by Duché's Anglican denomination) 'shed tears' as they listened to it.[29]

The British Parliament passed the New England Restraining Act and received King George's approval on March 30, 1775. This Act restricted all commercial trading in the colonies to England which was a serious threat to the economic condition in the colonies.

The Battles of Lexington and Concord were the first military engagements between Britain and the American colonies. The battles were fought on April 19, 1775 in Middlesex County in the Province of Massachusetts Bay. The goal of the British for these battles was to destroy American munitions in Lexington and Concord. Paul Revere and William Dawes alerted the Minutemen, and the British troops were prevented from succeeding.[30]

The Second Continental Congress was called for on May 10, 1775, in Philadelphia and George Washington was named Commander-in-Chief of the Colonial army. This Congress remained active until March 1, 1781. During those years, it adopted the Declaration of Independence, successfully managed the war efforts, drafted the articles of confederation, adopted the first U.S Constitution, and secured diplomatic recognition from other nations.

British General Gage initiated martial law on June 12, 1775, and, announced that any person helping Americans would be considered a traitor and a rebel. About that same time an Olive Branch petition was sent to King George III expressing loyalty to him and urging him to attempt reconciliation between Britain and the Colonies. The King rejected that petition and declared the Colonies in rebellion.

In early 1776, the British evacuated Boston. The Second Continental Congress declared independence and called for the adoption of a new constitution for the, now united, colonies as they formed the United States of America.

---

29   Barton, *The American Story*, 139, 141.

30   "Battles of Lexington and Concord," accessed February 10, 2021, https://en.wikipedia.org/wiki/Battles_of_Lexington_and_Concord#:~:text=The%20battles%20of%20Lexington%20and,day%20Arlington)%2C%20and%20Cambridge.

In 1777, the Americans adopted a flag and the war intensified! France and American colonists became allies in 1778, a pact that was negotiated by Benjamin Franklin. The war came to an end in 1783 when Congress ratified the articles of Peace, which included France, Britain, and America on April 15, and hostilities formally ceased. The war was concluded, and the United States of America was now established. Excitement reigned throughout the new nation and plans were now put in place to produce the governing documents of the new nation.

THE PATRIOT PREACHERS OF COLONIAL AMERICA

We are familiar with names such as George Washington, Thomas Jefferson, Benjamin Franklin, Daniel Boone, John Hancock, Alexander Hamilton, John Adams, and Patrick Henry. But the moral influence and passion of the war was driven mostly by unknown men – the patriot preachers of that era. Today these are largely obscure men. Though often unrecognized, they carried the emotional and spiritual strength of their faith and transplanted it into the hearts of those who led the battles of the Revolutionary War. They were giants of inspiration and motivation for the colonies. Their bold proclamation in the Election Sermons, especially, swung the momentum of the struggle to the colonists. Logically and rationally, the colonists did not stand a chance against the power of the British Empire. But prevail they did, as they were carried on the currents of those Election sermons. The names of some of these leaders are provided here along with a short biography:

1. Isaac Backus: born in 1724 in Norwich township, CT; converted to Christianity in 1741 because of the Great Awakening preaching of the theologian Eleazar Wheelock; pastor of Middleborough First Baptist Church for 50 years; died November 20, 1806. He is listed as a preeminent figure in the establishing of freedom of conscience in America.

2. John Leland: born in 1754; Baptist minister in Massachusetts and Virginia; close friend and ally of James Madison and greatly aided Madison's election in the first United States Congress in 1789; elected to the Massachusetts legislature, his second public office; died in 1841 at the age of 87.

3. George Duffield: born in October 1732; pastor of the Third Presbyterian Church in Philadelphia; died February 2, 1790, at age 58.

4. John Rodgers: born on August 2, 1727; in 1785, he went to New York and became pastor of Wall Street Presbyterian Church; died on May 7, 1811, at the age of 84.

5. James Dana: born in 1735; Congregationalist minister and graduate of Harvard; became pastor of First Church of New Haven in 1789 where he served until 1805; his most memorable message was delivered in 1791, "The African Slave Trade," a great message on the evils of slavery; he died in 1812 at the age of 77.

6. Oliver Hart: born in Warminster, PA, July 5, 1723; pastor of the Charleston Baptist Church in Charleston, SC for 30 years; died in 1795 at the age of 73.

7. Nathaniel Whitaker: born on February 22, 1732, in Long Island, NY; pastor of Third Church in Salem, MA; died January 21, 1795, at the age of 63.

8. William Gordon: born in Hitchin in Great Britain; arrived in New England in 1770 and pastor of the Third Church at Roxbury in 1772; he was chosen to be chaplain to the Provincial Congress of Massachusetts; died November 18, 1816, at age 87.

9. Jacob Duché: born in Philadelphia in 1730; chosen to open the Continental Congress with prayer in 1774; in 1776 he was appointed Chaplain to the Congress; died in 1798 at the age of 68.

10. **Samuel Langdon:** born in Boston, MA; graduated from Harvard in 1740; succeeded John Hancock as president of Harvard in 1774; died November 29, 1797, at age 74.

11. **Jonathan Mayhew:** born in 1720 into one of the most honorable families in New England; in 1747 he became pastor of the West Church in Boston, where he remained until his death on July 8, 1766, at the age of 46.

12. **Timothy Dwight:** born in 1752 in Northampton, MA; entered Yale in 1765 at the age of thirteen and graduated in 1769; Congregational pastor of Greenfield Hill Congregational Church; president of Yale from 1795 until his death January 11, 1817, at the age of 65.

13. **Benjamin Colman:** in 1699 became first pastor of Boston's Brattle Street Church; in 1724 he declined the presidency of Harvard but served as one of its trustees from 1717-1728 and remained an overseer (in addition to his ministry at Brattle Street Church), until his death in 1747 at the age of 74.

A few others included John Witherspoon, who was born in Scotland in 1723. He came to America in 1768 to be president of College of New Jersey (now Princeton University) a position he held until 1792, when blindness forced his retirement. He was elected to the Continental Congress in time to urge the adoption of the Declaration of Independence and to sign it. Witherspoon was the most influential professor in American history and was a brilliant writer and speaker. His students included a president and a vice-president of the United States, twenty-one senators, twenty-nine representatives, fifty-six state legislators, thirty-three judges, three of whom were appointed to the Supreme Court. He died November 15, 1794, at the age of 71.

Samuel Stillman was born on February 27, 1737, in Philadelphia, PA. He was the pastor of First Baptist Church in Boston, MA. Stillman was elected by the town of Boston to be a member of the Constitutional Convention for the adoption of the federal constitution in 1788. He died March 14, 1807, at the age of 70.

Joseph Lathrop was born in Norwich, CT in 1731, and was a graduate of Yale College in 1754. Lathrop was one of the most prominent preachers of his day who published more sermons than any Yale graduate before him. He pastored the Congregational Church in West Springfield, MA, until his death in 1820 at the age of 89.

Jonathan Edwards (Oct. 5, 1703 – March 22, 1758) and George Whitefield (December 17, 1714 – September 30, 1770) were two of the significant leaders in the First Great Awakening and were also prominent during the years leading up to the Revolutionary war.

There were two primary issues leading up to the American Revolution. The first one was that of religious liberty. This grew out of two conditions the people had lived under in Britain. One was the Established Church in Britain that was imposed upon all citizens. It was the utmost and arbitrary authority in all matters of religion. Along with this was the abusive actions and hypocrisy of the clerical hierarchy in Britain. The moral and theological extremes that resided in the established Church were unacceptable to the colonists. Thornton explains, "In substance the prelates claimed that every word, ceremony, and article written in the Book of Common Prayer, and in the Book of Ordination, was as faultless and as binding as the Book of God, and must be acknowledged as such . . . the prelates claimed in themselves . . . an infallibility of judgment in all things pertaining to religion, and these preposterous claims of the prelates rested upon acts of Parliament . . . the quarrel was in the church." [31]

The second issue was the problems arising from the monarchy of King George III. He claimed total authority over both civil and religious society in Britain. The colonists disputed his right to be an absolute monarch.

Because religious liberty was the biggest concern of the colonists, their primary promoters of the cause of independence were the ministers of the colonies. Sandoz explains, "'Religion gave birth to America,' Tocqueville observed long ago. On the eve of the revolution, in his last-ditch attempt to stave off impending catastrophe, Edmund Burke reminded the

---

31 Thornton, *The Pulpit of the Revolution*, xiii-xiv.

House of Commons of the inseparable alliance between liberty and religion among Englishmen in America."[32]

In the preface to "The Pulpit of the American Revolution" John Wingate Thornton declared, "They prepared for the struggle and went into battle, not as soldiers of fortune, but, like Cromwell and the soldiers of the commonwealth, with the Word of God in their hearts and trusting in Him. This was the secret of that moral energy which sustained the Republic in its material weakness against superior numbers, and discipline, and all the power of England."[33]

The earliest settlers who came to America arrived in search of a haven from the religious and civil conditions they had faced in Britain. Barton explains,

> A love of God and the Bible inspired many of the early explorers who came after Columbus. One was Richard Hakluyt (1552-1616), an English minister and prominent geographer in America's colonization period. For decades, he advocated that America become a haven for those persecuted in Europe. As he explained in his 1584 'Discourse on Western Planting', 'We shall by planting there (in America), enlarge the glory of the Gospel and from England plant sincere religion and provide a safe and a sure place to receive people from all parts of the world that are forced to flee for the truth of God's Word.'[34]

Over the next 200 years, seekers of religious liberty came from all over Europe. Barton comments, "Those who came included . . . Jews facing the Inquisition in Portugal (1654); Quakers fleeing England after some 10,000 had been imprisoned or tortured (1680); Anabaptists (Mennonites, Moravians, Dunkers, etc.) persecuted in Germany (1683); 400,000 Bible-believing

---

32 Sandoz, *Political Sermons of the American Founding Era, 1730-1805, vol. 1* (Indianapolis: Liberty Fund, 1998), xii.

33 Thornton, *The Pulpit of the Revolution*, iii.

34 Barton, *The American Story*, 37.

Huguenots persecuted in France after 110,000 of them were killed (1685); and 20,000 Lutherans expelled from Austria (1731); etc."[35]

One other matter is of utmost importance. Some have maintained that America was founded as a Christian nation, that the nation has always been filled with born-again believers who lived consistent and devoted Christian lives. The fact is that this has never been the case! America has never been filled with devoted believers in the Lord Jesus Christ. However, the miracle that emerged after the Revolutionary War is even more remarkable considering that fact. The colonies were filled with a great mixture of people. Some were devout believers, and some nominal believers. Others were dissenters with little or no faith at all, whose lifestyles reflected the basest of instincts of fallen human nature. In spite of these weaknesses, those colonists managed to deliver a constitution (with its Bill of Rights), solidly based on God's Word that was unequaled in history.

That is a miracle of divine intervention. The preachers of the Election sermons clearly did not paint a desirable picture of the citizens in the colonies. Samuel Langdon's Election sermon in 1775 is a strong example of this:

> We have rebelled against God. We have lost the true spirit of Christianity; though we retain the outward profession and form of it. We have neglected and set light by the glorious gospel of our Lord Jesus Christ, and his holy commands and institutions. The worship of many is but mere compliment to the Deity, while their hearts are far from him. By many the gospel is corrupted into a superficial system of moral philosophy, little better than ancient Platonism.[36]

In one Election Day sermon Pastor John Rodgers, pastor of Wall Street Presbyterian Church in New York, spoke of the spiritual condition of the colonies,

> I only add, once more, that the sons of profaneness cannot now sin at the cheap rate, in point of criminality, they were wont to do.

---

35 Barton, *The American Story*, 37.
36 Moore, *Patriot Preachers*, 7.

Your guilt is greater, in your neglect of God, and contempt of his Son Christ; in your profane cursing and swearing; your drunkenness, reveling and uncleanness; your sabbath-breaking, gaming and dishonesty in dealing; in a word, in your every species of impiety, than in years past, in proportion to the great things God has done for us, as a people, I beseech you, then, my dear brethren, by all these mercies of God, in addition to all the grace of the gospel of his Son Christ, that you break off your sins by repentance, and study to walk before him as it becometh those for whom the Lord hath done such great things.[37]

Conclusion

In his Election Sermon of 1775, William Smith declared, "We know that our civil and religious rights are linked together in one indissoluble bond, we neither have, nor seek to have, any interest separate from that of our country, nor can we advise a desertion of its cause. Religion and liberty must nourish or fall together in America. We pray that both may be perpetual."[38]

The conduct and character of Americans has always failed to live up to our ideals. However, the foundation of our nation was not built upon the actions, or even character, of the Founding Fathers or the people of the colonies, but on the clear teachings of Scripture. Therein lies our strength, our comfort, and our hope for the future! To the Election Sermons of the Colonial period and the early decades of our nation, we owe a great debt of gratitude for solidly calling for our polity, laws, and governing documents to be based upon the Word of God and to inspire us to build our lives on the principles of God.

---

37 Moore, *Patriot Preachers*, 21.
38 Ibid., 10.

CHAPTER 6

MAMMAS, DON'T LET YOUR BABIES GROW UP TO BE ETHICISTS, UNLESS...

Mark Coppenger

As I entered upon my graduate studies in philosophy in the early 1970s, the last thing I wanted to be was an ethicist (well, maybe, the next to last thing, for the thought of being a philosopher of mathematics, wrangling over Gödel's Incompleteness Theorem and such was even more uninspiring). I had several big problems with the discipline of ethics. It seemed to me that 1) right-minded Christians had pretty well sorted out the moral facts, and new thinking in ethics was akin to new thinking in theology, which was probably in error; 2) In the hands of its currently most influential practitioners, professional ethics looked askance at much of what I held dear and reasonable in my life and thought. As an ROTC grad during the Vietnam War, trained at Fort Benning and serving as a mechanized rifle platoon leader in the Tennessee National Guard, I was lumped in among the deplorables by Noam Chomskyites on campus and beyond; the Earth Day enthusiasts were marching us away from godly stewardship of resources to a sort of Gaia idolatry; Peter Singer's "animal liberation" movement was setting the stage for the insanities of PETA; 3) Our decadent society was going full Woodstock, with its fashionable glorification of extra-marital sex, drug "trips," and all sorts of cultural rebellion, expressed in many rock lyrics, so efforts to ingratiate oneself to those who earned their credentials by laughing or cursing at traditional convictions could only end badly; 4) On the other end, some of the loudest voices in evangelical Christendom were driving us toward a host of overreaching teetotalisms beyond alcohol (which I happily eschewed) and extending to proscriptions of trick-or-treating, attendance at movies, use of credit cards, enrollment in public schools, etc. Who wanted to jump into that mix, with any hope of saying something useful and compelling? It was a zoo.

But then God, in his providential humor, dragged me into the fray with an invitation from a professor to be his assistant, and subsequently the director with faculty status, under a National Endowment for the Humanities grant for The Nashville Human Rights Project. So I found myself running a booth at the Tennessee state fair showing films against strip mining (produced by SOCUM, "Save Our Cumberland Mountains") and deploring the ways "the poor pay more" (as in Korean convenience stores in ghettos, far away from the big box savings of the suburbs); taking professors from a dozen Nashville colleges into the community—to churches, community centers, libraries, television stations, school auditoriums—to do ethics from their areas of expertise, or at least ideology. Some of what they said was good (as in the visit from Boston University President John Silber), and some of it, not so much (as when the speaker disparaged parents who objected to forced school busing to achieve racial balance in public schools). A lot of it was innocuous, even moderately helpful, if only for the sight of academicians learning to speak clearly to townsfolk. Still, I was much keener on epistemology, upon which my dissertation focused, with its application to the meaningfulness and plausibility of the Christian faith.

About this time, another pro-ethics irritant came my way, thanks to a lifelong friend in the sociology doctoral program. I was a "G. I. Joe," and he the product of a Mennonite ("peace church") upbringing. Sharon and I spent a lot of time with him and his wife, playing the *Jeopardy* home game on weekends, traveling with them up the East Coast of America as he prepared to assume a teaching position in New York, attending Sunday school and church together across the street from their apartment.

When Nixon was running against McGovern in 1972, we talked about the pros and cons of the candidates, and he said he was favoring the

Democrat because he appreciated his concern with "justice." Well, I figured the Republican cared too, but I didn't have a clear idea of what it was that the two men did or didn't care about in this connection. 'Justice' is one of those words that sounds great but could use a lot of clarification (Witness the knee-jerk assent to the expression, 'social justice,' as if anyone with reservations were keen on anti-social justice, social-injustice, or anti-social injustice).

I had my puzzlement tucked away when I was hired by Wheaton College to teach philosophy. But it came to the fore when I learned I was slated to take a month-long course on the "integration of faith and learning" in the summer before my first fall class. A paper was required of us, so I decided to sort out my old confusion. I wrote a piece that issued in an article for the alumni magazine, which helped gain me a quarter-long alumni study leave (a month of which we spent with the aforementioned grad school friends on the East Coast), from which issued a 1983 Broadman book, *A Christian View of Justice*. At its core was a matrix grouping biblical types on a retribution model, with prescriptions for those earning deserved benefit (servants and stewards), deserved harm (offenders and fools), undeserved harm (victims), and undeserved benefit (beneficiaries). Two stipulations rounded out the approach: 1) The government (and not the vigilante) is the proper agent of justice; 2) It must do justice justly, without victimizing people along the way. In application, it stood for, among other things, the death penalty, safety-net welfare, acceptable disparities in wealth, and a good measure of libertarian freedom to "work out your ruination in fear and trembling, or giddy delight."

I think it holds up well, and I'm working currently on an update. What clearly held up was my interest in these matters, an interest that grew as I fielded teaching assignments in jurisprudence, social ethics, moral development, and the thought of Kant and Mill. One week, we'd be homing on Aquinas's treatment of natural law, another on the reasoning in *Roe v. Wade* or the Karen Quinlan case; and so on through the utilitarianisms of Bentham and Mill, the Categorical Imperative of Kant, the Stoic counsel of Epictetus, the legal realism of Holmes and Llewellyn, the just war writings of Suarez and Vittoria, etc.

I took my philosophy of law classes to sit in on Socratic-style tort instruction at the University of Chicago; wrote a piece on addressing world hunger for *Christian Scholar's Review*; argued for the validity of serious investment in the arts when many were in poverty. In short, the hook was set (or I was overtaken by a circumstantial wave). Either way, I found myself an ethicist of sorts.

I'm reminded of the remark of one of my FBC El Dorado deacons back in 1985, as we were about to head to the Southern Baptist Convention meeting in Dallas at the height of the struggle for the conservative resurgence. We knew the gathering would be a big one, but we didn't imagine it would be our largest, with over fifty-five thousand in attendance, with messengers sitting on the floor and others overflowing to an ancillary hall in the convention center. He said, "I feel like the Scotsman who said, 'I have to go to Glasgow this weekend to get drunk, and, O, do I dread it.'" So, yes, I seemed destined to do some ethics, and O, did I dread it . . . at least for a while.

Little did I know that I'd soon do another Wheaton-based book, *Bioethics: A Casebook* and then keep on plugging for decades through a range of ethical writings and presentations, including a book on "moral apologetics"; SBC resolutions on abortion and homosexuality; denominational newspaper columns on the race riot in Ferguson, cremation, and land claims of the Palestinians; seminary journal articles on divorce and remarriage, Israeli stewardship of the Holy Land, and the just war tradition; opinion magazine pieces on waterboarding, never-Trumpism, and Confederate statues; retreat talks on critical race theory and intersectionality; sermons on national decline and on tithing; and courses in environmental ethics, church-state relations, and the ethics of work and leisure, as well as survey courses covering both metaethics and normative ethics; and the Scudder Lectures at Midwestern Baptist Theological Seminary, upon which this essay is built.

Along the way, I've found a variety of reasons to caution folks not to go into ethics unless they can't help themselves, hence the title, "Mammas, Don't Let Your Babies Grow Up to Be Ethicists, Unless . . ." (The 'unless' refers to the good resources and rewards available to you if you do take that route). Of course, I should acknowledge that all of us are ethicists of one stamp or another. As G. K. Chesterton explained, if you don't have a well-thought-out philosophy, a philosophy will have you. We all take positions, either by conscious choice or default on countless matters of "ought" and "duty" and "permissibility" and "advisability" and some are matters of prudence (e.g., "Don't wear Crocs, a Speedo, and a tank top" to a bank teller interview; nothing evil in that unless you want to talk about a failure in the stewardship of an employment opportunity, but it's mainly just absurd).

But right away we find ourselves in situations where people judge our behavior as culpable or excusable, from litterbugging to shoplifting to exaggeration in a sermon illustration for the sake of greater effect. Some of the acts are internal (coveting, lusting, hating); others are external (stealing, abusing, assaulting). Some have to do with parenting (whether to spank or not; whether to let your kids play ball on Sunday); some with workplace protocols (lying for your boss when he tells you to tell someone on the phone that he's not in; baking a cake for a gay wedding). Some concern church (whether the "regulative principle" is binding in worship, and whether to support church discipline for those co-habiting without benefit of marriage). It goes on and on, and we become little ethicists just as surely as we become little theologians when we object to an eighth grade Sunday school teacher's urging her wards to develop a prayer language.

But it's another thing to presume to go public with ethical arguments, putting a target on your back. Yes, you can do this on a small scale, with letters to the editor or comments at a PTA meeting. But once you take up the vocational mantle, you need to know some things.

Playing a Prophet's Role, Might Pay a Prophet's Wage

The Bible is rich in examples of those who spoke truth to power and suffered the consequences: Jeremiah who was thrown in a cistern for his unhappy evaluation of the character and prospects on Jerusalem; John the Baptist, who was imprisoned and beheaded for faulting King Herod for taking his brother's wife for his own; Balaam's donkey, who took a beating for frustrating his master who was oblivious to the appearance of God's messenger; and, of course, our Lord, who went to the Cross for calling out the Pharisees. And these paid-in-the-coin-of-abuse, biblical spokesmen worked in the day before "cancellation" on social media, when, in our era, a single posting, however thoughtful, can cost you your job.

When I worked at the PR VP for the SBC Executive Committee in the 1990s, we started a new publication, *SBC LIFE*, which began as a tabloid but now appears in magazine form. As we ramped up the project, I, along with several from the (then) Baptist Sunday School Board (now LifeWay) traveled to New York for a workshop held by *Folio*, the magazine about magazines. Our teachers covered all sorts of angles, from business plans to the advantages of coated paper to editorial posture, and in this last connection, they spoke of a fundamental choice we needed to make: Would we have "edge" or not?

They explained this was a matter of having the power to offend. Magazines like *Reader's Digest*, *Christmas Ideals*, Saturday *Evening Post*, and *Martha Stewart Living* had their detractors and could generate occasional sparks, but that wasn't their aim. Rather, they had a more benign, come-together feel about them, more inspirational than confrontational. On the other hand, journals of strong opinion like *The Nation* and *National Review* were guaranteed to stir controversy.

So, the question lay before us, would SBC LIFE be strictly a happy-talk production, or would it run material inclined to put certain people on the defensive, prompting them to angrily dismiss or counter our perspective on hot button issues. Our answer was to salt provocative material into what was generally a good news journal. We majored on glad and intriguing reports, from the field, from the mission-planting fruitfulness of a church in Wyoming to the imaginative range of banner ministries in congregations across the land to our disaster relief efforts following an Iranian earthquake to the manifold baptisms issuing from the Kenyan Coastal Crusade. But we also took issue with those who gainsaid the cause of biblical inerrancy. The Convention had undergone over a decade of "conservative resurgence," and two split-off groups, the Cooperative Baptist Fellowship and the Alliance of Baptists were directing polemical fire our way, and we thought it good to venture some edgy counterargument, knowing that they and tender souls who'd remained with the Convention would find this upsetting.

The pastor/prophet has the same choice. Is he willing to show some edge in his preaching and leadership, not for the sake of provocation, but rather for the integrity of the church and its pulpit? Must his church more closely resemble Nerf baseball, with Styrofoam bats and balls, the sort of game you could play in the living room, surrounded by Hummel figures, where nothing gets broken? Or might he venture some innings of hardball, where things that need to get broken do indeed get broken? Does the so-called pastoral agenda always trump the prophetic call? If so, he may enjoy a long tenure, much beloved for not rocking the boat, but it's not clear that he was faithful to his high calling to share "the whole counsel of God." Charles Spurgeon called the pulpit, "The Thermopylae of Christendom," recalling the way that three hundred Spartans gave their lives to stymie the advance of a vastly superior Persian army, buying time for Greeks to get their military act together to defend the homeland.

Please understand that the converse of "All prophets get hurt"—namely "All who get hurt are prophets"—has no logical force. Some get fired because they were callously offensive instead of judiciously approachable in ministering the difficult truth; some are dismissed because they are less than diligent, majoring on the minor and minoring on the major, or just plain getting things wrong, so wrong that key people and those who respected their counsel took notice and pushed back; some are just creepy or knee-jerk. So, one should go slowly in deciding that a beating is a badge of honor. It can be tough to sort these things out, but they're worth the effort, remembering that unholy critics are pathologically averse to faulting the truthfulness of your content and adept as recasting your offense as a matter of style.[1]

---

[1] I once attended a Chicago meeting of one of our seminary accreditors, North Central Association. The keynote speaker said that schools had become overly concerned that they refrain from hiring administrators "in trouble." He argued, rather, that they should be glad to hire people "in the right kind of trouble." So too should we be ready to be in the right kind of trouble for the sake of biblical fidelity.

Mark Coppenger

OPPONENTS SOMETIMES PLAY DIRTY

Crack open a textbook on "informal logic," and you can read the game plan of many of those who resist, subvert, and even defame the good word you bring directly from scripture and from God-given reasoning. The use of *argumentum ad hominem* is rampant, wherewith they attack your credentials, character, personal history, style, associations, etc.—anything to avoid dealing with the question of the truth and plausibility. Given current obsession over feelings and woundedness, *argumentum ad misericordiam* (appeal to pity) is especially effective. (You may recall the youth who murdered his parents and then threw himself on the mercy of the court because he was an orphan). Play the "I'm broken hearted by what you say" card, and you're halfway home, as especially sensitive folks huddle around the poor "bullied" soul and glare at you. Of course, there's place for diplomacy and a Barnabas hug, but, if you're not careful, you leave the question of reality on the table. And there are plenty of English-language fallacies at their disposal, e.g., "special pleading" (conveniently deploying only favorable evidence) and "slippery slope" (declaring without justification that your preachment is a treacherous move in a slide to ruin, whether toward Pharisaism, theocracy, or bibliolatry).

Yes, biblically earnest disputants can lose their way and fall into bad, even cheap-shot, reasoning, but they can't enjoy it as much as their lost opponents can. Something about the conviction of the Holy Spirit and a frequent return to the sacred text, wherein they find correctives to their cheesy ventures into illogic. And soon they're confronted with the decision of whether they still have firm limits to what they'll do to ingratiate themselves to the peanut gallery. Yes, "we seek to persuade men," but not at the expense of discursive corruption.

Speaking of corruption, perhaps the most insidious form is the hijacking and perversion of language, whether through shameless euphemism—'pro-abortion' becomes 'pro-choice' and adultery' is rendered 'affair.' Then there's the "question-begging epithet," whereby you rig the argument by denigrating your opponent through the label you assign him—calling his holy moral indignation and justified alarm over destructive social agendas a "phobia," as in 'homophobia' and 'transphobia,' leaving him with a clinical problem rather than an honorable moral stance; engineering fine-sounding expressions into unrecognizable linguistic mutants, as in turning level-playing-field 'equity' into rigged-final-score 'equity,' regardless of actual performance on the field.

IN THE CHURCH, ONE MIGHT BE SURROUNDED BY DRAMA QUEENS, WELL-INTENTIONED DRAGONS, AND FAINTING FLOWERS. . .

Drama comes in many varieties. Of course, social media has taken it to a whole new level, but nuclear tweets have forerunners in letters to the editor, which often began with "I've never been so appalled" or "This goes against everything I believe in" or "No one who calls himself a Christian would . . .." To gin up interest and advance their ideological narrative, they favor "Demands" over "Requests," "Outraged" over "Upset," "Trauma" over "Unhappiness." I think, too, of those I call Flash-Bang ethicists, who have an initial fit and then go looking for justification for their fit. (I recall one fellow who cranked up hysterical tweets upon hearing of the 2010 Deepwater Horizon oil spill, exclaiming that Gulf of Mexico seafood was a thing of the past and offering other dire takes, which proved to be bogus).

This recalls the old fable about the princess and the pea. Skeptical over her claims to royalty, her hosts put a garden pea under a stack of mattresses on her guest bed, and, sure enough, in the morning she had a backache from the tiny bump in the bed, a bump that ordinary folks would not feel. So, it seems to me that we have a lot of princesses out there, who magnify their hurts, seek out micro-aggressions, look for safe spaces away from discombobulations to their emotions, surrounded by nurses ever ready to apply the balm of reassurance, vilification for the disturbers, self-flagellation, and even compensation. And by so doing, they cut folks off from important personal growth. Would that they would read Oswald Chambers' March 24 entry in *My Utmost for His Highest*, working from John 3:30: "Over and over again, we become amateur providences, we come in and prevent God; and say—'This and that must not be.' Instead of proving friends of the Bridegroom, we put our sympathy in the way, and the soul will one day say—'That one was a thief, he stole my affections for Jesus, and I lost my vision of Him.'"

For most, there's something a bit tawdry about defending your own honor and taking pay-back into your own hands—not well in synch with "turn the other cheek." But one can muster a great batch of self-righteous zeal in the cause of taking down someone who hurt another's feelings. You see this, for instance, when you cast biblical doubt upon a divorce-remarriage scenario so common in the church. You won't likely lose your head, as did John the Baptist, but you could lose a lot when the "victim" of your earnest and arguably sound exegesis and exposition stands by in sorrow as his or her champions step forth to make you suffer for their friend's disappointment. Understand that *they* aren't asking for personal favors; nothing so ignoble as that. Rather, they're standing up for the downtrodden against you, the downtrodder.

As for fainting flowers (or nervous Nellies), after your tempestuous, public exchange with critics, they can often be heard to say, privately in a whisper, with nervous glances all about, "I'm glad you said that." Of course, you're grateful for this, but you do want to ask, "Thanks, but where were you when the hail was falling on my head?" These are the folks who would do well to visit or revisit Teddy Roosevelt's "Man in the Arena" comments.

NOT TO MENTION QUISLINGS AND BREATHLESS INGRATIATORS

As if this were not enough, the church is now blessed with those who find more gratifying fellowship with the outside critics than with the inside sheep. They yearn for the day when we could be more likeable and more enlightened, and they push the faithful to be less off-putting, more attractive. If only we'd stop putting up barriers to the happy assimilation of seekers. Perhaps we should use their preferred pronouns. If Ze wants to be called Zir Ze, that had better happen, if one is "Christlike." If Bradley Manning visits, graciously call him Chelsea.

Mammas, Don't Let Your Babies Grow Up to Be Ethicists, Unless...

Be quick to repent of whatever the world says you need to repent of, whether the offense is proximate and ongoing or ancient and lapsed, whether the affront was justified or simply upsetting to the lost. Throw your saints under the bus when the clamor of sensitivities dictates. Don't you dare preach "hellfire and brimstone," "buttonhole" in evangelism, "Bible thump" to make a point, slip into SNL-Church Lady mode, or suggest "legalistic" church discipline for those cohabiting without-benefit-of-marriage. Save your harshest words for the brethren while giving their gainsayers a pass. And press your leaders to soften or jettison their pointed, biblical words when the world might deem them "phobic."

It's been said that mid-twentieth century evangelicals, including Southern Baptists, academics, would make a deal with theological liberals: "You call us scholars, and we'll call you Christians." Now, in a PR-obsessed church, we seem to be venturing another exchange: "You call us civilized [i.e., house-broken], and we'll call you admirable." Of course, the price for such "gratuitous ingratiation" is the incremental chipping away at the moral counsel of the canon, the result being an analogue to the Jefferson Bible, wherein our third president redacted the objectionable parts, retaining the passages that would play well in deist salons.

I'm reminded of a speaking engagement I had in support of the Annie Armstrong Easter Offering for Home Missions. An old college acquaintance had me down for a Sunday morning sermon in a fairly new church in an affluent suburb of Atlanta. Over lunch, I asked the pastor how it was that they'd enjoyed such a strong start, and he said that they'd gone door-to-door in the town, asking people who didn't go to church why they didn't. The most common answer was that churches were always asking for money (it's not clear how they knew this since they were not likely to have had broad experience with churches.) So, he concluded, they shouldn't press their congregants for money, and that seemed to go over well.

The previous December, we had received a Christmas letter from an old seminary friend who had been a successful pastor in California. He had sensed a call to foreign missions in Africa, and they were writing from Khartoum. It was a cheerful letter, full of interesting details on their life and work, and, in passing, his wife reported that she recently bought milk for her kids in the marketplace. The problem was, before she boiled it, she had to filter it through cloth to remove the donkey hairs. No big deal.

So, I was tempted to tell the Atlanta area pastor, "You should answer back, 'Sorry, but you don't understand. Christ is not just asking for your money. He's asking for your life.'" Try that for "outreach." Well, they certainly understand that demand in part of Pakistan and Myanmar. Just read an issue of *The Voice of the Martyrs* magazine. But we are very reluctant to get around to that, lest we turn off our prospects. On the other hand, we're not at all reluctant to torment a pastor who is so impolite to hang a plumb line up against the culture and our lives, suggest that things might be out of whack, and then urge us to repent in the face of Scripture rather than bow to the court of public opinion.

BEWARE THE ROCKS-ON-ONE-SIDE CROWD, NOT TO MENTION THE MIDDLE OF THE WINDING-ROADERS

Aristotle is famous for his Golden Mean, spelled out in his *Nicomachean Ethics*. His argument is that virtue lies between extremes—courage between foolhardiness and cowardice; a sense of humor between being a stiff and being a perpetual clown. And I think there is great wisdom there, consonant with the Bible, which urges "moderation." I used that notion in a talk to the Defense Intelligence Agency with the topic I called "Snowdenism," working from the practice of exposing top-secret material as with the likes of Eric Snowden, Julian Assange, and Bradley/Chelsea Manning. Regarding surveillance, I said there were "rocks on both sides," with the possibility of too much and too little scrutiny of the lives of the citizenry.

Of course, neither Aristotle nor the Bible would apply that to clear cut evil deeds. It is not as though a scrupulous person would make sure he wasn't committing too much or too little adultery or murder. Compromise and split-the-difference thinking on genuine transgressions is moral nonsense, but there are many biblical norms which admit of balance. Yes, we are to labor, but not to be "workaholics." Yes, we are to be patient, but there's a limit, a time when we should act decisively to put a stop to something.

But let me note another danger in middle-of-the-road thinking. In pitching our favorite view, we instinctively know that you can garner support by situating it between two extremes. People love to find themselves in the center, indifferent or hostile to the blandishments of the "far right" and "far left." We even label cities and states with that in mind—as the "Heart of Dixie" (Alabama), "Keystone State" (Pennsylvania), and "Gateway to the West" (Saint Louis). And it's a simple matter to "triangulate." You can always find someone to the right and another to the left. Furthermore, you can ignore the fact that the road is typically bending if not veering to the left, and so your split-the-difference approach takes you farther and farther away from where you were. What was middle-of-the-road in 1950 is not at all moderate in 2021. Some change is good but hewing to the center line will take you places you never imagined you'd go, a sad spectacle no matter how much respectability you retain or gain in the eyes of the culture.

This being said, let me bring up a kind of hermeneutic that can get us into trouble. It comes in twins—the "lighten up" and "tighten up" schools of exegesis and application. The first group pretty much finds a way to lump everything under "God is love" (making, as they say, "Love is God") and pointing to Christ's mercy toward the woman at the well as the paradigm. The other side looks for the hard road, the greatest degree of separation, as the way to pleasing God. Jesus' gobsmacking command to the Rich Young Ruler is a paradigm. But, as you see, the problem is that there is a time for each. When Jesus and His disciples were rebuked for picking some grain to eat on the Sabbath, He told His foes, "Lighten up." But when the Hillel party encouraged Him to "lighten up" on divorce and remarriage, He sided with the "tighten up" Shammai group. So, you need to take ethical matters on an issue-by-issue basis.

The Fundamentalists (with a capital "F," mind you) notoriously don't do this. In their second, third, and fourth degree separation, they look down on those who don't properly disassociate from those who don't properly disassociate from those who don't properly disassociate from . . . Well, you get the idea. As Timothy George once put it, your hat finally becomes your church.

And then there are the aforementioned teetotalists, those who chose H. R. Niebuhr's "Christ Against Culture" motif for all sorts of discretionary matters, whether dating, television ownership, or use of a social media account. Practitioners are much taken with regard for the "weaker brother," with assiduous attention to not doing anything that might cause the impressionable to stumble. But there can be problems with this unalloyed standard. "Weaker brothers" can turn into "sensitivity thugs," denying you the right to exercise otherwise licit freedom in Christ. And strict prohibitions against, for instance the use of a credit card, can make travel unnecessarily complex and daunting paths in the absence of a clear biblical prohibition. You must work with the whole counsel of Scripture. Leviticus 19:28 forbids tattoos, but the previous verse forbids trimming your beard. What's the Levitical context? And how do you square submission to verse 28 with indifference toward verse 27? It can take some work, but it's worth it.

Of course, one can "explain away" most every restrictive teaching in the Bible. The gay, Metropolitan Community Church explains that the sin of Sodom was inhospitality,[2] in that Lot refused to send his visitors out for harmless fellowship with the citizenry. And this same group argues, from Romans 1, that it's wrong for a gay man to engage in heterosexual activity because it would be "unnatural" for him to do so. Hermeneutically, nothing is foolproof since fools are so ingenious. Nevertheless, there are much better and much worse readings of biblical counsel, and biblical inerrantists need to be careful that they don't skew their application by the sort of malpractice that is the stock-in-trade of skeptics.

Consider the "Order of Battle"

The military expression, "order of battle," might seem to refer to the way the conflict unfolds, with attacks, withdrawals, counterattacks, envelopments, and such. But it means a roll call of forces arrayed against each other,

---

[2] "What Does the Bible Say about Homosexuality," accessed August 10, 2021, https://www.hrc.org/resources/what-does-the-bible-say-about-homosexuality.

e.g., in the old days, the US 2nd Armored Division versus the Soviet 3rd Tank Division.

When it comes to practicing Christian ethics today, the forces arrayed against us are formidable. Not quite Thermopylae, but stunning in breadth and depth. As Rod Dreher ventures in *The Benedict Option*, we've lost the culture war. Take, for instance, the cause of normalizing transgenderism (an oxymoron if ever there was one). Who will advance it? Who will resist it? Though it is early in the game, it seems that the government (state and federal), the media (both news and entertainment), sports, hi-tech engineers, big business, and academia are all on board. In this past hour, I've watched a trans commentator, Lynette Nusbacher (born Aryeh Judah Schoen Nusbacher) on *AHC* (*American Heroes Channel*) discuss the use of fire weapons in WWII, and then I read an opinion piece in the *Wall Street Journal* about Congressional hearings on an "Equality Act," which would follow California's lead in transferring males who self-identify as women into women's prisons. It's everywhere. When I attended the last, in-person American Philosophical Association meeting before the COVID19 pandemic, they offered me a choice of preferred-pronoun stickers at the registration desk. This is the same APA that publishes an LBGQT-issues newsletter, with articles such as "Puzzle Pieces: Shapes of Trans Curiosity" and "Without a Net: Starting Points for Trans Stories"—one essay published by a professor at a state university, the other from a professor at a private university with historic Methodist connections. And, in March of 2021, the Biden administration lifted the Trump administration's ban on transgenders in the military, putting in place a process whereby troops may "transition gender while serving."

Dreher's prescription is to shift focus to the Christian family, church, school, and community health, implementing analogues to St. Benedict's monastic rules, launching truth missiles from our enclaves and platforms, but abandoning, at least for now, the failed dream of effecting change at the controls of political power, as if the next election or court appointment could facilitate the appearance of a new golden age of national well-being.

Though Dreher disavows retreat and huddle-in-the-bunker thinking, his case lends itself to that interpretation, and I would argue for more of a both-and strategy, running away from society in some instances, running for office in others. But we can agree on the fact that the enemy has fielded a massive array of troops and weapons systems to crush dissent, whether through shaming, marginalizing, de-platforming, fining, firing, or imprisoning.

I mentioned the media, and I should note that a big part of my job as Vice President for Convention Relations (public relations) for the SBC Executive Committee put me daily in contact with the press. Among the many lessons I learned was that 'right' and 'left' meant "right of me" and "left of me." That's why you often read of the "religious right" but seldom about the "religious left." This is one reason that those who get their wisdom from the "ink-stained wretches" of journalism fall prey to the skewing of categories and language.

Having spoken of disincentives to the role of ethicist, let me mention some blessings you'll have to enable and advance your work. You might even come to sing, "Mammas, encourage your babies to become ethicists."

"Pity the Fool" Who Doesn't Have or Use the Bible

Okay, I seem stuck in the twentieth century, drawing the title for this piece from a song Waylon and Willie made famous in the 70s. And now I'm drawing a famous line from Mr. T (*Rocky III*; *The A-Team*) in the 1980s. But pitying fools in the context of this essay has biblical warrant. Oblivious or hostile to special revelation (and increasingly to general revelation), they can come up with interesting stuff (for this image, I draw on "Mr. Baptist," Herschel Hobbs, who said that, without the guidance of Scripture, we're like one of those wind-up rubber-band airplanes; launch them into the air, and they could land just about anywhere).

Let me return to the APA for three examples garnered, as I recall, in a single day at one of their meetings. Mid-morning, I sat in on a panel discussion held by the LGBTQ group. On the platform were two men dressed as women, both from state schools (paid by taxpayer money), one in California, the other in Canada.[3]

They were bemoaning the strait jacket of cisgenderism, utterly absorbed in the righteousness of their desires, insisting that they be regarded with solemn respect by people who presumed to be "lovers of wisdom" (from the Greek meaning of the word 'philosopher'), though there seemed to be scarcely enough wisdom at the dais to fill a thimble. And pity the person who might raise the gender binary flag in that hall or suggest that the APA needed to similarly host a pro-binarism panel down the hall. A lot of foolishness was in play at that session, foolishness that could have been avoided by consulting the first chapters of Genesis and Romans.

From that room, I hustled to another Bible-deaf panel discussion, this one devoted to imagined animal rights. Princeton professor Peter Singer had popularized the term 'speciesism' in the 1970s, and the notion that favoring men over animals was toxic had reached full flower therein. At one point, I raised the (I thought embarrassing) example of a PETA ad, picturing turkeys on one side and Jewish death camp, inmates on the other. The wording in the middle read, "Holocaust on a Plate," the point being that the upcoming holiday season would mean the slaughter of many birds, the moral equivalent of the operations at Auschwitz. If ever there was a reduction to absurdity of PETA's conceptual framework, this was it. But one of the panelists, a Purdue professor, said that one of his relatives died in such a camp and that he had no problem with the ad. You'd think that a Jewish thinker might appreciate Genesis 9, where God gave us animals for consumption.

Then, in an evening gathering of the anarchism study group, an anarchist professor reported on her year as a long-haul trucker, with emphasis on the way in which GPS tracking and strict scheduling had taken the romance out of the trade, robbing the drivers of the delight they used to enjoy in wandering side roads, lingering over a dessert at the truck stop, and sightseeing along the way. She also criticized CEOs for recruiting de-

---

3 The one, wearing pearls looked like Maude on *Golden Girls,* the other like Phoebe *on Friends.* And yes, they brought to mind the 1980s Aerosmith song, *Dude (Looks Like a Lady).* And yes, there I am again in the twentieth century. Please indulge this boomer, septuagenarian.

veloping-world drivers of questionable skill because they came cheap and depressed wages. We'll certainly, there is a place for attention to working conditions, road safety, and fair wages, but what does that have to do with anarchy? And couldn't she have saved herself a lot of trouble by absorbing Romans 13 and then appealing to those in power to do a better job of treating people right?

Imagine how lost at sea you'd be without Genesis 1, Romans 1, Genesis 9, and Romans 13. Well, it doesn't take much imagination, for all around us are people making things up in the absence of these passages and a thousand more. Thank God for the grace and mercy He's shown us in revealing His wisdom through the Bible.

ALLIES LIVING AND DEAD

As noted above, I was getting the impression in graduate school days that the venerated (ancient and modern) and currently working ethicists were counter-culture, counter, that is, to the culture of traditional/Christian thinking in which I had been raised. It seemed that attempts were being made in every arena to pry me away from allegiances to things I'd counted holy, reasonable, and salubrious. Woodstock and its adoring media were telling me the deliverances of Sunday School and Training Union were bogus. Environmentalists were snorting at my paltry efforts at nature stewardship through the Boy Scouts, pointing me toward higher walks in the company of pantheists. The cynicism of M*A*S*H mocked my R.O.T.C. commitments. And so on.

Though I wasn't knocked off my convictions, my interest in joining the prevailing conversation waned. But then, I began to discover a host of articulate spokesmen (living and dead) who well represented perspectives I had long known to be sound, and I began to take heart that public discourse on these matters was not a lost cause. Upon reflecting on these things, I'm reminded of Elisha's word to his servant who was panicked by the sight of the massive, encircling army from Aram: "Don't be afraid, for those who are with us outnumber those who are with them." And then there was the

Lord's word to Paul in a vision, while the apostle was engaging the Corinthians: "Don't be afraid but keep on speaking and don't be silent. For I am with you, and no one will lay a hand on you to hurt you, because I have many people in this city" (Acts 18:9-10).

Over the years, I've been tutored and bolstered by a wide range of voices, not the least of which belongs to Richard Land, whom we honor in this volume, who studied under a strong just-war theorist, Paul Ramsey, at Princeton. (Ramsey, I came to discover, worked in the long line of both Protestant and Catholic writers who provided criteria both for entering and conducting war—men like Augustine, Suarez, Vittoria, Grotius, Pufendorf, and Niebuhr). There are countless examples I could provide, including the Catholic priest who appeared on William Buckley's *Firing Line*, the one who argued that giving murderers less than the death penalty would devalue the lives of the victims; and in that same vein, the case for judicial retribution laid out by C. S. Lewis in "The Humanitarian Theory of Punishment."

Thank God, various think tanks and declarations have arisen to speak truth to cultural confusion, e.g., The *Danvers Statement* (for the sake of gender complementarity); the *Cornwall Declaration* (for biblically grounded environmental stewardship); the *Nashville Statement* (on gender integrity and sexual purity). And don't discount the contribution of non-Christians. I sometimes find more insight in Jewish writers such a Jonathan Sacks (from 1991 to 2013, Chief Rabbi of the United Kingdom and the Commonwealth of Nations) and Ben Stein (economist, columnist, game show host [*Win Ben Stein's Money*] and film star ["Bueller, Bueller"]) than in the writings of neo-Evangelicals. And who can forget the spectacle of atheistic humanist Nat Henthoff (editor of *The Village Voice*) lifting his voice against partial-birth abortion, while "mainline" church leaders were silent? As Augustine taught us, "All truth is God's truth," wherever you may find it.

Mark Coppenger

You Have a Swiss Army Knife at Your Disposal

Before the terrorists and TSA stopped me, I used to carry a Swiss Army Knife on my travels. It was a modest model, with fewer than ten functions, nothing close to the "SwissChamp" version, with over two-dozen components, including a can opener, wire stripper, fishhook disgorger, metal saw, ball point pen, and wood chisel. This fancier version gives a better picture of the tools available to the Christian ethicist about the business of what William James called (regarding philosophy in general) "the usually stubborn attempt to think clearly."[4]

I have spoken of the help we get from non-Evangelicals, even non-Christians, and I'll mention a philosophical benefactor who did his work hundreds of years before the word 'Christian' made sense – Socrates (469-399 BC). His dogged questioning in attempts to get at the essence of a matter, e.g., justice, knowledge, friendship, piety, and courage, gave us the "Socratic method" of teaching, most common in law schools. Today, students have been conditioned to take and regurgitate notes, often delivered in wall-to-wall lectures, often based on PowerPoint slides, perhaps with the professor fielding comments and questions at the end. These dialogue-averse classroom events have been increasingly normalized through online courses, with pre-recorded lectures still workable years after the professor has died. Yes, there are discussion strings, but they are a shadow of the sometimes-harrowing scrutiny to which Socrates would subject his interlocutors, such as Theaetetus, Lysis, Laches, Glaucon, and Meno. He'd challenge them to throw out an idea, and then he'd lead them in checking it out, down to the nth degree, calling himself a "midwife" seeking to deliver their thought-babies, checking them out to see if they're healthy or "wind eggs" (in effect, miscarriages).

---

4 "Definitions of Philosophy," accessed August 12, 2021, http://www2.hawaii.edu/~stroble/philosophy_definitions.html#:~:text=%22Philosophy%20is%20the%20unusually%20stubborn%20attempt%20to%20think%20clearly.%22&text=4.112%20Philosophy%20aims%20at%20the,of%20doctrine%20but%20an%20activity.

Mammas, Don't Let Your Babies Grow Up to Be Ethicists, Unless...

When we launch into such teaching, students find themselves at sea, impatient that their note-taking is chaotic as conflicting claims are thrown out there ("Wait! Which is it? What's the *right* answer, the one we can use in our own lectures and writing? Cut the nonsense and give me the truth package), anxious that their participating in the rough and tumble of discourse could expose them to embarrassment or worse, heresy of some sort, or perhaps there was irritation that the teacher was wasting time fielding the lame opinions of students when they had signed up for wisdom from *The Man*.

Something like this was in play one morning in a doctoral seminar, with a dozen or so professors-in-the-making, and I decided to jot down some lines of inquiry they might follow in sorting out the nature of art, knowledge, mathematics, worship, or whatever it was we were talking about:

Elements of Dialogue
1. Can you give an example? (illustration)
2. What's at stake? What difference does it make? (application)
3. Where are you going with this? (destination)
4. But wouldn't that mean . . .? (implication)
5. What exactly do you mean by . . .? (clarification)
6. So it is kind of like . . .? (analogy; comparison)
7. But what about . . .? (counter-example)
8. Wouldn't it be better to look at it this way? (alternative paradigm)
9. So you're saying . . .? (summarization)
10. But how does this square with . . .? (cohesion)

I explained that these would serve them well as entry points to the study of intellectual challenges along the way. And though none of the ten is explicitly Christian, but rather tracks with the sound operation of our God-given capacity to reason, #10 above opens the door wide for the question of whether a position coheres with the teaching of the Bible.

I used to think that ethicists and philosophers in general learned a lot of things in their undergraduate and graduate courses and then they talked about them for the decades to come. But I was quickly disavowed of this conceit in my first graduate class (on Plato), when the professor spent a whole opening session on one page in one dialogue. I did the math and wondered how in the world we'd get through my big book of dialogues at that rate. But then I figured it out—that we were going to *do philosophy*, and not just talk about it. And that is when this representative list of ten began to form in my mind.

Speaking of rubrics (or Swiss Army tools), I owe a debt to my department chairman at Wheaton College, Arthur Holmes. He sketched out a ladder on which ethical thinking is done, one that begins with a "meta-ethical" *base* (where one considers what is most fundamental to right moral thinking, whether the will of God, the maximization of happiness in the world, or something else); moves up to principles, typically expressed in a word or two (such as 'justice,' 'love,' and 'integrity'); breaks things down into *rules* (such as the Ten Commandments, the dictates of the Sermon on the Mount, or the specific instructions to the Church in Paul's epistles); and then gets down to tough *cases* (such as whether and when to lie, as did Rahab in protecting the Hebrew spies). Of course, one can invert the ladder, making the base the highest court of appeal, from which you "get down" to specific cases. Either way, you work up and down the ladder. For instance, you don't necessarily rebuke a church if they're slack with "holy kisses." Rather, you go with the deeper principle of brotherly affection, expressed physically, which can work itself out in "the right hand of Christian fellowship" or a hug.

Holmes also introduced me to the dichotomy of revelation, found in Thomas Aquinas's *Treatise on Law*. Drawing lines down left and right from a central bubble containing the words, 'Eternal Law,' we first see the path of General Revelation/Philosophy, down through Natural Law and Human Law. On the other side, we track Special Revelation/Theology down through Divine Law (Scripture) to Canon Law (Church Law). And, by Thomas's light, the two forms of revelation coincide, when properly understood. Nature teaches us that homosexuality is unnatural in that it falls outside the procreative realm, and Romans 1 shows that it is biblically illicit.

An Eager Audience

Decades ago, I was pitching a book idea to a Christian publisher, and he noted that ethics books were a hard sell. And, for reasons I gave early on, this was not surprising. But I'm finding that as the culture goes increasingly mad, there is a growing hunger for incisive and prophetic counsel on these matters. Yes, there is blowback and dismissal by many, but God's people, insofar as they are devoted to the Bible and filled with the Holy Spirit, "hunger and thirst for righteousness" and its conceptual framework. Of course, their hunger can drive them to grab unhealthy food from the buffet of opinion. Even more reason to be circumspect in your speaking and writing. But let's not abandon the opportunity for ministry out of fear that we'll misstep. If you do, say you're sorry and then get back at it. The church is dying for perceptive, courageous words on these issues. A good many media platforms have been built to get out the word, so when you have an insight, approach one or another and ask for a hearing. You might be surprised at how God will use you in this connection. As British philosopher and novelist Iris Murdoch phrased it, "Writing is like getting married. One should never commit oneself until one is amazed at one's luck." She was an atheist, so she had to stick with luck. For us, it's a matter of God-given inspiration and calling as "we feel a sermon coming on." If you do, and you're persuaded it's of God, then by all means preach, and if you're called to be an ethicist, get to it!

Chapter 7

Understanding the Difference Between Religious Liberty and Religious Autonomy

Daniel R. Heimbach

The conference occurred just following the fall of Communism in that country and was held to help Baptists there understand the vital importance of religious liberty. I was privileged to speak at that conference along with Richard Land, then President of the Ethics and Religious Liberty Commission of the Southern Baptist Convention. And it is fitting, in this essay, to recall that collaboration because it marked the beginning of a long personal friendship with Land and was the first of many joint projects on ethical issues emerging in contemporary culture both domestic and foreign.

It is hard to have a casual discussion of *religious liberty* because discourse on the subject is highly charged, and rightly so. The stakes are high and include such fundamental matters as personal conscience, accountability to God, duty to preach the gospel, the role, and responsibilities of government, and even questions of social survival. The view we take on *religious liberty* is shaped by how we think about the relation of morality to law, of ethics to government, and the enormous tension that always exists between necessities that drive and limitations that restrict responsible use of God-assigned power in the hands of governors to accomplish what the Bible calls approving good and avenging wrong (Rom 13:3-4), or restraining the wicked and favoring the righteous (Ps 82:3-4; 2 Chron 19:2; 1 Pet 2:14).

Daniel R. Heimbach

Religious liberty includes several foci that easily lead to opposing (or at least rather confused) views about what it means in the first place. So, while debating the merits of *religious liberty*, parties often talk past each other so completely as never to engage what the other affirms or denies. Lack of clarity at critical junctures about what one means by *religious liberty* can be dangerous if it leads to concessions that should never be made or hinders agreements that really are essential. Precisely because *religious liberty* is highly charged, we must approach it with careful attention to what is intended in specific circumstances.

While there certainly is a valid theoretical need to clarify what *religious liberty* means, the need for clarification is not just theoretical but intensely practical as well. Conflict arising from contrary notions of, and about *religious liberty* drives struggles around the world including some close to home. For example, a major division has arisen among Southern Baptists between those who espouse the sort of *liberty* from outside interference the Christian community needs to assure fidelity to the Word of God, and those who espouse a form of *autonomy* that severs individuals and congregations from accountability to God through His Word.[1]

Also consider the tension that rises between the pride Baptists have in having helped the American Founding Fathers assure *religious liberty* in the U.S. Constitution, and arguments set forth recently by Justice Antonin Scalia regarding the need responsible government has to prohibit using substances dangerous to human life and social order. On the first, historian Joseph Martin Dawson has said that, "If researchers of the world were to be asked who was most responsible for the American guarantee for religious liberty, their prompt reply would be "James Madison"; but if James Madison

---

[1] Gregory A. Wills, in an unpublished paper, has analyzed how Baptists in America started with a view of religious freedom that focused on ecclesiastical freedom to determine matters of doctrine and to exercise church discipline independent of state control. He goes on, however, to show that many Baptists over time came to a different view of religious freedom, one that insists, not on freedom *for*, but on freedom *from*, accountability and discipline in church life. His paper is titled: "That Altar to Freedom: Freedom, Authority, and Southern Baptists."

Understanding the Difference Between
Religious Liberty and Religious Autonomy

might answer, he would as quickly reply, "John Leland and the Baptists."[2] That is because Leland and Madison together led the charge that convinced the American Founders to guarantee the new nation would honor and protect the independence of religious conviction, expression, and practice.

The Baptist John Leland is famous for having once said that, "government has no more to do with the religious opinions of men, than it has with the principles of mathematics."[3] And Leland is largely responsible for convincing James Madison, a lifelong Anglican who represented Virginia at the Constitutional convention, that "religion and government will both exist in greater purity, the less they are mixed together."[4] In line with this heritage, Southern Baptists today affirm in *The Baptist Faith and Message* that we believe the state not only "has no right to impose penalties for religious opinions of any kind . . . (and) no right to impose taxes for the support of any form of religion," but also that "a free church in a free state . . . implies the right of free and unhindered access to God on the part of all men, and the right to form and propagate opinions in the sphere of religion without interference by the civil power."[5]

But, while maintaining our zeal for *religious liberty*, how should Baptists say our heritage accords with civil need to restrain religiously motivated activities threatening the common good? The U.S. Supreme Court, in 1990, considered whether government can ever justify restricting religiously motivated conduct, and Justice Scalia writing the majority opinion held that, under the U.S. Constitution, the American right to religious expression is not unlimited and that government interference is sometimes

---

2 Joseph Martin Dawson, *Baptists and the American Republic* (Nashville: Broadman, 1956), 117.

3 Quoted in H. Leon McBeth, *The Baptist Heritage* (Nashville: Broadman, 1987), 275.

4 "From James Madison to Edward Livingston, 10 July 1822," accessed August 17, 2021, https://founders.archives.gov/documents/Madison/04-02-02-0471#:~:text=And%20I%20have%20no%20doubt,less%20they%20are%20mixed%20together.&text=We%20are%20teaching%20the%20World,Kings%20%26%20Nobles%20than%20with%20them.

5 *The Baptist Faith and Message*, adopted by the Southern Baptist Convention, June 14, 2000 (Nashville: Southern Baptist Convention, 2000), 20-21.

warranted. In that case entitled *Employment Division v. Smith*, the Supreme Court held that states have a right to prohibit using narcotic drugs including peyote, even though some Native Americans have long used peyote for sacramental purposes.

Justice Scalia held that religious beliefs do not excuse individuals "from compliance with an otherwise valid law prohibiting conduct that the State is free to regulate . . . . (and) the mere possession of religious convictions which contradict the relevant concerns of political society does not relieve the citizen from the discharge of political responsibilities."[6] He denied unrestricted liberty of religious expression because, he said, such liberty produces "a right to ignore generally applicable laws" and "any society adopting such a system would be courting anarchy."[7] "We cannot," Scalia argued, "afford the luxury of deeming *presumptively invalid*, as applied to the religious objector, every regulation of conduct that does not protect an interest of the highest order."[8]

Thirdly, to further illustrate the need we have to clarify the meaning of *religious liberty*, consider the volatile and exceptionally dangerous tension we face these days between the sort of *religious liberty* we have in mind as Baptists, which sees no inconsistency with swearing to "support and defend the Constitution and laws of the United States of America . . . without any mental reservation or purpose of evasion,"[9] and a sort of *religious liberty* that denies civil authorities should ever hinder (or even monitor) the activities of Muslims who believe the Koran requires doing all in their power to impose Islamic rule on the rest of the world. The sort of *religious liberty* Baptists affirm is completely consistent with defending a constitution that says, "Congress shall make no law respecting an establishment of religion."[10] But because the Koran tells Muslims to "make war on the infidels (non-Muslims) who dwell around you" (Sura 9:123) and requires them to "fight . . .

---

6 Employment Division, Department of Human Resources of Oregon v. Smith (17 April 1990).
7 Ibid.
8 Ibid.
9 Naturalization Oath of Allegiance to the United States.
10 *The Constitution of the United States*, Amendment I.

Understanding the Difference Between
Religious Liberty and Religious Autonomy

until idolatry (non-Muslim religion) is no more and Allah's religion reigns supreme (politically and religiously)" (Sura 2:193), zealous Muslims cannot honestly swear to support the U.S. Constitution "without any mental reservation or purpose of evasion." *Autonomy* for Muslim activity in the United States means leaving ourselves vulnerable to activities aimed at destroying the American system of government and only allowing *religious freedom* for followers of the Muslim faith.

Do Baptists believe civil government should *never* hinder anything men do in the name of pursuing "access to God"? Are Baptists *unexceptionally* opposed to government *ever* restricting religiously motivated activities *however* interpreted, *whatever* they involve, and *no matter what* they threaten? Do Baptists espouse a version of *religious liberty* that insists on complete unaccountable independence from answering to *any external authority at all*? Do we defend what might be called *religious autonomy*? Or do we espouse something more limited, a view of *religious liberty* that assumes some basic level of common decency sufficient to keep society from trying to avoid chaos at the price of tyranny on one hand, and trying to avoid tyranny at the price of chaos on the other? In different terms, the fundamental issue Baptists must clarify when it comes to *religious liberty* in the face of religiously inspired terrorism is: *How are we to handle religious liberty for individuals and systems whose religion demands getting rid of the sort of religious liberty we believe in?*

We will proceed now to clarify the meaning of *religious liberty* by evaluating three questions: Why liberty? What liberty? and Whose liberty? The first question—Why liberty?—shows there are two fundamentally contrary approaches to *the value* of religious liberty touching the role and duties of responsible government. The second question—What liberty?—reveals two mutually incompatible concepts of liberty that affect the way we understand efforts to escape government regulation. The third question—Whose liberty?—highlights differences that arise between claiming exemptions that apply to institutions as opposed to individuals. And finally, we will show that combining these distinctions enables us to define four very different views about the fundamental meaning of *religious liberty*.

Daniel R. Heimbach

Why Liberty? Different Views on The Value of Religious Liberty in General

We turn now to consider what distinguishes *favoring* religious liberty as something valuable and necessary from *rejecting* religious liberty as something dangerously evil. For Baptists used to biblical categories, it must be said the sort of *freedom* with which we are dealing in this context is *not* what Paul had in mind writing to the church in Galatia where he said, "It is for freedom that Christ has set us free" (Gal 5:1). Paul was speaking there of the sinner's spiritual-moral freedom from bondage to the power and penalty of sin, a freedom won for us by Christ's death and resurrection, a freedom that can neither be guaranteed, restricted, nor removed by any human power. Is that the sort of *freedom* to which we refer in discussing *religious liberty* in temporal affairs, to the sort of *religious liberty* granted or denied by civil authorities? No, it is not.

To be sure, that is a very real sort of freedom. And that sort of *freedom* is certainly religious in nature. But it is not the sort of *religious freedom* with which we deal when advocating or defending independence from government interference. Spiritual-moral freedom from the power and penalty of sin is something God alone determines. That sort of *freedom* cannot be given or hindered by men no matter what they try, say, or do. By contrast, the sort of freedom addressed here—the sort of *religious liberty* for which Baptists have struggled for centuries, on many continents, and against many administrations of human government—is an affair of the social and civil order. It is more political than spiritual and refers more to ways in which groups or individuals relate to each other in space-time-material reality than to how they stand before God. And while this sort of *religious freedom* affects Christians and matters to the Church, it has no immediate relation to spiritual-moral freedom from the power and penalty of sin by which sinners escape the wrath of God.[11]

Moving now to what we mean by *religious liberty* in relation to government, our first defining question is: Why liberty? Addressed to the state,

---

11 For a more complete discussion see John Courtney Murray, *Religious Liberty*, ed. J. Leon Hooper (Louisville, KY: Westminster/John Knox Press, 1993), 140ff.

this question asks whether, and to what extent, government ought to protect and promote moral truth; and how we answer sets up a division distinguishing two opposing approaches: one favoring *religious idealism* in general, and the other favoring *religious liberty* in general.

THE CASE AGAINST RELIGIOUS LIBERTY IN GENERAL[12]

Religious idealism—an approach associated with pre-Vatican II Catholicism,[13] various parts of the Orthodox Church,[14] Saudi Arabia, Islamic terrorist groups linked to Osama bin Laden and Al Qaeda,[15] Japan prior to WWII, and ideological Communism—is characterized by a single overarching principle, that *only truth has rights, and error has no rights*.[16] This one key principle is judged to be universal and is thought applicable to social and political, as well as

---

12 Although I employ different terms, I here follow a distinction made by John Courtney Murray. Ibid., 97-113, and 130-151.

13 At Vatican II, the Roman Catholic Church shifted from traditional-historic commitment to *religious idealism* to instead favor and support *religious liberty*. This change was promulgated in "Declaration on Religious Freedom: On the Right of the Person and Communities to Social and Civil Freedom in Matters of Religion" (*Dignitatis Humanae*). This declaration appears in *The Documents of Vatican II*, ed. Walter M. Abbott, S. J., trans. Joseph Gallagher, (Rome: American Press and Association Press, 1966), 675-696.

14 For example, the Romanian Orthodox Church took the *religious idealism* approach when in 1994 it successfully pressured the Romanian government to cancel, on short notice, several previously approved Easter programs sponsored by the Evangelical Alliance of Romania that were scheduled to be aired on the government-owned, government-operated television station.

15 Documentation of this view can be found in John Kelsey, *Islam and War* (Louisville: Westminster/John Knox, 1993). Especially see his chapters on "The Islamic View of Peace" and "Religion as a Cause of War."

16 As an example of this view, Murray cites Pope Pius XII in *Ci riesce*, *Acta Apostolica Sedis* 45 (1953), 788-789, who states: "That which does not correspond to the truth and the norm of morality has, objectively, no right either to existence or to propaganda or to action" (Murray, *Religious Liberty*, 134).

theological, matters. Adherents may pursue this approach in ecclesiastical or secular forms, but all are convinced there is only room for one religious-moral ideology on earth.[17] In secular form, truth is interpreted by an ideological body, like the Communist Politburo of the former Soviet Union, that declares what must be applied to everyone else. In ecclesiastical form, truth claims issue from the head of a body of believers, such as the Pope speaking for the Catholic Church or Osama bin Laden claiming to speak for the *umma muslima*—the *universal community of faithful Muslims*. But whether in secular or ecclesiastical form, *religious idealism* always assumes that civil government must do all in its power to coerce conformity to one true faith and leaves no room for tolerating differences in theology or politics. *Religious idealism* is completely intolerant of ideological diversity so long as there is power enough to eradicate other views, and it tolerates dissent only so long as adherents are too weak to impose their view on others.[18]

The Case for Religious Liberty in General

The opposite position to *religious idealism* regarding the role of government in promoting religious-moral truth is, of course, to favor *religious liberty* in general. This approach—historically associated with Baptists and Anabaptists, and more recently with post-Vatican II Catholicism, the United States, and most Western European nations as well—supposes that everyone has a right to some degree of independence from government interference based on some notion of accountability to higher moral authority.[19] Whereas *re-*

---

17 Historic examples include the Catholic Pope, the Patriarch of the Greek Orthodox Church, the Islamic Caliph (before destruction of the Caliphate), the Ayatollah of Shiite Islam, or the Communist Party Politburo which ruled the former Soviet Union.

18 Murray explains, "The supreme juridical principle for the exclusive rights of truth, and its pendant distinction between thesis and hypothesis, establish a rule of jurisprudence with regard to intolerance and tolerance. This rule prescribes intolerance whenever possible; it permits tolerance whenever necessary" (Murray, *Religious Liberty*, 134).

19 Many examples, both theological and philosophical, could be cited in defense of *religious liberty*. Baptist minister Leonard Busher, in 1614, explained in

Understanding the Difference Between
Religious Liberty and Religious Autonomy

ligious idealism in general expects government to use coercive power to eradicate error at all levels, the approach favoring *religious liberty* in general limits the coercive power of government only to where needed to preserve basic (not ideal) social order.[20] Proponents of this approach expect governors to be humble enough to recognize their judgments are *not* God's judgments, even though they should cooperate *with* God to protect *religious*

---

a petition to King James I of Great Britain, that, "Kings and magistrates are to rule temporal affairs by the swords of their temporal kingdoms, and bishops and ministers are to rule spiritual affairs by the Word and the Spirit of God, the sword of Christ's spiritual kingdom, and not to intermeddle one with another's authority, office, and function" (Anson Phelps Stokes, *Church and State in the United States*, 3 vols. [New York: Harper, 1950], 1:113).

John Leland, another Baptist minister, writing at the time of the American Revolution argued saying, "I now call for an instance, where Jesus Christ, the author of his religion, or the apostles, who were divinely inspired, ever gave orders to, or intended, that the civil powers on earth, ought to force people to observe rules and doctrine of the gospels.... (T)here are many things that Jesus and the apostles taught, that men ought to obey, which yet the civil law has no concern in" (L. F. Green, ed., *The Writings of John Leland* [New York: Arno Press, 1969], 187).

In a break from previous Catholic tradition, Pope John XXII, in 1963, defended *religious liberty* saying, "the dignity of the human person requires that a man should act on his own judgment and with freedom. Wherefore in community life there is good reason why it should be chiefly on his own deliberate initiative that a man should exercise his rights, fulfil his duties, and cooperate with others in the endless variety of necessary social tasks.... it is clear that a society of men which is maintained solely by force must be considered inhuman" (*Pacem in terris*, *Acta Apostolica Sedis* 55 [1963], 265; also Murray, *Religious Liberty*, 137-138).

20 Thomas Jefferson, author of the "Bill for Establishing Religious Liberty" passed by the State of Virginia in 1785, argued that, "the opinions of men are not the object of civil government, nor under its jurisdiction; (and) ... to suffer the civil magistrate to intrude his powers into the field of opinion and to restrain the profession or propagation of principles on supposition of their ill tendency is a dangerous fallacy, which at once destroys all *religious liberty*, because he being of course judge of that tendency, will make his opinions the rule of judgment, and approve or condemn the sentiments of others only as they shall square with or differ from his own; (thus) ... it is enough for the rightful purposes of Civil Government for its officers to interfere when principles break out into overt acts against peace and good order" (Stokes, *Church and State*, 1:334).

liberty within general duty to preserve civil order. Favoring *religious liberty* in general does not deny that government has moral purpose nor suggest that government never punish evil or reward good. But it views the legitimate purpose of morally responsible government to be limited only to what is needed to maintain peace with justice in civil affairs.

According to this approach, the duties of responsible government do not include eliminating theological error, and do not include matters of religious discipline. These are left to religious institutions and individuals out of desire to honor boundaries making room for freedom of conscience and of religious competition within the civil order. This respect for *religious liberty* in general within the civil order does not deny the importance or reality of theological truth by which individuals are reconciled with God or the church pursuing its mission on earth. But it does give latitude for competition between competing religious convictions within the same civil order. Indeed, this approach presumes such trust in the power of truth over error that institutions and individuals with a strong sense of religious-moral conscience are given room by civil authorities to compete without interference from the government.

WHAT LIBERTY? FOR WHOM? DIFFERENT VIEWS ON THE MEANING OF RELIGIOUS LIBERTY ITSELF

The second question we must address to understand what *religious liberty* means is, What liberty? And responding to this question leads to recognizing two incompatible concepts of liberty: one we may call *ordered liberty*, and the other *autonomous liberty*.[21]

---

21 I am following a distinction described by Michael Novak in *The Catholic Ethic and the Spirit of Capitalism* (New York: Free Press, 1993), 93-99. Novak identifies two contrary concepts of liberty in chapter 4 titled: "The Second Liberty." Although he approaches liberty as a component of economic philosophy, he nevertheless takes time to discuss its religious dimensions. Thus, the distinction he makes between concepts of liberty does, in fact, pertain directly to the project addressed in this article.

*Understanding the Difference Between
Religious Liberty and Religious Autonomy*

Ordered Liberty

Ordered liberty is a concept of freedom that is restrained by moral obligations. Freedom from human authority is pursued to obey some higher moral authority—an authority that is by definition beyond being controlled by the institutions or individuals concerned.[22] This concept of freedom always involves freedom *for* as opposed to freedom *from*. It is freedom to do what *we ought*, not freedom simply to do what *we wish*. It is freedom to fulfill higher moral obligations and is not just a matter of avoiding accountability. Put differently, it is freedom *under a higher law*, not freedom *from any law at all*. *Ordered liberty* presumes that real moral authority is objective, enduring, and universal, and is certainly not anything controlled nor made up by those living by it. Not only is the source of moral authority considered to be outside and beyond the individual and outside and beyond institutions of religion, it is outside and beyond civil government as well.[23] This is the view of morally responsible *religious liberty* in relation to human government expressed throughout the Bible.[24] It is also the view that has most influenced the formation of English and American law.[25]

---

22 Novak calls this the "Anglo-American" conception of liberty and quotes Lord Acton who said, "The Christian notion of conscience imperatively demands a corresponding measure of personal liberty. The feeling of duty and responsibility to God is the only arbiter of a Christian's actions. With this no human authority can be permitted to interfere. We are bound to extend to the utmost, and to guard from every encroachment, the sphere in which we can act in obedience to the sole voice of conscience, regardless of any other consideration" (Novak, *Catholic Ethic*, 94; originally from Lord John Emerich Edward Dalberg-Acton, *Select Writings of Lord Acton*, 3 vols., ed. J. Rufus Fears [Indianapolis: Liberty Classics, 1988], 3:491).

23 Lord Acton said, "With this (religious freedom) no human authority can be permitted to interfere." Ibid.

24 For example, when the Sanhedrin banned Peter and John from preaching in the name of Jesus they replied, "Judge for yourselves whether it is right in God's sight to obey you rather than God (Acts 4:19-20).

25 This view is outlined by Novak and contrasted with European nations whose legal traditions descend directly from the Roman system (as opposed to the Anglo-American common law tradition) (Novak, *The Catholic Ethic*, 99-101; also

Daniel R. Heimbach

Autonomous Liberty

Standing in contrast to *ordered liberty* is a view we may call *autonomous liberty*.[26] This is a view of independence that arises from Roman law and that permeates continental European legal traditions.[27] The *autonomous liberty* view defines freedom as the absence of obligation. It is always freedom *from* and is never freedom *for*. Freedom, thus conceived, is defined by what it lacks—no limitations, no responsibility, no accountability—not by what it entails. This is not liberty under obligation to some higher law, but liberty that is essentially *lawless*.[28] According to this view, an individual or institution is never truly *free* unless independent from, and therefore unaccountable to, any limitation or accountability whatsoever—not merely civil, but ecclesiastical, moral, and social as well. Consequently, this view poses a dilemma—law must either deny *autonomous liberty* to maintain social order or allow *autonomous liberty* to increasingly undermine the rule of law leading eventually to complete social collapse.

WHOSE LIBERTY?

The third and final question we must ask to better understand *religious liberty* is, Whose liberty? This leads us to address the fact that *religious liberty* covers more than one sort of relationship, and often involves complex lev-

---

see Harold J. Berman, *Law and Revolution: The Formation of the Western Legal Tradition* (Cambridge, MA: Harvard University Press, 1983).

26 Novak describes this as the Roman or Latin concept of liberty and refers to it by the Latin "liberte" (Novak, *The Catholic Ethic*, 99). I prefer the term *autonomous liberty* because it defines the concept itself.

27 Ibid.

28 Novak says that "those who live in Latin countries in particular are accustomed to thinking of *liberte* as lawless. In Latin countries, many early leaders of the liberal party prided themselves on being anticlerical, atheistic, not infrequently amoral, and metaphysical skeptics. . . .. (Thus they) do not conceive of liberty as ordered by law, reason, and conscience, or recognize that, without law, liberty (in the Anglo-American sense) cannot be achieved." Ibid.

els of inter-related interests, responsibilities, and authorities. In particular, *religious liberty* concerns the way individuals and institutions relate to one another and to God. Each party in this complex bears responsibilities and duties in relation to all the others, and lines of relationship must be drawn that order these responsibilities and duties in ways that secure harmony, not conflict.

CONTRASTING VIEWS ABOUT THE SPECIFIC MEANING OF RELIGIOUS LIBERTY

Using the distinctions clarified above, it is possible to identify several specific categories of meaning for *religious liberty*, and when the distinction between individuals and institutions is combined with the distinction between *ordered liberty* and *autonomous* liberty, it yields four distinctly different concepts: (1) *ordered liberty for institutions*; (2) *autonomous liberty for institutions*; (3) *ordered liberty for individuals*; and (4) *autonomous liberty for individuals*.[29] We shall now look at each in turn.

View 1: Ordered Liberty for Institutions

Ordered liberty for institutions touches many important issues such as freedom of association, freedom of worship, freedom of the Church to maintain discipline, freedom to control religious education, freedom to set membership requirements, freedom to hire Church workers, and freedom to evangelize. While *ordered liberty for institutions* is characterized by obligation to a higher moral authority, and while standards of truth are treated as objective and enduring, an institution's perception of truth and its understanding of moral obligation—that is, its beliefs—can either be accurate or mistaken. That is,

---

29 Here I develop an original paradigm that goes beyond what is found either in the work of John Courtney Murray or Michael Novak. I rely on Murray's understanding of institutional as well as individual dimensions of *religious liberty*, and I borrow Novak's insight regarding differing concepts of liberty. But neither of these noted scholars considered the intersection of these distinctions.

they can be genuinely believed even if they lack a basis in fact. But whether beliefs are accurate or mistaken, *ordered liberty for institutions* means that desire, will and conduct, at the level of institutional leadership, are subject to convictions of religious-moral conscience; it involves an acceptance of corporate responsibility to be faithful to a higher source of religious-moral authority, a source that transcends the mere wishes of institutional leaders or the passing whims of institutional majorities. In American practice and tradition, this form of *religious liberty* has proven good and beneficial to society and supportive of civil order.[30]

View 2: Autonomous Liberty for Institutions

Autonomous liberty for institutions results from combining the claims of a religious body with the autonomous concept of liberty. This second view addresses concerns like the first—freedom of worship, group discipline, and institutional control of religious education and propagation. Nevertheless, the second view differs from the first in that the freedom claimed does not, even in the mind of institutional leaders, entail obligation to an authority beyond or above the personal authority of an institution's leaders. However, they are put, standards espoused by institutions holding this view are no more than ambitions, wishes, or desires held by leaders who do not believe they are under any constraint other than what they make up for themselves. Where this

---

[30] This traditional assessment was expressed by George Washington, partly in a letter of May 1789, sent to the United Baptist Churches of Virginia, and partly in his "Farewell Address." In the first he said, "If I could have entertained the slightest apprehension, that the constitution framed in the convention, where I had the honor to preside, might possibly endanger the religious rights of any ecclesiastical society, certainly I would never have placed my signature to it" (Stokes, *Church and State*, 1:495). In the second he added that, "Of all the dispositions and habits which lead to political prosperity, Religion and Morality are indispensable supports. In vain would that man claim the tribute of Patriotism, who should labour to subvert these great pillars of human happiness, these firmest supports of the duties of Men and Citizens. . . . Whatever may be conceded to the influence of refined education on minds of peculiar structure; reason and experience both forbid us to expect that national morality can prevail in exclusion of religious principle" (ibid., 1:494-495).

Understanding the Difference Between
Religious Liberty and Religious Autonomy

is genuinely the case, one cannot rightly speak of religious-moral *conscience* or the *rights of conscience*. That is because religious-moral conscience must by definition entail some sense of obligation to moral authority beyond one's own,[31] and there simply is no ground for claiming obligation to comply with conscience where there is no place for obligation to any authority beyond one's own desires. Without any sense of obligation to higher authority, the convictions of such institutions cannot be judged accurate or mistaken, and others can only evaluate their conduct as harmful, irrelevant, or helpful as it affects the civil order. We can conclude that institutions claiming to be *religious* while led under the rubric of *autonomous* liberty serve only the self-interests of institutional leaders. Where self-interests are benign, there is no real threat. But where they are not, the *autonomous liberty for institutions* view is surely hazardous to social order and civil tranquility. In extreme form, the influence and activities of such institutions will erode and not support social cohesion and will inevitably leave less assertive groups vulnerable to more assertive ones. That is because where groups are *free* to operate with no sense of responsibility to any authority beyond themselves, experience shows it will not be long before the common good comes under attack and the welfare of others is trampled.[32]

---

31 The rights of conscience have received critical attention in the defense and affirmation of *religious liberty* precisely because conscience is deemed to entail obligation to an authority beyond human control and ability to shape or determine. Reinhold Niebuhr, referring to human conscience, calls it "the sense of moral obligation laid upon one from beyond oneself and of moral unworthiness before a judge" (*The Nature and Destiny of Man*, 2 vols. [New York: Scribner's, 1941], 1:131). Like Niebuhr, I contend that conscience is a sense, or awareness, that our actions are known and judged from a standpoint beyond ourselves, beyond our social community, and beyond the realm of contingent reality itself. It is an awareness, at the edges of consciousness, self-understanding, that our lives, including every thought and action, are being examined from a transcendent perspective, by an authority we do not control but cannot ignore because we are in some way being held accountable whether we like it or not.

32 This tendency explains the atrocious behavior of ethnic cleansers in Bosnia, who sensed no moral obligation other than to what served the limited interests of their own select group.

Daniel R. Heimbach

View 3: Ordered Liberty for Individuals

Ordered liberty for individuals constitutes a third view regarding the meaning of *religious liberty*. Here we move from what freedom means in the life of religious institutions to the freedom of individuals in matters of religious conviction and religiously motivated conduct. The liberty involved includes such matters as personal choice of association, individual involvement in corporate or private worship activities, one's personal perception of right and wrong, as well as individual accountability to God as judge of every thought and activity. Like *ordered liberty for institutions*, *ordered liberty for individuals* also involves religious-moral conscience because an individual understands himself to be under some moral authority higher than himself, a moral authority he cannot himself control and to which he must submit. He is obligated to obey an authority that will not bend to fit personal desires. This third view argues that human government must not interfere with the obligation individuals have to live up to standards they do not control and to fulfill religious duties they cannot deny. At the same time, the sort of freedom involved in the *liberty for individuals* view strengthens respect for the moral purposes of government. Indeed, the moral purposes of government are thought to support, and never to oppose, efforts to conform with higher moral duties. Like *ordered liberty of institutions*, *ordered liberty for individuals* includes the possibility of honest error. It may involve adherence to genuine convictions that are misperceived. But even where misperception exists, individuals are not denying accountability to moral authority transcending their own. Consequently, this third view of *religious liberty*, like the first, has also proven to be good for society and supportive of civil order.[33] But while it supports the strength of responsible institutions,

---

33 This understanding was expressed in the 1866 edition of McGuffey's fifth reader which read that, "Religion is a social concern; for it operates powerfully on society, contributing, in various ways, to its stability and prosperity. Religion is not merely a private affair; the community is deeply interested in its diffusion; for it is the best support of the virtues and principles, on which the social order rests. Pure and undefiled religion is, to do good; and it follows, very plainly, that, if God be the Author and Friend of society, then, the recognition of him must enforce all social

it also threatens those that are irresponsible. Why? Because individuals are left to freely scrutinize moral failure in their leaders, whether they be leaders of religious institutions or leaders in government. Indeed, *ordered liberty for individuals* is the view expressed by heroic prophetic witness in the Bible.[34]

View 4: Autonomous Liberty for Individuals

A fourth view of *religious liberty—autonomous liberty for individuals—*applies the concept of lawless liberty to individuals within the civil order. Like the previous three views, *autonomous liberty for individuals* also demands a realm of independence for religious belief and expression. But like the second and opposed to the first and third, it involves no real sense of higher moral duty. Indeed, it proposes a more radical concept of *religious liberty* than even the second. By the rubric of *autonomous liberty for institutions*, individuals are at least still held accountable under the leadership of a religious body. But individuals claiming *autonomous liberty* are accountable to no authority at all. They claim a sphere of expression for which any irresponsibility will go unchecked. For this reason, proponents of this view, like those espousing *autonomous liberty for institutions*, cannot properly claim to be exercising a *right of conscience*. That is because the notion of *autonomous liberty* involves no measure by which to legitimize such claims. No one can ever assess whether alleged convictions are either valid or invalid, genuine, or mistak-

---

duty, and enlightened piety must give its whole strength to public order" (William H. McGuffey, ed., *McGuffey's New Fifth Eclectic Reader* [Cincinnati: Wilson, Hinkle & Co., 1866], 306).

34   The prophet Jeremiah offers one of the finest biblical examples of such witness. Scripture records that, "Jeremiah said to all the officials and all the people: 'The LORD has sent me to prophesy against this house (i.e., the king) and this city all the things you have heard. Now reform your ways and your actions and obey the LORD your God. Then the LORD will relent and not bring the disaster he has pronounced against you. As for me, I am in your hands; do with me whatever you think is good and right. Be assured, however, that if you put me to death, you will bring the guilt of innocent blood on yourselves and on the city and on those who live in it, for in truth the LORD has sent me to you to speak all these words in your hearing'" (Jer 26:12-15).

en. Self-generated convictions are so purely subjective they can be evaluated by others only regarding whether words are consistent with actions. But even though this view denies individual responsibility to any external authority—any authority outside the control of individuals concerned—the behavior of individuals in this category can still be assessed by others as to how they affect social stability and the welfare of others in the civil order. Being so thoroughly *autonomous*—even to the level of persons who recognize no moral authority beyond themselves—the *autonomous liberty for individuals* view serves no higher good at all whether social, political, or personal. It necessarily upsets theological-moral discipline in the Church and directly opposes government responsibility to maintain social-moral accountability in the civil order.[35]

SOME FINAL REMARKS

The views we have defined regarding four different ways of understanding the essential meaning of *religious liberty* each share the idea that matters of religious belief and religious expression should in some sense be left *free* of government limitation, regulation, or control. And yet, these four views do not carry the same level of legitimacy either in traditional Christian understanding, or in terms of political-social analysis. Where they affect legitimate duties and responsibilities of civil government, it is clear these views are not equally compatible. Two obviously strengthen and support the functioning of responsible government, while two serve only to undermine and threaten responsible government. Therefore, in assessing their practical implications, I conclude by offering four general principles. While these principles will not exhaust needed analyses, they do suggest some ways Baptists might proceed in defending *religious liberty* without

---

35 This view of *religious liberty* comports with complete anarchy; and should a government grant this view full protection under law, it would soon find itself helpless to maintain order at any level. Criminals could justify any action as a matter of pressing personal and self-defined religious conviction, while shifting their convictions to what seems convenient from situation to situation.

hindering God-assigned functions of responsible government in the face of religiously inspired terrorism.

First, *it is not within the competence of governments to distinguish between true or erroneous conscience.* Although governments can certainly distinguish institutions from individuals, they are not competent to discern when claims of religious-moral conscience are either accurate or mistaken. That is, they cannot tell when perceptions of duty owed to a higher source of moral authority are in fact true or false.[36] This means governments risk tyranny and oppression where they prefer one religious institution, or religious class, over others based solely on their own assessment of religious validity.

Second, *governments have very little, if any, ability to distinguish sincere from insincere claims of religious-moral conscience.*[37] I have suggested that the presence of religious-moral conscience is critical for distinguishing *ordered liberty* from *autonomous liberty* at all levels, and that distinguishing *autonomous* from *ordered* views of *religious liberty* does seriously affect the proper working of legitimate governmental responsibilities. But while the difference surely matters to government, civil government also lacks competence to recognize the most critical factor setting them apart. It cannot easily discern the difference between convictions of a genuine religious-moral conscience that truly submits to higher authority and insincere appeals to

---

36 Government simply has no way to render judgment between an authoritative or counterfeit experience of spiritual revelation. For example, government has no basis of meaningful authority by which to judge the validity of the vision reported by the apostle Paul to evangelize Macedonia (Acts 16:9) as compared to the spurious visions alleged by Joseph Smith to justify founding of the Mormon religion. That one might be true and the other false, or that both may be true or both false, are surely conceptual possibilities. But that determination is beyond the competence of government to prove or decide.

37 For example, government cannot genuinely discern by external observation when an objection to participating in war is truly a matter of a claimant's submission to higher moral authority, and when it is a matter of fear and self-interest cloaked in moralistic rhetoric. That such a distinction exists is clear enough. But where the difference is not readily apparent, the government is bound to grant claimants the benefit of a doubt or risk a serious violation of a genuine moral conviction.

alleged convictions of conscience made only to win license to indulge the desires of those who submit to no sense of higher authority at all.

Together, these first two principles mean that government cannot use evaluation of religious-moral conscience to separate between the four views of *religious liberty*. The best it can do is assume a particular claim is likely to be one variety or the other based on the appearance of sincerity and efforts to verify consistency. This impediment stands even though the different views offer radically opposed risk profiles. This means governmental efforts to judge the authenticity and validity of assertions regarding religious-moral conscience cannot completely avoid uncertainty and vulnerability. Efforts to judge the difference between sincere and insincere religious-moral conscience may be easier in more homogeneous religious environments, but they are still permeated with risk. And, of course, the more diverse the religious environment becomes, and the more radically different religious minorities involved happen to be, the more of a risk and more difficult it will be for government officials to make any satisfactory assumption regarding authentic claims of religious-moral conscience.[38]

Third, *while governments can distinguish between belief and action, they are not able to distinguish in a reliable way between authentic and unauthentic religious expressions*. Governments do not have the competence necessary to separate exercises that genuinely serve a higher authority from exercises that are merely fabrications of an autonomous human imagination.[39] This means that on matters of religious expression, as with claims of religious-moral conscience, civil governments can tell very little difference between dif-

---

38 For example, in early American society differences regarding contrary claims of conscience were for the most part limited to those that could be evaluated within the larger conceptual framework provided by the Judeo-Christian worldview. Hazardous as they are, government efforts to determine sincerity of conscience in such circumstances is easier than in a more radically pluralistic setting that must also evaluate conscience claims raised by Buddhists, Secular Humanists, Atheists, Wiccans, New Agers, and Neo-pagans.

39 For example, civil officials of a secular government are not able to distinguish persons who seek to smoke peyote because they truly think it is religious from persons who make religious claims merely as a stratagem to justify getting high on the drug's narcotic effect.

Understanding the Difference Between
Religious Liberty and Religious Autonomy

ferent views of *religious liberty* except where it concerns distinguishing individuals from institutions and evaluating consistency between words and actions. A government may feel very threatened by the risk of allowing freedom for persons or groups that sense no responsibility for anything beyond themselves. But it has no reliable way to assess the religious authenticity of exercises, the validity of which is subject only to the interpretation of those who engage in them. Because it cannot judge the authenticity of any particular source of religious authority, government cannot reliably use authenticity of religious expression to judge between the actions of *ordered* and *autonomous* liberty.

This brings us to the fourth principle for relating government to the various views identified. And it is, I believe, possibly the only principle that offers legitimately functioning governments a way to make meaningful distinctions within their competence to judge. *Governments are indeed (or should be) competent to judge between actions and expressions that are benevolent, benign, or malicious as to their effect upon civil peace, order, justice, and safety.* Since responsible human governments do have a God-assigned moral mission to punish evil and reward good so far as it concerns their civil responsibilities, they must try to pass and to uphold laws that serve to restrain behavior that is harmful and to promote behavior that is beneficial to the common good (whatever their motives). This means government can discern and should restrain malicious conduct that at times arises from institutional or individual views of *autonomous religious liberty*, even while it protects and rewards benevolent conduct whatever its origin.

As a practical matter, government must be able to protect the civil order from abuses committed in the name of *religious liberty*, and such abuses certainly can arise where latitude is granted individuals and institutions who, under no sense of transcendent moral obligation, are guided by nothing more than their own transitory wishes and desires. But where it acts to restrain such abuse, government, if it is to remain responsible, must take care to limit its power to only that which is necessary to prevent harm. Should it seek to order society by imposing a single view of religious truth, then it oversteps its moral mission, presumes to act *as God* (in God's place) rather than *with God* (in cooperation with God, or at least non-interference with God), and makes judgments that only deity can truly judge. When that happens, then not only does government become tyrannical, but it also undermines its own success by destabilizing society and marginalizing the moral influence of men and women who truly live by legitimate religious-moral conscience—those who truly live for something more than their own self-centered concerns and desires.

A government that restrains its power out of respect for the *ordered religious liberty* of citizens will be strong and stable. But a government that tries to control religious belief and expression —either from zeal for *religious idealism* or for fear of *religious autonomy*—will soon be tyrannical, however good its intentions. When a government hinders *ordered religious liberty*, it cannot be stable and eventually destroys itself because it loses the respect and support of the responsible, public-minded segment of its citizenry that produces and strengthens social cohesion.

Chapter 8
A Stealth Agenda

Michael Brown

Is there really a homosexual agenda?[1] Is there truly an insidious gay plot to undermine traditional values and subvert the American family? The very idea of it appears to be laughable – especially to the gay and lesbian community. According to one source, identified only as "L.," this is the menacing and dangerous "gay agenda":

The Gay Agenda

7:45 a.m. Alarm rings
8:00 a.m.–8:10 a.m. Take shower
8:15 a.m.–8:30 a.m. Dress and put items into briefcase
8:35 a.m. Leave house
8:45 a.m. Starbucks

---

1 https://www.peterlang.com/document/1051205, accessed January 06, 2022, cites from its source, "The 'gay agenda' is a rhetorical strategy deployed by the religious right and other social conservatives to magnify fear and hostility of queers." Also see Jack Nichols, *The Gay Agenda: Talking Back to the Fundamentalists* (New York: Prometheus Books, 1996), 81: "The 'gay agenda' is a term that has been coined for propaganda purposes by the forces of religious fundamentalism. To enhance what they would have others believe is the ominous dimension of this term, they also refer to 'the homosexual agenda.'"

9:00 a.m. Arrive at job
12:00 p.m. Lunch with a co-worker. Perhaps Chili's?
12:45 p.m. Return to job
1:30 p.m.–2:30 p.m. Meeting
5:00 p.m. Leave work
5:30 p.m.–6:30 p.m. Work out in gym
7:00 p.m. Return home
7:20 p.m. Prepare and eat dinner
8:00 p.m. Watch *Law & Order* on TNT
11:00 p.m. Go to sleep[2]

Do you detect just a little sarcasm? Then consider this anonymous, widely circulated posting:

The Gay Agenda:
Author Unknown

I know that many of you have heard Pat Robertson, Jerry Falwell and others speak of the "Homosexual Agenda," but no one has ever seen a copy of it. Well, I have finally obtained a copy directly from the Head Homosexual. It follows below:

6:00 a.m. Gym
8:00 a.m. Breakfast (oatmeal and egg whites)
9:00 a.m. Hair appointment
10:00 a.m. Shopping
12:00 p.m. Brunch
2:00 p.m.
  1) Assume complete control of the U.S. Federal, State and Local Governments as well as all other national governments,
  2) Recruit all straight youngsters to our debauched lifestyle,

---

[2] See, e.g., 'The Gay Agenda," accessed January 06, 2022, https://www.mcsweeneys.net/articles/the-gay-agenda.

A Stealth Agenda

3) Destroy all healthy heterosexual marriages,
4) Replace all school counselors in grades K-12 with agents of Colombian and Jamaican drug cartels,
5) Establish a planetary chain of homo-breeding gulags where over-medicated imprisoned straight women are turned into artificially impregnated baby factories to produce prepubescent love slaves for our devotedly pederastic gay leadership,
6) Bulldoze all houses of worship, and
7) Secure total control of the Internet and all mass media for the exclusive use of child pornographers.

2:30 pm Get forty winks of beauty rest to prevent facial wrinkles from stress of world conquest
4:00 pm Cocktails
6:00 pm Light Dinner (soup, salad, with Chardonnay)
8:00 pm Theater
11:00 pm Bed (du jour)[3]

A gay agenda? What a joke! Simply stated, a "gay agenda" does not exist anymore than a "Head Homosexual" exists – at least, that's what many gays and lesbians would surely (and sincerely) say.[4]

As expressed by the widely read, lesbian blogger Pam Spaulding, "The Homosexual Agenda" is an elusive document. We've been looking around for a copy for quite some time; the distribution plan is so secret that it's almost like we need a queer Indiana Jones to hunt the master copy down. The various anti-gay forces are certain that we all have a copy and are coordinating an attack to achieve world domination."[5] Right!

---

3   Quoted in "Anti-LGBT trolls face backlash after targeting Pride campaign," accessed October 14, 2021, https://www.pinknews.co.uk/2017/08/07/vodka-lovers-are-putting-down-these-anti-lgbt-trolls/comments/.

4   A search for the phrase "there is no gay agenda" yields multiplied thousands of hits on a wide variety of websites.

5   Quoted at https://americansfortruth.com/2006/11/22/gay-agenda-what-gay-agenda/, accessed January 06, 2022.

Of course, most gays and lesbians *do* have an "agenda." They want to live productive, happy, fulfilling lives, just like everyone else. Beyond that, they probably want others to accept them as they are. That would be the "agenda" of most homosexual men and women worldwide.[6] As stated (again, with real sarcasm) by a poster on the website of gay activist Wayne Besen, responding to a prior, negative comment by another poster, "Us faggots DO have a homosexual agenda. I'm risking my life by telling you, and the Council will revoke my license for sure, but I'm going to tell you exactly what it is. You ready? The insidious gay agenda is . . . We want you to leave us the [expletive] alone and to be treated like normal human beings with the same rights that YOU take for granted. THAT'S the gay agenda."[7]

What then are we to make of books written by conservative Christians with titles such as *The Agenda: The Homosexual Plan to Change America*, or *The Homosexual Agenda: The Principal Threat to Religious Freedom Today*, or *The Gay Agenda: It's Dividing the Family, the Church, and a Nation?*[8] Per-

---

6 As stated by Jeffrey-John Nunziata, "Homo-hatred in America," both accessed October 14, 2021: http://www.impactpress.com/articles/octnov97/homo-hate.htm, "We as a nation and a people have a long way to go in regard to treating our gay, lesbian, bisexual and transgender brothers and sisters as equals. All they want to do is live out their lives just like you do. All they want is to love someone and be loved . . . so what if it is with a member of the same sex." According to openly gay Congressman Barney Frank, (speaking on the heels of the repeal of "Don't Ask, Don't Tell"), "the radical homosexual agenda" is "to be protected against violent crimes driven by bigotry, it's to be able to get married, it's to be able to get a job, and it's to be able to fight for our country. For those who are worried about the radical homosexual agenda, let me put them on notice. Two down, two to go," http://www.advocate.com/News/Daily_News/2010/12/22/Barney_Frank_Reveals_Gay_Agenda/, accessed January 09, 2022.

7 See *A Queer Thing Happened*, accessed August 17, 2021, https://www.scribd.com/document/453037246/387573719-A-Queer-Thing-Happened-To-America-Michael-Brown-pdf.

8 Rev Louis P. Sheldon, *The Agenda: The Homosexual Plan to Change America* (Lake Mary, FL: Frontline, 2005); Alan Sears and Craig Osten, *The Homosexual Agenda: Exposing the Principal Threat to Religious Freedom Today* (Nashville: Broadman & Holman, 2003); Dr. Ronnie W. Floyd, *The Gay Agenda: It's Dividing the Family, the Church, and a Nation* (Green Forest, AZ: New Leaf Press, 2004). Sim-

haps the authors of these studies are delusional? Perhaps they are displaying symptoms of hysteria? Perhaps they are projecting their own homophobic fears? Maybe *they* are the ones with an agenda, an oppressive campaign to deprive gays and lesbians of their constitutional rights?

In September 2004, Salon Magazine quoted Sen. Tom Coburn as stating that, "The gay community has infiltrated the very centers of power in every area across this country, and they wield extreme power" and the "[gay] agenda is the greatest threat to our freedom that we face today."[9] Can such sentiments be taken seriously?

This much is sure: Even though the "homosexual community" is as diverse as the "heterosexual community," there is vast agreement among homosexuals that there is no such thing as a gay agenda. In fact, such terminology is to be studiously avoided, as noted by the following piece on "queercafe":

---

ilar is the statement of Janet L. Folger, *The Criminalization of Christianity* (Sisters, OR: Multnomah Publishers, 2005), 16: "The *greatest threat* to our freedoms comes from the homosexual agenda" (emphasis in the original). More extreme would be the comment of Scott Lively, *Reprobate Theology: The Homosexual Seduction of the American Church* (Citrus Heights, CA: Veritas Aeterna Press, 2003), 1, "The 'gay' activists will be satisfied by nothing less than the total capitulation of the culture to their agenda." Cf. also Congressman William Dannemeyer, *Shadow in the Land: Homosexuality in America* (San Francisco: Ignatius, 1989); Peter Spriggs, *Outrage: How Gay Activists and Liberal Judges Are Trashing Democracy to Redefine Marriage* (Washington, DC: Regnery, 2004). Also quite representative would be Rod Parsley, *Silent No More* (Lake Mary, FL: Charisma House, 2005), chapter 4, "Homosexuality: The Unhappy Gay Agenda," 69-88; David Kupelian, *The Marketing of Evil: How Radicals, Elitists, and Pseudo-Experts Sell Us Corruption Disguised as Freedom* (Nashville: WND Books, 2005), especially 17-38; Tristan Emmanuel, *Warned: Canada's Revolution Against Faith, Family, and Freedom Threatens America* (Canada: Freedom Press, 2006), especially 61-78; Roger Magnuson, *Informed Answers to Gay Rights Questions* (Sisters, OR: Multnomah, 1994), esp. 27-43, "The Agenda: What Homosexuals Really Want." See further O. R. Adams Jr., *As We Sodomize America: The Homosexual Movement and the Decline of Morality in America* (n.p.: n.p., 1998); note that this self-published study, available as an ebook, runs 649 pages.

9 "Anti-Gay Pol Reaches Out to GLBTs for Support Against ObamaCare," accessed October 14, 2021, http://www.edgephiladelphia.com/index.php?ch=news&sc=&sc2=&sc3=&id=97955 (October 21, 2009).

> OFFENSIVE: "gay agenda" or "homosexual agenda."
> PREFERRED: "lesbian and gay civil rights movement" or "lesbian and gay movement." Lesbians and gay men are as diverse in our political beliefs as other communities. Our commitment to equal rights is one we share with civil rights advocates who are not necessarily lesbian or gay. "Lesbian and gay movement" accurately describes the historical effort to achieve understanding and equal treatment for gays and lesbians. Notions of a "homosexual agenda" are rhetorical inventions of anti-gay extremists seeking to portray as sinister the lesbian and gay civil rights movement.[10]

There you have it – "Notions of a 'homosexual agenda' are rhetorical inventions of anti-gay extremists seeking to portray as sinister the lesbian and gay civil rights movement." Thus, there are no facts behind this claim, only *notions*; there is no substance to this charge, only *rhetorical inventions*; those behind these accusations are not balanced, well-meaning people, but rather *anti-gay extremists*; the movement in question is nothing less than a civil rights movement, and the only thing *sinister* about this movement is the way it is portrayed by the fanatical opposition.

As explained by the late Jack Nichols, a highly literate, pioneer gay-rights advocate:

> Propagandistic hate films touting a so-called gay agenda have been produced and circulated widely by the religious right. Each has been carefully edited so as to create false impressions of gay men and lesbians as well as the "evil" social program they are accused, en masse, of desiring. Fund-raising letters, couched in inflammatory language to frighten recipients, are sent out with the signatures of ministers. They promise to use the dollars sent to bring a halt to this imaginary gay agenda, one, they say, that favors a variety of outrageous proposals ranging from the "right" to molest children to a fondness for spreading AIDS.[11]

---

10 https://queercafe.net/language.htm, accessed January 06, 2022.
11 Jack Nichols, *The Gay Agenda: Talking Back to the Fundamentalists* (New

A Stealth Agenda

To restate the prevailing gay consensus: There is no such thing as a gay agenda, a fact underscored time and again by the common practice (especially among gays and lesbians) of putting this term in quotes. It simply doesn't exist. As stated succinctly by the Rainbow Alliance, "The 'Gay Agenda' is but one of the many lies promulgated by radical religious political activists."[12] In the words of a representative for Soulforce, a leading gay, religious organization, "It is only the extreme religious right who suggest that there is a homosexual agenda."[13] So there you have it!

Charles Karel Bouley II, writing on February 22, 2005, on Advocate.com, a leading gay website, put it like this:

> We've heard about it for years. Many have tried to define it, including 22 organizations that released a combined statement in January 2005 to outlets such as Advocate.com [for this statement, see below]. It's the Gay Agenda, and while many pontificate about it,

---

York: Prometheus Books, 1996), 81 (the used copy of the book that I purchased turned out to be signed by Nichols to a friend). Cf. also Didi Herman, *The Antigay Agenda: Orthodox Vision and the Christian Right* (Chicago: University of Chicago Press, 1997).

12 https://massresistance.blogspot.com/2005/03/gay-manifesto-not-satire.html, accessed January 06, 2022.

13 This was part of a response to an email from Bill Bonilla to Dr. Mel White, the founder of Soulforce, dated October 9, 2006, responding to a request to hold a campus debate with me about homosexuality and the Bible. Mr. Bonilla made the innocent mistake of referring to "the homosexual agenda," drawing this response from Kara, assistant to Dr. White: "You clearly show your bias against the LGBT community with these words. It is only the extreme religious right who suggest that there is a homosexual agenda. Just as any self-respecting black person would never deighn [sic] to discuss their humanity with the KKK, we do not choose to give fundamentalists a platform to promote their lies." In an email dated October 12, 2006, Kara added, "Anyone who says there is a homosexual agenda, clearly does not know any gay people. There is no more a homosexual agenda than there is a heterosexual agenda. There will be no debate, because we will no longer allow fundamentalists such as you, to call our faith and our lives into question." The response from Jeff Lutes of Soulforce, also on October 12, 2006, was much more gracious, as was his personal e-interaction with me.

condemn it, or allegedly try and further it, I as a gay man have yet to figure out what it is. Actually, let me flat-out say it: There is no gay agenda. I hate to break it to all those antigay organizations out there that have made such a myth the bedrock of their bigotry campaigns, but really, it just doesn't exist.[14]

In a speech on behalf of same-sex marriages delivered to the House of Representatives February 20, 1996, Iowa Republican Ed Fallon stated:

> Heterosexual unions are and will continue to be predominant, regardless of what gay and lesbian couples do. To suggest that homosexual couples in any way, shape, or form, threaten to undermine the stability of heterosexual unions is patently absurd. And I know, you'll say: "What about the gay agenda?" Well, just as there turned out to be no Bolsheviks in the bathroom back in the 1950s, there is no gay-agenda in the 1990s. There is, however, a strong, well-funded anti-gay agenda, and we have an example of its efforts here before us today.[15]

So then, the "gay agenda" is a myth? In response to the proposed ban on gay marriages in her state in 2004, Stacy Fletcher of the gay activist group Arkansans for Human Rights said, "We were not looking for this

---

[14] "The Gay Agenda Revealed," accessed January 06, 2022, https://www.advocate.com/politics/commentary/2005/02/22/gay-agenda-revealed. He states, "There is no gay agenda – this is so clear, and it's the stance we must take. But there is an American agenda, a promise made by the founders that we are still striving to fulfill. Gays and lesbians have merely started to pursue the freedoms and exercise the rights granted in that document that the president wants to amend. How we get and pursue those rights and freedoms remains up for debate, and while there is not real unity in the gay community, there is one thing that ties us in the United States together: We are Americans first. It's time to remind the Right that our agenda is not based on sexual orientation but on a political and social promise, set forth by a group of insightful men a couple hundred years ago."

[15] "A Speech by Ed Fallon in Opposition to an Iowa *Defense of Marriage Act*," accessed October 14, 2021, http://www.religioustolerance.org/hom_mar1.htm.

fight. There is no gay agenda. All our community was doing was working, paying taxes, and trying to live our lives."[16] The testimony is unanimous and unequivocal: There is a right-wing, bigoted, anti-gay agenda, but there is no gay agenda. Case closed. Or is it?

Is There More to the Story?

Pointing back to the turning point in modern homosexual history, the Stonewall riots in New York City in 1969, gay activist Marc Rubin asked in 1999, "How did that singular event in June 1969 become the fountainhead for so many of the changes that have made the world so different for queers thirty years later?" His answer? "It spawned the Gay Liberation Movement."[17] Rubin continues:

> First there was The Gay Liberation Front proclaiming loudly, clearly, and brilliantly, the truth that gay is good, that queers had embodied within them all of the genius of Humanity and owned all privileges of that status. . ... GLF, the Gay Liberation Front, was conceived as being part of the entire Liberation movement, one segment of a worldwide struggle against oppression. . . The Gay Activists Alliance stood for writing the revolution into law. Although individual members would ally themselves to causes not directly related to the oppression of homosexuals, the organization's single-issue focus enabled it [to] direct all of its energies toward working intensively in, on, with, and against "The Establishment" on issues effecting lesbians and gay men. It said, "We demand our Liberation *from* repression and *to* the point where repressive laws are removed

---

16 https://www.foxnews.com/story/gay-marriage-vote-in-11-states, January 06, 2022.

17 "The GAA Must be Restored to History," accessed October 14, 2021, http://www.gaytoday.com/garchive/viewpoint/071999vi.htm. My appreciation to Katie George and Kim Stephen Allison, FIRE School of Ministry grads and former staff, for drawing my attention to this article.

from the books and our rights are written into the documents that protect the rights of all people, for without that writing there can be no guarantees of protection from the larger society." The means to achieving these ends included, street actions famously defined as "zaps," marches, picket lines, political lobbying, education, active promotion of the need for lesbians and gay men to come out of their closets, and a constant in-your-face presentation of the fact that gay is good. Its goals were revolutionary in that it sought, through these means, to restructure society.[18]

Yes, society has been greatly restructured by gay "revolutionary" goals, *but there is no gay agenda*. Carl Wittman's landmark *Refugees from Amerika: Gay Manifesto*, dated Thursday, January 1, 1970, concluded with "An Outline of Imperatives for Gay Liberation":

1) Free ourselves: come out everywhere; initiate self-defense and political activity; initiate counter community institutions.
2) Turn other gay people on: talk all the time; understand, forgive, accept.
3) Free the homosexual in everyone: we'll be getting a good bit of [expletive] from threatened latents: be gentle and keep talking & acting free.
4) We've been playing an act for a long time, so we're consummate actors. Now we can begin *to be*, and it'll be a good show![19]

---

18 "The GAA Must be Restored to History," accessed October 14, 2021, http://www.gaytoday.com/garchive/viewpoint/071999vi.htm. This material is also treated in my book *Revolution in the Church: Challenging the Religious System with a Call for Radical Change* (Grand Rapids, MI: Chosen Books, 2002), 29-30. Also relevant is my lecture from February 20, 2007, "What the Church Can Learn from the Gay and Lesbian Community" (available only on DVD).

19 Available online at http://www.williamapercy.com/wiki/images/Refugees_from_Amerika.pdf, accessed October 14, 2021. Wittman died of AIDS in 1986; his manifesto has frequently been reprinted. See, e.g., Karla Jay and Allen Young, eds., *Out of the Closets: Voices of Gay Liberation* (New York: Douglas Book Corporation, 1972), 330-341.

A Stealth Agenda

But there is no gay agenda, despite a gay manifesto with a call to action for the purpose of gay liberation. In Chicago, Illinois, the 1972 Gay Rights Platform was formulated, including nine federal goals and eight state goals, some of which called for:

1) Issuance by the President of an executive order prohibiting the military from excluding for reasons of their sexual orientation, persons who of their own volition desire entrance into the Armed Services; and from issuing less-than-fully-honorable discharges for homosexuality; and the upgrading to fully honorable all such discharges previously issued, with retroactive benefits (1972 Federal-2).
2) Federal encouragement and support for sex education courses, prepared and taught by Gay women and men, presenting homosexuality as a valid, healthy preference and lifestyle as a viable alternative to heterosexuality (1972 Federal-6).
3) Repeal of all state laws prohibiting private sexual acts involving consenting persons; equalization for homosexuals and heterosexuals for the enforcement of all laws (1972 State-2).
4) Repeal of all state laws prohibiting transvestism and cross-dressing (1972 State-6).
5) Repeal of all laws governing the age of sexual consent (1972 State-7).
6) Repeal of all legislative provisions that restrict the sex or number of persons entering into a marriage unit; and the extension of legal benefits to all persons who cohabit regardless of sex or numbers (1972 State-8).[20]

But there is no gay agenda, despite a gay rights platform spelling out militant, comprehensive goals, including the repeal "of all laws governing the age of sexual consent" (an endorsement of pederasty!) and governmental

---

20 See, conveniently, "Homosexual Agenda Platforms from 1972-2000," accessed October 14, 2021, http://www.freerepublic.com/focus/f-news/908140/posts.

recognition of multiple-partner "marriages" (today called "polyamory") at both the national and statewide level.

Literature distributed at the 1987 March on Washington listed seven major demands, including the legal recognition of lesbian and gay relationships and the repeal of all laws that make sodomy between consenting adults a crime. The 1993 event was billed as the March on Washington for Lesbian, Gay, and Bi Equal Rights and Liberation. The opening item in the Platform Demands stated: "We demand passage of a Lesbian, Gay, Bisexual, and Transgender civil rights bill and an end to discrimination by state and federal governments including the military; repeal of all sodomy laws and other laws that criminalize private sexual expression between consenting adults." The third Platform Demand stated: "We demand legislation to prevent discrimination against Lesbians, Gays, Bisexuals and Transgendered people in the areas of family diversity, custody, adoption and foster care and that the definition of family includes the full diversity of all family structures."[21] *But there is no gay agenda!*

Expressing himself with great vigor – and perhaps an extremist tone even for gay activists – ACT UP leader Steve Warren intoned an ominous sounding alarm for religious Jews and Christians in his September 1, 1987 "Warning to the Homophobes." (Despite the threatening tone, this *was* published by *The Advocate*, the nation's most prominent gay publication.)

1) Henceforth, homosexuality will be spoken of in your churches and synagogues as an "honorable estate."
2) You can either let us marry people of the same sex, or better yet, abolish marriage altogether.
3) You will be expected to offer ceremonies to bless our sexual arrangements, whether or not you retain marriage as something to celebrate in your churches. You will also instruct your young people in homosexuality as well as homosexual behavior, and you

---

21 See "Platform of the 1993 March on Washington for Lesbian, Gay, and Bi Equal Rights and Liberation Action Statement Preamble to the Platform," https://www.thetaskforce.org/reflections-on-the-1993-march-on-washington/, accessed January 06, 2022.

will go out of your way to make certain that homosexual youths are allowed to date, attend religious functions together, openly display affection, and enjoy each others' sexuality without embarrassment or guilt.

4) If any of the older people in your midst object, you will deal with them sternly, making certain they renounce their ugly and ignorant homophobia or suffer public humiliation.

5) You will also make certain that all of the prestige and resources of your institutions are brought to bear on the community, so laws are passed forbidding discrimination against homosexuals and heavy punishments assessed. We expect and demand the same commitment to us that you made to blacks and to woman, though their suffering has not been as great as ours.

6) Finally, we will in all likelihood want to expunge numbers of passages of your scriptures and rewrite others, eliminating preferential treatment of marriage and using words that will allow for homosexual intrepations of passages describing biblical lovers such as Ruth and Boaz or Solomon and Queen of Sheba.

Warning: If all these things come to pass quickly, we will subject orthodox Jews and Christians to the most sustained hatred and Vilification in recent memory. We have captured the liberal establishment and the press. We have already beaten you on a number of battlefields. And we have the spirit of age on our side. You have neither the strength to fight us nor the will, so you might as well surrender now."[22]

Yes, Warren states clearly that gays are taking over, and religious people had better be ready for the radical changes that are coming. *But there is no gay agenda!*

In their pioneering 1990 volume *After the Ball: How America Will Conquer Its Fear and Hatred of Gays in the 90's*, Harvard-trained gay authors Marshall Kirk and Hunter Madsen offered a brilliant and comprehensive

---

22 http://community.fortunecity.ws/village/foster/263/queerf.html, accessed January 06, 2022.

strategy for changing America's attitudes towards homosexuality, as indicated by the subtitle, *How America Will Conquer Its Fear and Hatred of Gays in the '90s*. The book built on the authors' 1987 article, "The Overhauling of Straight America,"[23] and their six-fold plan has been referred to many times in the last two decades, especially by conservatives who have noted how successful this plan has been:

1) Talk about gays and gayness as loudly and often as possible.
2) Portray gays as victims, not aggressive challengers.
3) Give homosexual protectors a "just" cause.
4) Make gays look good.
5) Make the victimizers look bad.
6) Solicit funds: the buck stops here (i.e., get corporate America and major foundations to financially support the homosexual cause).[24]

Kirk and Madsen's strategies have been implemented with tremendous success, resulting in a major shift in the nation's perception of homosexuals and an equally major shift in the perception of those who oppose homosexuality. Indeed, these once-radical proposals seem utterly benign today. *But there is no gay agenda!*

In fact, the authors even stated that, "In February 1988 . . . a 'war conference' of 175 leading gay activists, representing organizations from across the land, convened in Warrenton, Virginia, to establish a *four-point agenda* for the gay movement"[25] – *but there is no gay agenda.*

In *Bashing Back*, Wayne Besen, founder of Truth Wins Out, stated:

> I am so proud to stand with you as a member of the gay, lesbian, bisexual and transgender community. Just to be here [at South Car-

---

23 See Marshall Kirk and Hunter Madsen, *After the Ball: How America Will Conquer Its Fear and Hatred of Gays in the 90's* (New York: Penguin, 1989).

24 For the 1987 article from which the outline is quoted, see http://library.gayhomeland.org/0018/EN/EN_Overhauling_Straight.htm, accessed January 06, 2022.

25 "What is the Gay Agenda?," accessed January 10, 2022, https://forerunnersofamerica.com/article/what-is-the-gay-agenda/, my emphasis.

A Stealth Agenda

olina Pride], out and proud, we have overcome obstacles and persevered against prejudice and persecution. We are robust and resilient; vibrant and vital. And we will succeed and create a new reality in America. But first, we must turn our pride into passion, and our passion into action. Our future is in our hands, and we must not drop the fragile object of freedom. One person can make a difference. Think of Gandhi, Martin Luther King, Susan B. Anthony, and Rosa Parks. Their singular acts of courage liberated the world and unleashed the soaring spirits of millions. While not everyone can lead a movement, we can all do our small part to move the world forward. Here are five things you can do:

1) If you have straight friends and family, ask them to support full equality. You have taken the courageous step to come out. Now it is time your friends and family step-up.
2) If you are a person of faith, don't let counterfeit Christians such as Jerry Falwell, James Dobson, and Pat Robertson hijack religion. Jesus never once mentioned homosexuality. Yet, these phoniest of Pharisees are obsessed with the issue. If you are a Christian, whose priorities do you trust? Jerry Falwell's or Jesus Christ's?
3) Look around you and you will see that there is strength in numbers. Join a gay civil rights group today because they need you and you need them. Together, we can win.
4) Get involved in the political process. I guarantee you that many of your representatives do not think that any GLBT people live in their districts. Come out to politicians in your area.
5) We can create a new reality, but first we must be real. Coming out turns the meek into mighty and turns the passive minority into the massive movement. Visibility is victory.

Be out. Be strong. Be vigilant, Be Proud. And be the best openly gay, lesbian, bisexual or transgender person God intended you to be. Thank You and Happy Pride Month![26]

---

26 Wayne Besen, *Bashing Back* (New York: Routledge, 2012), 156-57. For those few readers who might be ignorant of this, June has been widely designated

Michael Brown

On January 13, 2005, twenty-two national gay and lesbian organizations released a joint statement of purpose with eight goals. In an article on GayPeoplesChronicle.com noting that, "The 22 organizations signing the document include just about all of the major national LGBT [Lesbian, Gay, Bisexual, Transgender] groups."[27] The statement itself observed that, "The speed with which our movement is advancing on all fronts is absolutely historic. We are born into families as diverse as our nation ... We, literally, are everywhere." The eight goals were:

1) Equal employment opportunity, benefits, and protections.
2) Ending anti-LGBT violence.
3) HIV and AIDS advocacy, better access to health care, and LGBT-inclusive sex education.
4) Safe schools.
5) Family laws that strengthen LGBT families.
6) Ending the military's gay ban.

"Gay Pride Month," hence Besen's "Happy Pride Month." Note that, beginning in June 2009, President Obama officially recognized June as Gay Pride Month; see https://www.aclu.org/blog/lgbtq-rights/president-obama-proclaims-lgbt-pride-month, accessed January 06, 2022.

27 Cited in Brown, *A Queer Thing Happened*, 35, https://u1lib.org/book/2341228/b3e245, accessed January 10, 2022. The article is by Eric Resnick. The twenty-two organizations are: American Civil Liberties Union; Lesbian and Gay Rights Project; Equality Federation; Freedom to Marry; Gay and Lesbian Advocates and Defenders; Gay and Lesbian Alliance Against Defamation; Gay and Lesbian Victory Fund; Gay Lesbian and Straight Education Network; Human Rights Campaign; Lambda Legal; Log Cabin Republicans; Mautner Project; National Association of LGBT Community Centers; National Black Justice Coalition; National Center for Lesbian Rights; National Center for Transgender Equality; National Coalition of Anti-Violence Programs; National Gay and Lesbian Task Force; National Youth Advocacy Coalition; Parents, Family and Friends of Lesbians and Gays; Servicemembers Legal Defense Network; Sigamos Adelante – National Latino/Hispanic LGBT Leadership; Stonewall Democrats. A more recent and more comprehensive but similar list of goals can be found at https://www.americanprogress.org/article/improving-lives-rights-lgbtq-people-america/, accessed January 10, 2022.

A Stealth Agenda

7) Exposing the radical right's anti-LGBT agenda and fighting their attempts to enshrine anti-gay bigotry in state and federal constitutions.
8) Marriage equality.

The article reporting this on GayPeoplesChronicle.com was entitled "The Gay Agenda" – *but there is no gay agenda.*

An August 11th, 2010, article on the National Review Online noted that, "Nine college and university presidents gathered in Chicago over the weekend and decided to form a new organization that will promote the professional development of gay academics as well as work on education and advocacy issues." The meeting was hailed as "the first attempt to gather the growing number of out college presidents (25 were invited)," and, according to the report, "participants said in interviews after the event that they wanted to encourage more gay academics to aspire to leadership positions and wanted to *push higher education to include issues of sexual orientation when talking about diversity.*"[28] So, openly gay college and university presidents have decided to work together to "promote the professional development of gay academics as well as work on education and advocacy issues," including pushing higher education to make sexual orientation a core part of "diversity." *But there is no gay agenda.*

The Human Rights Campaign (HRC), founded in 1980 and described on its website as "America's largest gay and lesbian organization," provides "a national voice on gay and lesbian issues. The Human Rights Campaign effectively lobbies Congress; mobilizes grassroots action in diverse communities; invests strategically to elect a fair-minded Congress; and increases public understanding through innovative education and communication strategies."[29] It does all this with an annual budget of more than $35 million

---

28 See "LGBTQ Presidents in Higher Education," accessed August 24, 2021, http://www.nationalreview.com/phi-beta-cons/242996/lgbtq-presidents-higher-education-thomas-shakely, my emphasis. For this use of the word "diversity," see more fully, Chapter 8 of my *A Queer Thing Happened.*

29 https://books.google.com/books?id=-GMEAAAAMBAJ&pg=PA31&lpg=PA31&dq=%22a+national+voice+on+gay+and+lesbian+issues.+The+Hu-

and a staff or more than 110. And for three years, Joe Solmonese, the president of the HRC, hosted a radio show called "The Agenda." *But there is no gay agenda.*

The National Gay and Lesbian Task Force (NGLTF), founded in 1974, and with an annual income more than $3.5 million states, "The mission of the National Gay and Lesbian Task Force is to build the power of the lesbian, gay, bisexual and transgender (LGBT) community from the ground up. We do this by training activists, organizing broad-based campaigns to defeat anti-LGBT referenda and advance pro-LGBT legislation, and by building the organizational capacity of our movement."[30] So, there is a national gay, lesbian, bisexual, and transgender task force, an organizing and training program, a policy institute, and an annual "Creating Change" conference. *But there is no gay agenda.*

ILGA (The International Lesbian and Gay Association) is a world-wide network of national and local groups dedicated to achieving equal rights for lesbian, gay, bisexual, and transgendered (LGBT) people everywhere. Founded in 1978, it now has more than 1,766 member organizations. Every continent and around 168 countries are represented. ILGA member groups range from small collectives to national groups and entire cities.[31]

More specifically, "ILGA is basically a network of activists, and our success lies to a large extent in the achievements and progress of our many member groups."[32] *But there is no gay agenda.* The mission statement of

---

man+Rights+Campaign+effectively+lobbies+Congress;+mobilizes+grassroots+action+in+diverse+communities;+invests+strategically+to+elect+a+fair-minded+Congress;+and+increases+public+understanding+through+innovative+education+and+communication+strategies%22&source=bl&ots=2AaBSJm8gX&sig=ACfU3U30YJaOhpd5ZwbxTz7U06PvNGsBEQ&hl=en&sa=X&ved=2ahUKEwiv_5b2qKX1AhUxMX0KHTCUCzMQ6AF6BAgEEAM#v=onepage&q=grassroots&f=false, accessed January 09, 2022.

30 http://www.oldcambridgebaptist.org/about-us/our-tenants/item/national, accessed January 09, 2022, but carrying other information now, although, as with the HRC website, similar statements can be found throughout their website.

31 https://ilga.org/, accessed January 9, 2022.

32 Quoted in Brown, *A Queer Thing Happened*, 37, https://u1lib.org/book/2341228/b3e245, accessed January 09, 2022.

A Stealth Agenda

Lambda Legal, with an income of better than $10 million annually, explains: "Lambda Legal is a national organization committed to achieving full recognition of the civil rights of lesbians, gay men, bisexuals, transgender people and those with HIV through impact litigation, education, and public policy work."[33] In an oft-quoted statement, Paula Ettelbrick, the former legal director of the Lambda Legal Defense and Education Fund, once said, "Being queer is more than setting up house, sleeping with a person of the same gender, and seeking state approval for doing so. ... Being queer means pushing the parameters of sex, sexuality, and family, and in the process transforming the very fabric of society."[34] *But there is no gay agenda.*

Another major player is PFLAG (Parents, Families & Friends of Lesbians & Gays), with an annual income just under $2.5 million. PFLAG describes itself as "a national non-profit organization with over 200,000 members and supporters and over 400 chapters in the United States."[35] Its website offers clearly articulated statements of Vision, Mission, and Strategic Goals, including "full civil rights" for GLBT people (which, of course, would include the "right" to same-sex marriage) and the "full inclusion of gay, lesbian, bisexual and transgender persons within their chosen communities of faith" (which would imply some of those communities having to modify their standards and beliefs).[36] *But there is no gay agenda.*

Working in the educational system is GLSEN (pronounced "glisten"), with an annual budget of almost $6 million. Its mission statement explains: "The Gay, Lesbian and Straight Education Network strives to assure that each member of every school community is valued and respected regardless of sex-

---

33 http://www.lambdalegal.org/, accessed August 24, 2021; note also that there is a strong, pro-homosexual slant among lawyers in the ACLU; see now Alan Sears and Craig Osten, *The ACLU Against America* (Nashville: Broadman & Holman, 2005).

34 See Paula Ettelbrick, "Since When Is Marriage a Path to Liberation?", in William Rubenstein, ed., *Lesbians, Gay Men and the Law* (New York: The New Press, 1993), 401-405. Dr. Ettelbrick has been a Professor of Law at the University of Michigan since 1994. Her comments here have often been quoted and turn up in many Internet articles on both sides of the issue.

35 https://pflag.org/, accessed January 09, 2022.

36 https://www.pflagla.org/z-mission-statement/, accessed January 09, 2022.

ual orientation or gender identity/expression."[37] This includes training teachers in what is called "gender speak,"[38] recommending textbooks such as the famous (or, infamous) *Heather Has Two Mommies*,[39] encouraging children to question their parents' non-gay-affirming views,[40] and sponsoring an annual "Day of Silence" to draw attention to what is referred to as the widespread oppression and persecution of gays and lesbians[41] – *but there is no gay agenda.*

The gay campus organization Campuspride.net offers specific strategies for events during what has been dubbed "Gaypril," announcing, "If April showers brings May flowers, then Gaypril brings campus queers. . .. April is the time to celebrate, educate and stimulate for campus Gay Pride!" The organizers urge student groups to: "Create Visibility," "Create Awareness," and "Foster Community."[42] Under the first category, they suggest:

» **Information Tables** – display fliers or pamphlets about LGBT and Ally resources, groups, and community outreach, etc.
» **Write letters** to your school and/or local newspapers about LGBT and Ally issues.
» **Poster Campaigns** – get together with other LGBT and Ally students, faculty and staff and make posters that display positive slogans relating to the LGBT and Ally community (i.e. "Gay is Great!", "Trans Rights are Hu-

---

37 http://www.glsen.org/cgi-bin/iowa/all/about/history/index.html, accessed October 20, 2021.

38 See Chapter 3 of my *A Queer Thing Happened* for more on this.

39 Ibid.

40 "GLSEN's materials regularly undermine both parental authority and religious teaching. They seek to separate children from their families and from their faith upbringing" – See Brown, *A Queer Thing Happened*, 605, fn 46, A Queer Thing Happened And What a Long, Strange Trip Its Been by Michael L. Brown (z-lib.org).pdf , accessed January 10, 2022. See also Indoctrination by Sara Dogan at file:///C:/Users/melma/Desktop/IndoctrinationTheLeft-sAttackonourPublic-Schools__4_.pdf, accessed January 10, 2022.

41 See Chapter 3 of my *A Queer Thing Happened* for more on this.

42 Cited in Brown, *A Queer Thing Happened*, 39, https://u1lib.org/book/2341228/b3e245, accessed January 09, 2022.

man Rights", "Loud and Proud"). Make sure to hang them all over campus (the inside doors of bathroom stalls are a great place to advertise!). Be aware that the posters may get ripped down or defaced.

» **Create a policy where any posters found with graffiti on them are returned to you** – use this to show other students and the administration the extent of homophobia on campus.
» **Chalking** – get out the old box of Crayola chalk and hit the concrete. Advertise your events and positive slogans. Make sure you find out what the "chalking" policy is on your campus before you start.
» **Fly the Flag** – you can't get more visible than flying the rainbow flag from the school's flagpole. Use your faculty and staff allies to help you lobby the administration to make this happen.
» **Condoms/Dental Dams . . .** – promote safer sex by distributing or selling (at a reasonable price or for donations) materials at your events and information tables.
» **Give-aways** – You can use almost any type of give-away to create attention and excitement: Rainbow Ribbons, Buttons, Bumper Stickers…the possibilities are endless. It helps to be creative. . ..[43]

So, there is a specific plan of attack with targeted goals – indeed, the gay flag should be flown throughout the month of April and the call for "Trans-Liberation" must be loud and clear. *But there is no gay agenda.*

The mission statement of the Gay & Lesbian Alliance Against Defamation (GLAAD), whose own annual budget exceeds $4 million, states: "GLAAD rewrites the script for LGBTQ acceptance. As a dynamic media force, GLAAD tackles tough issues to shape the narrative and provoke dialogue that leads to cultural change."[44] *But there is no gay agenda.*

---

43   https://www.campuspride.org/resources/planning-for-the-month-of-gaypril/, accessed January 09, 2022.

44   https://www.glaad.org/about, accessed January 09, 2022.

Michael Brown

Upon becoming GLAAD's president in 2005, Neil G. Giuliano, declared in an open letter:

> We must also continue to reach the moveable middle with our message of non-discrimination based on sexual orientation and gender identity/expression. Make no mistake, those who seek to further deny us full equality are powerful adversaries, and we must prepare better, communicate better, and go beyond our efforts of the past if we are to succeed and steadily advance. I am genuinely looking forward to working with my colleagues at other LGBT organizations to do just that – succeed and advance. . ..
>
> Our efforts will be the same: neither the first nor the last, yet inspiring and significant because it is our time to march, to make a lasting difference for lesbian, gay, bisexual, and transgender Americans. We will because we must.[45]

But there is no gay agenda – despite the impassioned vision to "succeed and advance," despite the call "to march" and "make a lasting difference for lesbian, gay, bisexual and transgender Americans."

When the Human Rights Campaign held its $195-a-plate, fundraising dinner in Charlotte in 2005, gay campus activist and Charlotte resident Shane Windmeyer stated that the event "offers an opportunity for us to come together and look at how we want Charlotte to be in five or 10 years."[46] *But there is no gay agenda.* So, there are well-funded, highly-motivated, sharply-focused gay activist organizations such as HRC and NGLTF

---

45 Cited in Brown, *A Queer Thing Happened*, 40, https://u1lib.org/book/2341228/b3e245, accessed January 10, 2022. The article was found at http://www.glaad.org/about/pres_letter.php, accessed August 29, 2006, but subsequently removed.

46 Cited in my article "Charlotte Pride or Charlotte Shame," accessed September 15, 2010, http://www.icnministries.org/revolution/CharlotteShame.htm, but is no longer available online; the citation can also be found in Brown's *A Queer Thing Happened.*

and PFLAG and GLSEN and GLAAD and Lambda Legal – just to mention a few – but there is no gay agenda.

WHY DENY THE EXISTENCE OF A GAY AGENDA?

What is behind this consistent and concerted denial of a gay agenda?

Could it simply be a matter of semantics since it would be more accurate to speak of a gay and lesbian civil rights movement rather than a gay agenda? Hardly. The civil rights movement, both past and present, has freely and unashamedly spoken of a "civil rights agenda."[47] To give some representative examples, a piece by Jesse Jackson reads, "In fact, in 1830 the first series of national meetings of Colored men began with a civil rights agenda . . . ." and " . . . it will require the willingness to support all relevant strategies, including civil methods of lobbying, demonstrations and other methods of nonviolent social change to affect public attention to our agenda . . ."[48]

Walter Williams wrote an important article in *Capitalism Magazine* (November 12, 2001) entitled "The Unfinished Civil Rights Agenda."[49]

---

[47] See further, below, Chapter 6 of my *A Queer Thing Happened*, where the "Gay is the new black" argument is analyzed.

[48] Jesse Jackson, "The Fight for Civil Rights Continues," https://books.google.com/books?id=wsoDAAAAMBAJ&pg=PA68&lpg=PA68&dq=-Southern+Methodist+University+%2B+To+pressure+the+government+and+-Congress+to+act+more+quickly+on+the+civil+rights+agenda,+a+massive+march+on+the+nation%E2%80%99s+capital+was+planned,+scheduled,+and+carried+out+on+August+28th,+1963.+According+to+estimates,+over+250,000+participated+in+the+peaceful+demonstration+which+culminated+in+the+speech+given+by+Reverend+Martin+Luther+King.%E2%80%9D&source=bl&ots=276uyDFd05&sig=ACfU3U309uaKmRPeZ6W0r_ug0kA4xw-f7UA&hl=en&sa=X&ved=2ahUKEwiqu9-32aX1AhUxHzQIHaweBJ8Q6AF-6BAggEAM#v=snippet&q=agenda&f=false, accessed January 09, 2022, pp. 108 and 115, respectively, my emphasis.

[49] Walter Williams, "Unfinished Civil Rights Agenda," accessed October 24, 2021, http://capmag.com/articlePrint.asp?ID=1211.

Joyce A. Ladner's 2000 article in the *Brookings Review* (vol. 18, 26-28) was entitled, "A New Civil Rights Agenda: A New Leadership Is Making a Difference," in which she also speaks of the "Unfinished Civil Rights Agenda," stating, "Two issues remain on the civil rights agenda. The first is addressing the persistence of racial disparities. The second is redefining the agenda to fit a vastly changing American demographic profile."[50] It appears that people are not hesitant to speak of a civil rights agenda.

The same can be said of the feminist movement, which freely speaks of a feminist agenda. The phrase "feminist agenda" (in quotes) yielded 397,000 hits on Google (January 10, 2022), including websites such as Coalition for a Feminist Agenda (and others) which announces, "We are a coalition of feminist women committed to working with like-minded others to create a new and fairer global agenda, with women's voices at its centre."[51] Also notice the National Organization for Women (NOW) website which features articles such as, "NOW's Progressive Feminist Agenda for Peace"[52] and "Feminist Agenda Rising: Our Time is Now (NOW National Conference)."[53] The feminists are not hesitant to speak of a feminist agenda! The same can be said of moral conservatives, who also speak freely of an agenda (indeed, as illustrated in some of the citations, above, gays frequently refer to this "conservative" or "right wing" or "radical right" agenda).

There is nothing wrong with having an agenda, as civil rights leaders, feminist leaders, and conservative leaders would readily agree. Why then is it taboo to speak of a gay agenda?

---

50 https://www.brookings.edu/articles/a-new-civil-rights-agenda-a-new-leadership-is-making-a-difference/#:~:text=A%20New%20Civil%20Rights%20Agenda%3A%20A%20New%20Leadership%20Is%20Making%20a%20Difference,-Joyce%20A.&text=Few%20issues%20in%20American%20life,on%20which%20it%20was%20founded, accessed January 09, 2022. A Google search for "civil rights agenda" on January 10, 2022, yielded 130,000 hits.

51 See https://esvc004736.swp0002ssl.server-secure.com/, accessed January 09, 2022.

52 Mentioned in https://laidbare.pressbooks.com/chapter/revised-is-there-really-a-gay-agenda/#footnote-230-5, accessed January 09, 2022.

53 https://now.org/update/feminist-agenda-rising-our-time-is-now-now-national-conference/, accessed January 09, 2022.

A Stealth Agenda

If the goal of this agenda was simply to achieve "civil rights" for gays, lesbians, bisexuals, and transgender people, why refuse to speak of an agenda? That *was* the agenda of the civil rights movement: civil rights! Yet when the gay community strives for what it believes to be these very same rights, it refuses to call this an agenda. Why?

There is a gay revolution, a gay liberation movement, a plethora of gay activist organizations with clearly identified missions and goals, but no gay agenda. There is a civil rights agenda, a feminist agenda, a conservative agenda, but no gay agenda. How can this be?

Why is there such a unified gay denial of such an obvious gay agenda? Why the claim, quoted above, that, "Notions of a 'homosexual agenda' are rhetorical inventions of anti-gay extremists seeking to portray as sinister the lesbian and gay civil rights movement"? Why not state that the so-called gay and lesbian civil rights movement has a definite agenda? Why not articulate what this agenda includes?

Perhaps the answer is provided by gay columnist Charles Bouley:

> Those who think [a gay agenda exists] are giving gays and lesbians too much credit. For there to be a gay agenda, there would have to be immense unity among us since we would have to agree across the globe on said agenda. It might even have to be put up for a vote. Only then could it be disseminated to community leaders as well as the millions of gays and lesbians scattered across the world. Frankly, that does not, will not, and cannot happen. Gays and lesbian are a diverse community, composed of many voices with many ideas on how to achieve goals. We don't all agree on any issue, be it same-sex marriage or the usefulness of pride festivals. We're not all of the same political ideology (yes, for some reason, there are still gay Republicans—but then again, the world is filled with oxymorons), and many of us still keep our sexuality private or hidden. No, there is no consensus among us, let alone an agenda.[54]

---

54 https://www.advocate.com/politics/commentary/2005/02/22/gay-agenda-revealed, accessed January 09, 2022. Note that Bouley's reference to gay Republicans as oxymoronic points to his assumption that the expected political allegiance of

Is this, then, the reason that gays and lesbians insist that there is no gay agenda, namely, the lack of "immense unity" among them on a global level? While Bouley might be quite sincere, his thesis is untenable. Since when does an agenda require "immense unity" on a global level? How many groups have this? Certainly not conservatives, who disagree on a multitude of religious, political, and social issues – yet no one denies that there is a conservative agenda. And there has always been great diversity among leaders in the civil rights movement – think of the differences between Malcolm X and Dr. Martin Luther King, Jr. – yet hardly anyone would deny that there has been a civil rights agenda. And, realistically, no agenda comes from the people as a whole. Rather, it comes from the activists who seek to represent what they believe to be in the best interests of those people. So "immense unity" on a global scale is hardly required.

Ironically, when it comes to *denying* the existence of a gay agenda, there *is* "immense unity" in the gay community. Why? *It is because the denial of that agenda is part of the agenda* (although for some, it might be a sincere, heartfelt denial). That is a necessary piece of the puzzle: It must be a stealth agenda. Otherwise, its progress will be thwarted, and its success greatly impeded, because the open, unambiguous, full disclosure of the goals and ramifications of the gay agenda would stop that agenda in its tracks.[55]

---

most gays is *not* with the Republicans, for obvious reasons.

55 In a mock – but quite realistic – confession of "a large group of same-sex-marriage activists . . . to a group of same-sex-marriage skeptics," Stanley Kurtz puts these words on the lips of the same-sex-marriage activists: "As gay marriage gains acceptance, we're going to have a polygamy-polyamory debate in this country. And among those sponsoring that debate will be many of the very same people and groups who've already pushed for same-sex marriage. "So why haven't we told you all this before? Simple. We've been censoring ourselves for fear of scaring away public support for same-sex marriage. You see, it's all about timing. Our plan is to establish same-sex marriage first, and then, as our next step, to demand that the rights and benefits of marriage be accorded to all types of families. After all, when the call for yet another radical redefinition of marriage comes from married same-sex couples, it's going to be that much more persuasive. Up to now, truth to tell, if any same-sex marriage backers pushed this radical agenda in public, we pressured them to keep silent. But now we're telling you the truth." See "The Confession," October 31, 2006, https://www.

Am I claiming that all gay organizations work in unison together? Certainly not. Am I claiming that all gays and lesbians embrace the same societal goals? Not at all. Am I claiming that most major gay organizations agree on certain fundamental goals and that most gays and lesbians support those goals? Absolutely.[56]

Just look at the mission statements of the primary gay advocacy and lobbying groups, the primary gay educational groups, the primary gay media-related groups. They are in fundamental harmony, and they are all devoted to bringing about societal change. That constitutes an agenda. Then read the primary gay publications – the leading gay magazines and newspapers, the most visited gay websites, the most respected gay scientific journals – and they too are in fundamental harmony as far as viewpoints, issues of concern, and points of action. That constitutes an agenda. Then look at what is proclaimed loudly and clearly at gay pride events, with clear calls for political action for major gay causes. The message is consistent, and the demands are clear. That constitutes an agenda. And then research the writings and messages of gay religious groups, both Jewish and Christian, and they too share a fundamental harmony in their primary theological positions, clearly believing that their fellow-religionists who do *not* share these views are wrong and need to change. That constitutes an agenda.

Do you think I'm taking things too far? Perhaps, some might argue, the real issue is that this so-called agenda is not an agenda at all. Perhaps the reason for the consistent gay denial of a gay agenda is that the extent of that agenda is simply: Please leave us alone and let us just live our lives in peace. Once again, we beg to differ. That is not the only thing all the gay organizations and individuals are fighting for. To the contrary, the *legitimizing* of homosexuality as a perfectly normal alternative to heterosexuality also re-

---

nationalreview.com/2006/10/confession-stanley-kurtz/, accessed January 09, 2022.

56 See Stanley Kurtz, "The Confession II," November 1, 2006, https://www.nationalreview.com/2006/11/confession-ii-stanley-kurtz/, accessed January 09, 2022, quotes the "conservative" gay advocate Evan Wolfson who acknowledged that, "Ninety percent of what's in that document could have been signed onto by virtually every person working in the gay movement today."

quires that all opposition to homosexual behavior must be *delegitimized*. At the very least, the gay agenda requires this (and let recognized gay leaders renounce this if it is not so):

1) Whereas homosexuality was once considered a pathological disorder, from here on those who do not affirm homosexuality will be deemed homophobic, perhaps themselves suffering from a pathological disorder.[57]
2) Whereas gay sexual behavior was once considered morally wrong, from here on public condemnation – or even public criticism – of that behavior will be considered morally wrong.[58]
3) Whereas identifying as transgender was once considered abnormal by society, causing one to be marginalized, from here on those who do not accept transgenderism will be considered abnormal and will be marginalized.[59]

IMPLICATIONS OF THE GAY AGENDA

This is all part of the mainstream gay agenda, a necessary corollary to the call for "gay and lesbian civil rights." In keeping with this:

---

57 For psychological effect, students in Framingham, MA "were forced to answer a questionnaire that openly challenged the validity of their heterosexuality," or at least, was intended to demonstrate to them that homosexuality was just as innate and natural as heterosexuality and that all forms of "homophobia" were completely baseless, https://ia601303.us.archive.org/7/items/TheHomosexualAgenda-ExposingThePrincipalThreatToReligiousFreedomToday/The-Homosexual-Agenda-Exposing-the-Principle-Threat-Alan-Sears.pdf, accessed January 10, 2022, 62.

58 See, e.g., Hans Clausen, "The 'Privilege of Speech' in a 'Pleasantly Authoritarian Country': How Canada's Judiciary Allowed Laws Proscribing Discourse Critical of Homosexuality to Trump Free Speech and Religious Liberty," https://www.thefreelibrary.com/The+%22privilege+of+speech%22+in+a+%22pleasantly+authoritarian+country%22%3A+how...-a0132299649, accessed January 10, 2022. See further Chapter 14 of my *A Queer Thing Happened*.

59 See Chapters 14 and 15 of my *A Queer Thing Happened* for more on this.

A Stealth Agenda

1) When the father of a six year-old child in Lexington, MA, notified his son's school that he wanted prior notification if anything related to homosexuality was to be taught in his son's first-grade class, he was rebuffed by the superintendent of schools who informed him that the court had ruled that it was more important to teach "diversity" – with specific reference to homosexuality – than to honor the requests of the parents.[60] So much for parental rights! As expressed by a concerned San Francisco mother, "My children's teachers say they want students to think for themselves, but when my children say they think they should obey their parents or God, they're ridiculed. What kind of diversity can you have when children are pressured into thinking the same things?"[61]

2) A Swedish pastor in his seventies was given a prison sentence for simply *preaching a sermon in his own church* on sexual ethics in which he stated that all non-marital sexual relations (including homosexual acts) were sinful, since his message was said to offend gays. The verdict, which was ultimately overturned by the Swedish Supreme Court, was supported by the Swedish Ambassador, Cecilia Julin, who said, "Swedish law states that public addresses cannot be used to instigate hatred towards a certain group."[62]

3) A Christian leader in Pennsylvania was charged with "Disorderly Conduct" and "Disrupting Meetings and Processions" for trying to read a passage from the New Testament that dealt with homosexual practices during his designated speaking time at a city council meeting (he was shut down before he could read the

---

60 For more on this, see Chapter 3 of my *A Queer Thing Happened*.

61 See Debra J. Saunders, "Diversity Training," *The San Francisco Chronicle*, 23 June 1996, cited by Josh McDowell and Bob Hostetler, *The New Tolerance* (Wheaton, IL: Tyndale House, 1998), 75.

62 See Folger, *Criminalization*, 17-18, with references. In 2003, these views were written into the Swedish constitution; see also Chapter 14 of my *A Queer Thing Happened*.

passage). Assistant District Attorney Alyssa Kunsturiss explained that the borough president, Norman Council, "perceived what he was reading as hate speech. It would be homophobic today. They couldn't let him go on. You can't go up to the podium and start reading from the Bible."[63] Yes, this is an accurate quote from an attorney right here in America, supposedly "one nation under God" and the home of free speech – as long as that speech does not challenge or differ with the gay agenda.[64]

4) In Boise, Idaho, an employee of Hewlett Packard was fired for posting Bible verses on his cubicle after a pro-gay poster was placed near his workspace. According to the Ninth Circuit Court of Appeals, "An employer need not accommodate an employee's religious beliefs if doing so would result in discrimination against his co-workers or deprive them of contractual or other statutory rights." In response to this, author Janet Folger (now Porter) asks, "The homosexual agenda trumps an employee's religious beliefs?"[65] But of course! (note that even if Folger's rhetorical question was rephrased to read, "Gay rights trump religious rights?", the answer would be the same).

5) In England, a bishop in the Anglican Church was "ordered to undergo equal opportunities training and to pay a gay youth worker nearly £50,000 [roughly $80,000] for refusing him a job because of his sexuality." According to a report in the *Telegraph*, the youth worker "took the Hereford Diocesan Board of Finance to an employment tribunal and said today he was 'delighted' with the payout. . . . Ben Summerskill, chief executive of the gay rights pressure group Stonewall, added: 'We're delighted that the

---

63 See Folger, *Criminalization,* and Chapter 14 of my *A Queer Thing Happened.*

64 Ultimately, under federal pressure, the Borough Council had to apologize to Michael Marcavage, the Christian leader in question, since the charges against him were found to be without merit. See http://www.alliancedefensefund.org/news/story.aspx?cid=3689, accessed October 14, 2021.

65 See Folger, *Criminalization*, 20-21.

A Stealth Agenda

tribunal has sent such a robust signal, both to the bishop and other employers. The substantial level of compensation sends out a very clear message. Not even a bishop is above this law.'"[66]

6) The Associate Vice President of Human Resources at the University of Toledo, an African American woman, was fired from her job "for stating in a guest column in a local newspaper that choosing homosexual behavior is not the same as being black or handicapped."[67] The university president stood behind the decision to dismiss her.

You can be assured that there has been no widespread gay outcry over these court rulings, arrests, fines, firings, and reprimands, most of which were instigated by offended members of the GLBT community, since (to repeat) full recognition of "gay rights" means limited recognition of the rights of others. That's why these rulings are celebrated as victories among gay activists since this is all a necessary part of the agenda. The rule of thumb for gay rights can therefore be stated as follows: "We have the right to be ourselves, even it offends you, but you do not have the right to be yourselves or to be offended. And under no circumstances do you have the right to offend us."

Shockingly, the examples just cited are only the tiny tip of a massive iceberg. Here are just a few more. Were you aware of things such as:

1) A "reeducation class" to ensure that foster parents embrace the gay agenda (California)?
2) Public schools with a mandated pro-homosexual ["antidiscrimination"] policy that sends objecting students to "appropriate counseling" without notifying their parents (California)?
3) Being put out of business (with a $150,000 fine) for firing a man in a dress (California)?

---

66 Nick Britten, "Bishop Fined in Gay Discrimination Case," accessed October 14, 2021, http://www.telegraph.co.uk/news/uknews/1577982/Bishop-fined-in-gay-discrimination-case.html.

67 See chapter 14 of my *A Queer Thing Happened* for details.

4) Being told by a judge that you can't teach your daughter anything "homophobic" (Colorado)?[68]

THE INEVITABLE PROGRESSION OF GAY ACTIVISM

All this is part of an inevitable process which can be summarized with this progression:

First, gay activists came out of the closet; second, they demanded their "rights"; third, they demanded that everyone recognize those "rights"; fourth, they want to strip away the rights of those who oppose them; fifth, they want to put those who oppose their "rights" into the closet.[69]

Look again at the statement on the GLSEN website: "The Gay, Lesbian and Straight Education Network strives to assure that each member of every school community is valued and respected regardless of sexual orientation or gender identity/expression." In contrast, it does *not* strive to assure that each member of every school community is valued and respected regardless of religious beliefs, moral convictions, or different views on sexual orientation. In fact, it has vigorously opposed the views and activities of groups that differ with the gay agenda, protesting the presence of such

---

68 All these are cited verbatim from Folger, *Criminalization*, 26-27; see further Sears and Osten, *Homosexual Agenda*, for numerous examples, assembled carefully and without exaggeration by the authors, both of whom are attorneys. More broadly, see now Rev Donald E. Wildmon, *Speechless: Silencing the Christians* (n.p.: Richard Vigilante Books, 2009). Even if some of the specific instances cited in these books could be challenged in terms of there being another side to the story, or if, in some cases, the Christians involved were not entirely "Christian" in tone, what cannot be denied is that: 1) There are many, undeniable cases of attempts to eradicate or greatly curtail the constitutional liberties guaranteed by our nation; and 2) free speech is not protected only when the speaker's tone is civil and gracious.

69 It has been suggested to me by a conservative attorney that "full circle" would be this: In the past, gays were put into jail for their open demonstrations and violations of the law; in the future, those who oppose them will be put into jail!

things as ex-gay material (i.e., literature from former homosexuals) in any school discussion of sexual orientation, where GLSEN believes that only the pro-gay position can be represented.

As stated explicitly by GLSEN founder Kevin Jennings, "Ex-gay messages have no place in our nation's public schools. A line has been drawn. There is no 'other side' when you're talking about lesbian, gay and bisexual students."[70] And did I mention that on May 9, 2009, the Department of Education appointed this gay activist leader, Kevin Jennings, to serve as Assistant Deputy Secretary for the Office of Safe & Drug Free Schools?[71]

It would appear, then, that "civil rights" for some means "limited rights" for others, and *that* by specific design. As stated explicitly in a teacher's lesson aid published by the Gay and Lesbian Educators [GALE] of British Columbia: "We must dishonour the prevailing belief that heterosexuality is the only acceptable orientation even though that would mean dishonouring the religious beliefs of Christians, Jews, Muslims, etc."[72] All this is part of the gay agenda.

Does this surprise you? If so, bear in mind that these are *not* predictions. They are statements of fact, a recap of what has already taken place in America and what is currently taking place around the world. Even our vocabulary is being affected,[73] as the gay agenda has produced these new definitions and concepts:

1) From here on, embracing *diversity* refers to embracing all kinds of sexual orientation, (homo)sexual expression, and gender iden-

---

70 Quoted in George Archibald, "Changing minds: Former gays meet resistance at NEA convention," *The Washington Times*, July 27, 2004, p. A2.

71 For a thorough critique of Jennings' appointment, see Peter Sprigg, "Homosexual Activist Kevin Jennings not Fit for Dept. of Education," https://www.scribd.com/document/47535564/Homosexual-Activist-Kevin-Jennings-Not-Fit-for-Dept-of-Education-Sprigg, accessed January 09, 2022.

72 Cited in Clausen, "Privilege of Speech," 447, n. 21. The lesson aid is entitled *Counseling Gay and Lesbian Youth*, accessed January 10, 2022, https://www.thefreelibrary.com/The+%22privilege+of+speech%22+in+a+%22pleasantly+authoritarian+country%22%3A+how...-a0132299649.

73 See Chapter 9 of my *A Queer Thing Happened* for more on this.

tification but rejects every kind of religious or moral conviction that does not embrace these orientations, expressions, and identifications.[74]

2) From here on, *tolerance* refers to the complete acceptance of GLBT lifestyles and ideology – in the family, in the workplace, in education, in media, in religion – while at the same time refusing to tolerate any view that is contrary.[75]

3) From here on, *inclusion* refers to working with, supporting, sponsoring, and encouraging gay events and gay goals while at the same time systematically refusing to work with and excluding anyone who is not in harmony with these events and goals.

4) From here on, *hate* refers to any attitude, thought, or word that differs with the gay agenda, while gays are virtually exempt from the charge of hate speech – no matter how vile and incendiary the rhetoric – since they are always the (perceived) victims and never the victimizers.[76]

And how does this activist, gay agenda work itself out in everyday life? Much of this is already taking place throughout the country.

1) Children in elementary schools will be exposed to the rightness and complete normality of homosexuality, bisexuality, and transgender expression – witness highly-praised academic books such as *The Queering of Elementary Education* – and opposing views

---

[74] See Chapter 8 of my *A Queer Thing Happened* for more on this.

[75] See Chapters 8 and 14 of my *A Queer Thing Happened* for more on this. Cf. also Robert Weissberg, *Pernicious Intolerance: How Teaching to "Accept Differences" Undermines Civil Society* (New Brunswick, NJ: Transaction Publishers, 2008); Brad Stetson and Joseph G. Conti, *The Truth about Tolerance: Pluralism, Diversity and the Culture Wars* (Downers Grove, IL: InterVarsity, 2005); Jay Budziszewski, *True Tolerance: Liberalism and the Necessity of Judgment* (Brunswick, NJ: Transaction Publishers, 2000); Amy Orr-Ewing, *Is the Bible Intolerant? Sexist? Oppressive? Homophobic? Outdated? Irrelevant?* (Downers Grove, IL: InterVarsity, 2005).

[76] See Chapter 2 of my *A Queer Thing Happened* for more on the accusation of "hate speech."

A Stealth Agenda

will be branded as dangerous and homophobic, to be silenced and excluded from the classroom.[77]

2) Middle schools, high schools, and colleges will go out of their way to encourage both the celebration of homosexuality and deep solidarity with gay activism – witness The Annual Day of Silence in our schools in recognition of "the oppression and persecution" of LGBT people[78] and the Lesbian, Gay, Bisexual and Transgender Students' Bill of Educational Rights in our universities, not to mention Queer Study Programs and the celebration of "Gaypril."[79]

3) The federal and state governments will legalize same-sex marriages – as has already been done in Massachusetts, Connecticut, Vermont, and Iowa – along with, currently, ten countries worldwide, including Canada and Spain in the same week in 2005 – meaning that all heterosexuals must accept the legality of these marriages and that anyone refusing to do so could be prosecuted for discriminatory behavior.[80]

4) Corporate America will embrace every aspect of non-heterosexuality (including bisexuality, transgender, and beyond) – calling for the dismissal of those who refuse to follow suit – and religious groups will no longer be allowed to view homosexual practice as immoral, branding such opposition as "hate speech."[81]

In the last four decades, major changes have taken place in: 1) the public's perception of homosexuality and same-sex relationships; 2) the educational system's embrace of homosexuality; 3) legislative decisions recognizing gays and lesbians as a distinct group of people within our society, equivalent to other ethnic groups; 4) the media's portrayal of GLBT people; and 5) corporate America's welcoming of what was once considered unac-

---

77 See Chapter 3 of my *A Queer Thing Happened* for more on this.
78 Ibid.
79 See Chapter 4 of my *A Queer Thing Happened* for more on this.
80 See Chapter 14 of my *A Queer Thing Happened* for more on this.
81 See Chapters 2 and 14 of my *A Queer Thing Happened* for more on this.

ceptable behavior. Is this simply one big coincidence? Did all this happen by chance? Don't these very results – which barely tell the story – give evidence to a clearly defined gay agenda?

Well, just in case you're not 100% sure, a leading gay activist has helped remove all doubt. Speaking shortly after the 2006 elections, Matt Foreman, then the executive director of the National Gay and Lesbian Task Force, had this to say: "You want to know the state of our movement on November 10, 2006? We are strong, unbowed, unbeaten, vibrant, energized and ready to kick some butt." And what exactly does this mean? "The agenda and vision that we must proudly articulate is that yes, indeed, we intend to change society."[82] Or, in the words of gay leader (and former seminary professor) Dr. Mel White, "It is time for a campaign of relentless nonviolent resistance that will convince our adversaries to do justice at last. They have assumed that we are infinitely patient or too comfortable to call for revolution. For their sake, and for the sake of the nation, we must prove them wrong."[83] So, the cat is out of the bag and the covert agenda is becoming overt, backed by a movement that proclaims itself "strong, unbowed, unbeaten, vibrant, energized and ready to kick some butt." It is nothing less than a gay revolution – and it is coming to a school or court or business or house of worship near you.

America, are you ready?

---

82 Foreman's statements make Kurtz's "gay" comments somewhat prophetic and more believable: "Up to now, truth to tell, if any same-sex marriage backers pushed this radical agenda in public, we pressured them to keep silent. But now we're telling you the truth." On October 20, 2006, in the gay *Washington Blade*, Wayne Besen was quoted as saying, "We're accused of having a gay agenda … but this is the time when we really need one," cited in https://americansfortruth.com/2006/10/20/homosexual-activists-already-planning-%E2%80%9C-gay-agenda%E2%80%9D-for-democratic-controlled-house/, accessed January 09, 2022.

83 Mel White, *Religion Gone Bad: The Hidden Dangers of the Christian Right* (New York: Jeremy P. Tarcher/Penguin, 2006), 7.

Chapter 9

A Life for Life: Dr. Richard Land's Legacy of Defending Pre-Born Persons

Sharayah Colter

Palms behind her on the doctor's pleather-upholstered table, a woman simultaneously lifts her frame and shifts her weight back and forth a few times to raise herself onto the thin paper covering, wrinkling, and crinkling it with each movement. Cold air filters in through the vent on the ceiling, adding a chill to the already cold and slightly sterile closet-sized room. Following instructions to lie backward, the woman lifts her shirt tail to reveal her bare stomach beneath while the doctor places more crinkling tissue paper into her waistband, talking about the weather as he stuffs and tucks. A quick, burbling squirt of warm jelly straight to the abdomen prepares a field for the ultrasound wand. The doctor flips a switch to turn on the large piece of equipment, pushing it back and forth to arrange it in the preferred position next to the rolling stool which a sign on the wall warns is for physician use only. As power illuminates the DOS-style screen that looks like it could display the 1970s version of Oregon Trail at any moment, all eyes focus in on the small, empty pie-shaped window, the doctor holding the wand just inches above the stomach.

At this point, the possibility of new life is a question mark. Perhaps a missed monthly cycle or even a pink line on a pregnancy test have made a woman and her mate suspect quite strongly that they have conceived a child, but even then, the potential new life seems abstract and unknown.

Within the space of a few heartbeats, however, the budding life has never seemed so real. So obvious. So undeniable. The empty, pie-shaped window fills with a shape that resembles a tad pole or a ping pong ball, and with it, the wish-wash-woosh of a heartbeat thuds through the static. This is new life.

While at some points in the history of the pro-life movement, the humanity of unborn babies has been hard to visualize without the benefit of ultrasound machines and Doppler tools, scientific advancement has become a friend of the fetus, testifying to the undeniable presence of new, unique life in a mother's womb. In the past, mothers and fathers lacked this clear confirmation of having created a new human being, but in the 21st century, with the wide availability of ultrasound machines and even laws requiring their use prior to abortion procedures in some states, women, doctors, and the rest of society are without excuse when it comes to protecting what can objectively be shown as a new human being (and therefore deserving of the right to life).

While efforts to protect unborn life have always been needed and noble, the same efforts in modern times hold the most promising opportunity to effect change. With science providing a rock-solid defense of the humanity of unborn children, never has there been a greater chance to end the American Holocaust that is abortion.

Dr. Richard Land's defense of unborn life as a leading Christian ethicist has likewise always been virtuous. Now, his work and scientific advancement join hands and give enthusiastic, realistic hope and energy to the pro-life movement.

THE PRO-LIFE CAUSE IN BIBLICAL HISTORY AND TEACHING

In its earliest renditions, the pro-life movement began on the banks of the Nile River a few thousand years ago in what today would be considered quite rudimentary birthing wards. Having received orders from Pharaoh to kill during delivery each male baby born to the Hebrew women, the Hebrew midwives employed what today would be called a "graded hierarchal approach" to ethics and lied to protect the lives of the babies. The midwives reported that the Hebrew women were expedient in labor and birthed the children before they could arrive to assist and subsequently carry out the ruler's orders (Ex 1:15-22). Moses' mother, too, sought to protect the life of her baby boy by placing him in a basket and setting him afloat down the river (Ex 2:1-10).

In addition to the anecdotal example of pro-life ethics provided by the account of the Hebrew midwives, Scripture also explicitly condemns both child sacrifice and the intentional harming of unborn children. The value of all life, including life in the womb, is abundantly clear throughout the pages of Scripture.

God, through the prophet Jeremiah, declared His disapproval of mothers and fathers burning their children:

> 'For the children of Judah have done evil in My sight,' says the Lord. 'They have set their abominations in the house which is called by My name, to pollute it. And they have built the high places of Tophet, which is in the Valley of the Son of Hinnom, to burn their sons and their daughters in the fire, which I did not command, nor did it come into My heart' (Jer 7:30-31).[1]

The book of Deuteronomy includes a similar reference, "There shall not be found among you anyone who makes his son or his daughter pass through the fire…" (Dt 18:10a).

Though not an exhaustive listing, Scripture also marks as evil the practice of killing children, especially as a sacrifice to idols: see Lev 18:21, Dt 12:31, Ezek 16:20-21, Lev 20:1-5, and 2 Kings 21:6. David, writing in Psalm 139, acknowledges God's work in creating new human life inside the womb:

---

1 While there may be references to Scripture in this chapter, any actual citations are from the NKJV, unless otherwise noted.

> For You formed my inward parts; You covered me in my mother's womb. I will praise You, for I am fearfully and wonderfully made; Marvelous are Your works, and that my soul knows very well. My frame was not hidden from You, when I was made in secret, and skillfully wrought in the lowest parts of the earth. Your eyes saw my substance, being yet unformed. And in Your book they all were written, the days fashioned for me, when as yet there were none of them (Ps 139:13-16).

Additionally, note the biblical account of Mary, the mother of Jesus, visiting her relative, Elizabeth—who was six months pregnant with the baby who would come to be known as John the Baptist—the man born to prepare the way for Christ (Mark 1:1-7):

> Now Mary arose in those days and went into the hill country with haste, to a city of Judah, and entered the house of Zacharias and greeted Elizabeth. And it happened, when Elizabeth heard the greeting of Mary, that the babe leaped in her womb; and Elizabeth was filled with the Holy Spirit. Then she spoke out with a loud voice and said, 'Blessed are you among women, and blessed is the fruit of your womb! But why is this granted to me, that the mother of my Lord should come to me? For indeed, as soon as the voice of your greeting sounded in my ears, the babe leaped in my womb for joy. Blessed is she who believed, for there will be a fulfillment of those things which were told her from the Lord' (Luke 1:39-56).

The Old Testament instructions for how to handle the harm or death of an unborn child mandate "life for life," indicating capital punishment for causing the demise of a pre-born baby. While the eye-for-an-eye passages apply differently to people living after the crucifixion and resurrection of Christ, under redemption and grace, the principle remains that taking the life of a person, even a person yet to be born, is a severe crime requiring a severe punishment. Exodus 21:22-23 provides this standard of justice: "If men fight, and hurt a woman with child, so that she gives birth prematurely, yet no harm follows, he shall surely be punished accordingly as the woman's husband imposes on him; and he shall pay as the judges determine. But if any harm follows, then you shall give life for life." (Ex 21:22-23).

In addition to these specific instances where Scripture addresses unborn life and the killing of children, the Bible is replete with the admonition that human life is made in the image of God (Gen 1:27, Gen 9:6), that to take the life of another human on purpose is murder, which is prohibited in God's law (Ex 20:13, Ex 21:12-14), and that a man or woman who chooses to kill another human should receive the death penalty as punishment (Lev 24:17, Ex 21:12). While our culture debates the practice of abortion—whether it is an acceptable choice or an egregious evil—the Bible demonstrates God's heart on the matter clearly: the murder of a pre-born life is sinful and demands a just response in certain punishment.

THE PRO-LIFE MOVEMENT IN THE MODERN ERA

Though the use of ultrasound imaging in prenatal care has become standard and routine in the 21st century, the technology only arrived in medical practice in the mid-1950s.[2] In the next decade, the medical field saw the introduction of the Doppler ultrasound monitor, a device used to detect a fetal heartbeat audibly.[3]

Prior to these inventions, the doctrine of "quickening," or the point in pregnancy at which a mother can begin to feel fetal movement in her

---

2 Tanya Lewis, "5 Fascinating Facts About Fetal Ultrasounds," Live Science, May 16, 2013, accessed June 26, 2021, https://www.livescience.com/32071-history-of-fetal-ultrasound.html.

3 Saeed Abdulrahman Alnuaimi, Shihab Jimaa, and Ahsan H. Khandoker, "Fetal Cardiac Doppler Signal Processing Techniques: Challenges and Future Research Directions," National Center for Biotechnology Information, December 22, 2017, accessed June 26, 2021, https://www.ncbi.nlm.nih.gov/pmc/articles/PMC5743703/.

abdomen, dictated the legal window for abortion.[4] Typically, a mother begins to detect movement of a baby in her womb between 14 to 26 weeks' gestation. In the 1800s, American abortion law reflected that of British common law which designated abortions carried out after "quickening" as a misdemeanor crime.[5] Historians say pre-quickening abortion was common before 1840 in America, with women using herbal abortifacients—also known as a medical abortion—to end their pregnancies and prevent their babies from reaching full gestation. Abortions occurring after quickening are said to have been illegal due to the greater danger they posed to the mother rather than any moral opposition.[6]

After the point of quickening, an unborn baby typically has grown too large and too developed to abort chemically and must be removed from the womb surgically—also known as surgical abortion. As is true in the 21st century, a surgical abortion carried increased risk of injury and death for the mother—a reality that leads some to surmise that the reason for the quickening doctrine had the safety of the mother in mind more than that of the developing child.[7] Between 1840 and the turn of the 20th century, legislators began passing more laws regulating abortion. The impetus, however, came more from physicians' desire to eliminate the competition they found in lay healers and midwives by seeking government regulation and licensing. Connecticut saw the nation's first law against abortion in 1821.[8] In 1856, Dr. Horatio Storer established the American Medical Association (AMA) to work toward ending legal abortion, which at that point was either legal or only a misdemeanor in all states. By 1890, legal advances had led to abortion being regulated according to guidance from the AMA. To obtain

---

4   Jennifer L. Holland, "Abolishing Abortion: The History of the Pro-Life Movement in America," Organization of American Historians, accessed June 26, 2021, https://www.oah.org/tah/issues/2016/november/abolishing-abortion-the-history-of-the-pro-life-movement-in-america/.

5   Ibid.
6   Ibid.
7   Ibid.
8   Ibid.

an abortion, a woman would have to have two physicians attest that the procedure was medically necessary to preserve the life of the mother.[9]

Of note, some 21st century physicians say abortion is never medically necessary, even to preserve the life of a mother. A doctor may perform a pre-term delivery, which the child may or may not survive, but the baby should never be killed on purpose. Even in the case of an ectopic pregnancy, the intention of medical intervention should never be to kill the child, though the child's life may indeed be lost.[10]

By 1900, every state in the nation had outlawed abortion at any stage with an exception that became a frequently seized loophole: the life of the mother. With this loophole, physicians became the arbiters of when an abortion could be performed legally. Illegal abortions increased in the early 20th century in response to the widespread passage of abortion laws. Some 15,000 women per year are estimated to have died from abortions by the 1920s.[11] A group representing the American Law Institute offered in 1959 a proposal that became a model for state legislators in how to pass laws that would permit abortions in the cases of rape, incest, fetal abnormality or when the life of a mother was at stake. The feminist movement and the population-control movement both began to contribute support for repeal or reform of abortion laws.[12] In the 1960s, the sexual revolution ignited, bringing with it second-wave feminism, increased promiscuity, and the

---

9 "Timeline of abortion laws and events," Chicago Tribune, March 29, 2001, accessed June 26, 2021, https://www.chicagotribune.com/sns-abortion-timeline-story.html.

10 Live Action, "The Pro-Life Reply to: 'Abortion Can Be Medically Necessary,'" published July 30, 2019, video, 4:48, accessed June 26, 2021, https://www.youtube.com/watch?v=5TmomK2RB2A&t=220s.

11 Katha Pollitt, "Abortion in American History," The Atlantic, May 1997, accessed June 26, 2021, https://www.theatlantic.com/magazine/archive/1997/05/abortion-in-american-history/376851/.

12 Mary Ziegler, "A brief history of US abortion law, before and after Roe v Wade," History Extra, June 21, 2019, accessed June 26, 2021, https://www.historyextra.com/period/20th-century/history-abortion-law-america-us-debate-what-roe-v-wade/.

introduction of the birth control pill. The vacuum-style aspirator abortion method also began to gain popularity in Europe.[13]

Some say that with increasing liberalism and efforts to liberalize abortion laws in the 1960s, this decade serves as the true origin of the pro-life movement, which emerged in greater visibility than before to respond to the growing threat to unborn life.[14]

In 1961, President John F. Kennedy used the platform of the presidency to call for the repeal of abortion laws.[15] While politicians began to push for abortion law reform to make the procedure more readily available and legal, pro-life advocates began to band together to oppose those efforts. The years 1967 and 1968 saw the organization and founding of The National Right to Life Committee (NRLC) when doctors, lawyers, and housewives, aided by the support of the National Council of Catholic Bishops, began to organize themselves in the fight against abortion.[16] The formation and mission of the National Right to Life Committee is described on the organization's website:

> Founded in 1968, National Right to Life, federation of 50 state right-to-life affiliates and more than 3,000 local chapters, is the nation's oldest and largest grassroots pro-life organization. Recognized as the flagship of the pro-life movement, NRLC works through legis-

---

13 "Timeline of abortion laws and events," Chicago Tribune, March 29, 2001, accessed June 26, 2021, https://www.chicagotribune.com/sns-abortion-timeline-story.html.

14 Jeremy L. Sabella, "Pro-Life and Rescue Movements," Association of Religion Data Archives, accessed June 26, 2021, https://www.thearda.com/timeline/movements/movement_31.asp.

15 The Editors of Encyclopedia Britannica, "President's Commission on the Status of Women," Britannica, April 26, 1999, accessed June 26, 2021, https://www.britannica.com/topic/Presidents-Commission-on-the-Status-of-Women.

16 Jennifer L. Holland, "Abolishing Abortion: The History of the Pro-Life Movement in America," Organization of American Historians, accessed June 26, 2021, https://www.oah.org/tah/issues/2016/november/abolishing-abortion-the-history-of-the-pro-life-movement-in-america/.

-lation and education to protect innocent human life from abortion, infanticide, assisted suicide and euthanasia.[17]

Mildred Jefferson, a female physician who served as president of the NRLC from 1975-1978, is remembered by colleagues as one of the most persuasive and articulate advocates the pro-life movement has ever had. Working with great determination and eloquence of speech, Jefferson traveled around the nation speaking on behalf of the movement. In an audio recording published by the NRLC, Jefferson can be heard offering a rationale for her dedication to the pro-life movement, "I am a physician, a citizen, and a woman, and I am not willing to stand aside and allow this concept of expendable human lives to turn this great land of ours into just another exclusive reservation where only the perfect, the privileged, and the planned have a right to life," Jefferson said.[18]

Jefferson, who graduated high school at age 15, earned two college degrees before becoming the first African American woman accepted to Harvard medical school—an accomplishment she achieved at age 20. Jefferson went on to become the first woman accepted into a surgical internship program with Boston City Hospital and the first female doctor at the former Boston University Medical Center.[19]

By 1970, abortion laws began to fade, beginning with Hawaii allowing abortions before 20 weeks' gestation. New York soon followed in repealing its criminal abortion law. In another year's time, four states permit-

---

17 "History of National Right to Life," National Right to Life, accessed June 26, 2021, https://www.nrlc.org/about/history/. Concurrently, abortion advocates founded the National Abortion Rights Action League (NARAL), known at first as National Association for Repeal of Abortion Laws, in 1969. The organization later amended its name again in 2000 to NARAL Pro-Choice America ("The Fight for Our Lives," NARAL Pro-Choice America, accessed June 26, 2021, https://www.prochoiceamerica.org/timeline/).

18 National Right to Life, "National Right to Life Remembers Dr. Mildred Jefferson," published June 23, 2011, video, 11:26, accessed June 26, 2021, https://www.youtube.com/watch?v=UB3o-QazcNg.

19 "History of National Right to Life," National Right to Life, accessed June 26, 2021, https://www.nrlc.org/about/history/.

ted abortion, and 14 allowed them under some circumstances.[20] 1971 saw the repeal of the Comstock Act, passed in 1873 as an "Act of the Suppression of Trade in, and Circulation of, Obscene Literature and Articles of Immoral Use." The act had essentially prohibited distribution of information about unlawful abortions and contraception.[21]

Jefferson, concerned with the increasing opposition to abortion laws and specifically efforts to alter Massachusetts laws governing abortion, became one of the founders of the Massachusetts Citizens for Life, later joining the board of the National Right to Life Committee in 1971.[22] The Local Public Broadcasting Station (PBS) affiliate in Boston hosted Jefferson on a program called "The Advocate," in 1972. Audiences nationwide tuned in to the program, and Jefferson's appearance there swayed the opinion of at least one politician regarding abortion—a victory that had positive repercussions for the pro-life movement for years to come.[23]

Jefferson received a letter dated January 17, 1973, from the persuaded politician. Ronald Reagan wrote:

> I hope you won't mind my writing to you, but I had to tell you how truly great you were in your testimony on the 'Advocate' program regarding abortion. Yours was the most clear-cut exposition on this problem that I have ever heard... Several years ago, I was faced with the issue of whether to sign a California abortion bill... I must confess to never having given the matter of abortion any serious thought until that time. No other issue since I have been in office has caused me to do so much study and soul-searching... I wish I

---

20 "Timeline of abortion laws and events," Chicago Tribune, March 29, 2001, accessed June 26, 2021, https://www.chicagotribune.com/sns-abortion-timeline-story.html.

21 The Editors of Encyclopedia Britannica, "Comstock Act," Britannica, April 26, 1999, accessed June 26, 2021, https://www.britannica.com/event/Comstock-Act.

22 National Right to Life, "National Right to Life Remembers Dr. Mildred Jefferson," published June 23, 2011, video, 11:26, accessed June 26, 2021, https://www.youtube.com/watch?v=UB3o-QazcNg.

23 Ibid.

could have heard your views before our legislation was passed. You made it irrefutably clear that an abortion is the taking of a human life. I'm grateful to you.[24]

Reagan's enlightenment and course correction concerning the ethics of abortion demonstrate the efficacy of communication and advocacy. Many pro-life-minded citizens ask what they can do in the fight against abortion. Jefferson's work provides a sterling example of the difference one convictional, courageous, articulate person can make by speaking out into whatever areas of influence he or she may have. Jefferson's compelling appearance on a single televised program allowed her to indirectly influence public policy, thereby contributing tangibly to the effort to save babies from abortion. Twenty-first century pro-life advocates can glean from Jefferson's example the encouragement to speak, write, and create social media posts in defense of unborn life, knowing that the efforts are not in vain.

With the Roe v. Wade decision by the United States Supreme Court, the year 1973 stands as one of the most well-known years in the pro-abortion versus pro-life battle. On Jan. 22, 1973, Justice Harry A. Blackmun issued the majority opinion in the Court's decision ruling "that unduly restrictive state regulation of abortion is unconstitutional."[25] Here's the rest of the story.

Norma McCorvey, familiar to many as Jane Roe of the originally anonymous Roe v. Wade case, was pregnant and single, living in Texas, and desiring an abortion. State law, however, dictated that a physician could only perform an abortion in cases where the mother's life was at stake. Elective abortions were a crime. At first, McCorvey claimed she was raped, hoping the Court would make an exception and allow her an abortion under such a circumstance, but in 1987, McCorvey recanted the rape claim, admitting she had merely alleged rape as a means of securing the desired

---

24 Glenn Sunshine, "Christians Who Changed Their World: Mildred Fay Jefferson (1926-2010)," BreakPoint, February 22, 2017, accessed June 26, 2021, https://www.breakpoint.org/mildred-fay-jefferson-1926-2010/.

25 "Roe v. Wade," Encyclopedia Britannica, April 26, 1999, accessed June 26, 2021, https://www.britannica.com/event/Roe-v-Wade.

abortion.[26] Ultimately, in a ruling based on a woman's right to privacy, the United States Supreme Court heard and adjudicated the case, determining that women in America have a constitutionally protected right to privacy which allows legal termination of first trimester pregnancy via abortion.[27] The National Right to Life Committee estimates, based on data from the Centers for Disease Control (CDC) and the Guttmacher Institute, that more than 62 million babies have been aborted since the Supreme Court delivered the Roe v. Wade decision.[28] That death toll exceeds the number of Jews killed in the Holocaust by a multiplication factor of more than 10.

Also in 1973, a United States Supreme Court ruling in the case of Doe vs. Bolton struck down a Georgia law requiring a woman to obtain approval from three separate doctors before having an abortion.[29] Ten months after the Supreme Court ruled in Roe v. Wade, a group of 30 advocates of the pro-life movement met in Washington D.C. in the home of Nellie Gray, a federal government lawyer, to discuss the first anniversary of the Court's decision. In January 1974, the first March for Life took place in the nation's capital to lobby congressional leaders to support the sanctity of human life. Gray determined that the march should be held every year until Roe v. Wade is overturned.[30] She quit her job to become the full-time volunteer

---

26 Kenneth B. Noble, "Key Abortion Plaintiff Now Denies She Was Raped," The New York Times, September 9, 1987, accessed June 26, 2021, https://www.nytimes.com/1987/09/09/us/key-abortion-plaintiff-now-denies-she-was-raped.html.

27 Kimberly Kutz Elliott, "Due process and the right to privacy: lesson overview," Khan Academy, accessed June 26, 2021, https://www.khanacademy.org/humanities/us-government-and-civics/us-gov-civil-liberties-and-civil-rights/us-gov-due-process-and-the-right-to-privacy/a/lesson-summary-due-process-and-the-right-to-privacy.

28 Sam Dorman, "An estimated 62 million abortions have occurred since Roe v. Wade decision in 1973," Fox News, January 22, 2021, accessed June 26, 2021, https://www.foxnews.com/politics/abortions-since-roe-v-wade.

29 "Timeline of abortion laws and events," Chicago Tribune, March 29, 2001, accessed June 26, 2021, https://www.chicagotribune.com/sns-abortion-timeline-story.html.

30 "About the March for Life," March for Life, accessed June 26, 2021,

A Life for Life: Dr. Richard Land's Legacy of Defending Pre-Born Persons

president of March for Life when it incorporated as a non-profit organization.[31] March for Life has continued its annual presence in Washington, D.C., into the 21st century, welcoming as speakers, for the first time in history, the nation's most senior leaders. Mike Pence became the first United States vice president to speak at the demonstration during the 44th annual March for Life in 2017.[32] Donald Trump became the first United States president to do so in 2020 at the 47th annual march.[33] "Today, as president of the United States, I am truly proud to stand with you," Trump said in his 2020 speech. "We're here for a very simple reason: to defend the right for every child, born and unborn, to fulfill their God-given potential."[34]

The Hyde Amendment, passed in 1976 as part of the appropriations bill for what became the Department of Health and Human Services, prohibited federal tax-payer funding of abortion through Medicaid.[35] The Amendment, named for former Representative Henry Hyde, a Republican from Illinois, is estimated to have prevented a significant number of abortions, according to the Guttmacher Institute which said in 2009 that "approximately one-fourth of women who would have Medicaid-funded

---

https://marchforlife.org/about-the-march-for-life/.

31 Bethany Peck, "Women of the Pro-Life Movement: Nellie Gray," March for Life, March 20, 2014, accessed June 26, 2021, https://marchforlife.org/women-of-the-pro-life-movement-nellie-gray/.

32 Bethany Peck, "Vice President Mike Pence to Speak at the 44th Annual March for Life in Washington, D.C. on January 27," March for Life, January 27, 2017, accessed June 26, 2021, https://marchforlife.org/mike-pence-to-speak-at-march-life/.

33 Ritu Prasad, "Trump first president to attend anti-abortion rally," British Broadcasting Corporation, January 20, 2020, accessed June 26, 2021, https://www.bbc.com/news/world-us-canada-51239795.

34 Dennis Sadowski, "Trump tells March for Life crowd he welcomes their commitment," National Catholic Reporter, January 24, 2020, accessed June 26, 2021, https://www.ncronline.org/news/people/trump-tells-march-life-crowd-he-welcomes-their-commitment.

35 Maggie Astor, "What Is the Hyde Amendment? A Look at Its Impact as Biden Reverses His Stance," The New York Times, June 7, 2019, accessed June 26, 2021, https://www.nytimes.com/2019/06/07/us/politics/what-is-the-hyde-amendment.html.

abortions instead give birth when this funding is unavailable."[36] The Charlotte Lozier Institute, in a 2016 report entitled "Hyde @ 40: Analyzing the Impact of the Hyde Amendment," estimates a 60,000 per year reduction in abortions, noting a 13 percent increase in births among those receiving Medicaid assistance 'post Hyde.'[37]

In commemorating National Sanctity of Human Life Day in 2021, then-United States President Donald Trump cited a 24 percent decrease in abortion in America between 2007 and 2016. He noted that teen pregnancies had experienced an overall decrease as well.[38] For perspective, the Guttmacher Institute reports that 862,320 babies were aborted in 2017.[39] These statistics and others like them provide helpful insight to the pro-life movement as some believe the incremental approach to ending abortion has not been successful in reducing the number of overall abortions.

The 1980s also saw the emergence of the Rescue Movement, which as its name suggests, included men and women who set out to rescue babies from being aborted and mothers from committing abortions. The movement's tactics included civil disobedience in the form of blockading abortion clinics to keep providers and patients from entering. Organizers built the movement, which began around 1985, upon the conviction that fetuses are human and that killing them is equivalent to killing an already-born person of any age—a premise that provides the foundation for the abolition

---

36 Stanley K. Henshaw, Theodore J. Joyce, Amanda Dennis, Lawrence B. Finer and Kelly Blanchard, "Restrictions on Medicaid Funding for Abortions: A Literature Review," Guttmacher Institute, June 2009, accessed June 26, 2021, https://www.guttmacher.org/sites/default/files/report_pdf/medicaidlitreview.pdf.

37 Michael J. New, "Hyde @ 40: Analyzing the Impact of the Hyde Amendment," Charlotte Lozier Institute, September 2016, accessed June 26, 2021, https://s27589.pcdn.co/wp-content/uploads/2016/09/OP_hyde_9.28.3.pdf.

38 Sharayah Colter, "Small wins in pro-life effort must breed sober hope and increased action," Sharayah.org, accessed June 26, 2021, https://www.sharayah.org/post/small-wins-in-pro-life-effort-must-breed-sober-hope-and-increased-action.

39 "U.S. Abortion Statistics: Facts and figures relating to the frequency of abortion in the United States," Abort73.com, accessed June 26, 2021, https://abort73.com/abortion_facts/us_abortion_statistics/.

of abortion movement as well. In 1988, national attention turned to the Rescue Movement when a series of protests known as the "Siege of Atlanta," took place for five months. Police made 1,300 arrests in Atlanta, and as the protests spread to other cities, the arrest total grew to 11,500 in the year 1988 and 12,000 in 1989. The movement declined in the 1990s but influenced the pro-life movement for decades, having demonstrated the importance of keeping the issue of abortion in national attention as well as the effectiveness of tactics such as picketing. Eventually, the movement lost momentum and began to decline when some veered toward violence as part of the rescue missions and others remained committed to non-violent actions, leaving the group in an untenable tension. The Freedom of Access to Clinic Entrances Act of 1994 also played a role in the decline of the Rescue Movement by answering blockade activities with large fines.[40]

In 1992, the same year Americans elected Democrat William "Bill" Clinton as United States president, the United States Supreme Court handed down the Planned Parenthood of Southeastern Pa. v. Casey decision. While the ruling affirmed the Roe v. Wade decision, it adopted a doctrine of "undue burden," permitting states to regulate abortion so long as the regulation did not impose an "undue burden," on women seeking abortions. This ruling provided pro-life supporters an avenue by which to promote legislation against abortion in the careful crafting of legal actions and public messaging.[41]

Writing for National Review in a 2017 article, Michael J. New explained the benefits of the Casey ruling for the pro-life cause:

> Under this new standard, the *Casey* decision upheld most of the provisions included in Pennsylvania's Abortion Control Act, including the

---

40 Jeremy L. Sabella, "Pro-Life and Rescue Movements," Association of Religion Data Archives, accessed June 26, 2021, https://www.thearda.com/timeline/movements/movement_31.asp.

41 Michael J. New, "Casey at 25: Pro-Life Progress Despite a Judicial Setback," National Review, June 29, 2017, accessed June 26, 2021, https://www.nationalreview.com/2017/06/planned-parenthood-v-casey-1992-pro-life-incremental-approach-decline-abortion/.

parental-consent provision, the reporting requirements, the waiting period, and the informed-consent language. Only the spousal-notification requirement was struck down. The constitutional protection that *Casey* granted these laws, coupled with pro-life gains in numerous state legislatures since the 1990s, has led to a substantial increase in the number of state-level pro-life laws. Since 1992, the number of states with parental-involvement laws has increased from 20 to 37. The number of states with informed-consent laws pertaining to abortion has increased from 18 to 35. In recent years, 20 states have banned abortions that take place at or after 20 weeks' gestation, based on the unborn child's scientifically documented ability to feel pain. Even more important, after *Casey*, many states strengthened existing pro-life laws. Several states improved their informed-consent laws by including more information about health risks, fetal development, and sources of support for single mothers.[42]

The "undue burden" standard established by the Casey decision was revisited again by the Supreme Court when it ruled in the case of Whole Woman's Health v. Hellerstedt in 2016. Though the "State has a legitimate interest in seeing to it that abortion . . . is performed under circumstances that insure [sic] maximum safety for the patient," as stated by the Supreme Court in 2015, the Court decided in the Hellerstedt case that a Texas law requiring an abortionist have admitting privileges at a nearby hospital and that abortion centers meet the minimum standards for ambulatory surgical centers imposed an undue burden on women seeking abortions.[43] Thus, the 1992 Casey decision continued its reach into 21st century abortion permission.

During the early 1990s, pro-life advocates sought successfully to wed the anti-abortion effort into conservative politics and the Republican Party. Assistant Professor of History at the University of Oklahoma Jennifer L.

---

42 New, "Casey at 25."

43 Whole Woman's Health et al. v. Hellerstedt, Commissioner, Texas Department of State Health Services et al., United States Supreme Court, 2016, accessed July 2, 2021, https://www.supremecourt.gov/opinions/15pdf/15-274_new_e18f.pdf.

Holland, writing for the Organization of American Historians, dissected the effort to comingle pro-life efforts and conservative politics:

> The radical and moderate groups differed in terms of strategy, but together they succeeded at reorienting the conversation about abortion. Both types of groups worked to make pro-life politics central to social conservatism and by extension the Republican party. They made fetal life central to how many Christians viewed their religion and their politics. They asked conservative children to think of themselves as "survivors of the Abortion Holocaust." And they helped new "family values" constituents consider the fetus a member of the family and legal abortion the biggest challenge facing the modern family. In all these efforts, activists were successful, not for all Americans but for enough to build an expansive movement with the defense of fetal life as its core.[44]

Some 21st century evangelicals have expressed disdain for Christian involvement in politics, a few even criticizing those promoting the Republican Party and its platform as a means of advocating for babies' rights to life. Considering that the melding of the pro-life cause and the Republican Party was part of an intentional effort among pro-life advocates to harness political influence for the advancement of the pro-life cause and ultimately the saving of lives, many pro-life supporters have rejected the notion that Christians should abstain from politics. The question has risen whether those advocating such an abstention have the pro-life movement's best interest in mind, or if perhaps some advocates within the movement are less committed to its success than they purport to be. With fetal life positioned at the center of political conservatives' priorities, pro-life advocates continue to see efforts to influence abortion in America through a legislative challenge to Roe v. Wade as both a worthwhile and virtuous endeavor.

---

44 Jennifer L. Holland, "Abolishing Abortion: The History of the Pro-Life Movement in America," Organization of American Historians, accessed June 26, 2021, https://www.oah.org/tah/issues/2016/november/abolishing-abortion-the-history-of-the-pro-life-movement-in-america/.

As rhetoric intensified and tensions continued to rise between pro-life and pro-abortion supporters, 1993 and 1994 saw instances of violence against abortion doctors and prosecution of the individuals committing those crimes. The year 1995 tells a story some may find surprising however, as the national director of Operation Rescue befriended Norma McCorvey (Jane Roe). McCorvey accepted Jesus Christ as her Lord and Savior, and the Operation Rescue leader baptized her.[45] McCorvey went on to refer to herself as pro-life and expressed regret for "her role in the landmark case," according to the Chicago Tribune.[46] She never actually had the abortion which she sought and which became the impetus for the Supreme Court decision that opened the floodgates for abortion in America since her child was born before the case was decided and then placed for adoption. Pro-life organizations lauded McCorvey for her public reversal regarding abortion, speaking fondly of her and her work for life in the days after her death in 2017.[47] McCorvey's deathbed confession, however, made public in a 2020 documentary—three years after her death—left the world uncertain as to whether her faith conversion and pro-life advocacy had been genuine.[48]

The 1990s saw the abortion debate shift to a discussion about partial-birth abortion, an abortion technique in which, as the name suggests, an abortionist allows a baby to be partially born—feet, legs and trunk delivered—before inserting scissors into the base of the baby's skull, opening the scissors to widen the hole, using a catheter to suction the baby's brain from

---

[45] "Timeline of abortion laws and events," Chicago Tribune, March 29, 2001, accessed June 26, 2021, https://www.chicagotribune.com/sns-abortion-timeline-story.html.

[46] Ibid.

[47] Matt Hadro, "Life, conversion of Roe v. Wade's Norma McCorvey remembered," Catholic News Agency, February 20, 2017, accessed June 26, 2021, https://www.catholicnewsagency.com/news/35480/life-conversion-of-roe-v-wades-norma-mccorvey-remembered.

[48] Jessica Gresko, "Film: 'Roe' plaintiff says her anti-abortion switch was act," Associated Press, May 21, 2020, accessed June 26, 2021, https://apnews.com/article/norma-mccorvey-us-news-ap-top-news-courts-supreme-courts-25a89c-0caf19df066ccfa8dc18e22a1a.

the skull, and then evacuating the baby from the birth canal.[49] Though partial-birth abortion is not a legal or medical term, the phrasing is used to refer to the intact dilation and extraction abortion method, not to be confused with dilation and evacuation method in which the baby is dismembered inside the uterus and removed by a combination of instruments and vacuum suction. Though Congress passed a bill to outlaw the partial-birth abortion procedure in 1996, President Bill Clinton vetoed the measure.[50] Clinton vetoed a similar bill the next year. Congress passed yet another bill outlawing partial-birth abortion in 2003, which became law when United States President George W. Bush affixed his signature.[51] The Supreme Court upheld the law in the 2007 decision, Gonzalez v. Carhart.[52]

By the turn of the century, abortion continued to become increasingly central to the Republican Party platform. The ideological divide grew, generally separating pro-choice Democrats from pro-life Republicans. In elections for United States president, NARAL Pro-Choice America endorsed Democrat Barack Obama and later Hillary Clinton. The National Right to Life Committee offered endorsements to Republican Mitt Romney and later Donald Trump. Abortion has been an issue included in the official platforms of both major political parties, one for and one against, solidifying it as a dividing line in American politics and public policy. While some discourage Christians from involvement in politics—some pastors even declining to mention "political issues" from the pulpit—others see every political

---

49 Janice Hopkins Tanne, "US Supreme Court approves ban on 'partial birth abortion,'" National Center for Biotechnology Information, April 28, 2007, accessed June 26, 2021, https://www.ncbi.nlm.nih.gov/pmc/articles/PMC1857800/.

50 Melissa Healy, "Clinton Vetoes Ban on Procedure in Late Abortions," Los Angeles Times, April 11, 1996, accessed June 26, 2021, https://www.latimes.com/archives/la-xpm-1996-04-11-mn-57381-story.html.

51 Dana Milbank, "Bush Signs Ban on Late-Term Abortions Into Effect," Washington Post, November 6, 2003, accessed June 26, 2021, https://www.washingtonpost.com/archive/politics/2003/11/06/bush-signs-ban-on-late-term-abortions-into-effect/22d3c373-ae0a-4e6b-8e3e-a06b040c2ae6/.

52 Janice Hopkins Tanne, "US Supreme Court approves ban on 'partial birth abortion,'" National Center for Biotechnology Information, April 28, 2007, accessed June 26, 2021, https://www.ncbi.nlm.nih.gov/pmc/articles/PMC1857800/.

issue as a biblical and moral issue.[53] Many contend that if Scripture addresses an issue, Christians should also be willing to address those issues as well.[54]

The Family Research Council released a guide to help Christians navigate what role they should play in the political process. A portion of that guide written by David Closson reads:

> In summary, as the means by which we order our shared lives, politics occupies a significant place in society and is an unavoidable, central area of Christian concern. Because government and its laws are an inextricable part of our lives, there is no way to avoid some level of involvement. This is true for Christians, who, though 'sojourners and exiles' (1 Peter 2:11) in this world, are nevertheless citizens of the "City of Man" as well as the "City of God." Christians ought to endeavor to be good citizens of both cities and leverage their influence for the advancement of laws, policies, and practices that contribute to the flourishing of our neighbors. Thus, Christians have a biblical obligation to engage in politics and the political process.[55]

Historically, Christians in many generations have embraced as a duty their role in government. The British, for example, noted such involvement during the American Revolution, labeling government-minded ministers as the "Black Robed Regiment," without which some say the Revolution

---

53 Jeff Brumley, "Outgoing SBC president affirms conservative values while decrying legalism," Baptist News Global, June 15, 2021, accessed June 26, 2021, https://baptistnews.com/article/outgoing-sbc-president-affirms-conservative-values-while-decrying-legalism/#.YN__Ei1h3GI.

54 Emily Robertson, "Liberty University Think Tank Rebrands to Standing for Freedom Center," Liberty Champion, March 29, 2021, accessed June 26, 2021, https://www.liberty.edu/champion/2021/03/liberty-university-think-tank-rebrands-to-standing-for-freedom-center/.

55 David Closson, "Biblical Principles for Political Engagement," Family Research Council, accessed June 26, 2021, https://downloads.frc.org/EF/EF19G02.pdf.

may not have occurred.[56] The National Black Robed Regiment, a 21st century organization formed to honor and promote the same courageous spirit that embodied many ministers of the 1800s, describes ministerial involvement in the formation of the United States:

> The American clergy were faithful exponents of the fullness of God's Word, applying its principles to every aspect of life, thus shaping America's institutes and culture. They were also at the forefront of proclaiming liberty, resisting tyranny, and opposing any encroachments on God-given rights and freedoms.[57]

In the 20th century and strengthening into the 21st century, reflecting Christian engagement of eras-past, several factors propelled Christians further into advocacy of the pro-life movement in political and cultural spheres.

Live Action, which regards itself as having the largest online following among pro-life organizations, formed informally in 2003 and formally in 2008.[58] The organization, founded and led by advocate Lila Rose, seeks to expose the evil of abortion and to affirm the life of every child. Through their educational videos, many featuring former abortion doctors, minds have been changed regarding the cruelty of abortion. The group's website recounts some of the testimonies of those whose opinions have shifted:

> "Thank you for getting the truth out. You changed my mind." … "I was pro-choice up to a certain amount…until seeing the video … it changed my mind completely." … "I never had a firm position in either camp. But because of this video, I am 100% pro-life."[59]

---

56 "History of the Black Robed Regiment," National Black Robe Regiment, accessed June 26, 2021, https://nationalblackroberegiment.com/history-of-the-black-robe-regiment/.

57 Ibid.

58 "Our Story," Live Action, accessed June 26, 2021, https://shop.liveaction.org/pages/about-live-action.

59 Ibid.

In addition to video animations describing the barbaric process of abortion, including the dilation and evacuation procedure in which a doctor dilates the cervix, forcibly tears the limbs from the baby's body one at a time, crushes the skull with metal forceps, and suctions the baby's remains from the uterus, pro-life advocates have employed photographs of aborted babies as a means of demonstrating the humanity of a baby killed in an abortion. Many have reported that seeing a fully formed human baby, bloody and pieced together on a medical tray, has conveyed to them for the first time the horror of abortion. The clear presentation of scientific realities has led to minds being changed and lives being saved.

In 2015, abortion activist and citizen journalist David Daleiden, a part of the investigative group called The Center for Medical Progress, released undercover video footage of Planned Parenthood representatives discussing the practice of selling aborted baby parts for money. The videos, which also included what many found to be heartbreaking discussion about the ruthless killing of babies, shocked much of America, ignited a social media firestorm, became the subject of congressional debate, and led to Daleiden facing significant legal opposition.[60] The group's efforts continued in the years following the initial video releases and remain a source of frustration for abortion advocates espousing the narrative that Planned Parenthood primarily focuses on family planning and that the pro-abortion movement is a pro-woman movement.[61]

While the abortion industry purports to care about women and their "rights," Americans in the 21st century increasingly have become suspicious of those claims and wise to the truth that abortion is the murder of innocent life committed in an inhumane way that would not even be acceptable behavior toward a sea turtle. A Florida news outlet reported in 2015 that, "under state law, destroying a sea turtle nest or eggs is a third-degree felo-

---

60 Jennifer Ludden, "Undercover Video Targets Planned Parenthood," National Public Radio, July 15, 2015, accessed June 26, 2021, https://www.npr.org/sections/thetwo-way/2015/07/15/423212004/undercover-video-targets-planned-parenthood.

61 "Planned Parenthood Fact vs. Myth," Minnesota Family Council, accessed June 26, 2021, https://www.mfc.org/ppfacts.

ny, punishable by up to a $5,000 fine and/or five years in prison."[62] In most cases, destruction of a human through abortion carries no legal repercussion in the United States.

When Virginia Governor Ralph Northam said in an extemporaneous response on a radio show that if a baby survives a third trimester abortion, the child may be left to die, effectively condoning infanticide, Americans began to awaken to the depths of the depravity fueling the pro-abortion movement.[63] While at one time the pro-abortion mantra had been that abortion should be safe, legal, and rare, pro-abortion advocates continue to clarify, intentionally or unintentionally, that the goal is for a woman to have the legal clearance to rid herself of the responsibility and perceived inconvenience of being a mother despite science declaring the undeniable humanity of unborn babies.[64] The myth that an unborn baby is only a clump of cells, has been debunked as advancements in the medical field can demonstrate that a baby's heart beats at approximately 21 days into a mother's pregnancy—often before the pregnancy can even be detected by an at-home pregnancy test. By six weeks, brainwave activity begins, and eyelids have formed. By 12 weeks, a baby can feel pain.[65] Yet, the blatant disregard for the humanity of a fetus in the early days of gestation comes as no surprise. Congress has more than 75 times declined to consider a bill ensuring that babies born alive in failed abortions are cared for and protected instead

---

62 "Stiff penalty for disturbing sea turtle nests," Spectrum News, July 14, 2015, accessed June 26, 2021, https://www.baynews9.com/fl/tampa/news/2015/7/14/stiff_penalty_for_di.

63 Alexandra Desanctis, "Virginia Governor Defends Letting Infants Die," National Review, January 30, 2019, accessed June 26, 2021, https://www.nationalreview.com/corner/virginia-governor-defends-letting-infants-die/.

64 Emma Green, "Science Is Giving the Pro-life Movement a Boost," The Atlantic, January 18, 2018, accessed June 26, 2021, https://www.theatlantic.com/politics/archive/2018/01/pro-life-pro-science/549308/.

65 "Fetal Development," Pro-Life Future, accessed June 26, 2021, https://prolifefuture.org/abortion-facts/fetal-development/.

of being left to die.[66] If politicians can ignore the plight of a fully developed baby lying helpless and hurting in a medical facility, can a fetus hidden and muted in the womb possibly elicit any more compassion?

The implementation of ultrasound machines, which began in earnest in American hospitals in the 1970s, marked a critical milestone in the pro-life movement by allowing parents and doctors to see an image of a baby in the womb.[67] Scientific developments in the field of fetal surgery have emerged as well, with the first documented human fetal surgery performed in 1963.[68] In the cases of fetal surgery, the fetus is considered a patient—a stark contrast to the fetus not even being considered a person with rights when presented by a mother for an abortion procedure rather than for fetal surgery. This non-scientific double standard can also be seen in the legal realm in that the homicide of a pregnant mother warrants that the perpetrator be arrested and tried on murder charges for both the mother and baby, while in many situations a baby of the same gestation can be killed by a doctor at the mother's request with no legal repercussions for either party.[69]

Ultrasound technology and other advancements in science pick up the abortion debate and set it back down in a completely different legal environment than that of the days preceding Roe v. Wade. Because of this evolved environment, pro-life activists in the 21st century now see a path

---

66 Rebecca Angelson, "Latta Signs Discharge Petition to Force House Vote on Born-Alive Abortion Survivors Protection Act," Bob Latta, April 14, 2021, accessed June 26, 2021, https://latta.house.gov/news/documentsingle.aspx?DocumentID=402446.

67 Tanya Lewis, "5 Fascinating Facts About Fetal Ultrasounds," Live Science, May 16, 2013, accessed June 26, 2021, https://www.livescience.com/32071-history-of-fetal-ultrasound.html.

68 Kathleen O'Conner and Erica O'Neil, "Fetal Surgery," The Embryo Project Encyclopedia, January 11, 2012, accessed June 26, 2021, https://embryo.asu.edu/pages/fetal-surgery.

69 "State Laws on Fetal Homicide and Penalty-enhancement for Crimes Against Pregnant Women," National Conference of State Legislatures, May 1, 2018, accessed June 26, 2021, https://www.ncsl.org/research/health/fetal-homicide-state-laws.aspx.

to outlawing abortion in working with the arguments made in the Roe v. Wade decision and the existing 14th amendment to the United States Constitution. Where another constitutional amendment was once thought necessary, some within the pro-life movement realize that operating within the current legal framework, using science to prove the humanity and personhood of unborn babies may provide a reasonable path toward abolishing abortion in America. As recently as 2021, United States Senator Rand Paul, (R-KY), along with the National Pro-Life Alliance, urged pro-life-minded Americans to support the Life at Conception Act:

> A Life at Conception Act declares unborn children 'persons' as defined by the 14th Amendment to the Constitution, entitled to legal protection. This is the one thing the Supreme Court admitted in Roe v. Wade that would cause the case for legal abortion to 'collapse.' When the Supreme Court handed down its now-infamous Roe v. Wade decision, it did so based on a new, previously undefined "right of privacy" which it "discovered" in so-called "emanations" of "penumbrae" of the Constitution. Of course, as constitutional law, it was a disaster. But never once did the Supreme Court declare abortion itself to be a constitutional right. Instead, the Supreme Court said: 'We need not resolve the difficult question of when life begins... the judiciary at this point in the development of man's knowledge is not in a position to speculate as to the answer.' Then the High Court made a key admission: 'If this suggestion of personhood is established, the appellant's case [i.e., "Roe" who sought an abortion], of course, collapses, for the fetus' right to life is then guaranteed specifically by the [14th] Amendment.'[70]

The personhood perspective frames the pro-life movement in a way that mirrors the movement to abolish slavery. Ultimately, American slaves were freed and gained citizenship and voting rights through the combination of the 13th, 14th, and 15th amendments. Modern-day abolitionists

---

70 Rand Paul, e-mail message to constituents, June 29, 2021.

are increasingly hopeful that the 14th Amendment and recognition of personhood status will afford the same protective result for pre-born humans. Though pro-life advocates generally share the same end goal of eliminating abortion, debate exists within Christendom of whether only total abolition can be sought, or if incremental, pro-life measures have merit as well. Those hesitant to adopt the abolitionist mindset say the perspective paints with too broad of a brush, not leaving room for cases in which the life of the mother is at stake. Conversely, those representing the abolition effort say the life of the mother argument is a misnomer that only creates a loophole. While both segments of the pro-life movement hold a foundational desire to save the lives of unborn babies, the groups continue to debate what is the most effective and most ethical method to accomplish that shared goal.

Concluding Remarks

Noble are the souls who would stand against the cultural milieu and guaranteed backlash associated with defending the sanctity of life. The evil that fuels the pro-abortion movement wafts up toward earth from the depths of hell where atrocities such as parents killing their own children are birthed and planted into the hearts of fallen humanity. The battle is spiritual. The most important weapon is prayer (Eph 6:12; 2 Cor 10:3-5). Standing in prayer and seeking God's divine intervention are the people willing to speak and act on behalf of the speechless and most vulnerable (Prov 31:8-10).

Dr. Richard Land has been one such leading defender of the sanctity of human life. In 2020, Land commented about the scientific backing now present for a move toward ending abortion—a "crime against humanity" that he notes was responsible for killing more people in the world in 2019 than any other cause of death:

> *Every abortion stops a beating heart, and God had a plan and a purpose for every one of* those hundreds of thousands of babies who are killed each year in the United States and the millions of babies killed around the world. Don't take my word for it. Look it up in a biol-

ogy textbook. Abortion on demand is a grotesque atrocity, a crime against humanity and a stain on our nation's moral conscience. It must come to an end.[71]

Land, who led the Southern Baptist Convention's ethics and public policy arm for many years, noted in a 2003 interview with Baptist Press that the issue of life in the womb largely had been considered a Catholic issue until the 1973 Roe v. Wade decision. When Baptists in the pew came to understand, through the national attention brought to the issue, what was happening regarding abortion in America, they took notice and began to lead the SBC toward a more overt support for a conservative pro-life stance. Until that shift, the SBC had adopted resolutions affirming, "legislation permitting abortion for reasons nearly as expansive as those the Supreme Court eventually would allow in Roe v. Wade and its companion ruling, Doe v. Bolton. Resolutions in 1974 and 1976 did little, if anything, to move the SBC beyond that statement," according to reporting by Baptist Press.[72]

Baptist Press continued its report, describing the effect grassroots Baptists and subsequently a movement known as the Conservative Resurgence had on the evolving pro-life perspective in Southern Baptist life, polity, and influence:

While that transformation began occurring in many pews and pulpits in the 1970s, the SBC's entities did not follow along as quickly. Some denominational leaders even defended the abortion-rights position. In 1977, Foy Valentine, longtime head of the SBC's eth-

---

71 "Southern Evangelical Seminary President Richard Land: 'Abortion on Demand is a Crime against Humanity and a Stain on Our Nation's Moral Conscience,'" Hamilton Strategies, January 20, 2020, accessed June 26, 2021, https://hamiltonstrategies.com/southern-evangelical-seminary-president-richard-land-abortion-on-demand-is-a-crime-against-humanity-and-a-stain-on-our-nations-moral-conscience/.

72 Tom Strode, "Southern Baptists transformed as U.S. grappled with Roe v. Wade," Baptist Press, January 22, 2003, accessed June 26, 2021, https://www.baptistpress.com/resource-library/news/southern-baptists-transformed-as-u-s-grappled-with-roe-v-wade/.

ics commission, and four seminary professors signed a document for the then-named Religious Coalition for Abortion Rights that affirmed the Roe v. Wade ruling, as well as government funding of abortions for the poor. Shut out at the denominational level, some pro-lifers in the SBC started a non-convention organization, Southern Baptists for Life, to proclaim the sanctity-of-life message. Change at the national level began in 1979 with the election of the first of an ongoing series of SBC presidents who strongly defended biblical inerrancy, as well as the pro-life position.[73]

As leaders in the SBC's Conservative Resurgence began populating trustee boards of Convention entities with more conservative representatives, those trustees eventually began making personnel changes which in turn effectuated the Resurgence as seen in policy decisions and cultural influence. In 1988, trustees of the Christian Life Commission—now known as the Ethics and Religious Liberty Commission—elected Richard Land as president. From that post, the Oxford and Princeton-educated, convictionally pro-life Land provided leadership that has helped Southern Baptists speak in a united and influential manner on behalf of those who cannot speak for themselves. May the Lord raise up ten thousand more articulate and courageous men and women to follow in his legacy—a life for life.

---

73 Strode, "Southern Baptists transformed."

Chapter 10

Christian Leadership in the Public Square

Janice Shaw Crouse
Gilbert L. Crouse, Sr.

Dr. Land's record of accomplishments is broad and deep as well as widely known. The influence of the Southern Baptists' Ethics and Religion Liberty Commission (ERLC) was never more impactful or respected than during Dr. Land's tenure. His books, articles, and other writings reveal a theologian and statesman of stature and significance in the public square as well as within the church and Christian circles.

What is not so well-known is that while he was in D.C., Dr. Land worked in many areas that, while very important with significant ramifications in terms of public policy, were not high-profile involvements. For that work behind the scenes, Richard Land remains a well-known, well-respected leader among the pro-family, religious freedom, anti-trafficking, and pro-life activists and policy leaders. We had the privilege of working with him in pivotal task forces that increased the ERLC's influence among grassroots churches and the public in addition to political and religious leaders.

Dr. Land was remarkable in his ability to work across racial, religious, and political divides in seeking common ground on the social issues. Despite his impressive degrees, he was respectful of diversity and differences of opinion; more importantly, he was respectful, collegial, and friendly with the minority members. Often public figures are willing to lend their names to task forces, but they think they are far too important to do the work of getting to know the other participants and work with them toward the goals of the task force. Richard Land was not only present, but he participated as an equal, and stayed with the process until the end. It was clear that he was not merely giving "lip service" to goals of inclusion and diversity; he was willing to devote the time and commit to the process to see the mission accomplished.

* * *

INTRODUCTION

Within the Christian community, it is not uncommon for people to expect, without proper consideration of the Bible's teaching on gifts, that any exemplary Christian will be a good leader. It may be true that "everyone has an obligation as well as the privilege of leading something."[1] The term "leader" is used to describe a wide variety of people in responsible positions – from committee chairs to the organization's president and from a team captain to owner of the team franchise.[2] Some people use the term to describe certain traits or anyone having an outgoing, take-charge kind of personality. Kouzes and Posner's, *The Leadership Challenge*,[3] described leadership happening when an individual makes a difference, with leadership not being limited by age, one's position, degree of authority, or power. For instance, individuals under thirty years of age typically identify a family member as the most influential person in their life. The second most influential person is typically a coach or teacher and the third a community or religious leader. For individuals over thirty, second place is usually a business leader.[4] Parents have the privilege and responsibility for leading their family; older children end up leading their younger siblings. The smallest task undertaken by a group

---

1 Charles E. Jones, Chief Executive Officer, FirstEnergy Corporation, 2015 – 2020.

2 Jerome Adams and Janice D. Yoder, *Effective Leadership for Women and Men* (New York: Ablex Publishing Company, 1985), pp. 1-35.

3 James M. Kouzes and Barry Z. Posner, "Business Book Summaries," *The Truth about Leadership: The No-Fads, Heart-of-the-Matter Facts You Need to Know* (San Francisco, CA: Jossey-Bass, 2010), accessed August 13, 2021, https://www.ebscohost.com/uploads/corpLearn/pdf/TruthAboutLeadership_BBS.pdf.

4 Kouzes and Posner, *The Truth about Leadership*.

Christian Leadership in the Public Square

requires someone to take leadership. Leadership at the public level, however, has added dimensions and different requirements.

Some people question whether a Christian should aspire to public, political careers or leadership positions in "the public square." The Bible is clear: Christians are instructed in the Holy Scriptures to "go into all the world to preach the gospel;" (Mark 16:15-16)[5] presumably that commandment includes the public square. Still today, there is a wide range of opinions about the complex question of political involvement by Christians. Despite that controversy, there is no question about the link between Christianity and political thought, about the influence of Christianity on America's founding, nor the continuing impact of Christianity on political development in this country. The very purpose of government is to ensure individual freedom including the basic, fundamental freedom of religion. Consequently, Christians have a vested interest – indeed, a responsibility – to participate in national governance and public policy endeavors to ensure that such protections continue.

Some words of caution are in order. Sometimes Christian groups declare a leader they have selected to be "God's choice" even when that the person blatantly is not the right person for a specific time or a unique challenge or when the person obviously lacks the strengths, competencies, and gifts necessary for a particular situation. It is inevitably harmful to assume God's authorship and blessing on a leader just because he or she has been elevated to a certain position of authority or responsibility. Likewise, it is harmful to place the mantle of "Christian" on an individual in leadership (thus leading to unreasonable expectations and inevitable disappointment) when that person has made no profession of faith.

A further caution: There are always *faux-leaders* – those who push their way into leadership merely to be "in charge." William Safire makes a distinction between "being a leader" and the "act of leading." He contends that we should not "confuse getting *in front* with getting *out front*. That's the difference between a principal and a spokesman, between a mover and

---

5   While there may be references to Scripture in this chapter, any actual citations are from the KJV, unless otherwise noted.

a shaker."[6] Taking the lead is to accept the challenge at hand (crisis, problem, or sense of drift) and "meeting it with your solution or your dream." The faux-leaders who lack a larger purpose – those who have no vision beyond getting "in front" and being in charge – are like a child's top which stops spinning but, against all odds, remains delicately balanced. Inevitably, something wreaks havoc on such an unstable equilibrium. By contrast, the true leader – one whose vision, faith, and commitment puts him or her "out front" – is like a spinning top: able to maintain balance even when circumstances transform a stable, solid position into a risky tightrope.

Historically, Aristotle and other classic philosophers centered on the "good" and the "great-souled man" which became the "Great Man" theory. Others focused on the "Crisis Event" theory where leaders were propelled to the front by a crisis. Contemporary definitions are more collegial and emphasize the importance of servant leadership and empowerment as conferred by followers. But the social science study of leadership shows that leaders come in an amazing variety of types and styles. Over the years more than 300 different explanations of leadership have emerged in the literature. Bennis and Namus's study of 90 leaders identified no unique collection of characteristics or qualities that set leaders apart from others.[7] More recently, D. Michael Lindsay interviewed 550 top CEOs and senior officials, including two former U.S. presidents and numerous Fortune 100 leaders and, likewise, found a significant variety of personalities and styles of leadership, though top executives shared specific principles of leadership.[8]

Even charisma – that nebulous quality so often sought in leaders – comes in a variety of forms and sometimes evolves because of position and effectiveness rather than being an innate characteristic. Even so, one factor remains constant – leaders lead. That is, leaders go before to show the way, or they guide and direct the course of action or opinion. Obviously, "show-

---

6 William Safire and Leonard Safir, *Leadership* (New York: Simon and Shuster, 1990), p. 13.

7 Warren Bennis and Burt Namus, *Leaders: The Strategies for Taking Charge* (New York: Harper & Row, Publishers, 1985), 223.

8 D. Michael Lindsay with M.G. Hager, *View from the Top: An Inside Look at How People in Power See and Shape the World* (Hoboken, NJ: John Wiley & Sons, 2014).

ing and guiding" requires an understanding of the objective sought. In other words, one cannot lead without insight. Thus, vision is the *sine qua non* of true leadership. Managers preside over the status quo, but leaders move people and organizations toward a particular goal or mission; they mobilize the people and resources necessary for achieving those objectives.

Visionary leadership moves with direction and purpose while those who are control-oriented seek primarily the gratification of being in charge. Without vision, the merely "in control leader" is unable to comprehend the factors that are critical to the fulfillment of the institution's mission. Further, public institutions thrive or weaken to the degree that the vision of its leaders captures the hearts and minds of the public; to the degree that vision inspires a hope that they will see their deepest, most important needs met; and to the degree that vision challenges them to be involved in a redemptive, life-changing ministry. To paraphrase the biblical truth, "Without vision, the institution perishes."[9] The institution, then, loses its focus just as a fecund, vigorous shrub that is never pruned will, in time, lose its shape and cease to fulfill its proper role in the landscaping scheme of which it was meant to be a part. At worst, without vision's rekindling sense of purpose, vitality wanes, inertia provides what direction there is, and mediocrity and stagnation become the norm.

This chapter seeks to describe how vision enables and empowers leadership in activities and accomplishments that are not only creative, transforming and revitalizing, but also redemptive. We describe that type of leadership through its "voices."

THE FOUR VOICES OF VISIONARY LEADERSHIP

We picture four voices of visionary leadership, which, if properly balanced and harmonized, can translate the *de jure* mission of an institution into its *de facto* mission. These voices are the philosophic, the prophetic, the pragmatic, and the poetic. If visionary leadership were a musical performance,

---

9 Prov 29:18.

the philosophic voice would be the composer who writes, orchestrates, and sometimes directs the music; the prophetic voice would be the soloist whose dramatic talent highlights the music's message at strategic points; the pragmatic voice would be the staging and sound system for optimal acoustics for the performance – those practical elements that enable a quality performance – and the poetic voice would be the descant or counterpoint which enhances and enriches the theme.

Institutions flourish when leadership embodies an appropriate balance among the four visionary elements. An institutional mission is diminished when any of the four elements becomes distorted or overly emphasized, and it falters when leadership relies exclusively on any one element or ignores the importance of appropriate interaction among the elements.

I. Philosophic Voice

The philosophic voice is analogous to the composer/conductor of a musical chorus or orchestra. The philosophic voice shapes, interprets, and articulates the mission. The key word for the philosophic voice is *significance*. That is, the philosophic voice comprehends values and beliefs; it seeks global perspective; it establishes priorities for accomplishing the mission. The philosophic leader sees the overarching concerns of the institution and can discern the unseen forces which will, in time, become apparent as their impact is felt in individual circumstances and decisions. The philosophic voice focuses on ideas and understands their significance in the pursuit of issues of transcendent value. Just as the creation of a symphony requires a composer with the ability to hear the music and understand the capacity of the various instruments to produce all the requisite melodies, harmonies, and dissonances and then a conductor who has the capacity to direct and inspire the players of the orchestra, so Christian institutions need leaders who have the ability, first, to see what the paramount needs are that the institution has the opportunity and obligation to address and, second, to envision the potential for meeting those needs through persons and groups acting individually and cooperatively.

Authenticity in principled, philosophic, or theological leadership is not optional; for a leader to lead he or she must be real – through and through. That does not mean being perfect. At the same time, it is more than not being a phony or merely not being a hypocrite. People want the real thing. They want someone real, consistent, and authentic in Christian leadership. People understand mistakes and failures; they do not expect anyone to be perfect – an automaton. No one is perfect, and a leader who recognizes his or her shortcomings or weaknesses and works to overcome them is a strong leader.[10]

Being philosophic means that the beliefs that anchor the leader are real; the leader is principled and authentic. The Christian community – especially, but, every institution and organization – expects authenticity in its leaders, most especially those in the public eye. Moral authority – standing on principle regardless of the cost – is incredibly persuasive. It can be and often is squandered carelessly; when lost, moral authority is very difficult, if not impossible, to regain.

Billy Graham, famously, is known for his authenticity and the principled living out of his faith; there were no scandals associated with him or his ministry.[11] He is known for his trustworthiness; he was believable and persuasive because he embodied the truths he proclaimed. Graham put into place systems and policies to protect and ensure transparency and accountability. While that is true of hundreds and perhaps thousands of leaders, there are exceptions. The public square is littered with scandals of Christian leaders who have been spectacularly exposed as inauthentic – even frauds – to the worldwide public.

Is it any wonder, then, that for many people, the word, "Christian," is "virtually synonymous with hypocrisy."[12] Reinder Bruinsma, former Pres-

---

10 Andy Stanley, *Next Generation Leader: Five Essentials for Those Who Will Shape the Future* (Colorado Springs, CO: Multnomah Books, 2003), 26.

11 Franklin Graham, "My Father, Billy Graham, avoided scandal by being transparent – and never alone with women," *Think: Opinion, Analysis, Essays*. May 1, 2018, accessed August 13, 2021, https://www.washingtonpost.com/religion/2019/03/01/independent-report-finds-allegations-against-willow-creek-founder-bill-hybels-are-credible/.

12 Reinder Bruinsma, "How to Become an Authentic Christian Leader," Ministry: International Journal for Pastors, July, 2009, accessed August 13, 2021, https://www.ministrymagazine.org/archive/2009/07/how-to-become-an-authen-

ident of the Seventh–Day Adventist Church in the Netherlands, compared untrustworthy leaders to the fake "products one can buy from street smart vendors: expensive watches for very little money." He adds "When things prove to not be genuine, this can be a serious matter."[13]

As "PKs" (preacher's kids) growing up with an inside view of Christian organizations, movements, and institutions, we can attest that sometimes the most pious–appearing leaders are often the stingiest givers, the most difficult board members, the meanest committee heads, the gossipiest neighbors or sometimes the ones most likely to be abusive at home. We cannot count the number of churches, institutions, and organizations that have been torn apart by an affair, dishonesty, greed or an indiscretion between church members, leaders, staff, or members.

As Bruinsma said, the consequences of moral failures in Christian leadership are, indeed, serious. Numerous churches and organizations have failed because of leadership failures. Numerous believers have become apostate because of the hypocrisy of a previously admired leader. It is no exaggeration to say that disillusioned believers litter the landscape after leaders have fallen, and the cause of Christ suffers an inevitable setback.

One of the saddest failed leadership examples in our experience is a man who was much loved by everyone, with multiple gifts and seemingly unlimited potential in leadership. His problem was that he wanted to please others so much that he readily agreed with whoever was presenting ideas to him. Consequently, nobody could predict where he stood at any particular moment on any issue; nor could they count on the decisions that he supposedly made. He could be influenced toward another direction by the next person to visit his office. He was not authentic; he was whatever someone else wanted him to be at any point in time.

The highly–rated classic book on authentic philosophical Christian leadership by Aubrey Malphurs[14] defines "the uniquely Christian leader from the inside out, from godly character and commitment to pure motives

---

tic-christian-leader.

13 Bruinsma, "How to Become an Authentic Christian Leader."

14 Aubrey Malphurs, *Being Leaders: The Nature of Authentic Christian Leadership* (Grand Rapids, MI: Baker Books, September 1, 2003), 244, Kindle.

and a servant attitude. He examines the leaders of the first-century church and then discusses qualities such as credibility, capability, and influence that are essential for successful leadership."[15] These are all qualities of authenticity; regardless of leadership style or type of leadership position, the Christian leader must exhibit authenticity. To put it bluntly, if we are more like Christ, we will be more authentic; more principled. For a Christian leader, Christ-centered authenticity is not optional; it is the key to effectiveness.

One last word on this topic: The philosophic voice – even if authentic and principled – if left to itself, however, will not always have the drive and persistence needed to wrestle a dream into a reality. Often it must have assistance if it is to translate its vision into a workable program. At its worst, it can sometimes be content to have discussed a problem and its solution or to have generated a perfect conceptualization of a great initiative. We have all observed leaders who have clear principles and authentic faith, but are ineffectual, impractical, or inconsistent in actually leading. Thus, the philosophical voice, even when principled and authentic, must be balanced by other voices to prevent its thoughts and its discussion from being a substitute for action.

II. Prophetic Voice

The prophetic voice is driven by a sense of calling. The prophetic voice seeks transformation of the institution in some dimension. The prophetic voice looks to a new future and articulates this vision with passion and conviction. This statement is timeless: "The purpose of leadership is to create a legacy, not a legend." Leadership is about pursuing a sharply defined purpose; it's about staying tightly focused on the institution's mission. It is about leading the organization, not building the leader's reputation. The focused leader builds the organization rather than allowing the organization to become the PR vehicle for the leader's personal enhancement. Obviously, if the organization flourishes, the leader's reputation grows. But

---

15 Malphurs, *Being Leaders*, 244.

the driving force behind the leader's decision–making must be fulfilling the institution's mission; this can often involve saying no to attention-getting initiatives which would compete for resources needed for the institution's main purpose.

Prophetic leaders push the organization or institution forward toward a specific vision. Organizations typically resist change, and any leader frequently hears, "But we've always done it this way." Most people like stability; ironically though, progress requires change and growth, or an organization becomes stagnant. Taking a first step toward change requires courage in leadership if that change is to gain support and become a reality. Successful leadership is always a balancing act, but nothing is more challenging than to balance "playing it safe" versus "taking a risk." Courage, as the wisdom goes, is not the absence of fear, but the courage to overcome the fear to take a risk. Max De Pree put it this way: "An unwillingness to accept risk has swamped more leaders than anything I can think of."[16] Gilbert Murray, who wrote about Athens after the Peloponnesian Wars, declared that ultimately, loss of vitality or disintegration of an organization is "the failure of nerve."[17]

Another dimension of courage is the ability to take command of the schedule and say no to extraneous, non–productive people and meetings. Warren Bennis in his classic *Why Leaders Can't Lead* advised that unless a leader wrestles his or her schedule into submission, he or she will be on an unending, unproductive cycle of meetings, phone calls, correspondence, and routine matters that will trap the leader in routine.[18] Bennis determined that it takes extraordinary courage (and discipline) to take control and prioritize the important factors.[19] As the old saying goes, "Whatever gets our attention, gets us!"

The easiest path is always the one with less risk, but there is much truth in the cliché, "Nothing ventured; nothing gained." President George

---

16 Max De Pree, *Leadership Jazz* (New York: Doubleday, 1992), 144.
17 As quoted in, John W. Gardner, "The Tasks of Leadership," *Leadership Papers/2*, Independent Sector, The Carnegie Corporation, March 1986, 8.
18 Warren Bennis, *Why Leaders Can't Lead: The Unconscious Conspiracy Continues* (San Francisco, CA: Jossey-Bass Publishers, 1989), 14.
19 Ibid., 19.

H. W. Bush was not well served by the policies of speechwriting leadership. Janice was privileged to be a Presidential Speech Writer during his presidency. While the experience of working in the White House with unlimited access to the West Wing and being part of history was incredible, the speechwriters' lack of control over the manuscript made it less than a professionally rewarding job. Every speech went through "clearance" which meant any of the 20–30 people who were on the list to preview speeches could – and did – add, delete, or edit passages.[20] As a result, the first President Bush's speeches lacked unity and flow. Worse, beautiful rhetoric would be interspersed with jarring political declarations or irrelevant statements. The President, having not seen the new insertions previously, stumbled over the incongruities, thus contributing to his reputation for "lack of eloquence." The lack of manuscript control undermined the President's effectiveness and contributed to his perceived "lack of vision."

Courage comes in varieties; there is moral courage and physical courage. One of Janice's favorite stories about her father comes from his years as a student pastor during college. He went back to school on the GI Bill when he was called to preach. Even though he had four children at the time, he instinctively knew that he needed to be prepared for the task to which God had called him. He started college full-time and on campus when Janice was 11 years old and ultimately graduated from Emory University with an MA in Theology the year she graduated from high school. His life was amazingly courageous, but when he served a country church as an undergraduate student in Kentucky, there was a man who loudly claimed he would "shoot any preacher who dared to show up at his door." Charles Shaw took on the challenge, went to see the man and won him to Christ. The scary, threatening man became a new man in Christ and a leading layman in that local church – all because of a courageous student pastor.

Her father's story illustrates an important difference between leadership that focuses merely on the characteristics of leadership and that lead-

---

20 The clearance process was different when Janice was writing speeches and Opinion Articles for Secretary Louis Sullivan at the U.S. Department of Health and Human Services. All input from clearance went to the speechwriter who had the responsibility of incorporating or ignoring the suggestions as he or she deemed best.

ership stemming from the internal power of a leader who is free to move forward courageously because of the power of God in their lives. In their book, *Lead Like Jesus (Revisited),* Ken Blanchard, Phil Hodges, and Phyllis Hendry write, "When a leader chooses to allow Jesus to transform him or her from the inside out, . . . Jesus frees us to reach heights of influence we never would be able to reach on our own."[21]

We must remember, however, that extreme versions of the prophetic voice cannot make accommodation to alternative but equivalent formulations of their vision which may be more feasible. Some may not be open to any correction no matter how benign the intent or how true it is to reality. In his book, *Leadership: Managing in Real Organizations,* Leonard R. Sayles differentiates between rhetoric and reality in leadership with the admonition that a leader's rhetoric must be firmly grounded in reality.[22] Finally, the truly prophetic voice is sometimes counterfeited by the "you can if you think you can" or "we will be who we think we are" type of baseless motivational hype.

III. Pragmatic Voice

The appropriate function for the pragmatic voice is a support and accompaniment role once the mission of the organization has been identified. The managerial function's role vis-à-vis the leadership role is a subordinate one. In other words, management functions support the dominant leadership role. Brave new initiatives are not in its nature. Problems arise when the pragmatic element with its need for order and efficiency does not remain in the service of the mission, i.e., if it usurps and dominates the process of defining and setting priorities.

All too often the practical mindset of the pragmatic voice tends to focus on what cannot be done and why it cannot be done. It frequently lacks

---

21 Ken Blanchard, Phil Hodges, and Phyllis Hendry, *Lead Like Jesus Revisited: Lessons from the Greatest Leadership Role Model of All Time* (Nashville: W Publishing, 2016), xi.

22 Leonard R Sayles, *Leadership: Managing in Real Organizations* (New York: McGraw-Hill Book Company, 1989), 8-13.

the imagination to see beyond the resources that are already in hand. Thus, if given the dominant role in decision-making by virtue of its experience in making the wheels go round, it will concentrate primarily on how to make the wheels go round as smoothly as possible. Madeleine F. Green postulates that we are now in the post managerial era, in which good management is a necessary but not sufficient condition for effective leadership.[23]

Two basic requirements of pragmatic leadership are competence and expertise. For the Christian leader, exercising the gifts of competence and expertise involves a special sensitivity. Dr. Howard Hendricks, known for his exemplary leadership, stressed the importance of a leader's "central focus." That central focus was the place where the leader was most competent, the place where he "adds the most value" (as John Maxwell puts it). A leader who knows his or her greatest competencies and focuses on those is effective and stays on track to succeed.[24] That point is like the popular distinction Peter Drucker makes: "Efficiency is *doing the thing right*, but effectiveness is *doing the right thing*."[25] A leader focuses on doing the right thing!

One of the most competent Christian leaders in the public square is John C. Bowling, who was installed as president of Olivet Nazarene University in 1991 and retired in 2021. In addition to his university responsibilities, Dr. Bowling is very active in his city and on international educational and Church of the Nazarene boards. He has received numerous awards for his public service beyond the university. In the foreword of Bowling's book on leadership, James H. Diehl described four examples from John Bowling's experience leading Olivet. He concluded, "I can follow a leader like that." or "I can listen to a leader like that."[26] The Spring 2021 issue of *Olivet: The*

---

23 Madeleine F. Green, ed. *Leaders for a New Era: Strategies for Higher Education* (New York: American Council on Education – Macmillan Publishing Company, 1988), 13-30.

24 As quoted in Stanley, *Next Generation Leader, 33.*

25 As quoted in De Pree, *Leadership is an Art* (New York: A Dell Paperback, 1989), 19.

26 John C. Bowling, *Grace-full Leadership: Understanding the Heart of a Christian Leader* (Kansas City, MO: Beacon Hill Press, 2011). The Foreword was written by James H. Diehl.

Magazine, highlights "The Bowling Era."[27] The Editorial Board summarized the impact of John and Jill Bowling, showing why people follow and listen to the Bowlings:

> The Bowlings came, they stayed, they served, they built, and they altered the trajectory of Olivet forever. They surrounded themselves with an outstanding leadership team, a gifted faculty, and an effective staff. They insisted the entire campus community stay focused each day on the success of Olivet students and the purposes of Jesus Christ. They taught us how to do things well and with style, sophistication, and an unwavering commitment to quality. They modeled humility and dedication to their craft, and we admired them, we wanted our friends and family to meet them and to hear Dr. John Bowling speak.[28]

Bowling's example points out some of the competency skills that are hard to quantify in leaders. Some of the seemingly nebulous skills of competence are the hardest ones to discern in a candidate. For instance, can the leader analyze complex problems and quickly master new information or cutting-edge technology? Is the person decisive and able to facilitate change and new initiatives while involving and motivating others and building collaborations? Those skills come in varieties of personalities and can better be observed than measured. The same is true of personal competencies, such as self-control, ability, and willingness to seize opportunities, capacity for managing personal life and balancing the professional obligations with family and other responsibilities. Is the potential leader capable of seeing the "big picture" and adapting to changing circumstances? In the book, *Lead Like Jesus*,[29] the authors describe "ego" as "edging God out" and calls ego the biggest addiction of all for leaders. Leaders like John Bowling show what it means to be there to serve others.

---

27 *Olivet: The Magazine*, "The Bowling Era: President John C. Bowling," Spring 2021.
28 Ibid., 1.
29 Blanchard, Hodges, and Hendry, *Lead Like Jesus*, 259.

Competence is also rather complicated. A leader can be competent in one area and incompetent in another. A leader can be effective in one position and incapable in another. Further, competence involves learning from mistakes and continuing to move forward from those mistakes rather than repeatedly making the same ones.

Janice has been privileged to serve on several Presidential Search Committees for universities and non-profit organizations. Three stand out. The first example of a leadership search resulted in the choice of a strong Christian man who was a good public speaker with a charismatic personality. He lasted only a couple of years because he was autocratic in his interactions with subordinates, lacked interpersonal communication skills and knew little about building a team. In short, he didn't have the skill sets necessary for the job. The second search that stands out ended with the choice of a quiet man who initially seemed rather unimpressive. He was, however, thoroughly professional in his interactions, and it was quickly obvious that he knew how to build a team to "get the job done." He quickly took the organization "to the next level." He wasn't obviously a leader, his speaking style was thoughtful and deep rather than dynamic, but he knew how to mobilize people and inspire them for the tasks that needed to be done. Another search that stands out from Janice's experience resulted in rather contentious discussions about the leading candidate. Some feared the man would be dictatorial. Janice's assessment that he was assertive, but consultative prevailed. He was appointed and proved to be a superb leader, taking the organization to international prominence, and building a strong team of leaders dedicated wholly to the mission and goals of the organization.

Competency means understanding the organization or entity the leader is responsible for leading and making it the best it can be. It means representing that organization appropriately and being the "face" of the organization. It does not mean changing the organization into the leader's image. That is, of course, difficult, because the leader must have the vision and strategies for shaping the organization for new challenges and new times, but that must be done within the parameters of the organization's mission and goals. The purpose is to build the organization not to build a monument to the leader's ego or shape the organization in his or her image. John Bowling, President of Olivet Nazarene University, expressed this thought beautifully when accepting an award for Lifetime Achievement. He described effective leaders as "always needing to be looking out toward the horizon." He described his job as being "to facilitate and enable [the organization] to adapt and evolve with the changes of the world without changing its mission and values."[30]

The emphasis here on visionary leadership is not meant to deny an appropriate role to the management function. When effective day-to-day operations are tangible expressions of the central mission of the institution, the pragmatic voice is indispensable and influential. Still the practical, managerial aspects of keeping an institution functional–while necessary and valued–can never substitute for visionary leadership. In his book, *Why Leaders Can't Lead*, Warren Bennis states it well, "Routine work drives out non routine work and smothers to death all creative planning, all fundamental change in the university–or any institution."[31] Keeping the wheels turning in an institution cannot replace the focused, forward thrust necessary for a truly vital institution.

IV. Poetic Voice

The poetic voice understands and appreciates the beauty and power of symbols, images, and ceremony. D. Michael Lindsay, in his book, *Faith in the Halls of Power*, devotes a whole chapter to the role of the artistic in leadership.[32] Various artists and leaders attest to the power of the "imagining process" as the means of being authentic in their leading, writing and worldview. When their leadership is framed as a "calling," artistry becomes transcendent. "This quest for transcendence and creative inspiration draws

---

30 Taylor Leddin, "Lifetime Achievement: John Bowling." Daily Journal, Kankakee, IL. February 6, 2021, accessed August 13, 2021, https://www.daily-journal.com/news/local/lifetime-achievement-john-bowling/article_4b875924-60c6-11eb-bbc8-4f1417951272.html.

31 Bennis, *Why Leaders Can't Lead*, 15.

32 D. Michael Lindsay, *Faith in the Halls of Power: How Evangelicals Joined the American Elite* (Oxford University Press, 2007, Part III), 117-157.

many evangelicals ... to the religious practices and beliefs [that] ground their ambition for greater cultural influence."[33]

The poetic voice creates something from nothing. Poetic leaders inspire and influence feelings through new approaches. They push their vision forward with creativity and thinking outside the box. They are innovative in utilizing ceremony and tradition. The poetic voice sees beauty in the variety of many diverse people's contributions; it can revel in even the minor roles in the accomplishment of the "big picture." Susan Ivey of the Reynolds Tobacco Company compares leadership and power to salt and pepper – we shake on salt to enrich the flavor of food, but just a sprinkle of pepper provides strong and sharp enhancement.[34] I think her comparison is apt in relating to the voices of leadership as we describe them. The "salt" of leadership is the leader's philosophy, prophetic vision, and pragmatic management; the "pepper" is the use of the poetic voice. Obviously, the first three voices are essential to getting the job done while the poetic voice empowers and inspires.

The focus of the poetic voice is the "polishing, liberating and enabling"[35] of the constituency of the institution so that they can produce quality. Peters and Waterman remind us, "We desperately need meaning in our lives and will sacrifice a great deal to institutions that will provide meaning for us."[36] Throughout their classic book on leadership, Peters and Waterman refer to "respectful treatment," "people orientation," "worker motivation," and "value systems." Successful companies, institutions and organizations value their employees, staff, and constituencies and provide recognition and a sense of belonging.

Bottom–line, out–front concerns are still very real, but the leader with poetic insight defines reality in ways that recognize the importance of

---

33 Lindsay, *Faith in the Halls of Power*, 140.

34 Lindsay and Hager, *View from the Top*, 56.

35 Max De Pree, *Leadership is an Art* (East Lansing, MI: Michigan State University Press, 1987), 10.

36 Thomas J. Peters and Robert H. Waterman, Jr., *In Search of Excellence: Lessons from America's Best-Run Companies* (New York: Harper & Row Publishers, 1982), 56.

the shadings and variations in the background of the picture. Just as a good carpenter or woodworker must be able to "see" the end product, just so a good leader must be a good judge of people – the raw material of an organization, company, or institution.[37] It takes a poetic eye to see potential in people and to see the long-term positive results of a project and importance of the steps that it will take to get a desirable end result.

When Gilbert was Vice President for Business and Finance at Taylor University, the institution was approaching an accreditation evaluation, having been warned during several previous evaluations that a new library was essential for accreditation. No previous plan had been approved by the Board, and the university was facing a potential crisis. Gil developed a detailed proposal including potential financial backing and other specifics for a new library and asked the architect to construct a mockup of the proposed new building. During the Board presentation, the new library mockup sat in the middle of the table for all the Trustees to see. The Board of Trustees, seeing both a fully developed proposal and a visualization of the building, voted to begin building immediately and the new library became a reality by the time the accreditation team visited campus. Being able to visualize the actual building and having a feasible plan for its completion were key factors in moving the project forward. The poetic voice can be very powerful to envision, transform, empower, inspire, and equip people for a project or endeavor.

The poetic voice sees the effectiveness of the ceremonial, of stories, and of relationships. On a recent road trip, we listened to the audio version of David S. Reynolds's book, *Abe*.[38] Reynolds notes that other lawyers at the time surpassed Lincoln in knowledge of the law. Lincoln, though, in addition to understanding the law, understood the importance of emotions and stories in persuading people. He was a master storyteller and thus a master at winning cases tried by a jury. Long after Lincoln's death, Alan H. Monroe introduced his Motivated Sequence[39] which pioneered the proposition that

---

37 Blanchard, Hodges, and Hendry, *Lead Like Jesus*, 174.

38 David S. Reynolds, *Abe: Abraham Lincoln in His Times* (New York: Penguin Press, 2020).

39 Monroe's Motivated Sequence, MindTools, accessed August 13, 2021,

listeners are not motivated to act solely through logical arguments (which are necessary to convince but are not enough to motivate), but when emotional appeals in the form of stories and "visualization" are added to logical arguments, people can be motivated to perform the desired action.

The institutional culture, mission, purpose, and values – all those "soft" aspects of its identity –are not typically "transmitted through formal written procedures." Instead, they are "diffused" through stories, myths, legends, and metaphors. In addition, these stories are often found in the annual reports. "Frito-Lay tells service stories. J&J tells quality stories. 3M tells innovation stories." These "socially-integrating myths" provide "uplift and idealism" along with conveying the "aims and methods of the enterprise."[40]

In his book, *View from the Top*, Michael Lindsay interviewed top CEOs and national leaders for an inside look at how people in power "see and shape the world." In telling their stories, he advocates for a creative, innovative, "more substantial" and "nobler" leadership.[41]

Several books focus attention on the poetic dimension of leadership: Max De Pree's *Leadership is An Art*,[42] Rosabeth Moss Kanter's *When Giants Learn to Dance*,[43] and the American Council on Education book, *Leaders for a New Era*, edited by Madeleine F. Green,[44] are examples of approaches to leadership which recognize the significance of people and programs, ceremony, and symbolism. Screenwriter Brian Godawa told Michael Lindsay, "The Bible is 80% story and visual . . . God communicates more through story than he does through propositional truth . . . [we tend to focus on propositional truth and logic] but story changes the world."[45]

---

https://www.mindtools.com/pages/article/MonroeMotivatedSequence.htm.

40 Peters and Waterman, *In Search of Excellence*, 282.
41 Lindsay and Hager, *View from the Top*, 141.
42 Max De Pree, *Leadership is an Art*.
43 Rosabeth Moss Kanter, *When Giants Learn to Dance: Mastering the Challenges of Strategy, Management, and Careers in the 1990s* (New York: Simon and Schuster, 1989).
44 Madeleine Green, *Leaders for a New Era*.
45 Lindsay, *Faith in the Halls of Power*, 148-149.

The danger of poetic vision in the extreme is that it can become empty image. It can focus on creativity until it degenerates to a pursuit of the novel, unconventional and *avant garde*. It can produce movement, change and innovation, without direction and without purpose; in such instances it is ultimately destined to crash.

The Synergy of Combining the Four Voices

When the poetic voice combines with one or all the other elements the result is stronger, more creative leadership. The addition of the philosophic element produces change that is not merely new, but which is also vital and significant. The prophetic dimension in combination with the other elements leads to change that can be transforming and redemptive. Add to the combination of other elements the requisite amount of the pragmatic and the changes will be implemented efficiently and economically. In summary, when all four elements are linked and balanced, the result is significant, redemptive transformation of situations and circumstances. Green explains it this way,

> An examination of the various tasks of leaders reveals that the requirements of leadership today and tomorrow will require not only vision and courage, but much skill in communicating ideas, selling them to various constituencies, catalyzing others to action, and building teams. A leader without constituents or followers has no one to lead. A leader who cannot mobilize the many different constituents toward a common agenda cannot lead.[46]

A few years back a quote that reechoed in the leadership literature was "A good leader is the one who, when the job is done, leaves the people saying, 'look what we have done.'" The loftiness of visions and the clarity of

---

46 Madeleine Green, *Leaders for a New Era*, 11.

mission statements count for nothing if staff members are not motivated by them to diligent involvement. In the final analysis, a leader is not a leader, if no one is persuaded to follow. A leader is as dependent upon the members of the group for implementation as the group is dependent on the leader for direction and motivation.

In one institution or organization after another, examples abound of what happens when leaders lack: a vision which keeps them focused on the institution's highest priorities and its central mission, or the wisdom to prune back activities which do not support the institution's central purpose, or the courage and commitment to say no to violations of the institution's Christian principles and heritage. It is inevitable that competing purposes and priorities will be championed – often by good people with initiative, but without the discernment to differentiate between what is merely good and that which is vitally important. Not only will "bad money drive out good money," but as we have noted, low priority activities will drive out high priority ones. The Christian leader with vision will have to guard the institution's highest priorities from being counterfeited by less urgent ones. If purposes of secondary importance are allowed to proliferate unchecked, the time and energy of the staff will become misdirected. With the resources marshaled to accomplish the institution's mission dissipated, the weakened institution will not realize its potential.

Vision, like common sense, is not very common and hence is a stranger, not often encountered and not easily recognized. Vision is usually better understood in the long-run when it is manifested after–the–fact by the results it produces. It is intriguing that vision which consists, in large measure, in seeing those things that are hidden from the casual gaze, is itself largely hidden from view. In contrast, managerial skills with their immediate and tangible results are more easily recognized and more readily appreciated. For these reasons, perhaps vision will never sell for its true value, will often be counterfeited, or will sometimes be dismissed as impractical and frivolous. But experience has shown us enough examples to prove that balanced visionary leadership can transform an institution, inspire new vigor, and breathe new life into the institutional mission; in short, the influence of a leader with vision can be incalculable.

Janice Shaw Crouse & Gilbert L. Crouse, Sr.

Is A Perfect Leader Possible?

An astute reader will notice that the description of each "voice" ends with a few lines about the weaknesses or danger of that "voice" in the extreme. Further comment is necessary because, bluntly, there are no perfect people, no perfect leaders. All of us are flawed individuals. The Scriptures are clear: "For all have sinned and come short of the glory of God" (Rom 3:23).

Numerous studies have found that leaders share common failures. Jack Zenger and Joseph Folkman identified in the *Harvard Business Review* 10 leadership shortcomings that they found common in their study of 450 Fortune 500 executives, along with 11,000 other leaders.[47] Because such failings are a significant risk for organizations, MITSloan Management Review published an article to help with early detection and provide better support systems.[48] They are especially concerned about the leaders who have a "track record of success" but "suddenly and unexpectedly" have an "abrupt and unpredictable form of leadership failure – which we refer to as leader derailment."[49] Such leaders have "the kind of confidence that can turn to arrogance and the kind of boldness that can lead to impulsiveness."[50]

A lack of accountability is very dangerous for Christian leadership. There are a "sickening number of opportunities" to fall into "moral traps" or to "develop a false sense of power"[51] or invincibility. The Evangelical landscape is littered with the tragedies of derailed leaders whose confidence turned to arrogance and bold defiance of their stated beliefs and calling. Ravi

---

[47] Jack Zenger and Joseph Folkman, "Ten Fatal Flaws that Derail Leaders," *Harvard Business Review,* June 2009, accessed August 13, 2021, https://hbr.org/2009/06/ten-fatal-flaws-that-derail-leaders.

[48] Morela Hernandez, Jasmien Khattab, and Charlotte Hoopes. "Why Good Leaders Fail," *MITSloan Management Review*, April 12, 2021, accessed August 13, 2021, https://sloanreview.mit.edu/article/why-good-leaders-fail/.

[49] Ibid., 1.

[50] Ibid., 4

[51] Austin J. Walker, "The Necessity of Leadership Accountability," *The Startup,* February 17, 2020, accessed August 13, 2021, http://austinjwalker.com/2020/02/17/the-necessity-of-leadership-accountability/.

Zacharias International Ministries (RZIM) stunned the global evangelical movement when they released a 12-page investigative report[52] shortly after the death of their founder, world-famous Christian apologist Ravi Zacharias, confirming earlier allegations that both Ravi and the ministry had previously denied.[53]

The international Hillsong Church, a megachurch based in Australia, was rocked by revelations of the "decadent lifestyles" of ministers – including celebrity pastor in New York City, Carl Lentz. The church is facing $20 million in lawsuits for "damages and immoral acts."[54] The founder and global senior pastor, Brian Houston, has "transitioned into a supporting role"[55] because of the barrage of accusations, lawsuits, and reports of immoral behavior among church leaders.

Before Hillsong, the Evangelical world was shocked by the Willow Creek Community Church Scandal[56] where Senior Pastor Bill Hybels was

---

52 Lynsey M. Barron, Esq. and William P. Eiselstein, Esq., "Report of Independent Investigation into Sexual Misconduct of Ravi Zacharias," Miller and Martin, Inc., February 9, 2021, pp. 1-12, accessed August 13, 2021, https://s3-us-west-2.amazonaws.com/rzimmedia.rzim.org/assets/downloads/Report-of-Investigation.pdf.

53 Daniel Silliman and Kate Shellnutt, "Ravi Zacharias Hid Hundreds of Pictures of Women, Abuse During Massages, and a Rape Allegation," *Christianity Today*, February 11, 2021, accessed August 13, 2021, https://www.christianitytoday.com/news/2021/february/ravi-zacharias-rzim-investigation-sexual-abuse-sexting-rape.html.

54 Hannah Frishberg, "Tithe Money funded Hillsong pastors' luxury lifestyles: former members," *New York Post,* January 26, 2021, accessed August 13, 2021, https://nypost.com/2021/01/26/former-hillsong-members-detail-pastors-lavish-lifestyles/.

55 Ibid., "Hillsong founder, Brian Houston moving into 'support role' amid church scandal," *New York Post*, February 15, 2021, accessed August 13, 2021, https://nypost.com/2021/02/15/hillsong-founder-brian-houston-moving-away-from-current-role/.

56 Emily McFarlan Miller, Religious News Service. "Misconduct allegations against Willow Creek founder Bill Hybels are credible, independent report finds," *The Washington Post,* March 1, 2019, accessed August 13, 2021, https://www.washingtonpost.com/religion/2019/03/01/independent-report-finds-allega-

revealed as having long been involved in sexual harassment and abuse of power; further, those abuse accusations had been known and mishandled by church authorities.[57] And, the most recent headline scandal involves Jerry Falwell, Jr, President of Liberty University, who is being investigated for "possible financial mismanagement at the university" rather than for his and his wife's personal conduct that has been in the media's focus.[58] Those are just the most recent high-profile scandals. Earlier, well-known televangelist Jim Bakker – founder of Praise the Lord (PTL) ministries, a multi-million-dollar empire – was indicted on eight counts of mail fraud, fifteen counts of wire fraud and one count of conspiracy. In plain terms, in 1988, Bakker bilked believers out of millions of dollars in donations and money.[59]

While the above-mentioned leaders are famous and make headlines, relatively unknown derailed Christian leaders also leave behind numerous disillusioned former believers.

Conclusion

The value of Christian leadership in the public square is profound. It is worth protecting. "Values always decay over time. Societies that keep their values alive do so *not* by escaping the processes of decay but by powerful processes of regeneration. There must be perpetual rebuilding. Each generation must rediscover the living elements in its own tradition and adapt

---

tions-against-willow-creek-founder-bill-hybels-are-credible/.

57 Ashley May, "Willow Creek church pastor, board resign amid sexual misconduct investigation of founder," *USA Today*, August 9, 2018, accessed August 13, 2021, https://www.usatoday.com/story/news/nation-now/2018/08/09/willow-creek-pastor-board-resign-bill-hybels-sex-scandal/944310002/.

58 Maggie Severns, "Falwell invites students to 'real Liberty graduation' at his home," *Politico,* 4/30/2021, accessed August 13, 2021, https://www.politico.com/news/2021/04/30/jerry-falwell-liberty-graduation-485112.

59 Lauren Effron, Andrew Paparella, and Jeca Taudte, "The Scandals that brought down the Bakkers, once among US's most famous televangelists," ABC News, December 20, 2019, accessed August 13, 2021, https://abcnews.go.com/US/scandals-brought-bakkers-uss-famous-televangelists/story?id=60389342.

them to the present realities."[60] That, simply, is today's imperative for Christian leaders in the public square. They are charged with the responsibility of affirming our Christian values as well as our national values. "They do so not only in verbal pronouncements but in the policy decisions they make, the kinds of people they surround themselves with and the way they conduct themselves. . . .. Values decay 'out there' – in the marketplace, the law office, the press – and they must be regenerated out there. They must be reflected in actual behavior, embedded in our laws and institutions."[61]

Warren Bennis echoed that same theme: "As a nation cannot survive without virtue, it cannot progress without some common vision, and we haven't had a real sense of purpose, as a people, since the 1960s."[62] While some people might debate Bennis on the particulars, there is no denying the rapid disintegration of American culture and the accompanying decline in church attendance and Christianity's influence in the public square. Amazingly (since the book was published in 1989) Bennis's laments are relevant today. He notes, "There was a time when CEOs were civic leaders and corporate statesmen. Today, they have no interest in anything but their own bottom lines."[63] Of course, now corporations and CEOs are also very political and, typically, are social justice warriors who are quick to pounce on the latest "woke" fad or the newest farfetched environmental, gender, or social trend.

Alexander Solzhenitsyn gave the Commencement Address at Harvard College in 1978. During that address he talked about the limitations of laws, especially the limitations of a society based solely on the "letter of the law." Such cold and formal rules and legalistic relationships, he declared, are not sufficient. They, he believed, "engender spiritual mediocrity" and "paralyze men's noblest impulses." Instead, leadership should "take advantage of the full range of human possibilities" so that there is a "commitment to ideas, to issues, to values, to goals and to the management processes." Such an environment enables work to have meaning and fulfillment.[64]

---

60 Gardner, "The Tasks of Leadership," 8-9.
61 Ibid., 9.
62 Bennis, *Why Leaders Can't Lead*, 41.
63 Ibid., 65.
64 As told in De Pree, *Leadership Is an Art,* 59-60.

Leaders need to create an environment of "shared ideals, shared ideas, shared goals, shared respect, a sense of integrity, a sense of quality, a sense of advocacy and a sense of caring. Such an environment cannot be "generic; it must be explicit."[65]

> Thus, precisely at the time when the trust and credibility of our alleged leaders are at an all-time low and when potential leaders feel most inhibited in exercising their gifts, America most needs leaders – because, of course, as the quality of leaders declines, the quantity of problems escalates. As a person cannot function without a brain, a society cannot function without leaders. And so the decline goes on.[66]

In the world of today, dominated by social media, a leader must be able to transcend the hubbub that is today's public forums. John Gardner reminds us that we need someone to explain what is happening in a world that is changing so rapidly.[67]

D. Michael Lindsay ends his study of evangelicals in the halls of power by writing:

> Evangelical public leaders have brought faith convictions to bear in their respective spheres of influence. History will be the judge of whether this contribution to a more enlightened democracy where engaged citizens use their faith to serve the common good, or whether we have merely witnessed the triumph of another interest group with a distinctive vision for society. What cannot be denied is that these leaders have brought evangelical faith – once confined to the lower ranks of society – into the very halls of power.[68]

The revival preachers of our past often spoke of preferring to "burn out" rather than "rust" as Christians. Likewise, John Mason Brown, Amer-

---

65 De Pree, *Leadership Is an Art*, 90.
66 Bennis, *Why Leaders Can't Lead*, 66.
67 Gardner, "The Tasks of Leadership," 18.
68 Lindsay, *Faith in the Halls of Power*, 230-231.

ican drama critic and author, wrote, "The only true happiness comes from squandering yourselves for a purpose."[69] The truly "called" Christian leader is so consumed by his or her purpose that their happiness comes from pouring everything they have into their high calling for an institutional or organizational mission and its goals.

Pastor Mike Colaw, of the Trinity Wesleyan Church in Indianapolis, IN, spoke about the kind of leader who is most effective – the person people want to follow. He said,

> It's not necessarily the one with all the degrees. It's not necessarily the person who is the most eloquent by nature. We want to follow people who have been truly transformed by the majesty of Jesus Christ to the point that the way they interact with people, the way they view their community, and their transparency about their process is what helps them usher people into the presence of Jesus Christ. That's a person who has truly been transformed by Jesus Christ and you can see it in every aspect of their life.[70]

---

69 "Why Can't Leaders Lead?," accessed August 13, 2021, https://archive.org/stream/whycantleadersle00benn/whycantleadersle00benn_djvu.txt.

70 Mike Colaw, Joanne Solis-Walker, Mike Dwyer, Jo Anne Lyon. "Four Perspectives on Authentic Christian Leadership," The Wesleyan Church, May 2, 2013, accessed August 13, 2021, https://www.youtube.com/watch?v=GmN-WOV5CnE4.

Chapter 11

An Understanding of Evangelical Christian Support for Israel

James Showers
Christopher J. Katulka

A Brief History of Evangelical Support for Israel

We minister with one of the older U. S. Christian-based ministries to the Jewish people, The Friends of Israel Gospel Ministry, Inc. It was founded by a group of evangelical Christians in the city of Philadelphia, Pennsylvania, out of a concern for Jewish refugees who were under the severe persecution of the Nazi Holocaust. As World War II drew to a close, the ministry's focus expanded, and it grew into a worldwide Christian organization, proclaiming biblical truth about Israel and the Messiah, while bringing physical and spiritual comfort to the Jewish people.

In our work with the Jewish community, Jewish people often ask us, "How long have there been Christians who support Israel?" Over the years, we have come to appreciate why they ask. History teaches that Christians, more than any other people group, have persecuted and tortured the Jews for the past two millennia. Almost any Jewish person will tell you the Holocaust was a Christian event.

But the issue goes much deeper than the atrocities of World War II. Christianity has been at the forefront of Jewish persecution for much of the

Church Age. The rise and prominence of Replacement Theology in the second and third centuries turned the church's love and appreciation for the Jewish people into hatred and rejection.[1][2]

Over time, the legal sanction and eventual prominence of Christianity, combined with the church's disdain for the Jewish people and its view that it had superseded Israel, coalesced into anti-Semitism, and led to violence against the Jews in the name of Christ. This legacy of Christian anti-Semitism has taught Jewish people to be extremely cautious, if not fearful, of Christians.

It is no wonder they are often surprised to learn *The Friends of Israel*

---

1 This chapter focuses primarily on evangelical Christianity in America. References to evangelical Christians or evangelicals assume an American context unless otherwise noted. References to Israel indicate the Jewish people individually, the Land of Promise, and the nation (Israel Inside, dir. Wayne Kopping, perf. Tal Ben Shachar, Jerusalem Online U, digital download, 2012, makes the point that the word *Israel* speaks of the Jewish people, the land of covenant promise, the national State of Israel, and all that makes the Jews a unique people in a diverse world). The context indicates whether one, two, or all three definitions apply. Actually, all three make up the larger definition of the word *Israel,* and reference to one or more of the subsets is common throughout the Bible.

Over the past few years, several surveys of evangelical support for Israel have been conducted, including Pew Research in 2013 and Lifeway Research in 2013 and 2017. Each of these surveys revealed consistently similar attitudes regarding evangelical support. Due to the similarity, this paper utilizes the 2017 Lifeway Research survey results (Lifeway Research (2017), *"Evangelical Attitudes Toward Israel: A Representative Survey of 2,002 Americans With Evangelical Beliefs,"* Lifeway Research, accessed March 19, 2021, http://lifewayresearch.com/wp-content/uploads/2017/12/Evangelical-Views-on-Israel.pdf. The respondents were slightly more female (54%) than male (46%) and comprised many denominations with Baptists (32%) the largest, followed by non-Denominational (19%). Two-thirds attends church once a week or more. There was a fair representation between age cohorts, although the 18-34 (20%) were the smallest and the 50-64 (33%) was largest. Spread across four U. S. regions, the South (54%) had the greatest participation, followed by Midwest (20%), West (16%) and East (10%)) unless specifically stated otherwise.

2 Ronald E. Diprose, *Israel and the Church* (Rome, Italy: Evangelical Biblical Institute of Italy, 2000), 69-71.

An Understanding of Evangelical Christian Support for Israel

Gospel Ministry began in 1938, ten years before the modern State of Israel came into existence; and yet, from its inception, the words *The Friends of Israel* have been a part of our ministry name. Therefore Jewish people also ask us, "You mean before there was a modern State of Israel, there were friends of Israel?"

Despite the prominent view held by many Christians that the church has taken Israel's place in God's promises, evangelical Christians have long felt an affinity for Israel. This affinity is not a recent phenomenon, nor did it begin in 1938. The apostles and early church fathers looked favorably on Israel, as seen in the New Testament. This outlook is also evident in more modern church history, dating to the Reformation.

A turning point in church history came during the Reformation, with the invention of the printing press, which published translations of the Bible in the common man's language at an affordable cost, putting the Word of God into the hands of the masses. No longer did they have to rely on what the church leaders taught them about God and the Bible. In fact, they learned to read and write using the Bible as a textbook.

For the first time, ordinary people could read and study the Scriptures. The open study of God's Word in the 16th and 17th centuries led many European Christians to reject the teachings of the Roman Catholic Church and define their faith based on a literal reading of the biblical text. Through their study, many came to see a future for the Jewish people, clearly defined and taught within the Word of God.

Former Israeli Ambassador Michael Oren's insightful, historical work, *Power, Faith, and Fantasy: America in the Middle East: 1776 to the Present*, masterfully shows that the connection between America and the Middle East is part of our historical, religious, and cultural fabric, dating back to the founding of our great nation. Many early settlers seeking religious freedom in the New World saw parallels between the Israelites fleeing the bondage of Egypt and their flight from the bondage of Europe. The Atlantic Ocean voyage was their "wilderness wandering," and America was their promised land.[3]

---

3 Michael B. Oren, *Power, Faith, and Fantasy: America in the Middle East: 1776 to the Present* (New York, NY: W.W. Norton & Company, 2007), 83-85.

The Great Awakenings that swept across the country in the 18th and 19th centuries sparked the evangelical church in America. The word *evangelical* identifies the church as an entity that shares or takes the Good News of the gospel to a lost and dying world, and it emphasizes the duty of believers to share this great message of hope in Christ with anyone who will listen.

The Second Awakening in America, which began at the beginning of the 19th century, raised up missionaries with a vision to take the gospel to the world, particularly to the Middle East. There was a growing heart and burden for both Arabs and Jews to come to faith in the Messiah, Jesus Christ. Many thought this missionary movement would lead to the restoration of a Jewish nation that would be ready for the Second Coming of Christ. This concept came to be known as Restorationism, and it was profoundly influential in churches.

However, life in the 19th-century Middle East was difficult and took its toll on many missionaries who ventured there. Disease and death overcame some, while disillusion and discouragement chased others back home. The culture, the land, and the people were so much different from the world the Americans knew.[4] Despite the failures of many of these missionaries, the concept of Restorationism—of a restored Jewish nation according to Scripture—remained in the consciousness of many believers in America.

Restorationism is, perhaps, the reason Charles Nelson Darby's Dispensational[5] teaching was so well received and embraced when he came to America in the mid-19th century. Although many factors brought about

---

4 Oren, *Power, Faith, and Fantasy,* 86–97.

5 Dispensationalism is a theological system that employs a literal, historical, and grammatical hermeneutic to interpret Scripture. Dispensationalism rejects the spiritualizing or allegorizing of Scripture, particularly biblical prophecy, unless it is supported by the context of a passage. Dispensationalism holds to a future, literal, 1,000-year restored Millennial Kingdom of God on earth following the return of Christ, and thus is premillennial. Charles Nelson Darby was a famous Plymouth Brethren orator and theologian from England; and though not the father of Dispensationalism, he was extremely influential in teaching it in churches and schools in Europe and North America in the 1860s and 1870s.

Israel's rebirth, Dispensationalism played an important role in the process. Darby's dispensational teaching made a significant impact on the church in America and won a number of converts. Dispensationalists became advocates for Zionism—the Jewish people's return to the Land of Promise to become a sovereign nation again—just as God had promised through the prophets.

Is it any wonder the Zionist movement of the 19th century began first in the evangelical church before it took hold in the Jewish community?[6] Perhaps the most famous Christian Zionist, although not the first, was William E. Blackstone, born in 1841. He was a very successful Chicago businessman turned evangelist. Blackstone, an evangelical Christian from age 11, committed his life to preaching and writing about the premillennial restoration of Israel and the Rapture of the church. He authored *Jesus Is Coming*, a popular dispensational book that deals with the return of Christ.

In 1888 Blackstone visited the Holy Land with his daughter at a time when Jewish people in Russia were suffering greatly under the pogroms.[7] His visit left him convinced that the only possible answer to ending the severe persecution of the Jewish people was their return to the Promised Land where they could defend themselves.[8]

Upon his return to the United States, Blackstone organized and held the pro-Zionist Conference on the Past, Present and Future of Israel at the First Methodist Episcopal Church in Chicago in November 1890. This was seven years before Theodor Herzl would hold the first World Zionist Congress in Basel, Switzerland. Blackstone's conference, attended by both

---

6 Thomas D. Ice, "Christian Zionism," Article Archives. Paper 30. (2009): 4, accessed November 10, 2015, http://digitalcommons.liberty.edu/pretrib_arch/30.

7 *Pogrom* is a Slavic term used to describe the 19th- and 20th-century violent riots aimed at the massacre or expulsion of Jewish people in Russia. The pogroms led to the deaths of thousands and made many more thousands homeless. The term has come to be used universally of riots that primarily target Jewish people, but it also can include other ethnic groups. "Pogrom," *Wikipedia*, accessed March 10, 2021, https://en.wikipedia.org/wiki/Pogrom.

8 David B. Green, "This Day in Jewish History an American Cleric Presents His Own 'Balfour Declaration,'" *Haaretz*, March 5, 2014, accessed September 14, 2015, http://www.haaretz.com/news/features/this-day-in-jewish-history/.

Jewish and evangelical Christian leaders, called for the world powers to return the land of Israel to the Jewish people.[9]

In 1891, Blackstone began a petition supporting the call to return the Holy Land to the Jews. It came to be called the Blackstone Memorial. Four hundred thirty-one prominent American-Christian and Jewish leaders signed the petition, including John D. Rockefeller, J. P. Morgan, Cyrus McCormick, senators, congressmen, the chief justice of the United States, leaders of all major denominations, university and seminary presidents, and editors of major newspapers—including *The Boston Globe, New York Times, Chicago Tribune, Washington Post, Philadelphia Inquirer,* and many others. Calling on America to support the Jewish restoration to Israel, Blackstone presented the Memorial petition to U. S. President Benjamin Harrison in March 1891.[10]

In 1916, at the behest of Supreme Court Justice Louis D. Brandeis, Blackstone updated his Memorial petition, which carried the endorsement of the Presbyterian Church, and presented it to U.S. President Woodrow Wilson. The petition was influential in gaining the president's support for Zionism and, in time, America's support for the Balfour Declaration in 1917.[11]

The popularity of prophecy conferences in the late 19th and early 20th centuries fueled the Zionist support of evangelical Christians, as they learned of the significant role Israel plays in God's future plans to complete His redemptive program. Jewish mission organizations, such as the Cleveland Hebrew Mission, American Board of Missions to the Jews, American Messianic Fellowship, and The Friends of Israel Relief Society (later renamed The Friends of Israel Gospel Ministry) began to minister to the Jewish people. Many were instrumental in helping the disenfranchised children of Jacob flee the clutches of Adolf Hitler.

Following World War II, evangelical Christians threw their support behind the formation of the modern State of Israel. President Harry Truman, a Southern Baptist who knew the Bible, spoke favorably of the Jewish nation being reborn and was quick to recognize Israel shortly after David Ben-Gurion declared its independence on May 14, 1948.

---

9 Green, "This Day in Jewish History."
10 Ibid.
11 Ibid.

An Understanding of Evangelical Christian Support for Israel

Sensing he was president of the United States "for such a time as this," and knowing his State Department opposed the formation of a Jewish nation, Truman moved quickly when news of Israel's proclamation arrived at the White House on the evening of May 14. Truman immediately composed a statement and released it to the public before the U.S. State Department could intervene.[12] America officially recognized Israel eleven minutes after Israel declared independence. Everything was done so quickly that Truman's handwritten edits became part of the released statement. U.S. recognition of the newly formed Jewish state was vitally important to Israel's legitimacy, as other key nations soon followed Truman's lead and issued their recognitions as well.

Evangelical Christian support for Israel continues to this day and is expressed by many who feel a responsibility to act on Israel's behalf. David Brog, former chief of staff for then Pennsylvania Senator Arlen Spector, once said that when important issues related to Israel arose, the senator's office would receive ten phone calls from Christians in support of Israel for every call from a Jewish constituent. David Brog went on to direct Christians United for Israel (CUFI), the largest pro-Israel group in the United States educating and directing Christians to speak in support of Israel. Founded by John Hagee in 2006, it has grown to 10 million members.[13]

Why is it that evangelical Christians, more than any other group both within and outside the church, are highly supportive of Israel? The answer is part theological, part political, and part experiential. To say it another way, the evangelical foundation of support for Israel is varied.

---

12 President Truman had very little support from his cabinet on the U.S. recognition of Israel. In the days following the passage of UN Resolution 181 in November 1947, which called for the partition of Palestine into one Jewish and one Arab state, Truman's advisors opposed any formal recognition of Israel when it declared independence. They believed Israel would be steamrolled by the much larger and better equipped Arab armies that surrounded Israel. Fearing her elimination hours after declaring independence, they reasoned the United States would have blood on its hands if it validated the new state by formal recognition.

13 Christians United for Israel, accessed, June 10, 2021, https://cufi.org/about/mission/.

James Showers & Christopher J. Katulka

FOUNDATIONS OF EVANGELICAL SUPPORT FOR ISRAEL

A Heartfelt Affinity for Israel

Experientially, evangelical affection for the Jewish people emanates from an appreciation for what the Jewish people have done to bless Christians and all the families of the world (Gen 12:3b).[14] Not only did God raise up Israel to record His written Word and preserve it with extreme accuracy, but He also used the Jewish people to bear the promised Redeemer of the world. It is that special encounter with a Jewish Savior that makes every believer eternally indebted to the Jewish people. Without Israel, there would be no Bible and no Savior.

Bible-believing evangelicals will always have a difficult time escaping the Jewishness of Scripture. A natural affinity for Israel and the Jewish people occurs by simple osmosis of the text. Time and time again, passages in the Old and New Testaments remind readers that God chose Israel from among the nations (Dt 7:6; Rom 9:4-5), loves Israel (Dt 10:15; Zech 2:8; Rom 11:28), protects Israel (Ps 121:4), and has a divine plan for Israel (Gen 12:1-3; Rom 11:12, 15).

Heartfelt fondness for Israel arises from a spirit of gratitude and indebtedness that God would raise up the Jewish people to inculcate the world with the message of God's plan of redemption through His Son, Jesus Christ—the Jewish Messiah. In addition, God's faithfulness is manifested by the very fact that the Jewish people still exist despite centuries of severe persecution and that Israel as a nation has been reborn, as the prophets promised.

Furthermore, God used Jewish people to pen the Bible. In a span of 1,600 years, God used forty divinely inspired Jewish men from all walks of life to produce the canon of Scripture. From Moses in the Torah to John in Revelation, a common thread seamlessly connects the two Testaments. Israel's Messiah and the Messianic Kingdom promised in the Old Testament

---

14 While there may be references to Scripture in this chapter, any actual citations are from the NKJV, unless otherwise noted.

become tangible in the New Testament in the person of Jesus Christ. God wove everything together with the common thread of His covenant with Abraham and Abraham's descendants through Isaac and Jacob.

Heartfelt evangelical affinity for Israel also emanates from the fact that Jesus was Jewish. This simple fact is often neglected. The genealogies in Matthew and Luke both trace Jesus' lineage through Abraham, Isaac, Jacob, David, and Joseph, qualifying Him as the Messianic heir. As Luke wrote, when the census was taken, Joseph went to Bethlehem because "he was of the house and lineage of David" (Luke 2:4). In addition, Jesus was circumcised eight days after He was born (v. 21) to fulfill the rite that was the sign of the Abrahamic Covenant (Gen 17), signifying that Jesus was religiously considered a Jew. Under the provisions of the Abrahamic Covenant, He was part of the community of Israel.

Jesus did not revolt against Judaism. He embraced His Jewish heritage, an acceptance that can be seen in the way He celebrated Jewish festivals, taught in synagogues, honored Jewish rituals, and valued the Law of God. He embraced His Jewishness, but He was extremely critical of the way Judaism was practiced in His society, especially by the religious leaders.

The people to whom Jesus ministered recognized Him as a teacher of the Law, a "rabbi," and a prophet from God (Matt 21:10–11; Mark 8:28; 9:5; John 3:2). Religiously speaking, Jesus was a Jew because He lived in obedience to Scripture—based on faith in God. His sole purpose in life was to do God's will (Matt 26:39). He interpreted the Law according to God's intention, which was based on God's covenantal love for the Israelites. In contrast, the Pharisees, being far from God in their hearts, twisted the Law to establish their own righteousness. Jesus wanted the Jews to live in obedience to God from a pure heart, as Deuteronomy 6 teaches (cf. Mark 12:28–34). In this respect, Jesus was in line with ideal Judaism.

Evangelical affinity for Israel and the Jewish people is also wrapped up in Christ's sacrifice, which is grounded in the system of substitutionary atonement that originates in the Mosaic Law. Evangelicals who read the Scriptures plainly are fully aware of the linkage that exists between the blood of bulls and goats that was spilled continually for Israel's sins in the past and the blood of Christ that was poured out once for all to cleanse them of their sins for eternity.[15]

Because of this connection, Jesus Himself interpreted all the prophetic promises as being fulfilled in Him. Jesus was God's beloved Son (Matt 11:25–27; John 5:31–47; cf. Ps 2:7; 89:19–29; Isa 42:1); the prophesied Messiah (Matt 22:44; Luke 4:18; cf. Ps 110:1; Isa 61:1–2); the Son of Man (Mark 2:10; 14:62; cf. Dan 7:13); the Suffering Servant (Luke 22:37; Mark 10:45; cf. Isa 53:10–12); and, ultimately, Lord (Mark 2:28). Jesus' unique interpretation of the Old Testament was based on His authority, given to Him by God the Father. His assumption of this authority ultimately led the religious leaders to challenge His ministry.

Finally, evangelicals empathize with Israel because of the land itself. Israel is more than a random geographical location. It is the one place on the face of the earth that was purposefully chosen by God as the center of the world, where redemption's story would be told for all to hear (Ezek 5:5). The land plays a critical role in God's plan for the ages. It is inextricably tied to the promise God made to Abraham that, through him, all the families of the earth would find blessing (Gen 12:1–3). When the Israelites dwelt in the land, their presence was associated with God's hand of blessing on them (Dt 28:1-14). By the same token, their exile from the land was associated with His divine judgment (vv. 15–68). The tension of spiritual obedience and disobedience, of dwelling and exile, drives Israel's biblical-historical narrative; and the land is at the center of it all.

In the New Testament, Jesus mourned over Jerusalem: "If you, even you, had only known on this day what would bring you peace—but now it is hidden from your eyes" (Luke 19:42). He mourned over the peace the Jewish people neglected. This peace encapsulates all the promises of God that include salvation, deliverance, restoration in the land of Israel, and establishment of God's Kingdom on Earth as the prophets promised.

When the apostle Paul noted in his letter to the Romans the role Israel plays in future redemption, he quoted Isa 59:20-21: "The Deliverer will come out of Zion; he will remove ungodliness from Jacob. And this is my

---

15 See especially Hebrews 9 – 10.

covenant with them when I take away their sins" (Rom 11:26-27). The physical location of Zion, also known as Jerusalem, still matters in Paul's eschatological framework. Christ will return to the Mount of Olives (Zech 14:1-4; Acts 1:9-12).

Evangelicals see that God has protected, preserved, and restored His ancient people to their Promised Land. No people group in world history other than the Jews have been expelled from their land, scattered throughout the nations, and returned home 2,000 years later to become a major player in the global community. Today, pilgrims travel to Israel from around the world to walk in Jesus' footsteps or traverse the paths of the patriarchs. Sites in the Bible that seem almost mythical become real in Israel. Nearly 4.5 million tourists visited the Jewish state in 2019 alone. And it's no wonder. The heartfelt affinity for Israel deepens as Scripture comes to life, and God's faithfulness is tangibly seen in the people and land of Israel.

Evangelicals believe God's promise to Abraham that He will bless those who bless the Jewish people (Gen 12:3) and curse him who curses them. The Abrahamic Covenant informs us all how God wants people to treat Israel. When presented with a choice between being blessed or cursed, evangelicals choose blessing. Jesus promised that when He returns, He will judge the nations for the way they treated His family—His Jewish brethren (Matt 25:31-46).

DEFINING ISRAEL – READING THE BIBLE WITH A LITERAL EYE

The Biblical Case for Israel

Historically, evangelical theology has been framed by reading the Word of God with a literal, grammatical, historical hermeneutic. A literal reading of Scripture in the 16th and 17th centuries revolutionized the church and fueled the fires of the Reformation as people began to question the Church's teaching after comparing it to God's Word.

One of the things they discovered was that the Bible teaches God is not yet finished with Israel. In fact, God never says He has rejected or replaced Israel or made the Church the recipient of His covenant promises to Israel. In taking the words of the Bible in a literal fashion, people discovered passages that spoke of Israel playing a vital role in the restoration of God's Kingdom on Earth with Messiah ruling from Jerusalem.

They learned that, when the Bible is read with a literal eye, it is evident God has a plan to restore the Jewish people to their Promised Land and bring Israel to faith in His Son, the Messiah. God has made important promises to Israel that are yet to be fulfilled. By simply taking Scripture for what it says, evangelicals could see the key role Israel plays in God's redemptive plan.

Reading with a literal eye, Israel easily is understood to mean the physical descendants of Abraham, Isaac, and Jacob, rather than the Church—as Replacement Theology teaches. For example, when the apostle Paul asked, "Has God cast away His people?" (Rom 11:1), the context argues that Paul had the Jewish people in mind as "His people" and not the Church. Not only do the two previous chapters of Romans deal with Israel's past and present, but immediately following his question in verse 1, Paul identified himself as an Israelite—a physical descendant of Abraham, from the tribe of Benjamin. Paul's reply to the possibility that God rejected the Jewish people was emphatic: "Certainly not!" He removed all doubt by adding, "God has not cast away His people whom He foreknew" (v. 2). What could he possibly have said to make God's stance any plainer?

Those who believe God has rejected Israel because the Jewish people rejected Christ at His first advent see the Church as the ultimate fulfillment of God's redemptive plan. But a literal eye cannot find a single verse in Scripture where God says He has cast away or rejected Israel. Nor are there verses that teach God will use the Church to heal this world of sin and its curse. The church's mission is to make disciples (Matt 28:19) and bring citizens into God's Kingdom through faith in Jesus Christ. It is not the church's mission to restore the Kingdom. That mission awaits the return of the only one capable of accomplishing the task – Jesus Christ.

Important promises in the Bible flow through Israel, with whom God made covenants. From the time God cut a covenant with Abraham in

An Understanding of Evangelical Christian Support for Israel

Genesis 12, He revealed His plan to bless the entire world with the gospel through a descendent of Abraham: "In you, all the families of the world will be blessed" (v. 3; 22:18). Paul reaffirmed that God, foreseeing He would justify Gentiles by faith, preached the gospel to Abraham when He said, "In you all the nations shall be blessed" (Gal 3:8). This statement aligns with Paul's declaration that the covenants and promises belong to Israel (Rom 9:4). In Romans 11, Paul taught that Gentiles, pictured as wild olive branches, are grafted into the olive tree that is rooted in God's covenant promises to Israel.

In the covenant God made with Abraham, God had in view the period of time that has come to be known as the Church Age, when salvation through His Jewish Son would be shared with the world. But God never said the church would replace Israel in His redemptive plan. In fact, without the covenant promises God made to Abraham, God's written Word never would have been revealed to mankind, the Messiah never would have been born, and Gentiles never would have received the gospel.

In God's wisdom, grace, and mercy, He chose to share His salvation with the whole world at Israel's expense. Paul made the point that God has chosen not to remove Jewish blindness to the gospel until His program with the Gentiles is fulfilled. This fact does not mean God has rejected Israel. Rather, it means God is working His plan to share the gospel with the world. And part of His plan is to restore Israel eventually to the place of blessing because the promises of God are irrevocable (Rom 11:29).

Nothing speaks of God casting Israel away but, rather, of folding Gentiles into the spiritual promise given to Israel of salvation through the Jewish Messiah. Even the removal of the natural branches in Romans 11 is for a limited time so that the wild branches (Gentiles) can be grafted in. Paul said the natural branches will someday be grafted back into the tree (v. 24). Drawing from the Psalms and the prophet Isaiah, Paul said a day is coming when "All Israel will be saved" (v. 26).

Paul's point is that God has done something unnatural by grafting wild branches into a natural olive tree so that Gentiles can participate in the same spiritual blessings that are available to Israel through faith in the Messiah. This was always God's plan before the beginning of time. Taken literally, the Bible defines the church as separate and distinct from Israel but related to Israel through the spiritual promises God made to Israel.

A literal understanding of Scripture teaches salvation came to us through the Jews, not the Gentiles. Jesus declared, "Salvation is of the Jews" (John 4:22). Gentiles cannot replace Israel because God has not replaced Israel. This fact speaks to the essence of why Israel exists: she is uniquely raised up to be God's instrument through whom He will redeem the world from the curse of sin.

Imposing anything less than a literal understanding on these and so many other key passages concerning Israel is to force one's viewpoint onto Scripture, rather than to let the Bible speak for itself. It is intellectually alluring to be creative and spiritualize key passages through allegorical interpretation. But unless the context argues for allegory, anything other than a literal interpretation renders a meaning that is contrary to what God is saying.

Spiritualizing Scripture, the idea that there is a higher spiritual meaning to God's Word than the literal meaning, was brought into the church by those who rejected Israel and argued that God had done likewise. In the early days of the church, Christianity was an illegal religion in the Roman Empire; and it faced severe persecution. Even though the book of Acts reveals that large numbers of Jewish people initially accepted the gospel, most Jewish people rejected it. This situation threatened the church's viability during its early days. The church responded by reasoning it was a sect of Judaism, a religion that was legal in the Roman Empire. But the Jewish leaders did not support this assertion; and the Romans rejected the church's claim, bringing a great deal of Roman persecution against the church.

The Jewish community's lack of support for Christians and its mass rejection of the gospel led to resentment on the part of church leaders in the early centuries. That resentment grew into hatred. In time, these leaders argued that God had rejected Israel, and so should Christians. However, reading with a literal eye shows the Bible teaches otherwise. The apostles all believed in a future for Israel, as is evident in their epistles and their question to the resurrected Christ: "Lord, will You at this time restore the kingdom to Israel?" (Acts 1:6). Allegory provided a way to reinterpret God's literal promises to restore and bless Israel into God's rejection of Israel. It laid the foundation for replacing Israel with the church. In time, the church came to be viewed as true or spiritual Israel. Unfortunately, allegory also led to bad theology that produced hatred and physical violence by the church against the Jewish people over the past two millennia.

Reading the Bible with a literal eye leads to the undeniable conclusion that God still loves Israel, has not rejected Israel, and has future plans for Israel. In fact, His redemptive plan flows directly through Israel. It is the repentance of the Jewish people and acceptance of their Messiah that will initiate Jesus Christ's return (Zech 12:10–14; 14:1-5; Acts 3:19-21).

Not surprisingly, the Bible has the greatest influence on evangelical beliefs about Israel because evangelicals generally read the Bible with a literal eye. A measure of the Bible's importance to evangelicals is seen when they were asked what influenced their view of Israel the most, the Bible (45 percent) was three times greater than the second choice, the media (15 percent).[16]

God Gave the Promised Land to Israel

The promise of land that God made to Israel, as recorded in the Bible, is never-ending. The promise lasts forever and cannot be withdrawn, canceled, or transferred to anyone else (Gen 17:2, 7–8; Ps 105:7–12). God's land promise was given to all the Jewish people and not merely to the remnant of Israel—the true believers among Israel who walk by faith. Nor was the promise for a "spiritual" land, as some argue. It was for physical real estate on earth that God chose with clearly identifiable borders (Gen 13:14-17; 15:18). Sixty-three percent of evangelicals believe the Bible says God gave the land of Israel to the Jewish people.[17]

Evangelical support for Israel's right to the Promise Land emanates from the Land Covenant God made with Israel. Although God warned the Jewish people that their privilege of living in and enjoying the land was contingent on obedience to His commands (Dt 28 – 30), He never revoked Israel's everlasting right to that particular piece of real estate in the Middle East. Through the prophets, God told the people of Israel they would one

---

16 Lifeway Research (2017), 9.
17 Ibid., 17.

day return to the Promised Land from the four corners of the earth where He had scattered them (Dt 30:3; Isa 11:12; 43:5; Jer 29:14; 31:8-10).

Replacement Theology teaches that the church took Israel's place in the promises God made to Israel—but that Israel keeps the curses. There are several basic problems with this view. Nowhere in Scripture does God say His covenants can be split and the promises transferred to another. Nor is there any passage that says the church replaced Israel in God's covenants. This cherry-picking takes the best parts of the covenants (the promises) and leaves the worst parts (the curses) for Israel. If it were possible for the church to appropriate Israel's promises, then it would also have to appropriate the curses.

This belief that the church replaced Israel led theologians to redefine *Israel* from meaning the physical descendants of Abraham, Isaac, and Jacob to meaning spiritual descendants only. The church came to be viewed as the covenant community. However, this understanding pushes the beginning of the church from Acts 2 back to Genesis 12 and the Abrahamic Covenant. It confuses the clear distinction the Bible makes between Israel and the church. The word *Israel* in Scripture now becomes defined as the true believers in God. However, this interpretation renders many passages incomprehensible because one cannot make sense of many references to *Israel* unless the word refers to the physical descendants of Abraham, Isaac, and Jacob.

Once the church was seen as Israel, then it was believed the Law still applied to the church. The church came to define obedience to the Law as simply keeping the Decalogue, the Ten Commandments. Redefining Israel also led the church to believe priests were still necessary to intercede between man and God, making the church the dispenser of grace and elevating the two ordinances of baptism and communion into sacraments of grace.[18]

It took the Reformation to correct some of this bad theology. However, the reformers brought the basic tenets of Replacement Theology, the belief that the church superseded Israel, with them into the reformed churches. To this day, many mainline denominations hold to Replacement Theology and fail to see any biblical support for the modern State of Israel

---

18 Diprose, *Israel and the Church*, 169-71.

An Understanding of Evangelical Christian Support for Israel

Israel is the Historic Homeland of the Jewish People

Empires, nations, and peoples have disputed the Jewish people's legitimate claim to the land of Israel. In May 2021, the Jewish state again was under attack as Hamas terrorists in Gaza launched more than 4,300 rockets into the country.[19] Hamas was emboldened by its mission to cleanse the land of Jews and reclaim what it believes rightfully belongs to the Arabs. But on what basis do Arabs make such a claim? Historically, Israel is Jewish land.

The international 1920 San Remo Conference was convened following World War I to determine how to divide the conquered Ottoman Empire. The conference Mandate Resolution formally recognized the Jewish right to the Promised Land under international law and incorporated the Balfour Declaration into the British mandate for Palestine.[20]

Israelis trace their ownership of Israel to the biblical promise God made some 4,000 years ago. Arabs, on the other hand, argue their descendants owned the land before Israel declared its independence in 1948. Consequently, legal ownership can only be determined through a historical record, one that predates both Jewish and Arab occupation of the Holy Land.

The only such record that exists is the Word of God. In 1947 a Bedouin boy in the Judean desert stumbled on a pre-Christian, 2,000-year-old Hebrew Bible now known as the Dead Sea Scrolls. The timing of this discovery was divine and providential. That year, the United Nations voted on Resolution 181, a partition plan permitting the Jewish people to establish a state in their ancestral homeland. The discovery of the Dead Sea Scrolls was like uncovering the unimpeachable, ancient deed connecting the Jewish people to their land.

---

19 Sebastein Roblin. "How Hamas' Arsenal Shaped the Gaza War of May 2021," *Forbes.com*, Forbes, 25 May 2021, accessed August 4, 2021, https://www.forbes.com/sites/sebastienroblin/2021/05/25/how-hamass-arsenal-shaped-the-gaza-war-of-may-2021/?sh=6df09ab379df.

20 "Pre-State Israel: San Remo Conference," accessed March 10, 2021, https://www.jewishvirtuallibrary.org/the-san-remo-conference.

The truth is, neither Israel nor the Palestinians originally owned the land. It is God who owns it, as well as the whole earth. It is His name etched on the title deed (Ex 9:29; 19:5; Lev 25:23; Ps 24:1). God in His kindness and wisdom chose the nation that would receive the right to His land; and He bestowed that right on Israel (Dt 7:6–7).

Two biblical pacts detail in legal terms Israel's entitlement to the land: the Abrahamic Covenant and the Land Covenant. These agreements delineate Israel's boundaries and mark out the specific portions God set aside for His people Israel. The size of the land grant was determined "according to the number of the children of Israel" (32:8). God's decision to give the Jewish people the land on which the State of Israel rests today was made millennia ago in His promise to Abraham.

In the Abrahamic Covenant, God gave the land of Canaan to Abraham and his son Isaac (Gen 17:19–21) and to Isaac's son Jacob (26:3; 28:13) and his descendants (Ps 105:7–11) as an eternal possession in perpetuity (Gen 12:7; 13:15; 17:8). Canaan is legitimately and legally owned by Israel today. The covenant is unconditional, which means its viability rests exclusively in God's faithfulness to fulfill it. No responsibility rests with Israel. As the writer of Hebrews puts it, "For when God made a promise to Abraham, because He could swear by no one greater, He swore by Himself" (6:13).

The thrust of the Abrahamic Covenant (a promise of land, descendants, and blessing) continues through the Torah and was confirmed in what is known as the Land Covenant, also made with the nation of Israel (Dt 28-30). Through Moses, God stipulated the spiritual standards Israel was required to maintain to be blessed in the land. However, He warned that Israel's rebellion would lead to the nation's exile and dispersion. Yet, because of God's unconditional promise to Abraham, Isaac, and Jacob, the covenant also provided for restoration to the land through repentance. Interestingly, Jeremiah's prophetic vision of a New Covenant is related specifically to Israel's covenant unfaithfulness and God's desire to establish a New Covenant that would protect the nation from perpetual dispersion and destruction (Jer 31:31-40).

The unconditional nature of the Abrahamic covenant can be seen even in the New Testament events that surrounded the births of Jesus and

An Understanding of Evangelical Christian Support for Israel

John the Baptist (Luke 1:67–73). Seeing the coming of his son and the birth of Jesus the Messiah, Zacharias, John's father, felt compelled to say that God raised up a horn of salvation "to remember His holy covenant, the oath which He swore to our father Abraham" (vv. 72–73).

When the apostle Peter preached to the Jews in the Temple, he encouraged them to repent and said through their repentance, the times of restoration and refreshing would come because "You are the sons of the prophets, and of the covenant which God made with our fathers, saying to Abraham, 'And in your seed all the families of the earth shall blessed'" (Acts 3:25).

The apostle Paul clearly knew Israel's future was tied to God's covenant faithfulness. He called his brethren "my countrymen according to the flesh, who are Israelites" (Rom 9:3-4) and said to them belong "the adoption, the glory, the covenants, the giving of the law, the service of God, and the promises; of whom are the fathers and from whom, according to the flesh, Christ came, who is over all, the eternally blessed God. Amen" (vv. 4-5).

When Paul highlighted the covenants, promises, and patriarchs, he drew a line back to the Abrahamic Covenant—which included land, descendants, and blessing. The Covenant is why Paul called them *Israelites*, a term linked to their national identity. He could have used the term *Jews*, which would have identified them ethnically wherever they lived. But he chose *Israelites* to connect them to the land God promised them.

Paul stated emphatically that God's plan for Israel was not finished even though Christ died, was resurrected, and had ascended: "I say then, has God cast away His people? Certainly not! For I also am an Israelite, of the seed of Abraham, of the tribe of Benjamin. God has not cast away His people whom He foreknew" (11:1-2).

To this day, Israel remains the historic homeland of the Jewish people. Their identity with the land is divinely woven into the ancient biblical promise, along with historical and archaeological proof. Even through the millennia of dispersion, a continual Jewish presence in such cities as Jerusalem, Tiberias, and Safed has kept the Jewish identity grounded in the Promised Land.

James Showers & Christopher J. Katulka

Israel Plays a Vital Role in Future Prophecy

Evangelicals consider Israel important, not only in the past, but also in the present and future. Slightly more than half of evangelicals (52 percent) believe Israel is essential in fulfilling biblical prophecy. But a whopping eight in ten evangelicals believe modern Israel's rebirth is a fulfillment of prophecy and a sign the return of Jesus Christ is getting closer.[21]

God promised in the Tanakh (Old Testament) that He would redeem a remnant of Israel from Gentile oppression and reestablish the Jewish people in their own land. That promise will be fulfilled when the Messiah returns to rule the world from David's throne in Jerusalem.

The prophet Micah revealed the details of this prophetic event of renewal and restoration (Mic 4:1-13). His vision was a microcosm of Israel's bright, prophetic future. Micah began by defining the timing of these events: "In the last days" (v. 1). This will be a traumatic time in Israel's future— a time of great tribulation, which will occur immediately prior to Christ's Second Coming to restore the nation and establish Jerusalem as the center of His divine rule on Earth. Before Israel entered Canaan, even Moses in the Torah prophesied concerning this tribulation and restoration (Dt 4:30).

As the tribulation comes to an end, God will establish His rule on Earth through the reign of His Son, Jesus Christ. The pre-exilic prophet Zechariah envisioned the mountains and hills surrounding Jerusalem, where the Temple once stood, flattening when Messiah returns (14:4). The city, as well as the Temple Mount, will be elevated above the surrounding area. The vision also illustrates the meteoric rise of Jerusalem above all other cities, to become the Kingdom capital that will receive the attention of all nations.

Nations will stream to Jerusalem to worship God, "And peoples shall flow to it. Many nations shall come and say, 'Come, and let us go up to the mountain of the LORD, to the house of the God of Jacob'" (Mic 4:1-2). In the "last days," all roads will lead to Israel as people around the world will encourage one another to go up to worship in Jerusalem. The prophet

---

[21] Lifeway Research (2017), 7, 17.

Zechariah saw a day when the nations will go to Jerusalem for the Israelite festival of Sukkot, the Feast of Tabernacles (Zech 14:16-19), to celebrate God's eternal presence among them.

The nations will be taught by the Lord at the Temple in Jerusalem: "'He will teach us His ways, and we shall walk in His paths;' for out of Zion the law shall go forth, and the word of the Lord from Jerusalem" (Mic 4:2). Revelation on how to live a righteous life and keep the Lord's commandments will radiate from Jerusalem.

Biblical peace, justice, and righteousness will emanate from the city: "He shall judge between many peoples, and rebuke strong nations afar off; they shall beat their swords into plowshares, and their spears into pruning hooks; nation shall not lift up sword against nation, neither shall they learn war anymore (v. 3). As a result, nations will live in safety and security. "Everyone shall sit under his vine and under his fig tree, and no one shall make them afraid" (v. 4). This terminology used to describe peace, plenty, and prosperity (1 Kings 4:25).

Micah compared the remnant of Israel that will be restored to a flock of sheep that was lame, sick, afflicted, and dispersed—which is best understood as Israel's condition during the Great Tribulation (Matt 24:15-28). Afterward, God will regenerate and restore the Jewish population (Zech 13:9). When Messiah Jesus returns, this remnant of Israel will look upon Him whom they pierced, and all of Israel will be saved, having the veil of unbelief lifted from their collective eyes as they find true salvation in their Messiah (Zech 12:10; Rom 11:26).

When the Messiah returns to Jerusalem, He will restore the daughter of Zion to her "former dominion" (Mic 4:8) and guarantee the nation of Israel protection, peace, political power, and prosperity. The picture is reminiscent of the early Davidic dynasty, which was united, strong, steadfast, and resistant to attacks from other nations. Micah's prophecy gave hope to a nation that would soon suffer the pain of destruction and captivity.

Unlike past Davidic kings, however, Messiah Jesus will rule from Jerusalem with justice and righteousness (Isa 9:6-7). He will not be held captive by the human desires of lust, power, and greed, which crippled David and his descendants. Instead, God will "raise up the tabernacle of David, which has fallen down, and repair its damages; I will raise up its ruins and rebuild it as in the days of old" (Amos 9:11-12).

Nations will stream to Jerusalem to see the King of kings, and Israel will experience a glorious victory over her enemies and enjoy redemption through her Messiah. Then Jerusalem will be exalted as the capital of the world.

Through the prophet Amos God declared, "'I will bring back the captives of my people Israel; they shall rebuild the waste cities and inhabit them; they shall plant vineyards and drink wine from them; they shall also make gardens and eat fruit from them. I will plant them in their land, and no longer shall they be pulled up from the land I have given them,' says the LORD your God" (vv. 14-15). Israel has a glorious prophetic future that awaits her (Rom 11:26).

God Commands Christians to Love Israel

The simple fact that God loves Israel with an everlasting love (Jer 31:3) and promises to bless Gentiles who bless Israel (Gen 12:3) is sufficient motive for many to support Israel. Christians are to love what God loves, and 42 percent of evangelicals believe the Bible instructs Christians to support Israel.[22] Though some claim the promise of receiving blessing in return for blessing Abraham's descendants is motivated by selfish gain, God is clear that He wants the nations to treat His Chosen People favorably. They are His instrument through whom He is blessing the nations; and He expects the nations to respond by blessing the Jewish people. Someday He will judge the nations on that basis (Joel 3:1-3; Matt 25:31-46).

Former Israeli Prime Minister Benjamin Netanyahu has said, "Evangelical Christians are Israel's best friends in the world!"[23] Former Israeli Ambassador to the United States Ron Dermer was quoted as saying, "People

---

22 Lifeway Research (2017), 17.

23 Remarks made during an address to participants at the Christians United for Israel convention in July 2017. Rebecca Shimoni Stoil, "Netanyahu: Evangelical Christians are Israel's Best Friends," accessed March 26, 2021, https://www.timesofisrael.com/netanyahu-evangelical-christians-are-israels-best-friends/.

have to understand that the backbone of Israel's support in the United States is the evangelical Christians. It's true because of numbers and also because of their passionate and unequivocal support for Israel."[24] This "passionate and unequivocal support" does not stem from politics. It stems from a God-given mandate that spans generations: "Bless those who bless you" (Gen 12:3) and "Pray for the peace of Jerusalem! May they prosper who love you!" (Ps 122:6).

THE UNCERTAIN FUTURE OF EVANGELICAL SUPPORT FOR ISRAEL

The presumption that things will continue as they have is a mistake. Strong evangelical Christian support for Israel in the past does not ensure strong evangelical support in the future. Already, we are seeing signs that younger evangelicals are not nearly as supportive of Israel as past generations.

A poll of young evangelical Christians between the ages of 18 and 29, conducted by Barna Group in March and April 2021, shows a marked decrease in support for Israel in the "Israel-Palestinian dispute" over the past three years. Only 33.6 percent favored Israel, which is down from 69 percent in 2018. That is a startling drop. Conversely, support for the Palestinians rose from 5.6 percent in 2018 to 24.3 percent. Those who favored neither side rose from 25.3 percent to 42.2 percent.[25]

Although young evangelical Christians do not represent the majority of the evangelical community, they accentuate the challenge of maintaining strong evangelical support for Israel over the long haul. If such downward trends hold, in a few years evangelical support for Israel will be markedly lower and could eventually decline to a level of insignificance. It is dangerous to assume that because older generations strongly support Israel, younger generations will do likewise.

---

24 Jacob Magid, "Dermer Suggests Israel Should Prioritize Support of Evangelicals Over US Jews," accessed May 10, 2021, https://www.timesofisrael.com.

25 Jacob Magid, "Support for Israel Among Young US Evangelical Christians Drops Sharply – Survey," accessed May 25, 2021, https://timesofisrael.com.

This decline in young-adult, evangelical support indicates the church is failing to teach the important role Israel plays in God's redemptive plan. In siding with Israel's enemies, young evangelicals fail to see the Arab-Israeli conflict in biblical terms of the greater battle between God and Satan. In addition, the powerful, well-developed Arab narrative paints the Palestinians as victims of Israeli oppression; and a strong sense of social justice attracts young evangelicals to the Palestinian cause.

The church has a big task to accomplish. Helping younger evangelicals understand the biblical teaching that ultimate and lasting social justice awaits Israel's repentance and Jesus Christ's return is a first step toward restoring strong evangelical support among the younger generation. In God's economy, Israel is the key and not the obstacle to everlasting social justice.

Chapter 12

Against the Tide: The Role of Distinctive Identity in the Great Commissionion

Charles S. (Chuck) Kelley

Cannon to right of them,
Cannon to left of them,
Cannon in front of them
Volleyed and thundered;
Stormed at with shot and shell,
Boldly they rode and well,
Into the jaws of Death,
Into the mouth of hell
Rode the six hundred.[1]

Meandering about a place one has never been while on vacation can lead to interesting discoveries and unexpected delights. While exploring the Lake District in England one summer, we happened upon a cottage converted into a small museum dedicated to the works of William Wordsworth, famed British poet of the Romantic period. As we prepared to leave, we noticed a small exhibit focusing on one of my favorite poets, Alfred, Lord Tennyson. To our surprise, the exhibit included a rare audio recording of Tennyson himself reading one of his most famous poems: "The Charge of the Light Brigade." Listening to that scratchy recording of the

---

1 "The Charge of the Light Brigade" by Alfred, Lord Tennyson, accessed October 19, 2021, https://www.poetryfoundation.org/poems/45319/the-charge-of-the-light-brigade.

poet's voice reading the poignant lines that immortalized a tragic moment in British military history is an experience I never expected to have and will never, ever forget.

Due to a battlefield miscommunication, a brigade of light cavalry, designed to harass an enemy retreating from battle, was instead sent to charge heavily fortified enemy artillery with deeply entrenched cannons on three sides of a valley. All knew they could not win, and very heavy casualties would result, but "All in the valley of death rode the six hundred." From the time the few survivors returned to their lines, even to this present day, the profound question was: Why were they sent out on an impossible mission? Because the key person involved in the mistake was killed in the battle, the truth will never be known. The valor of those who made the charge and fought anyway was world news then, and with Tennyson's poem the hopeless cavalry charge became forever famous. This moment in history raises a question that goes far beyond the battlefield. Can there be any useful result in fighting battles one cannot win?

Those moments of standing in a corner of that small museum with headphones on, listening to the poet's interpretation of this profound battlefield moment aroused an ongoing reflection on the meaning of fighting impossible battles that cannot be won. The Southern Baptist Convention assignment for the Ethics and Religious Liberty Commission, brings to my mind the unwinnable fight scenario. According to the Organizational Manual of the Southern Baptist Convention, the ERLC has four ministries:

1) Assist churches in applying the moral and ethical teachings of the Bible to the Christian life;
2) Assist churches through the communication and advocacy of moral and ethical concerns in the public arena;
3) Assist churches in their moral witness to local communities;
4) Assist churches and other Southern Baptist entities by promoting religious liberty.[2]

---

2   2021 Book of Reports of the Southern Baptist Convention, 176.

Against the Tide: The Role of Distinctive Identity in the Great Commissionion

To summarize, the ERLC is charged to present, explain, and defend Baptist perspectives on moral, ethical, and religious liberty issues, driven by a biblical worldview, to a secular and increasingly hostile culture that likely has little or no respect for Christ and the teachings of Scripture, and to help SBC churches know how to do the same. Such a task is very much an uphill battle.

The public presentation of Baptist positions on moral and ethical issues from the perspective of a biblical worldview opens wide the floodgates of the secular world for charges of being intolerant, narrow-minded, and so forth. It does little good to be able to make clear what the Bible teaches on moral and ethical issues, when those in opposition could care less about biblical teachings. Added to attacks from the secular world are attacks from liberal denominations who have abandoned confidence in the Bible's inspiration and the traditional Christian worldview. Leaders from the world of mainline denominations are just as likely to vehemently disagree on many issues with the ERLC as secular authorities. Vociferous disagreement can also come from inside the big tent of Southern Baptists. With more than forty thousand churches and fourteen million members, vigorous debates among Southern Baptists are not rare. Moral and ethical issues tend to be controversial issues that generate strong feelings. Many in SBC circles say that whoever leads the ERLC will inevitably find himself in trouble with some segment of the Convention at all times. Generating controversy goes with the territory. With attacks on the Southern Baptist perspective on moral and ethical issues likely to come from the secular world, the religious world, and the Southern Baptist world, there is little chance that attacks and controversy will ever cease. When your point of view is judged wrong because it is faithful to Scripture and to Baptist heritage, advocating that point of view is a very difficult battle to win. As with "The Charge of the Light Brigade" in a completely different context, unrelenting attack, not victory is the expectation.

If one cannot expect a victory, is a battle worth fighting? In the case of presenting Baptist perspectives from a biblical point of view, absolutely! Many would say the truth is always worth defending and championing no matter what the cost. However, what I appreciate most is how the work of the ERLC during the twenty-five-year tenure of Dr. Richard Land played a role in the Great Commission efforts of Southern Baptists. Seldom noticed and even more rarely discussed is the energizing effect of the moral and social stands taken by the ERLC on mobilizing Southern Baptists to share their faith and seek to win others to a saving faith in Jesus Christ. This is the subject of this essay. Getting the attention of our neighbors and our nation requires having a distinctive identity within our culture that others will notice. Being noticed creates the opportunity to further explain who we are and why we are distinctive. Those conversations can then lead into gospel conversations, introducing others to Jesus. Distinctiveness in the way Baptists live and the positions Baptists advocate is a crucial element of fruitfulness.

Knowing Who You Are Is Essential for Asking Others to Become Like You

From their earliest beginnings, Baptists have been the "bad boys" among the Protestant families of churches. Emerging during the 16th and 17th centuries, people knew Baptists were different because the earliest Baptists marched to the beat of a different drummer and lived out their faith in ways unlike those around them who also called themselves Christians. Baptists insisted that only those who believe in Christ as their Savior should be baptized, which means they reject the popular practice of infant baptism. During the Reformation era, Anabaptists were the earliest precursors of Baptists. The fury over their insistence upon believer's baptism caused both the Catholics and the Reformers to persecute the Anabaptists relentlessly. In introducing a 2012 Radical Reformation Day on his campus, Truett-McConnell University's President Emir Caner noted that the average lifespan of Anabaptists in the Reformation era was about 18 months following their baptism. These early Baptists also rejected the notion of a state church whose legitimacy can only be determined by the government. They found the idea that the state should collect a tax on the population to fund the operation of a church noxious. Every person should be free to worship or not worship according

Against the Tide: The Role of Distinctive Identity in the Great Commissionion

to the dictates of his conscience. Every church should be free to determine its own affairs. These Baptist ideas were very radical, and they threatened the foundations of the established church.

To discourage others from joining them, emerging Baptists, who were both men and women, were beaten, arrested, tortured, drowned, burned at the stake, put to the sword, and humiliated in every possible way by the authorities. Yet the very public and vicious attacks seemed to do more to attract followers rather than discourage them. In England, Baptists were often imprisoned and otherwise harassed for preaching without a license and other offenses against the official state church as they insisted on believer's baptism and fought for religious liberty and a free church. The Baptist preacher and poet John Bunyan wrote *Pilgrim's Progress*, one of the most widely read and influential Christian books of all time, while languishing in prison for acting on his Baptist convictions.

Many are unaware that the idea of having one official church for the state followed colonists to America. Some of the original American colonies had a single state church. Baptists were forbidden to preach, but they preached anyway, going to jail, and suffering a variety of persecutions. John Leland and other Baptist leaders engaged the political process as the United States was born, and they won approval for the First Amendment to the U. S. Constitution guaranteeing religious liberty and the separation of church and state. These "bad boy" Baptists going against the tide had a distinctive identity and stood out in the culture as unlike other families of churches.

Against the anvil of opposition, Southern Baptists hammered out a theological, missiological, and moral identity that was distinctively different than that of other Baptists in America, especially as theological liberalism made inroads into American Christianity. Their theological identity was a total commitment to the inspiration, authority, and sufficiency of the Bible. Their missiological identity was the necessity to call every person in the nation and the world to salvation through repentance from sin and faith in Jesus Christ, whose life, death, and resurrection make transformation into children of God possible. Their moral identity was the call to live a life of discipleship in accordance with the teachings of Jesus and the Bible. Although their implementation of all three components of this identity was far from perfect, the striving toward this identity was enough to make many Southern Baptists quite distinctive within their communities. They became known as "Bible Thumpers" who took the teachings of the Bible very seriously. They became known as "Zealots" who always wanted to talk about Jesus. They became known as "Teetotalers" who did not drink alcohol and were conservative on moral issues. As one wag noted about the Baptist attitude toward dating:

"I don't dance, and I don't chew [tobacco], and I don't go out with those who do!"

Any identity is always more complex than its essence, and Southern Baptists were more than the sum of these three components, but these three components were generally present to some extent when people thought about the Southern Baptists' identity.

There can be no conversion unless people know what they are not. You cannot experience a Christian conversion unless you know first that you are not a Christian. The path to conversion starts when one recognizes what a Christian is clearly enough to ask himself is that who I am? If not, is that who I want to become? With no clear understanding of what you could become, you are unlikely to seriously consider changing who you are. For most people in the world, religious identity is a matter of birth. The family or nation into which you are born determines your religious identity. Southern Baptists are different. You are born without Christ in your life. You must be changed, transformed to become a Christian. Ideally, from their earliest years, children born into SBC homes are taught both who they are and who they are not, with the hope they will one day turn away from who they are without Christ to become transformed into who they can become in Christ. Without a clear sense of who they are and why they are in Christ, Baptists cannot hope to draw others in the community into their churches and a relationship with Christ.

The work of Richard Land and the Ethics and Religious Liberty Commission (ERLC) became one means by which Southern Baptists could clarify their identity. By addressing the moral and ethical issues of the day on behalf of the SBC, the ERLC revealed the distinctive identity of Southern Baptists even when the stands taken aroused hostility and ridicule.

Against the Tide: The Role of Distinctive Identity in the Great Commissionion

Where we stand on this or that moral, ethical issue is a result of who we are in Christ. Taking a public stand during a national conversation is making an application of our theological, missiological, and moral identity. Taking such stands not only reveals something to Baptists about who we are as Baptists and Christians, it also reveals something to non-Baptists about who they are and who they are not. Thus, one Great Commission value of the ERLC is to continually remind Southern Baptists to know who we are and to show non-Baptists our distinctiveness in opinions and lifestyles. For those who do not share our perspective on this issue or that issue, the differences may lead to curiosity on why Baptists would take what seems to be such an odd position, perhaps creating the possibility for a gospel conversation. Being distinctively different from those around you can be a good thing, even a necessary thing, when you are seeking to introduce people to Jesus.

Embracing Who You Are Is the Test for Knowing Who You Are

There is a cost that comes with being out of step with the surrounding culture or with other Christian bodies. You may want to buy a new car, but when you go to the dealer and see the actual price of the car, you face the decision on whether the car is worth the cost necessary to buy it. That is the difference between being a car shopper and a car buyer. For much of the world's population, religious identity is largely determined by birth: the family or country into which you were born gave you a religious identity as a Catholic or Muslim, a Hindu, or an Anglican. Baptists have a different starting point for religious identity. Conversion rather than birthright or country of origin makes one a Baptist. Being born into a Baptist family can give you a start toward becoming a Baptist, but one never actually becomes a Baptist until one makes the decision to turn away from sin, place his faith in Christ, and be baptized as a believer into the church. The choice to be born again and then become a Baptist is not the only choice a Baptist must make. The historic practice of Baptists being the "bad boys" out of step with the culture and with the practices and views of other Christian bodies suggests that Baptists today will likely have to choose between conformity with the culture or distinction from the culture, blending in or standing out.

As life unfolds, there are choices to make that will indicate whether one embraces their religious identity, ignores that identity, or rejects that identity. Making those choices is not unlike the differences between being a car shopper and a car buyer. There is a cost involved in purchasing a car, and there is a cost involved in embracing the Baptist identity. I lived in New Orleans, LA for forty-three years. New Orleans was founded and settled by Catholics, and the Catholic church remains a huge influence in New Orleans today. I soon learned that it was not unusual for those who were born into Catholic homes but led to a personal relationship with Christ by Baptists to take years before being baptized and joining the church. They would faithfully attend worship and Bible Study in their Baptist church, and they would participate in many church activities. People in the church who did not know the details would often assume such folks were members because of their level of engagement.

Baptism for such people was the defining issue that would make them distinctively Baptist. It could lead to family tension and even formal ostracism, and thus baptism was a very costly choice to make. When a Catholic adult was baptized, he was doing more than joining a Baptist church. He was embracing a Baptist identity despite the cost. In the United States today, people are no longer beaten, thrown in jail, or burned at the stake for becoming Baptists. Still, some are reluctant to fully embrace a Baptist identity because social pressure in all its forms has a way of challenging those who would become true Baptists. It is one thing to be a Baptist. It is another to live out your Baptist convictions, whatever the cost.

Moral and ethical issues that become part of the national cultural conversation are always issues of significance going far beyond discussions at the dinner table, the classroom, or the small group. They have a way of popping up frequently, sometimes in the most unexpected ways. Homosexuality, transgenderism, racial reconciliation, social justice, and abortion are examples of current topics debated by politicians, lawmakers, office workers, athletes, friends, families, and people in almost any social setting.

Against the Tide: The Role of Distinctive Identity in the Great Commissionion

To take a position on such issues is to disagree with others in your social or family circle. Such disagreements can and usually do produce tensions. When the Bible speaks to such issues, Baptists are responsible to teach their people what God says and to speak God's Word into the culture even if that message is considered undesirable. In so doing, they are encouraging people to embrace fully and publicly their Baptist identity. The prophets of the Old Testament brought the Word of God to disinterested kings of Judah and Israel and to nations who worshipped pagan gods. When God speaks, His people must pass it on. The prophets took a stand on "Thus saith the Lord. . ." and called all who heard them to repent and believe. Those who followed the Lord were expected to be distinctive voices and distinctive lives within their culture.

Baptists of old did more than recognize their Baptist identity. They embraced it, even when doing so carried an enormous cost. By insisting baptism was for believers only, they risked jail, torture, and death. Neighbors and other family members thought they were putting the eternal souls of their children at risk of going to Hell for failing to baptize them. By crying out for a free church and the freedom for every person to worship when and how they pleased with no coercion from the state, even if they chose not to worship at all, Baptists were attacked and vilified for disrupting community life and national affairs. If one declared themself to be a Baptist, it would cost them physically, financially, and socially. A person would never be a Baptist unless he or she embraced all that being a Baptist meant. People knew who Baptists were because of the price Baptists were willing to pay to embrace and live out their faith. By completely embracing their Baptist identity, they encouraged others to become Baptists as well.

The ERLC is charged with speaking to such issues on behalf of Southern Baptists and with speaking to Southern Baptists to help them understand and frame the issues for the church. For a quarter century, Richard Land and his team could be found speaking before Congressional committees, having private conversations with Presidents, and conducting interviews with publications like the *New York Times*, *Washington Post*, or *Wall Street Journal* even as they spoke to pastors, churches, state conventions, and SBC leaders. What Land would not do is let a significant national issue go unnoticed or let the Southern Baptist voice go unheard. By identifying the moral and ethical issues of the day and clearly articulating a Baptist perspective from a biblical worldview, he created a decision for his Baptist hearers. Embrace your Baptist identity or ignore it. His ceaseless work encouraging Baptists to embrace their Baptist identity and the biblical perspective even when doing so put one out of step with the culture, friends, coworkers, and family. It is one thing to read the condemnation of homosexuality in the Bible. It is another to continue to recognize homosexuality as sin when a child tells you he is gay. Knowing you are a Baptist is one thing. Embracing fully that Baptist identity when it is costly to do so is another. Those who embrace fully their Baptist identity are more likely to live out their Baptist faith in all areas of life. They are more likely to have gospel conversations with others as they explain what they believe and why. One of the biggest challenges facing the Southern Baptist Convention is the need to encourage its members to embrace fully who they are as Baptists. Being a Baptist is about more than where the pew you occupy on Sundays is located. It is also about what positions you occupy in moral and ethical discussions of the day. The willingness to embrace fully a Baptist identity is a larger factor in Great Commission engagement than most realize.

Baptists of today are becoming less willing to embrace fully their Baptist identity. A growing number of churches are removing "Baptist" from their name, not wanting to be recognized in the community as a Baptist church. Churches making this decision often cite the Great Commission as their reason. They feel the Baptist name has such negative connotations to lost and unchurched people in the community, that incorporating it into the name of the church would make reaching those people more difficult and make the gospel less attractive to the lost. When informing their congregations that they would be nominated as a candidate for the Convention presidency, the last two SBC Presidents felt the need to include a reminder in the announcement that their churches were Southern Baptist churches for those members who did not know this fact. Most of the churches started under the auspices of the SBC's own North American Mission Board do not include Baptist in the name of the new church, ostensibly because of the negative connotations in the community.

Against the Tide: The Role of Distinctive Identity in the Great Commissionion

After all these centuries, controversy is still associated with the Baptist name. Southern Baptists are still the "bad boys" of the Protestant world. The controversial aspects of the Southern Baptist name today include the following. Some find the geographical appendage "Southern" to be a problem. If you live in Idaho or New York, why would you want to be a member of the "Southern" Baptist Convention? Often unmentioned in this discussion over geography is that most SBC churches have never included "Southern" in the name. The standard practice has been to use only "Baptist" in the formal name. It is not using the identity "Southern Baptist" that churches are seeking to avoid. It is the "Baptist" identity they would rather not use.

Others cite the racist associations with Southern Baptists in the minds of many from their acceptance of slavery prior to the Civil War and their opposition to the Civil Rights movement in the sixties. The near total embrace of abortion by the Democratic Party pushed Southern Baptists toward the Republican Party because of its Pro-Life stance, causing some to believe a conservative political image makes evangelism difficult. The insistence that the Bible is the inspired, inerrant Word of God, that there is no salvation apart from faith in Jesus Christ and that believers must be baptized to be members of a Baptist church are a theological scandal to some, causing them to ignore the SBC and its churches.

The insistence upon believer's baptism has become a particular sticking point for one group of people in many communities. As mainline denominations have become more and more liberal, they are losing members by the thousands. Active, conservative Christians in those churches started looking around for new church homes in churches that were biblically sound and theologically conservative. Having been baptized as infants in a non-Baptist church, the idea of being baptized again as an adult believer can be very unappealing and a barrier to churches reaching some who would otherwise be great church members. Unlike Baptists in the past, several contemporary Baptist churches are hoping to avoid these and other controversies by avoiding the use of the Baptist name. Such churches may have a Baptist identity, but they are not fully embracing it.

However, as this modern trend of a diminished embrace of Baptist identity grew, so did the decline of Southern Baptists. For the last decade, baptisms, membership, worship attendance, giving, and the number of international missionaries sent abroad are all down. The number of new churches started by the North American Mission Board as they have moved away from using a Baptist identity has dropped by nearly fifty percent in ten years despite tripling the size of the budget for church planting. Virtually all statistical measurements of the health of SBC churches are in decline and have been for several years. A few years ago, I was having lunch with an SBC President who had come to New Orleans Baptist Theological Seminary (NOBTS) to preach in a chapel service. A major political election year was unfolding, and he expressed some surprise at not having many inquiries from the national press about Southern Baptists and the elections. I suggested he think of SBC as now standing for the Smaller Baptist Convention. Our numerical decline and ebbing influence means less attention from the world. For those outside the SBC, the decline appears to be even greater than it is. As churches take "Baptist" out of their name, they no longer appear to be associated with the SBC. When people drive past church signs in a community, they do not see as many Baptist churches as they once did. Mission accomplished for those wanting to downplay their Baptist identity. They have succeeded. Fewer Baptist churches using the name "Baptist" create the perception of fewer Baptist churches existing across the United States.

Earlier Baptists experienced severe persecution, including imprisonment, torture, and execution. Despite such widespread hostilities, those Baptists fully embraced their identity and continually called people to join their ranks. People became Baptists when they embraced the Baptist identity. Explosive growth was the result. When the physical persecution was replaced with social pressure and cultural disdain, Southern Baptists continued to embrace their identity and invite others to join them anyway. By the mid-twentieth century, the SBC became the largest Protestant denomination in the United States. The social pressure did eventually take its toll, and a slow backing away from a clear Baptist identity began to unfold. The era of diminished embrace of Baptist identity was born, and so was the era of Southern Baptist decline.

The chart below shows a statistical snapshot of the last decade in Southern Baptist life. Southern Baptists had become accustomed to signif-

Against the Tide: The Role of Distinctive Identity in the Great Commissionion

icant growth for much of their history. When the growth began to slow, most SBC churches would remain approximately the same size. Even if they were not growing, they were holding steady. As the chart below indicates, those days of either growing or holding steady have passed for now. The addition of some two thousand churches while at the same time losing nearly two million members and one million worship attenders is not encouraging for a denomination that has longed taken pride in its evangelism efforts. The steady decline in annual baptisms and the worsening of the ratio of baptisms per member is without precedent.

Statistical Snapshots of the SBC (2010-2020)[3]

Year	Total Churches	Church Plants	Total Members	Total Baptisms	Baptism Ratio	Worship Attendance	SBC Share of CP	SBC CP
2010	45,727	769	16,136,044	331,008	1:49	6,195,449	38.32%	$191,763,153
2011	45,764	1,003	15,978,112	333,341	1:48	6,155,116	38.20%	$186,386,036
2012	46,034	927	15,872,404	314,956	1:50	5,966,735	38.77%	$186,640,481
2013	46,125	936	15,735,640	310,368	1:51	5,834.707	38.03%	$183,419,803
2014	46,499	985	15,499,173	305,301	1:51	5,674,469	37.80%	$180,971,579
2015	46,793	926	15,294,764	295,262	1:52	5,577,088	38.75%	$183,771,302
2016	47,272	732	15,216,978	280,773	1:54	5,200,716	40.08%	$190,468,781
2017	47,544	691	15,005,638	254,122	1:59	5,320,488	41.49%	$191,948,826
2018	47,456	624	14,813,234	246,442	1:60	5,297,788	41.30%	$191,257,988
2019	47,530	552	14,525,579	235,748	1:62	5,250,230	41.31%	$190,967,403
2020	47,592	588	14,089,947	123,160	1:114	4,439,797	41.23%	$187,806,636

The reality of both a decreased commitment to an SBC identity and increased SBC decline among SBC churches has made the role of the ERLC even more important to fuel the Great Commission fire in Southern Baptist life. The engagement of the ERLC in highly visible cultural conversations with a distinctively Baptist perspective is a means to encourage Southern Baptists to embrace their Baptist identity. This era in the national life of the United States has become well known for its polarizing discussions.

---

3 Table created by Dr. Chuck Kelley, New Orleans, Baptist Theological Seminary, May 2021 from data in the Annuals of the Southern Baptist Convention (2010-2020).

Controversies abound and are virtually impossible to avoid. Identifying the issues that call for a biblical response, articulating clearly that biblical response, and promoting the awareness of why there is a distinctively Baptist and biblical perspective in this or that discussion is crucial. Southern Baptists need to know who we are in the face of this cultural tumult. We need to be confident and assured that we are standing in the right place for the right reasons.

When Southern Baptists resonate with a position taken by the ERLC in an important national discussion, they are encouraged to embrace their Baptist identity and to carry that Baptist identity into discussions with family, friends, and others. Southern Baptists are unlikely to invite others to their Savior and to their churches if those Baptists do not have a clear knowledge and understanding of who they are as Baptists and if they do not embrace what they know. The ERLC provides tools for using the current cultural conversations to open doors for gospel conversations for those who are willing to embrace their Baptist identity.

DEMONSTRATING WHO YOU ARE IS THE BRIDGE TO WINNING OVER THE RELUCTANT

To look back at the severe persecution endured by early Baptists makes the explosive growth of Baptists through the years even more impressive. For those of us fortunate to live in a nation where the engagement of Baptists in the political process helped to win constitutional guarantees for religious liberty and the separation of church and state, it is difficult to imagine what life would be like if we had to endure suffering and death because of embracing religious convictions. One cannot help but wonder why people would choose to be persecuted. When the consequences for being a Baptist were swift, certain, and deadly, why would anyone but a fanatic become a Baptist? If being a Baptist were to make you socially disdained in the opinion of people you care about, why would you ever embrace being a Baptist? To understand the answer to this question, one must understand how people come to Christ and why they join a church.

Against the Tide: The Role of Distinctive Identity in the Great Commissionion

First and foremost is the issue of truth. As Baptists proclaimed God's Word to others, the Holy Spirit gave it the ring of truth in the soul of their hearers. To paraphrase the Gospel of John, the Holy Spirit brings deep conviction about sin, righteousness, and judgment (John 16:8-11). One reason people are willing to choose discomfort, even danger, over peace and security is a recognition that whatever is true is real and must be acknowledged and acted upon no matter what the consequences. Ulrich Zwingli was one of the major Reformation personalities. He began teaching some bright young men the Greek New Testament and talking to them about the authority of Scripture superseding all ecclesiastical authority. As those young men studied the New Testament, they found the Greek they were learning from Zwingli made the meaning of Scripture very clear. Baptism was for believers only, not for unknowing infants who were incapable of understanding its meaning. Zwingli rejected this insight as too radical, but his students insisted it was true because it was biblical. They became mortal enemies. Conrad Grebel and his fellow students all died a martyr's death over baptism. The issue was truth, and they were willing to oppose a respected teacher and to die for it. One would do well not to underestimate what people will do when they think the truth is at stake. People will not knowingly give their lives for an error, but both the New Testament and Baptist history have shown that they will give their lives for the truth.

Knowing that the Bible is true is why Baptists seek to frame discussions of faith and practice, doctrine, and discipleship in light of what the Bible teaches. Baptist scholars study the history and traditions of the church, and they consider the insights professional theologians and philosophers may bring to religious conversation. However, Baptist scholars are like Baptist pastors, Baptist Bible study teachers, and the typical Baptist church member. The perspective that matters most is that of God's Word, the Bible.

Richard Land is a very highly educated theologian who is as at home in the rarified company of academic elites, as he is in the ordinary halls of a rural Baptist church. The Bible is at the heart of the positions he takes on the significant moral and ethical issues of the day. That is why scripture references accompany all position papers, brochures, and written materials the ERLC published under Land. In his presentations on moral and ethical issues, the Bible is presented as the foundation of the Baptist perspective. The Bible is at the heart of every sermon he preaches. The issue is truth, and the truth is what appeals to people who face uncomfortable decisions for the sake of their faith.

The other major factor in why people would choose the uncomfortable path and become Baptists is the power of a human connection. Ideas are powerful, more powerful than many realize, but ideas given flesh are often exponentially more powerful still. John tells us that when God revealed Himself and His salvation:

> "The Word was made flesh, and dwelt among us, (and we beheld his glory, the glory as of the only begotten of the Father,) full of grace and truth." (John 1:14, KJV).
>
> "That which was from the beginning, which we have heard, which we have seen with our eyes, which we have looked upon, and our hands have handled, of the Word of life; (For the life was manifested, and we have seen it, and bear witness, and shew unto you that eternal life, which was with the Father and was manifested unto us)" (1 John 1:1-2).

God's revelation became complete when He took upon Himself flesh and blood, clarifying the truth revealed in His Word through a human connection with those He came to save. From their earliest days, Baptists preached. They wrote pamphlets, tracts, and books to explain who Baptists were and what God expected of those He saved. At the same time, they also lived normal lives among the people they sought to reach. They married, had children, and worked. William Carey, the Father of the Modern Missionary Movement, was a shoe cobbler. John Bunyan was a tinker who repaired household utensils for people, although he is far better known today as a writer and preacher. Many Southern Baptist pastors were also farmers, schoolteachers, or businessmen. Baptist thought incorporated the texture of life. People recognized themselves in the Baptists they knew.

From time to time, surveys are conducted to ask people what drives their decision to join a particular church. The common answers include worship style, preaching of the pastor, programs for children, and so forth. However, the most popular answer is usually the presence of friends or family members who are already in the church. The personal connection is often the factor of greatest influence in decisions about church. I observed this in New Orleans with Catholics who decided to become Baptists. In every case I can recall, people making that kind of transition in the face of significant social resistance had a husband, a wife, or a very close friend who were already active Baptists. They heard the truth and they saw the truth demonstrated.

Persecution did not stop the growth of Baptists in the days when it was so severe in part because of the interactions people had with Baptists. Communities saw what kind of people Baptists were, and they saw how they lived their lives. When political and state church officials attempted to justify the extreme persecutions with descriptions of how terrible Baptists were, the characterizations did not match up with the Baptists people knew. The lives they lived gave the Baptist message a ring of truth in many cases. When social disdain replaced physical persecution, people in a community may have noticed what appeared to be odd habits or different ways in the lives of Baptists. Yet they also noticed the kindness to others. They noticed who showed up when trouble came. They noticed their neighborliness. I have few memories about being in the homes of my high school friends, but all my friends have memories of visiting in our home and eating around our table. The authenticity of Baptist lives and the authenticity of the message they preached, wrote, and published drew more and more people who were willing to cast their lot with the persecuted. The demonstration of Baptist convictions in the normal lives of Baptists has long been a crucial aspect of persuasion.

To at least some extent, the structure of the ERLC reflects the importance placed upon the demonstration of Baptist convictions in the life of the Baptist people. The ERLC was not intended to be an evangelical "think tank" where specialists in moral, ethical, and religious liberty issues would gather and use the interplay of their research, writing, and discussion with one another to hammer out Baptist perspectives and positions on important issues of the day. Public announcements and press conferences were never intended to be the primary vehicle for making known Baptist positions on moral and ethical issues. To be sure, Land would periodically host gatherings of specialists for thorough discussions on key topics, but it was always with a view toward the church and ordinary Baptists having to face these issues in their community context. He issued many public statements to media, appeared as a guest on many radio and TV programs, and hosted scores of press conferences during his years of leading the ERLC, but Land and his staff would also go to local churches, area associations, state conventions, and the national meeting of the SBC to share their perspectives with the Baptist rank and file. Materials and training were offered for interested Southern Baptists to dig in and become better informed to share insights with people in their churches or other Baptists in their area. Yes, Richard Land wanted the nation and its leaders to know where Baptists stood on critical moral and ethical issues. More importantly, he wanted typical Baptists in the pew to fully understand and embrace how their faith and biblical worldview applied to this issue or that issue in the cultural conversations of the nation.

A part of the genius of Richard Land was the ability to combine his thorough knowledge of the Baptists in the pew and their normal life in the world with his deep knowledge of moral and ethical issues to produce an aphorism that expresses the Baptist perspective in a concise, memorable way almost impossible for his hearers to forget. Here is a classic example. The setting was his report to the thousands of messengers attending the annual meeting of the Southern Baptist Convention. The very loud issue demanding attention that year was homosexuality. The Disney corporation was adding fuel to the fire of this very controversial issue by using their theme parks to promote the homosexual lifestyle. Disney characters are popular in many American homes. For decades Mickey Mouse, Minnie Mouse, Donald Duck, and the big dog Goofy have entertained children and adults. Here is Land's summary of the frustrations Southern Baptists were feeling toward Disney's efforts to mainstream homosexuality: "Disney is telling us that Mickey Mouse left Minnie for Donald. That's Goofy!"

In that simple statement, pastors had a summary of the homosexuality discussion to take back to their churches, knowing every parent in the congregation would understand, agree, and use this point in conversations with their friends.

The ERLC never hesitated to take a position representing biblical, Baptist perspectives on moral and ethical issues in the national conversation because they were helping ordinary Southern Baptists who were the human face of the Convention understand the issues and how to address them in their circle of friends and family. This information was an important way to help Southern Baptists embrace their identity as Baptists and carry Baptist perspectives with them into the marketplace of life. The human factor is a vital link to connect the gospel with those who are lost and outside the influence of any church. If Southern Baptists are not noticed and respected by their neighbors, they are unlikely to influence the openness of their neighbors to the gospel. If Southern Baptists are not willing to embrace their Baptist identity, they are less likely to care about participation in the advance of the gospel by letting the Word become flesh in them.

Conclusion

For a quarter of a century, Richard Land occupied one of the hottest seats in the circle of Southern Baptist leadership. Controversial topics and complex issues, any one of which on any given day, could put the leader of the Ethics and Religious Liberty Commission at the center of a maelstrom that could consume one in a deluge of criticism from all sides. As many have said about leading the ERLC: If you are not in trouble with somebody every day, you are probably not doing your job. Some would say, the ERLC is a job for someone who loves a good fight. Not so. If you love a good fight, this job would keep you in so many fights you would never do anything else. This job is for someone who understands controversy can be a means to a necessary and significant end. If you know Richard Land, you know of the breadth and depth of his amazing intellect. You know of his incredible ability to create an impromptu aphorism on the spur of a moment, cutting to the heart of a matter in a clear and memorable way with just one sentence. You know of his prodigious work ethic and continual productivity. You know of his relentless focus and unfailing love for the Bible, its inspiration, authority, and sufficiency and for Southern Baptists and their history and churches. Hopefully you also know of his terrific marriage, his wonderful children, and his obnoxious passion for all things Texas. What you may not know is the depth of his passion for the salvation of the lost. Whatever Richard Land does, he does with the Great Commission in mind.

Richard Land diligently worked to connect the efforts of the ERLC with the people in the pews of SBC churches. Moral and ethical issues are not solely the domain of philosophers and theologians. Such issues define and express how we live, and those who follow Christ ought to be living distinctive lives. All our Great Commission efforts will be given greater power, greater energy, and greater impact when our neighbors notice us and see "the Word made flesh" as we embody our faith in our lifestyles. This is the heritage of Baptists. As the "bad boys" of the Protestant Reformation, Baptists were persecuted relentlessly by both the Catholics and the Reformers, but despite the danger, people became Baptists by the hundreds and the thousands. Physical persecution and social disdain followed Baptists to America, making them the "outsiders" of the religious scene. Those obstacles were overcome when Baptists embraced their identity as Baptists and won over their critics by the way they lived among their neighbors.

Richard Land has been right to fight for Baptist perspectives in the arena of public opinions all these years. It was a Great Commission battle. If we can get our people to embrace their Baptist identity and live distinctively, we will eventually draw attention to the gospel and have opportunities to invite others to Christ. The future will belong to the best teachers.

The moral and ethical issues of the day provide an opportunity to teach the people in our pews what it means to be a Baptist by applying the Bible and Baptist heritage to the questions that float around our homes, schools, and offices. The cultural conversation of our nation can be the launching pad for raising up a new Great Commission army who know who they are and are willing to call others in their communities to join them in following Jesus. Thank you, Dr. Richard Land for showing us that giving attention to moral, ethical, and religious liberty issues can also be another way for us to stimulate interest in reaching the world for Christ.

Against the Tide: The Role of Distinctive Identity in the Great Commissionion

Thank you for undertaking that mission even though it cost you dearly and you faced such small prospects of winning the field against relentless secular and religious critics. The battle was worth it. I hereby name you an honorary member of the Light Brigade, and I give Alfred, Lord Tennyson the last word on your significance as a member of that immortal band:

> *Cannon to right of them,*
> *Cannon to left of them,*
> *Cannon behind them*
> *Volleyed and thundered;*
> *Stormed at with shot and shell,*
> *While horse and hero fell,*
> *They that had fought so well*
> *Came through the jaws of Death,*
> *Back from the mouth of hell,*
> *All that was left of them,*
> *Left of six hundred.*
> *When can their glory fade?*
> *O the wild charge they made!*
> *All the world wondered.*
> *Honor the charge they made!*
> *Honor the Light Brigade,*
> *Noble six hundred!*[4]

---

4 "The Charge of the Light Brigade" by Alfred, Lord Tennyson.

CHAPTER 13

A RUDDER FOR A HISTORIAN AND ETHICIST: THE AVOCATION OF EVANGELIST

Paige Patterson

Perhaps everyone remembers playing the game Red Rover in elementary school. When we grow to adulthood, life continues to be a high stakes game of Red Rover. Dr. Richard Land is the player almost everyone wants on his team. Should opposing teams make the mistake of shouting "Let Richard come over" in this high stakes game of Red Rover we call "life," Richard Land becomes a nearly irresistible thunder bolt hurtling toward the opposition line. When opponents run against your team defense, you always want the steady hold of Land's apologetic grasp to resist even the cleverest of arguments. And through the entire contest, Land will usually demonstrate that he is the most optimistic and enthusiastic player on the team.

For me, Richard Land has been an inevitable encourager. He has served to challenge my positions and stir me to think more profoundly about the most difficult, as well as the most obvious, problems. By the consistency of his moral conduct, he has challenged my heart. As I have studied the man, I have learned to teach and to preach more effectively. As a husband and as a father, he has inspired me repeatedly. Sometimes we have disagreed, but never have those moments diminished our love and appreciation for one other. Richard Land is a man on mission with the eternal God.

* * *

The longer I have known Richard Land, the more intriguing he has become. In 1969, I was an advanced Th.M. student at New Orleans Baptist Theological Seminary and was informed by attorney Paul Pressler that a recent graduate of Princeton University was matriculating. Pressler, a new acquaintance for me, assured me that I would find young Richard to be an irresistible intellect. Pressler hinted at the possibility that Land would need an ombudsman to assist the youth in mastering the caves and dens of seminary life and suggested that I make myself available to the fellow Texan.

Richard needed assistance at seminary like my dog pined for guidance chasing rabbits. He found his fellow students delectable whatever their background and belief. His professors invigorated him except for a rare exception or two that did not fare so well in comparison with his Princeton dons. And books? He consumed them like they were wedge salads; and he digested the footnotes, indices, forewords, title pages, and all, remembering lonely footnotes decades later to query incredulous students in his quizzes over their reading. "I can't believe that Professor Land asked about footnote 486! It was the last footnote in the book," a distraught young preacher fumed.

Comfortable with almost any subject, Richard waxed eloquent about the class of recruits at the football program of the University of Texas, the presidents of the United States including the one that got stuck in the bathtub and had to be larded out, and the Black Regiment of Divines who led the fight of the colonists for independence. He roared aloud as he relived the heroic efforts of Sir Winston Churchill and did not miss a beat in extolling the virtues of Blue Bell Ice Cream.

What curled even my kinky red hair was that subject matter for discussion was not Land's concern. Someone else could choose, but before the discussion ever rang up midnight Land had launched into some ethereal discussion of an aspect of the debate at hand that has totally eluded the rest of us. He proceeded to provide some novel insight; and some of us would whisper, "Look, the kid is only 21. Princeton or no Princeton, nobody can know that much!"

Pursuing his D.Phil (1980) at Oxford in England effected little change in the young man other than that he now excelled on the questions of Baptist history. The product of what most would call an ordinary home of wage earners, Richard grew up in a small South Houston Baptist church, loyal to Southern Baptists. He spoke lovingly about Sunday School, Training

A Rudder for a Historian and Ethicist: The Avocation of Evangelist

Union on Sunday nights, and Royal Ambassadors on Wednesday nights. But he was likely the only kid in that Sunday School who featured intense antagonism to racism. Not only did he see the "log" in the Southern Baptist eye on that one, but he also determined that if ever given the chance, he would make a difference.[1] In short, Richard was just like the youngsters attending church and school with him, yet he was as distinct as Iguacu Falls in Argentina is from Pine Island Bayou in southeast Texas.

As I watched Richard Land develop across the years, I sought to understand what characterized the man. Brilliance was clearly present, and I watched him develop into a versatile orator and lecturer. Totally at home in the pulpit of the small Baptist Church, he became equally adept in the classroom lecture hall or the senate chamber of the Statehouse in Austin, TX. One of Richard Land's greatest contributions to the Southern Baptist Convention was his service on the 1999 presidentially appointed committee to revise the *Baptist Faith and Message*, the confessional statement for Southern Baptists. In this monumental augmentation to the denomination's confession, Land, together with two other men, adroitly defended the work of the committee on the floor of the convention. This lasting contribution is of major consequence.

---

[1] For an introduction to Land's effort to effect change, see Kimberly Lynn Pennington's dissertation entitled "Blueprint for Change: A History of Efforts by Southern Baptist Leaders to Reform Southern Baptist Culture on Race Relations" (Ph.D. Dissertation, Southwestern Baptist Theological Seminary, 2016), 214-277. Pennington writes of Land: "In a book commemorating Land's twenty-five years at the helm of the Commission, Gary Frost, Land's ally in orchestrating the 1995 Resolution of Racial Reconciliation, recounted their efforts in bringing the resolution to pass and said the respect he gained for Land during that process remained intact years later. Land's work on race relations was also recognized during a retirement dinner sponsored by Commission trustees. They bestowed upon him the honorary title of President Emeritus of the Commission and donated $250,000 to the Richard Land Center for Cultural Engagement at Southwestern Baptist Theological Seminary. The Washington D.C.-based Family Research Council, an evangelical public policy institute with whose leadership Land had worked closely with through the years, awarded Land their annual Watchman Award citing his work on racial reconciliation as one motivation for granting him the honor," 275-276.

Unlike most Texans, he loved New York and Washington, D.C., but still found Terlingua, TX, chili capital of the world, fascinating. Often, it occurred to me that enormous intellectual curiosity must have sparked his astonishing grasp of history, politics, and statesmanship. But while assuring myself that intellectual curiosity reigned on the throne of his mind, I had the sensation that I was missing something—something as decisive as the engine in an automobile or the gills on a fish. Gradually, by observation I discovered what I had continually overlooked. A series of events brought this to my attention. At the time I was pastor of Bethany Baptist Church, located a few blocks away from New Orleans Seminary, where we were both in attendance. I asked Richard if he would become Minister of Evangelism at Bethany Baptist Church for a salary of $5 per week. The Princetonian accepted!

For several months, Land worked in the middle-class community of New Orleans as Minister of Evangelism. He had written a superb bachelor's Dissertation at Princeton entitled, *Crisis of Conviction: The Social, Ethical, and Theological Thought of Representative Baptist Leadership, 1840-1865*. Now he was sharing his witness about Christ door-to-door. While this appeared odd, the matter seemed less astonishing when he told me that the Vieux Carre Baptist Church, a small church located in the midst of New Orleans French Quarter, wanted him to be their pastor. For two years Land witnessed and preached the faith of Christ to the French Quarter (1970-1972).

Richard Land was developing four great intellectual loves in his life: history, politics, ethics, and the pulpit. And as I observed, evangelism and the redemptive work of Christ emerged as the cement that held the citadel together. Land believed that a measure of success in the human race was possible with human endeavor; but for ultimate realization there would have to be regeneration, an encounter with Christ and, hence, evangelism. The remainder of this essay will assess the impact of evangelism on the four consuming interests of Richard Land.

A Rudder for a Historian and Ethicist: The Avocation of Evangelist

EVANGELISM AND POLITICS

Evangelical attitudes toward politics are varied. The conviction that politics is dirty and inevitably selfish pushes not a few to the sidelines, and some even refuse to participate in casting of ballots. Others enter the political game hesitantly and participate as little as possible while still others, admitting the wickedness of much that is political, believe that one cannot effect change without involvement and therefore participate as fully as possible. Some Anabaptists of the Reformation viewed the holding of political office as sinful. The Joint Decree for the Suppression of the Anabaptists issued on September 9, 1527, states,

> They hold and teach without any qualms, also presume to maintain with Holy Scripture, that no Christian may be a magistrate. And although the government could not be preserved nor exist without the duty and bond of the oath, still they teach and hold without any exception or distinction that no Christian nor anyone else may swear an oath (even to the government), all to the offense and displacement of Christian and orderly government, brotherly love, and general peace.[2]

But some Anabaptists such as Balthasar Hubmaier saw things differently and so paved the way for American Baptist patriots in the encounter for freedom in early colonial America.

> In addition, we confess publicly that there should be a government which carries the sword, that we want and should be obedient to the same in all things that are not contrary to God, and the more the same is Christian the more it desires from God to rule with the wisdom of Solomon so that it does not deviate either to the right nor

---

2 Leland Harder, ed., *The Sources of Swiss Anabaptism: The Grebel Letters and Related Documents* (Scottdale, PA: Herald Press, 1985), 509.

to the left against God. Therefore, we should also seriously and with great diligence pray to God, for it so that we may lead a peaceful and quiet life together in all blessedness and uprightness.[3]

Pilgram Marpeck, lay theologian of the vital Anabaptist movement in Augsburg and Strasbourg, set the whole matter in clear perspective:

> I admit worldly, carnal, and earthly rulers as servants of God, in earthly matters, but not in the kingdom of Christ; according to the words of Paul, to them rightfully belongs all carnal honor, fear, obedience, tax, toll, and tribute. However, when such persons who hold authority become Christians (which I heartily wish and pray for), they may not use the aforementioned carnal force, sovereignty, or ruling in the kingdom of Christ. It cannot be upheld by any Scripture. To allow the external authority to rule in the kingdom of Christ is blasphemy against the Holy Spirit, who alone is Lord and Ruler without any human assistance.[4]

Richard Land belongs to the Hubmaier/Marpeck contingency. First, God is the architect of government. The civilization of the world after the fall of man was anything but civil. To protect the denizens of that social order and every subsequent habitat, law, and government became essential. These verses make it certain that God is the source of the law and of government:

> "What purpose then *does* the law *serve*? It was added because of transgressions, till the Seed should come to whom the promise was made; *and it was* appointed through angels by the hand of a mediator" (Gal 3:19),[5] and "Let every soul be subject to the govern-

---

[3] H. Wayne Pipkin and John H. Yoder, trans. and eds., *Balthasar Hubmaier: Theologian of Anabaptism* (Scottdale, PA: Herald Press, 1989), 98.

[4] William Klassen and Walter Klaassen, *The Writings of Pilgrim Marpeck* (Scottdale, PA: Herald Press, 1978), 150.

[5] While there may be references to Scripture in this chapter, any actual citations are from the NKJV, unless otherwise noted.

ing authorities. For there is no authority except from God, and the authorities that exist are appointed by God" (Rom 13:1).

Only redemption in Christ can assuage the wickedness of the human heart. But until that transaction is complete, the onslaught of wickedness was (and is) impeded by the presence of government and law. The appropriate posture for a believer is that of cautious participation. This is observable in the pages of Scripture. Land himself, noting the work of Francis Schaeffer to establish "true truth," said that Schaeffer . . .

> . . . helped Evangelicals jettison a deep strain of pietism that had misled them to believe they shouldn't be involved in politics and other "worldly" activities. He helped an entire generation of Christians to understand their biblical responsibility to be salt and light in society—and, of course, salt has to touch what it preserves; light has to be close enough to the darkness that it can be seen.[6]

Multiple biblical concepts inform this posture. The doctrine of the temptation and fall of man guarantees that there will be no utopia, no perfect society or sinless world. The doctrines of the giving of the law and its enforcement provide an outline for a social order and augur for political involvement of believers to place the best conceivable leaders in public office. The doctrine of the cross of Christ, which provides a remedy for the manifold failures of politics and biblical instruction in eschatology, generates hope for the intervention of God in the affairs of men.

The Scriptures underscore such political activity. David served as king over Israel. Despite his well-known failures, overall, he provided moral and spiritual direction. Psalm 51 alone is an instruction manual in how to approach God. Daniel, Hananiah, Azariah, and Mishael are pressed into government service on behalf of their captors. Subject even to the cruelty and possible mutilation associated with being made eunuchs, they labored for the good of all and became major influencers in Babylon and Persia.

---

6 Richard Land, *The Divided States of America* (Nashville: Thomas Nelson, 2007), 9.

The New Testament and early Christian literature recount not a few examples, though servants of Rome remain fervent in their service to Christ. Politics is not essentially a game of compromise. Rather politics is the challenge of passionate and constructive leadership on behalf of the people.

In 1980, Uganda, in the tragic days following the escape of dictator Edi Amin from certain execution, was one of the first countries I visited in Africa. Amin, the Butcher of Uganda as he became known, was no more intrinsically evil than anyone else as a young leader, but over 300,000 people died at his hand during his evil reign.

Immediately to the south of Uganda is the kingdom of Zambia. Levy Mwanawasa was born in 1948 and died prematurely on August 19, 2008. As president of Zambia, Mwanawasa received Christ as his Savior through the witness of Rodney Masona and others and was baptized by Masona. Until his untimely death, he labored to rid Zambia of all corruption and establish equitable rule in Zambia. The contrast between Amin and Mwanawasa on the continent of Africa establishes the difference that is made by a godly ruler. As the Bible says, "When the righteous are in authority, the people rejoice; but when a wicked man rules, the people groan" (Prov 29:2).

Appropriate political action prevents coercive evangelism. But proper political perception guarantees freedom of faith and consequently leaves open the liberty to speak of Christ and His remedy for the sinfulness of humankind. And an altered life dedicated to Christ establishes principles of righteousness on which any nation prospers.

EVANGELISM AND ETHICS

At Princeton, Land minored in religion under the watchful oversight of Paul Ramsey, noted for his labors in biomedical ethics and Just War theory. The mentoring of this professor underscored the interest that Land had developed in ethics. Acknowledging the intrinsic evil of war, Land followed Ramsey and became a spokesman for the unavoidability of war in rare instances. But the subject of race became the area in which he would make his greatest contribution, although abortion was also prominent in his think-

A Rudder for a Historian and Ethicist: The Avocation of Evangelist

ing. In 1988 elected to the presidency of the Christian Life Commission[7] of the 12-million-member Southern Baptist Convention in 1988, Land, against the advice of others, tackled the question of racism in the Southern Baptist denomination and then served as a major player in electing Dr. Fred Luter as the first black president of the convention.

This effort to reestablish Southern Baptists as a convention of churches free of racial animus was attempted at a moment when racists still held sway even in conservative, otherwise Bible-believing circles. For example, when I accepted the presidency of Southeastern Baptist Theological Seminary in 1992, about my second week I discovered a large confederate flag displayed in the school cafeteria. This was followed by a large crowd at a night meeting. Queried, the response was that this was a regular meeting of the Sons of the Confederacy, and "they are good customers." I explained that they *had been* good "former customers," much to the chagrin of one in charge of food services. Later, I had to abandon my membership in a "conservative Baptist church" when a deacon refused to allow a black woman to enter. Land led the SBC to new heights in the battle against race in difficult times and under staunch criticism.

But whereas Land believed in societal action, he knew that George Washington Carver spoke the truth when he said, "Divine Love is destined to rule the world, I believe, despite the many things that often irritate and depress us."[8] Thus Land saw that the only resolution to racism worldwide was conversion to Christ.

For Land, the state of the nation is ominous. In 2002, he wrote:

> So where are we? The media bombards us with sex and violence, the traditional family is fractured by sex and violence as a direct result, and the government that should protect us has turned the chicken coop over to the foxes, ironically abandoning the Judeo-Christian traditional values our freedoms were built upon—in the name of

---

7 Later in 1997 the name was changed to the Ethics and Religious Liberty Commission under Land's leadership.

8 John Perry, *Unshakable Faith: Booker T. Washington & George Washington Carver* (Sisters, OR: Multnomah Publishers, 1999), 13.

freedom. The First Amendment has been turned on its head. If I weren't a Christian, I'd be worried. Honestly, deep down inside, I do fear for the future of our country and our cherished freedoms and way of life, which is without a doubt the richest and freest in the history of the world.[9]

Nevertheless, Land spoke of the family as an effective witness for Christ. He also wrote,

> Few things are a more effective witness, a more effective way to be salt and light to both your children and community, than to have the marriage God wants you to have and for you to be the husband or wife God wants you to be. But as we've seen, the traditional family is under fire like never before in American history. There's little point in debating for long the problems and challenges American families face because they're well documented already.[10]

Moral leadership in the political arena or any other has become a rare spectacle. Andrew Mangione notes that . . .

> America prospers when presidents are good moral leaders. This prosperity is evidenced financially, which is important, but is also supported by a morally straightforward culture. Robust societies are built upon the foundation of good moral leadership. Strong moral presidents have the courage to intrepidly provoke the angst that is troubling their people in pursuit of achieving what is best for the country. Fortunately, they are guided by the Constitution, which, as John Adams said, "was made only for a moral and religious People. It is wholly inadequate to the government of any other."[11]

---

9 Richard Land, *For Faith & Family: Changing America by Strengthening the Family* (Nashville: Broadman & Holman Publishers, 2002), 7.

10 Ibid., 8.

11 Andrew Mangione, "Morality and Leadership," in *The Amac Magazine* (April 2021): 54.

A Rudder for a Historian and Ethicist: The Avocation of Evangelist

A major issue that occupied much of Richard Land's time and attention is the sanctity of life in general and in particular the lives of innocent pre-borns. Land, joined by many evangelicals, believes that from the moment of conception, the pre-born is a life sacred to God.

In Wayne Grudem's extensive tome entitled *Politics According to the Bible*, Grudem takes issue with these evangelicals based on his understanding of John MacArthur and Cal Thomas, who argue for a somewhat truncated perspective of Christian involvement in the political arena. Though it would be difficult to slide a quarter between their views, Grudem says,

> While I agree with Thomas and MacArthur on many other things, I cannot agree with their disparagement of the value of Christian political involvement for God's purposes on this earth. I think it represents too narrow an understanding of the work of God's kingdom and the nature of the Christian gospel message. "The Gospel" in the New Testament is not just "trust Jesus and be forgiven of your sins and grow in holiness and go to heaven" (though that is certainly true, and that is the heart of the Gospel and its foundational message). No, the Gospel is God's *good news* about all of life! Jesus said, "Go therefore and make disciples of all nations, baptizing them in the name of the Father and of the Son and of the Holy Spirit, *teaching them to observe all that I have commanded you*" (Matt 28:19-20).[12]

Though Grudem and Land probably do not agree on the fine points of every theological or political affirmation, I believe that Land would applaud Grudem's statement for Christian interaction. This position recognizes that the Gospel has a primary and a secondary application. Above all, the Gospel is forever the story of redemption. God's love for lost women and men led to the incarnation of Christ and His atoning death, the benefits from which can be appropriated by faith. However, this step of faith in Christ results in regeneration, which in turn affects every aspect of life.

---

12 Wayne Grudem, *Politics According to the Bible: A Comprehensive Resource for Understanding Modern Political Issues in Light of Scripture* (Grand Rapids, MI: Zondervan, 2010), 45.

As far as the issue of abortion is concerned because it is an issue of life, and at that, an issue of innocent life, the government has both the right and responsibility to protect life. However, just as police have the duty to protect human life, there is a limitation on their ability to do so. Consequently, the ability of the government to protect innocent preborn life is to some degree the result of the conversion of a sufficient part of the general population to become a societal conscience and thus provide the backdrop for both the underlying morality and the enforcement of pro-life activity. Consequently, the fight for life must proceed on political and moral levels but never to the neglect of the message of Christ's transforming love.

Evangelism and the Historian

The role of historian allows Richard Land to excel and to recount the exploits of Christian evangelization. British historian, Arnold Toynbee, in his monumental *A Study of History* prepared the way by his focus on the failure of science.

> But the scientist's conviction was vitiated by two fundamental errors. He was mistaken in attributing the relative well-being of the eighteenth-century and nineteenth-century Western world to his own achievements; and he was mistaken in assuming that this recently achieved well-being was going to persist. It was not the Promised Land but the Waste Land that was just round the corner.[13]

Like Toynbee, Land knew the history of science well and was cognizant of its limitations and failure. But he also believed that there was a form of faith that was transformative. He could focus on places like Nagaland. The Nagas represented eighteen fierce tribes of noted headhunters in 1850. Around 1903, missionaries from Assam determined that even if it cost them their lives, they would venture to the South and take the Gospel to the Naga

---

13 Arnold J. Toynbee, *A Study of History* (New York: Oxford University Press, 1957), 99.

tribes. In 2003, my wife and I attended the 100th anniversary of the coming of Christ to the Nagas and watched as several hundred men adorned as headhunters stood and sang a perfect rendition of Handel's *Halleluiah* chorus without instrumental accompaniment. Despite the desolations and horrors perpetrated by the Indian government chronicled in Kaka Iralu's book, the Nagas continue to maintain an Asian oasis of Christian love in a hostile environment.[14]

John Wolffe's challenging work on Wilberforce, More, Chalmers, and Finney provides another starling example of the fact that Christianity nullifies the most overt causes of evil such as slavery.[15] Murray Andrew Pura underscores a similar theme.[16] Wolffe demonstrates the power of the Gospel message when word of relatively mild reform in the slave trade reached Barbados. Missionary William Shrewsbury was attacked by white racists in the Methodist chapel and had to be transferred for his own safety. But such upheavals gradually succumbed to the force of the Gospel, and abolition became a reality.[17]

John Piper, writing in *The Roots of Endurance*, focuses on the devout training of John Newton's mother and its ultimate impact on Newton, the slave trader. Then caught in a violent storm at sea,

> He awoke that night to a violent storm as his room began to fill with water. As he ran for the deck, the captain stopped him and had him fetch a knife. The man who went up in his place was immediately washed overboard. He was assigned to the pumps and heard himself say, "If this will not do, the Lord have mercy upon us." It was the first time he had expressed the need for mercy in many years.[18]

---

14   Kaka Iralu, *Nagaland and India: The Blood and the Tears* (Nagaland: Kaka D. Iralu, 2000).

15   John Wolffe, *The Expansion of Evangelicalism: The Age of Wilberforce, More, Chalmers and Finney* (Downers Grove, IL: InterVarsity Press, 2007).

16   Murray Andrew Pura, *Vital Christianity: The Life and Spirituality of William Wilberforce* (Toronto: Clements Publishing, 2003).

17   Wolffe, *The Expansion of Evangelicalism*, 205.

18   John Piper, *The Roots of Endurance: Invincible Perseverance in the Lives*

This event led ultimately to his conversion and even beyond to his total renouncing of the slave trade. What science or social reform was unable to effect, the Gospel accomplished on a grand scale. Doubtless, the church has often failed. But when Christ's way is honored and followed, the achievements are nothing short of spectacular. Social reforms do not constitute the Gospel, but Land understands the power that resides within the Gospel to change hearts and lives.

The thesis of this writer is that Land's unique comprehension of the work of God in history provided motivation for understanding a call to the ministry. Political interest was present, and academic endeavors provided a world in which he delighted. But it was his understanding that the ministry would place him in the power stream of God and enable him to accomplish what might otherwise be little more than a dream, which together guided his call to preach.

The Pulpit and Evangelism

Richard Land, in my opinion, does not conceive of himself as having the gift of the evangelist. But if the gift of the evangelist is absent, the responsibility for evangelism is unavoidable and is tied in part to the call of God for him to be a public spokesman for God—a preacher of the Gospel. Few have articulated this perspective with more insight than Quaker philosopher Elton Trueblood. In his book *The Company of the Committed*, Trueblood notes the impact of the ministry of Timothy Dwight when the latter was appointed to the presidency of Yale College. "When the great Timothy Dwight took over the presidency of Yale College not one student would admit publicly to faith in Christ. When Dwight ended the presidency twenty-two years later, in 1817, the entire intellectual climate of the college had changed: it changed because Dwight did something about it."[19] This invincible record

---

of John Newton, Charles Simeon, and William Wilberforce (Wheaton, IL: Crossway Books, 2002), 48.

19 Elton Trueblood, *The Company of the Committed* (New York: Harper & Row Publishers, 1961), 6.

Dwight accomplished because he understood that there was a more crucial purpose for Yale than education. Men were to be changed not merely educated. And he comprehended the truth often absent from the minds of contemporary administrators—that evangelism begins with the president of the institution. He also apparently grasped the amazing fact that an exciting school basking in the glow of aggressive evangelism is an auto-recruiting juggernaut. Not only so, but also the vision for the souls of the lost tends to inform all other disciplines. In fact, Trueblood observed, "Many contemporary seekers cannot abide the Church as they see it, their dissatisfaction arising not from the fact that membership demands too much, but rather from the fact that the demands are too small."[20]

Land arrived at New Orleans Seminary possessed of a clear vision of God's call to preach. There was an urgency about this predilection that is also captured by Trueblood as he focused on evangelism.

> If I do not open the door for another, it may never be opened, for it is possible that I may be the only one who holds this particular key. The worker on the production line may have an entree to the life of his fellow worker on the line which can never be matched by any pastor or teacher or professional evangelist. The responsibility of each individual Christian is to do that which no other person can do as well as he can.[21]

Land, like Trueblood, had this urgency underscored by one more critical circumstance described in another book of Trueblood.

> Before Christians succumb to such pressures, they are wise to note that there is no cutting edge that is not narrow. There is no likelihood whatever that Christianity could have won in the ancient world as religion in general. It survived very largely because it accepted the scandal of particularity. It could not have survived had it not been sufficiently definite to be counted worthy of persecution.

---

20 Trueblood, *Company of the Committed*, 9.
21 Ibid., 56.

> A tolerant pantheism, which is the real core of some of the self-styled new theology, will never be persecuted because most people will never oppose anything so vague.[22]

The lack in much of Christianity and the vitality available in Land's perspective provided the impetus for Land's conviction that his pulpit ministry was vital. Land would serve the public interests through politics, ethics, and the teaching of history. But he would serve the church from the pulpit, accepting the self-imposed restriction of expository preaching. The task of the preacher is not to take a text and derive therefrom a pithy outline on the subject of his choosing. Rather the preacher's task is to explain and apply the text selected from the Bible, letting God Himself speak His message to His creation.

Conclusion

Colorful Roger Scruton notes what often transpires in the world of the Academy.

> A man might see all the patches of colour which make up a painted portrait and yet not see the face which it contains, even though no feature of the painting has escaped his attention. He sees all the details, but not the *portrait*. There is a way of understanding what he sees, and a way of responding to it, which for some reason has eluded him. Analogously, a scientist may observe in another all the workings of a human organism and avail himself of a complete account of the organism's structure and behaviour. And yet he may fail to see the person who this organism embodies. And just as the detailed scrutiny of coloured patches militates against the understanding of the portrait, so, it might be suggested, does the clinical

---

22 Elton Trueblood, *The Incendiary Fellowship* (New York: Harper & Row, 1967), 25.

A Rudder for a Historian and Ethicist: The Avocation of Evangelist

objectivity of the scientific observer damage his understanding of the person.[23]

A person who has spent much time in the academic sphere knows well the paralysis of minutiae. And too frequently this preoccupation with detail curtails understanding an author. Richard Land stretched his mental capacities in history and ethics at Princeton and Oxford. He honed his political instincts in the governor's office in Texas and at the Ethics and Religious Liberty Commission, spending credible time in the nation's capital. The commencing phase of Land's retirement ministry added a tenure as president of Southern Evangelical Seminary in North Carolina. But at no time in this sojourn did Land neglect the call of God to preach the Gospel. Piecing together the myriad details of his career, Land found cohesion in the Word of God. Pulpit labors accentuated the variegated colors of his training; and as Scruton says, you could not miss the Man in the picture. Jesus the Christ held it all together and explicated the whole.

---

23 Roger Scruton, *The Politics of Culture and Other Essays* (South Bend, IN: St. Augustine's Press, 2019), 183.

Chapter 14

Social Justice in Light of Scripture

Ronnie Rogers

Dr. Land,

You helped me to think. As difficult as it was to be a student in your Systematic Theology, Baptist Distinctives, Philosophy, and Cultural Milieu classes, I would not take anything for all that you taught me. In these succeeding decades of serving in our convention, I have continued to learn from your strong leadership and statesmanship. I am truly your debtor!

* * *

This chapter has two parts. Part one explains the fundamentals for understanding social justice. Part two gives an insight into the methodologies of cultural Marxism and social justice. This part illustrates how social justice works in real life. I will use the lens of Scripture to contrast the biblical perspective with that of social justice and highlight how social justice undermines biblical truth and corrupts the gospel of Jesus Christ. Theories enmeshed in this topic such as critical theory, social justice, critical race theory, and intersectionality have been taught in academia for decades. They are the basis of identity politics in the Democratic Party. Now we must face their presence in conservative, evangelical Christianity, and the Southern Baptist Convention (SBC). I believe genuine racism exists, but I do not think any of these theories are descriptive or reflective of the biblical meaning of race or true racism, nor can they offer an effective answer for stemming racism and creating unity.[1]

PART ONE: THE FUNDAMENTALS FOR UNDERSTANDING SOCIAL JUSTICE

Here are some definitions of key concepts that will be expanded upon in the rest of the chapter.

Genuine racism is the belief that one or more ethnicities or races are *inherently* inferior. Since the inferiority is innate, it cannot be overcome. Accordingly, anyone can be racist. If a person is genuinely racist, it will manifest itself in objective speech and acts.

Critical race theory, as defined in *The Encyclopedia Britannica*, is "the view that the law and legal institutions are inherently racist and that race itself, instead of being biologically grounded and natural, is a socially constructed concept that is used by white people to further their economic and political interests at the expense of people of colour."[2] Consequently, whites are racists, and blacks are not. Racism dominates virtually everything, and racism is *always* present in personal and structural interactions; it is systemic. Critical race theory critiques both structures and groups. There

---

1 To see more of this topic, see my book *A Corruption of Consequence: Adding Social Justice to The Gospel* (Eugene, OR: Resource, 2021).

2 Tommy Curry, "Critical Race Theory," *Encyclopedia Britannica*, accessed February 02, 2020, https://www.britannica.com/topic/critical-race-theory para. 1. In between the time when I originally cited this entry and the time of the publication of my most recent book, March 08, 2021, *A Corruption of Consequence*, the Encyclopedia Britannica's definition of the term "critical race theory" evidently changed, providing an interesting insight into the terminological fluidity regarding our time and this subject. Here is the original: "Race, instead of being biologically grounded and natural, is socially constructed; and that race as a socially constructed concept functions as a means to maintain the interests of the white population that constructed it."

are little or no individual responsibility factors, and everyone is judged by the group to which they belong. Critical race theorists say they seek to expose racism everywhere because critical race theorists believe it is always present, even when people are unaware of its presence.

Race defined biblically maintains that all people belong to the human race, and therefore, all are equal, being created in the image of God (Gen 1:26–28). God later created multiple languages and dispersed the people into different geographical locations (Gen 11:7–9). Out of this scattered, geographically diverse, and multilingual human race developed various biologically common traits for the many groups, as well as more languages, dialects, and subcultures, which became known as ethnicities, nationalities, and races. These are often associated with language, skin color, and geographical origin. Accordingly, all races and ethnicities are understood in the sense of Gen 1:26–28, Gen 11:7–9, and other biblical distinctions such as tribe, people, tongue, and nation (Rev 7:9; 11:9). We may, therefore, note five essentials that unite all human beings.

1. All people belong to the human race (Gen 1:26–28).
2. All people are created in the image of God (Gen 1:26–28).
3. All people are fallen in sin (Gen 3).
4. Christ salvationally loves and died for all people (John 3:16).
5. The saved are reconciled to God and each other and forgiven of *all* their sins (Rom 8:1; Eph 2:10–20).

Race defined biblically necessarily rejects *actual* racism. Merriam-Webster Dictionary defines racism as: "A belief that race is the primary determinant of human traits and capacities and that racial differences produce an *inherent superiority* of a particular race."[3] Genuine racism is the sin

---

3 "Racism," accessed February 05, 2020, https://www.merriam-webster.com/dictionary/racism. Emphasis added. As of February 25, 2021, Cambridge Dictionary defined racism as "policies, behaviors, rules, etc. that result in a continued unfair advantage to some people and unfair or harmful treatment of others based on race: harmful or unfair things that people say, do, or think based on the belief that their own race makes them more intelligent, good, moral, etc. than peo-

of partiality, which Scripture condemns (Lev 19:15; Jas 2:1–9; 3:13–18). Accordingly, the biblical perspective of race necessarily rejects race as defined by critical race theory or as popularly used in American culture, which reduces it to a weapon to divide and silence anyone who disagrees with liberal or socialistic policies.

Intersectionality is a term developed by Kimberlé Williams Crenshaw, a leading critical race theory scholar.[4] Intersectionality is defined in the Oxford Dictionary as "the interconnected nature of social categorizations such as race, class, and gender as they apply to a given individual or group, regarded as creating overlapping and interdependent systems of discrimination or disadvantage."[5] Consequently, minorities can suffer from multiple levels of discrimination. Since life experience provides a person with his own truth, people who have been oppressed less or not oppressed (according to critical theory) cannot understand or judge the truth of the oppressed.

Interest convergence means that anything and everything a white person might do for or with a person of color is motivated by the benefit it brings to the white person. Consequently, all white people are hypocritical and do not *truly* care about people of color.

Social justice racism is the belief that racism is determined structurally rather than individually because it is systemic. Everyone belonging to the majority privileged group is a racist. Thus, white people are white suprem-

---

ple of other races." "Racism," para. 1. Similar to the Encyclopedia Britannica update in an earlier footnote, the definition from Cambridge Dictionary was changed at some point. Here is the original as of February 05, 2020, "the belief that people's qualities are influenced by their race and that the members of other races are not as good as the members of your own, or the resulting unfair treatment of members of other races."

4   Crenshaw coined the term in 1989. She is a black, full-time professor at the UCLA School of Law and Columbia Law School. She is an American lawyer, civil rights advocate, and a leading scholar of critical race theory. She used it to demonstrate that social justice happens at multiple levels. Merrill Perlman, "The Origin of the Term 'Intersectionality,'" *Columbia Journalism Review*, October 23, 2018, accessed March 13, 2020, https://www.cjr.org/language_corner/intersectionality.php.

5   "Intersectionality," accessed June 18, 202, https://www.lexico.com/en/definition/intersectionality.

acists because of the group to which they belong and the privileges they are said to have experienced. Reverse discrimination is impossible since only those with white privilege and power can be racists.

Cultural Marxism, in contrast to classical Marxism's economic emphasis, stresses the importance of culture, changing cultural norms (nuclear family, education, religion, media, law), and incorporates Sigmund Freud's psychology and Max Webber's sociology. It proposes a clash between the oppressed (minorities) and the oppressor (majority). It focuses on changing structures and marginalizing individual responsibility by emphasizing group identity and responsibility. Cultural Marxism emphasizes that "majority groups are privileged, and oppressive and minority groups are typically underprivileged and oppressed."[6]

Social justice, in contrast to biblical justice, seeks justice by a forced transfer of power and wealth from the oppressor (majority) to the oppressed (minority). All disparities are assumed to be the result of social injustices inflicted by various majorities on their respective minorities (white/black, heterosexuals/homosexuals, cisgenders/transgenders) rather than other possible causes. Not all social justice advocates endorse riots, violence, and destruction of private and government property, but many do. At its core, social justice rejects capitalism and seeks a Marxian socialistic utopia.

The term *Woke* refers to being intensely aware of social injustices such as institutional and systemic racism. Wokeness includes seeing virtually all disparities as resulting from injustices (injustices as defined by social justice and critical race theory) and actively fighting against systemic racism and injustice. Wokeness for a white person is a life-long process because a white person never becomes fully woke—non-white.

Critical theory is different from traditional social theory.[7] Traditional social theory endeavors to understand society, whereas critical theory seeks

---

[6] TheNewCalvinist, "Stain of Mohler 3" *YouTube* November 25, 2019, accessed February 04, 2020, https://www.youtube.com/watch?v=MIlnLU-vt_g, 9:36–44.

[7] Max Horkheimer contrasted critical theory with traditional theories. Max Horkheimer, *Critical Theory: Selected Essays*, 1968. Translated by Matthew J. O'Connell, et. al. Reprint, (New York: Continuum, 2002), 188–243.

to change society. When someone uses social justice or intersectionality, like critical theory, these terms presume there are oppressors and those that are oppressed who need to be delivered. James Bohman says, "A theory is critical to the extent that it seeks human "emancipation from slavery," and acts as a "liberating . . . influence."[8] Thus, critical theory is designed to over-focus on problems while neglecting any positive attributes so that which is being critiqued can be destroyed. In this case, America and capitalism are critiqued and destroyed for the purpose of replacing them with a better society, which means socialism or communism. They problematize everything in an oppressor vs. oppressed paradigm.[9]

The origin of critical theory is a think tank called the Institute for Social Research at the Frankfurt School in Germany, which eventually became known as the Frankfurt School.[10] The expected utopia that was supposed to arise from classical Marxism never appeared.[11] Critical theory arose

---

8   "Such theories aim to explain and transform all the circumstances that enslave human beings." (Horkheimer 1972, 246). Quoted by James Bohman, "Critical Theory," *Stanford Encyclopedia of Philosophy*, March 8, 2005. Edited by Edward N. Zalta, accessed February 21, 2020, https://plato.stanford.edu/archives/win2019/entries/critical-theory/, para. 1.

9   Problematize means to make or treat everything as a problem. Critical Theorists seek to problematize society to change the entire society to socialism. They will use any and every area of life to do so; for example, see Marcuse's use of sexual mores to this end in Mike Gonzalez's book, *The Plot to Change America: How Identity Politics Is Dividing the Land of the Free* (New York: Encounter, 2020), 136.

10   There is a sense in which Karl Marx was the first critical theorist, at least in modern times, since he evaluated society to change it, and his evaluation was composed of oppressors and the oppressed.

11   Stephen Thomas Kirschner says, "Marx believed that feudalism would lead to capitalism. Capitalism would create massive inequality between the rich and the poor. The workers would all rise up and overthrow the hated 'bourgeoisie' (the upper class). There would then be a 'dictatorship of the proletariat' (the workers) which would ensure equality. Then that government would wear away and break down, and the world would be left with this utopian, egalitarian society. (Although, how and why government would break down and equality would be ensured was never clearly explained.)" Stephen Thomas Kirschner, "Cultural Marxism: The Origins of the Present Day Social Justice Movement, and Political Correctness," *The*

to correct the deficiencies of classical Marxism and, therefore, bring about a just society.[12] The change sought by critical theory entails deconstructing (destroying) the existing culture and ushering in what critical theorists believe is a more just society, which means a socialistic or communistic society. In critical theory, there is the assumption of oppressors and oppression. It advances its cause by comparing real-life capitalism with utopic socialism, which has never existed, nor shall it in this life.

In 1933, Hitler rose to power, and he viewed Marxism as an enemy, which resulted in several pivotal thinkers of the Frankfurt School fleeing to New York. There, they took teaching positions at Columbia University and ultimately other universities. Stephen Thomas Kirschner says, "The Frankfurt School was loosely reestablished at Columbia, this time focusing on America, rather than Germany."[13] After the fall of the Third Reich, all but Herbert Marcuse returned to Germany. Marcuse went on to teach at other universities. It was Marcuse and the Italian neo-Marxist Antonio Gramsci who produced what we know as cultural Marxism.

Senior Fellow at the Heritage Foundation, Mike Gonzalez comments, "Woke progressives take their ideological marching orders from European thinkers of decades ago, such as the Italian Antonio Gramsci and

---

Policy, February 14, 2017, accessed March 13, 20210, https://thepolicy.us/cultural-marxism-the-origins-of-the-present-day-social-justice-movement-and-political-correctness-ffb89c6ef4f1, para. 3.

12 Kirschner says, "In 1937, [Max] Horkheimer wrote about what is today known as 'critical theory.' Critical theory is a social theory which is about criticizing the way a culture and 'society as a whole' function, in order to change it. Contrast this with other social theories, which are more just about understanding and interpreting why things are as they are." Kirschner, "Cultural Marxism," paras. 20-22. In speaking of Horkheimer's writings, the Stanford Encyclopedia of Philosophy says, "Especially important in this regard are the writings from the 1930s, which were largely responsible for developing the epistemological and methodological orientation of Frankfurt School critical theory." J.C. Berendzen, "Max Horkheimer," *The Stanford Encyclopedia of Philosophy*, June 24, 2009, accessed February 08, 2021, https://plato.stanford.edu/entries/horkheimer/, para. 1.

13 Kirschner, "Cultural Marxism," para. 19.

the German-American Herbert Marcuse."[14] Kirschner says, "In the 1950s, Marcuse stated the Marxist revolution would not be brought about by 'the proletariat' but by a coalition of blacks, feminist women, homosexuals, and students. This is where the term 'Cultural Marxism' comes from, as it is applied to marginalized groups rather than class."[15] Antonio Gramsci is often considered the father of cultural Marxism, but he and Marcuse are the most significant neo-Marxists, framing cultural Marxism.

Similar to classical Marxism, there must be a clash between groups. In cultural Marxism, the groups are the oppressors (majorities) and the oppressed (minorities). Critical theory is the foundation and source of contemporary social justice and cultural Marxism. Social justice and cultural Marxism is the advocacy and application of critical theory. In the late 80s, critical race theory made a move away from its close connections with critical legal theory toward men like "Martin Luther King, Jr.,[16] W.E.B. Du Bois, Malcolm X,[17] the Black Panthers, and Frantz Fanon."[18] This does

---

14 Mike Gonzalez, "The Revolution Is upon Us," *Law & Liberty*, September 4, 2020, accessed February 11, 2021, https://lawliberty.org/the-revolution-is-upon-us/, para. 5.

15 Kirschner, "Cultural Marxism," para. 29.

16 MLK is said to have been against capitalism and to have been pro-socialism, accessed February 11, 2021, https://www.theadvocates.org/2019/02/remembering-malcolm-x-an-unlikely-advocate-for-capitalism/, para. 8.

17 Malcolm X is said in his early years to have declared himself a Communist. Jose Nino, "Remembering Malcolm X: An Unlikely Advocate for Capitalism," *Advocates for Self Government*, February 2019, accessed February 11, 201, https://www.theadvocates.org/2019/02/remembering-malcolm-x-an-unlikely-advocate-for-capitalism/, para. 4. Also, he "criticized the mainstream civil rights movement, challenging Martin Luther King, Jr.'s central notions of integration and nonviolence . . . In contrast to King's strategy of nonviolence, civil disobedience, and redemptive suffering, Malcolm urged his followers to defend themselves 'by any means necessary.'" After his departure from the nation of Islam, he became a Sunni Muslim and "he claimed that the solution to racial problems in the United States lay in orthodox Islam." Lawrence A. Mamiya, "Malcolm X," *Encyclopedia Britannica*, October 22, 2020, accessed February 11, 2021, https://www.britannica.com/biography/Malcolm-X, para. 7.

18 Tommy Curry, "Critical race theory," *Encyclopedia Britannica*, May

not mean that critical race theory separated from critical theory, but that it only separated from working within critical legal theory. Both critical race theory and intersectionality have continued to expand their applications, including structures and groups of individuals, so that the connections and overlaps with critical theory and cultural Marxism are evident.[19] Marxian concepts can be seen in critical race theory applications and with men like Du Bois, who hated capitalism and blamed racism on it. For example, Dr. Du Bois "concluded that 'capitalism cannot reform itself; it is doomed to self-destruction . . . Communism—the effort to give all men what they need and to ask of each the best they can contribute—this is the only way of human life.'"[20]

In her significant paper *Mapping the Margins,* Crenshaw says, "Intersectionality may provide the means for dealing with other marginalizations

---

28, 2020, accessed February 9, 2021, https://www.britannica.com/topic/critical-race-theory, para. 2.

19 "Critical Theory has a narrow and a broad meaning in philosophy and in the history of the social sciences. 'Critical Theory' in the narrow sense designates several generations of German philosophers and social theorists in the Western European Marxist tradition known as the Frankfurt School. According to these theorists, a 'critical' theory may be distinguished from a 'traditional' theory according to a specific practical purpose: a theory is critical to the extent that it seeks human 'emancipation from slavery,' acts as a 'liberating . . . influence,' and works 'to create a world which satisfies the needs and powers' of human beings (Max Horkheimer 1972, 246). Because such theories aim to explain and transform all the circumstances that enslave human beings, many 'critical theories' in the broader sense have been developed. They have emerged in connection with the many social movements that identify varied dimensions of the domination of human beings in modern societies. In both the broad and the narrow senses, however, a critical theory provides the descriptive and normative bases for social inquiry aimed at decreasing domination and increasing freedom in all their forms." James Bohman, "Critical Theory," *Stanford Encyclopedia of Philosophy,* March 8, 2005. Edited by Edward N. Zalta, accessed February 21, 2020, https://plato.stanford.edu/archives/win2019/entries/critical-theory/, para. 1.

20 Peter Kihss, "Dr. W. E. B. Du Bois Joins Communist Party at 93," *New York Times,* November 23, 1961, accessed February 10, 2021, https://archive.nytimes.com/www.nytimes.com/books/00/11/05/specials/dubois-communist.html, paras. 10–11.

as well. For example, race can also be a coalition of straight and gay people of color, and thus *serve as a basis for critique of churches* and other cultural institutions *that reproduce heterosexism.*"[21] Thus, intersectionality can be used against churches that teach the biblical truth about men and women. Both intersectionality and the amorphous (fluid) term *critical race theory* serve as the framework used in bias sensitivity training within our systems of government, education, and corporate America by people like Robin DiAngelo and her book *White Fragility*. Presently, *social justice* is the most common term used in America to express the essence of Marxian ideologies and cultural Marxism.

Consequently, when one hears the term social justice, one should think of critical theory, cultural Marxism, critical race theory, and intersectionality. You should not think justice as understood to mean equality before the law or even equality of opportunity; by equity and equality, social justice advocates mean equal outcomes—socialism.

Thomas Sowell, a Senior Fellow at the Hoover Institute, asks, "How does one explain the *origins* of something like inequality, which has been ubiquitous as far back as recorded history goes?"[22] His book demonstrates multiple factors that result in unequal outcomes rather than simplistically reducing inequality to one cause, such as social injustice. Unequal outcomes are true whether one is considering a particular family, country, or the world. Thus, he says, "The probability that all of these combinations and permutations would work out in such a way as to produce even approximately equal economic outcomes around the world is remote."[23]

Nevertheless, social justice reduces the cause of unequal outcomes (disparities) to social injustice, which Marxian socialism is supposed to cure even though it has never done so. Additionally, you should never equate

---

21 Kimberlé Williams Crenshaw, "Mapping the Margins: Intersectionality, Identity Politics and Violence Against Women of Color," *Women, Gender & Research* 2 (2006), 7–20, accessed February 4/, 2021, https://pdfs.semanticscholar.org/734f/8b582b7d7bb375415d2975cb783c839e5e3c.pdf. Emphasis added.

22 Thomas Sowell, *Wealth, Poverty, and Politics* (New York: Basic Books, 2016), 2.

23 Ibid., 20.

social justice with God's justice, as revealed in Scripture, because social justice is based on man, an erroneous definition of racism, a forced transfer of power and wealth, and materialistic cultural Marxism, and, it is, therefore, in fundamental opposition to biblical justice. It is quite understandable that some proponents of critical race theory, intersectionality, and social justice want to distance themselves from cultural Marxism, but the overwhelming and indisputable facts are against them.

I often use cultural Marxism[24] as an umbrella term along with conflict theory, critical theory, or social justice.[25] I do so for many reasons, but primarily so the Marxian ideological basis and framework of events, goals, and popular ideas such as critical race theory, intersectionality, and social justice can be exposed. These umbrella terms encompass various concepts, which can often be used interchangeably or overlappingly although not synonymously. These concepts include such terms and ideas as, wokeness, critical

---

24 My use of the term cultural Marxism and criticism of critical theory and the Frankfurt school does not include even the slightest hint of antisemitism or some non-evidential conspiracy theory. While some who critique these may be antisemitic, the charge that criticism of Frankfurt school is necessarily antisemitic ignores the Germanic influence and decidedly Germanic direction the Frankfurt school took. Regarding the charge of cultural Marxism being a "conspiracy theory," that is not applicable to the best use or my use of the term since it is evidence-based. One only needs to read Antonio Gramsci and Herbert Marcuse's actual writings to properly understand the term. Moreover, while I recognize there are false conspiracy theories, the characterization that something is a conspiracy theory does not make it one. For example, belief in the Genesis account of creation is also deemed a conspiracy theory by many who seek to undermine Scripture; this charge is baseless. Thus, I unreservedly disavow both the antisemitic and conspiratorial aspects that are sometimes associated with the term. The term as used by me is evidenced-based and essential to helping Christians and others see that anarchical ideas like social justice are reformed expressions of Marxism. Classical Marxism failed to spread to countries like Germany and England, and the Frankfurt School sought to understand why. While there are many reasons, probably the most prominent is that Marx made it entirely about economics when he should have included cultural and psychological factors. That is what Herbert Marcuse, Antonio Gramsci, and others did in transforming classical Marxism into cultural Marxism.

25 We can also use terms like conflict theory.

race theory, intersectionality, postmodernism's emphasis that everything is about power and knowledge, and knowledge is not objective but a construct of language. Other ideas include: America is systemically and structurally racist, people are divided into groups in which personal identity and responsibility are secondary to group identity and responsibility, all groups are divided under the labels of oppressor or oppressed, and racism is defined to make only those with power capable of racism.[26] Additionally, knowledge comes from a person's social standing, which is known as standpoint epistemology,[27] identity politics,[28] and all for the purpose of redefining such concepts as diversity, inclusiveness, equity, and equality to unalterably promote wokeness and prove systemic racism and systemic one-sided social injustice.[29]

---

26 Racism is not based on an individual's belief about races or even a person's objective or intentional actions (as is true of biblically or historically defined racism). Instead, it is based on skin color, majority group status, and that racism is systemic so that all structures in society are inherently racist. Therefore, all white people are racist because they live in America; racism is in America's DNA. Thusly defined, the question is not whether racism is present in interactions between whites and people of color, but rather how did racism manifest itself in that situation. Since racism is systemic, including every structure, even the church, all structures must be overturned before justice, the utopia, can be ushered in, i.e., social determinism.

27 Knowledge comes from your position in society (life experience) and is, therefore, your truth and is unchallengeable. Those who suffer oppression, or intersecting oppressions, are to be believed regardless of objective evidence to the contrary.

28 Identity politics divide people by their racial or sexual identities rather than by broad unifying identities such as being created in the image of God, being human, or being American. These racial and sexual identities are in some ways more meritorious than active meritorious achievement.

29 Diversity is diversity of identity and not ideas or ideology. Inclusiveness is the promotion of politically correct speech so that if you say things that make someone feel bad, you cannot be included—Christians with biblical conviction and language must be excluded. Equity means equality of outcome and may also include things like reparations. Equality does not mean equality before the law but equality of outcomes.

Here are some similarities between social justice and cultural Marxism, which justify using them interchangeably at times:

1. Both look to Karl Marx's ideologies and Max Horkheimer, Herbert Marcuse, and Antonio Gramsci, who were Neo-Marxists and founders of cultural Marxism.
2. Both advocate revolutionary and anarchist tactics.
3. Both agree classical Marxism failed to include the essential aspect of culture, hence the name cultural Marxism.
4. Both advocate socialism/communism.
5. Both are opposed to capitalism.
6. Both their views of justice conflict with biblical justice.
7. Both are connected to and employ critical theory.
8. Both believe the Marxian model can usher in utopia.
9. Both seek a redistribution of wealth and power by force to usher in a socialistic utopia.
10. Both divide the world into oppressors (whites and majorities) and the oppressed (blacks and minorities).
11. Both are composed of a disparate group of minorities such as women, blacks, homosexuals, transgenders, and other minority groups who are said to be oppressed by their majority counterparts.
12. Both are advanced by favoring one group (the oppressed/minority/non-sinners) and punishing the other group (the oppressors/majority/sinners) through the redistribution of wealth and power.
13. Both advance a form of social determinism.
14. Both believe the majority is racist regardless of an individual's belief, in contrast to biblical racism, which teaches that a person is racist if he views his ethnicity as inherently superior to another.[30]

---

30 "A belief that race is a fundamental determinant of human traits and capacities and that racial differences produce an inherent superiority of a particular race." "Racism," accessed March 4, 2021, https://www.merriam-webster.com/dic-

15. Both believe the minority cannot be racists—oppressors.
16. Both believe the majority (oppressors) must repent and be changed to usher in the utopia, but the minority (oppressed) do not need to repent or change.
17. Both advocate a clash between the oppressed (minorities) and the oppressor (majority).
18. Both typically define majority groups as privileged and oppressive, while minority groups are labeled as underprivileged and oppressed.
19. Both fail to sufficiently distinguish between being an American and being white.
20. Both fail to distinguish between American values (to which all can share and contribute) and white values.[31]

---

tionary/racism. See also "a belief or doctrine that inherent differences among the various human racial groups determine cultural or individual achievement, usually involving the idea that one's own race is superior and has the right to dominate others or that a particular racial group is inferior to the others." "Racism," accessed February 4, 2021, https://www.dictionary.com/browse/racism?s=t. I reject that America today is systemically racist (also called structural or institutional racism), which is not to deny the existence of racism, even significantly so in some areas. Systemic, or structural racism, is "a policy, system of government, etc. that is associated with or originated in such a doctrine and that favors members of the dominant racial or ethnic group, or has a neutral effect on their life experiences, while discriminating against or harming members of other groups, ultimately serving to preserve the social status, economic advantage, or political power of the dominant group." "Racism," accessed February 4, 2021, https://www.dictionary.com/browse/racism?s=t.

31 America was founded on a pioneer attitude, settled by those who broke from the most powerful empire, courageous men who went to war with the most powerful empire, encapsulated in sayings like "go west young man." American values are accessible to anyone, which is undeniably demonstrated by people from all over the world coming to America and succeeding. Some of these values used to be more reflective of Christianity (marriage, family, view of God, Christianity), and included such things as meritocracy, hard work, no one owes me anything, personal responsibility, free will, and the inspiring words of our founding documents that all men are created equal.

21. Both promote identity politics—identity measures status, merit, access to truth, and worth.
22. Both promote racial, sexual group identity over our universal human identity.[32]
23. Both define people by their experience rather than their humanity.
24. Both diminish the place of personal responsibility and elevate group identity.
25. Both seek justice for one group by punishing another group even if individuals in the groups are not personally deserving.
26. Both promote disparity as indicative of racism/injustice.
27. Both are worldviews.
28. Almost all speakers who seek to explain the most notable aspects of social justice (critical/conflict theory) refer back to Marxism and cultural Marxism.
29. Marx may generally be considered the first critical theorist.
30. Social justice is based on cultural Marxism and neo-Marxism.

Here is the biblical response to social justice's distorted view of racism and privilege: Biblically, anyone can be a racist or commit any other sin that humans can commit and then be forgiven, delivered, and given a new life (John 3:1–4; Rom 10:9–19). Racism is not determined by a person's past, group size, or skin color, but by his heart, as reflected in his actions (Matt 15:18–20). For example, murder and adultery are sinful desires of the heart even if there is no physical murder or adultery (Mark 7:21; Matt 5:27–32).

---

[32] Crenshaw says, "We all can recognize the distinction between the claims 'I am Black' and the claim 'I am a person who happens to be Black.' 'I am Black' becomes not simply a statement of resistance, but also a positive discourse of self-identification . . . 'I am a person who happens to be Black,' on the other hand, achieves self-identification ... by straining for a certain universality (in effect, 'I am first a person'),'" Kimberlé Williams Crenshaw, "Mapping the Margins: Intersectionality, Identity Politics and Violence Against Women of Color," *Women, Gender & Research* 2 (2006), 7–20, accessed February 4, 2021, https://pdfs.semanticscholar.org/734f/8b582b7d7bb375415d2975cb783c839e5e3c.pdf.

All are privileged in some way over other people. All people have some opportunities that others do not. Privilege does not equal oppression or make a person an oppressor. Having less privilege or opportunity does not necessarily mean a person or group is oppressed by the ones who have more. Abraham was wealthy (Gen 24:35), Israel was privileged by being God's chosen nation (Rom 3:1–2), and Paul was privileged as a Roman citizen (Acts 16:37–38; 22:28).[33] Thus, everyone experiences privilege in comparison to someone else. Privilege is not a sin, and therefore does not require a sense of guilt or repentance; it requires only faithfulness and good stewardship.

Opportunities (privilege) can be accepted and require only that the recipients be faithful as good stewards of the opportunity, which involves being thankful (Eph 5:20). That is the theme of the parable of the talents (Matt 25:14–30). The one who was given more talents did not have to repent of privilege, nor were the ones who received fewer considered victims. They were judged only on whether they were faithful stewards of what they had. This same truth is evident when the Jews were slaves in Egypt and the Babylonian captivity (Exodus and Daniel, respectively).

Additionally, this parable, history, and the rest of Scripture demonstrate that opportunity or privilege does not equal achievement. Many are given privileges or opportunities only to squander them. Privilege grants an opportunity for development, but it does not grant success. Achievement comes about by capitalizing on the opportunity. We also know that while we can give someone an opportunity, we cannot guarantee a probability of success because the opportunity is not the agent for success; that belongs to the individual. For example, we can give someone the chance to get an education or experience salvation through hearing the gospel. Still, we cannot guarantee they will be a good steward of that opportunity.

The most significant privilege and call to stewardship and faithfulness is the call to receive the gospel unto salvation (Prov 10:5; Ps 95:6–8; Isa 55:6;

---

33 Jews were also privileged in that salvation was of the Jew first, Rom 1:16, they were God's chosen (His) people (Rom 11:1), custodians of God's Word (Rom 3:2), and the people through whom Christ came (Rom 9:5), "Salvation is from the Jews" (John 4:22). In Paul's ministry he sought out the Jews first in every new city (Acts 13:5, 14; 14:1; 17:2, 10, 17; 18:4, 19; 19:8).

John 12:35–36; 2 Cor 6:2). In eternity, what the individual did with that opportunity will matter more than all others combined. Every person who hears the gospel is more privileged than if he were a billionaire and did not hear, although I believe every person hears the gospel.[34] Therefore, praise and thanksgiving should flow from every life who hears the gospel.

The very nature of social justice, critical race theory, and intersectionality is to cause a divide. They divide individuals, groups, and even Christians. Christians who advocate any of these are dividing non-Christians as well as Christians. Creating such divisions is antithetical to the gospel and Christianity (Eph 4:4–7). Rather than confronting individuals with their own sin and need of repentance lest they die and perish in hell (Luke 5:32; 13:3; Rev 22:7–8), cultural Marxism and intersectionality provide an excuse to blame others.

PART TWO:
AN INSIGHT INTO THE METHODOLOGIES OF CULTURAL MARXISM AND SOCIAL JUSTICE

It is essential to keep the following thoughts in mind as we consider how cultural Marxism and social justice work in real-life situations or crises like the death of George Floyd and the ensuing anarchy.[35] First, some events that social justice warriors deem an injustice and cultural Marxists stand against are actual injustices. Many who are not social justice warriors may see the same event and conclude it is an injustice that needs to be corrected.[36] Con-

---

34 See my book *Does God Love All or Some? Comparing Biblical Extensivism and Calvinism's Exclusivism* (Eugene, OR: Wipf & Stock, 2019).

35 The backdrop of this part is the death of George Floyd and resulting riots and anarchy that spread across America in 2020, but the explanations of how social justice works are applicable to similar events of racial conflict and rioting.

36 The Conservative Baptist Network provided a thoroughly Christian response to the George Floyd event. The statement equally condemned both the injustice by the police against George Floyd and the injustices resulting from some people who seek justice for the death of George Floyd by inflicting injustices on innocent people's lives and livelihood. Conservative Baptist Network, "Statement

sequently, even those who hold opposing beliefs may unite against real injustice. Furthermore, just because those who are not cultural Marxists fight the same injustice does not mean that cultural Marxists are not involved, employing their strategies, or seeking their ultimate goal of overthrowing capitalism and America. We should always keep foremost in our minds that the overthrow of America includes banning Christianity and the spreading of the gospel.[37] The co-founder of cultural Marxism, Antonio Gramsci, said, "Socialism is precisely the religion that must overwhelm Christianity . . . In the new order, socialism will triumph by first capturing the culture via infiltration of schools, universities, churches, and the media by transforming the consciousness of society."[38]

The motive and the methods utilized by social justice advocates (many of whom are Marxists or embrace many Marxian ideals) in attempting to right a wrong can be very different from those of ordinary citizens who share their beliefs. Some social justice advocates may use anarchist tactics that are approved of and promoted by social justice advocates who are not actually on the streets. These advocates are in academia, newsrooms, and places of power.[39]

Dr. Paul Kengor interviewed Dr. Richard Pipes, the "acclaimed historian and Harvard University professor of Sovietology . . . who [also] served on the National Security Council during the Reagan administration,"[40] and

---

Regarding George Floyd and the Ensuing Riots," May 30, 2020, https://conservativebaptistnetwork.com/statement-regarding-george-floyd-and-the-ensuing-riots/.

37 Of course, this would include all supernatural faiths since Marxism is a materialistic faith.

38 Roger Kiska, "Antonio Gramsci's Long March Through History," *Acton Institute*, 29:3 (December 12, 2019), accessed March 5, 2021, https://www.acton.org/religion-liberty/volume-29-number-3/antonio-gramscis-long-march-through-history, para. 5.

39 Samuel Chamberlain, "Riots Break Out across America after George Floyd Death," *Fox News*, May 29, 2020, https://www.foxnews.com/us/live-updates-riots-break-out-across-america-after-george-floyd-death.

40 Walter E. Williams, *Liberty Versus the Tyranny of Socialism: Controversial Essays* (Stanford: Hoover Institution Press, 2008), 24.

Pipes explained that there are not as many communists among academics as some think. Still, these academics are significantly sympathetic to Marxist ideas. Pipes said,

> While academic leftists, and I'd include their media allies, are not communists, they are anti-anti-communists. In other words, they have contempt for right-wingers, conservatives, or libertarians who are anti-communists. Why? Academic leftists and their media allies agree with many of the stated goals of communism, such as the equal distribution of wealth, income equality, and other goals spelled out in Karl Marx and Friedrich Engels' 'Manifesto of the Communist Party.'[41]

Consequently, when we ask how many Marxists are in academia, we will get the wrong answer because we have asked the wrong question. The question we should ask is, how many are sympathetic with Marxian socialistic goals. When I was in graduate school at Henderson State University, I asked the head of the sociology department how many sociologists were capitalists, socialists, and communists. He responded, "Ninety-percent are socialists, and ten-percent are communists." I immediately asked what about those that are capitalists? He said, "They are not statistically significant."[42] Social justice warriors seek to destroy America's capitalistic civil system as a necessary component to usher in a socialistic utopia.

Harvard professor Cornel West's remarks after George Floyd's death and the riots that followed condemned America's capitalistic system as a failure. West stated, "I think we are witnessing America as a *failed social experiment*. And what I mean by that is that the history of black people for over 200-something years in America has been looking at America's failure. Its capitalist economy could not generate and deliver in such a way that people could live lives of decency. The nation-state, its criminal justice system, its legal system could not generate protection of rights and liberties."[43]

---

41 Williams, *Liberty Versus Tyranny*, 24.
42 I attended Henderson State University in Arkansas 1986–88.
43 Samuel Chamberlain, "Riots Break Out across America after George Floyd

Notice that the rioters and looters are not to blame because everything is due to racial injustice, a Marxian paradigm. The social justice intellectuals make academic arguments for abandoning capitalism and replacing it with socialism, the social justice warriors on the street provide the terrorizing fear needed, and the white-guilted Americans supply the unjustified sympathy and leniency for those who destroy private property and kill innocent people. In contrast, those who are not social justice warriors but also see the injustice usually seek correction through the legal, legislative, and elective processes.

Shelby Steele explains white guilt as,

> the *vacuum of moral authority* that comes from simply *knowing* that one's race is associated with racism. Whites (and American institutions) must acknowledge historical racism to show themselves redeemed of it, but once they acknowledge it, they lose moral authority over everything having to do with race, equality, social justice, poverty, and so on . . . .. The authority they lose transfers to the 'victims' of historical racism and becomes their great power in society. This is why white guilt is quite literally the same thing as black power.[44]

Steele does not use white guilt to mean moral guilt. Instead, it is a willingness by white people and their institutions to do almost anything to avoid the stigmatization of being called racist. Steele maintains that white guilt produces only results like affirmative action.[45] For example, rather than

---

Death," *Fox News*, May 29, 2020, https://www.foxnews.com/us/live-updates-riots-break-out-across-america-after-george-floyd-death, paras. 5–6. Emphasis mine.

44 Shelby Steele, *White Guilt: How Blacks and Whites Together Destroyed the Promise of the Civil Rights Era* (New York: Harper Perennial, 2007), 24.

45 Outcome solutions are based on looking at the problem, like not having many black students in college, and assuming the point of disparity is the cause of the disparity, which is often not the case. Nevertheless, such outcome perspectives answer the problem of disparities by outcome approaches such as affirmative action or diversity emphasis. However, outside of the presence of actual racism, outcome approaches do not address the real problem, which may be factors as varied as a lack

a university accepting the two or three percent of black students who are qualified on their own merit (SAT scores), the university may set a standard (quota) of admitting seven percent of black students. The result is a predominately white institution doing whatever is needed, such as lowering standards, to ensure quotas are reached. These quotas effectively protect the university from the stigma of being racist, even if some are accepted who cannot do the required work.[46]

An example of the damage of affirmative action is when a black student is accepted into a university like Harvard or Cornell, in which the student would not do well, but would do well in ninety percent of the universities in America. It is not racist to say some are accepted who cannot do the work required because I can say the same about myself and countless other white students. Affirmative action detrimentally mismatches student capabilities with university requirements to meet the school's quota, which serves to insulate the university from the stigma of being a racist institution, even at the expense of the black students. Not only does it hurt the students who would have been academically better suited at a different university, but it also hurts the black students who were accepted on their own merit. Such practices are self-serving for white people (showing they are not racists) and denigrate black people; it also maintains the patronizing white deliverer model. Moreover, affirmative action helps those already doing well while making no impact for people of color struggling in inadequate public primary and secondary schools or crime-ridden neighborhoods.

Regrettably, I see white guilt in some of the SBC leadership as well when they emphasize color-based selection rather than merit-based.[47] Such is no less dishonoring to our black brothers and sisters than when secu-

---

of excellent primary and secondary schools to attend, out of wedlock pregnancies, and cultural values that favor rappers or criminals more than those that prioritize hard work and getting a good education.

46 At seemingly an opportune time to overturn the 1996 proposition 209 and reimplement affirmative action in 2020 with proposition 16, the proposition failed in liberal California; affirmative action was defeated again.

47 I have heard and read some calls for more diversity with no mention of qualified diversity.

lar society does it. It is racist not to select a black person who is the most qualified in both skillset and doctrine simply because he is black, and it is racism motivated by white guilt to choose lesser qualified blacks because of the color of their skin. As equal image-bearers of God, I assure you, we have many capable black people to speak and serve without resorting to guilt-motivated paternalism.

For example, some of the best preachers on planet earth are doctrinally sound black preachers—such as Dr. Lee Brand, Voddie Baucham, and the late E.V. Hill. We do not have to compromise doctrinally to find black preachers to endorse. We need not compromise by hiring black scholars who support such ideas as critical race theory and intersectionality to demonstrate we are not racists; to do so dishonors black scholars who have not so compromised, but, most of all, it dishonors Christ. There is nothing wrong, and everything right, with doing due diligence to make sure we are not using lesser qualified white leaders because of convenience while overlooking qualified conservative black preachers and scholars. But it is pandering and racist to choose or reject people based on skin color regardless of how sincere the motive.

Speaking of white guilt, Steele says, "It constantly portrays problems of minority under development as problems of injustice."[48] That is precisely what social justice does. White guilt results in creating such things as the Great Society and affirmative action, and now permitting the grossest of anarchical criminal behavior while decreasing police funding at one of the most violent times in American history, all to abolish America and capitalism.[49] All the while blaming everyone but the perpetrators of the anarchist action, which is often referred to by the left as protests or mostly peaceful protests. As a result, blacks are dehumanized, and the government has abandoned its primary responsibility of protecting its citizenry.

---

48 Steele, *White Guilt*, 64.
49 "The Great Society was an ambitious series of policy initiatives, legislation, and programs spearheaded by President Lyndon B. Johnson with the main goals of ending poverty, reducing crime, abolishing inequality and improving the environment." "Great Society," accessed July 27, 2021, https://www.history.com/topics/1960s/great-society, para. 1.

Significant black scholars and intellectuals such as Larry Elder, Thomas Sowell, Shelby Steele, Robert L. Woodson Sr., Walter Williams, Jason Riley, and Glenn Loury, as well as many other black people, are calling for personal responsibility as the principal answer to the problems in the black community.[50] As we have seen, that is contrary to the message of social justice and cultural Marxism, which bases everything on group identity instead of individual responsibility. Those who emphasize the solution as personal responsibility do not ignore the need for policy changes, but they reject social justice's emphases on political deliverance and social determinism.

Social justice blames lack of success in the black community on systemic racial injustice. Social justice warriors and the woke do not ask if racism is present; they always assume its presence. Critical Race Theory scholars Richard Delgado and Jean Stefancic state it this way, "First, racism is ordinary, not aberrational—'normal science,' the usual way society does business, the common, everyday experience of most people of color in this country."[51] The author of *White Fragility*, Robin DiAngelo, puts it this way, "The question is not '*did* racism take place'? but rather '*how did* racism manifest in that situation?'"[52] In such an environment, even to ask for evidence of systemic racism results in being called a racist, and white guilt keeps many white people from asking since they will do anything to avoid the racist label. Since white guilt is not descriptive of moral guilt, it may help to understand it is a concept that communicates white terror, terrified of being seen as a racist.

Additionally, systemic racism cannot be demonstrated by referring to the past, such as the times of slavery, Jim Crow laws (enacted to enforce

---

50 Many black people of all ages and backgrounds are saying the same. See https://www.facebook.com/nancy.rogerscrosby/videos/10220521552061505/UzpfSTEwMDAzMDY1NDc1MTI0NTozMDA3MDY2NDc2Mjc4MjU/ and https://www.facebook.com/nancy.rogerscrosby/videos/10220497769746962/?fref=mentions, both accessed June 30, 2021.

51 Richard Delgado and Jean Stefancic, *Critical Race Theory: An Introduction*, 2nd ed (New York: New York University Press, 2012), 7.

52 Robin D. DiAngelo, "Anti-Racism Handout," accessed September 7, 2021, https://robindiangelo.com/wp-content/uploads/2016/06/Anti-racism-handout-1-page-2016.pdf, para. 2.

segregation), or other events predating legal corrections.[53] Nor can it be evidenced by merely providing examples of actual racism, as people are prone to do. Systemic racism could be demonstrated by exposing legal discrimination, as has been true in the past. This demonstration would require laws that explicitly prohibit black people from something white people are permitted based solely on race. For example, before the civil rights movement of the 1960s, blacks were not allowed to eat in many white restaurants because it was illegal.

Consequently, if one has the courage, they should ask those who argue for the existence of systemic racism to define what they mean and to provide *incontrovertible empirical data* to prove it. That would include the idea that there are no other plausible reasons or factors to be considered. Systemic racism means that every system and structure of American society, including churches, is racist. It means that racism is *always* present. It means individual acts of racism or finding a person acting overtly racist is not necessary because racism is always present in everything. In other words, they have redefined racism and its presence by using critical theory, which in turn perpetuates the advancement of critical theory. The assumption is that racism is present in every act that can even remotely be construed to be racist; they assume its obviousness and undeniability.

An example of falsely accusing people of racism based on social justice, which assumes that all disparities are due to social injustice, racism, can be seen in the following. Cab drivers have been accused of racism for picking up a white customer and passing by a black customer. Or pizza delivery drivers refuse to make home pizza deliveries in a black residential area, but they make them in white neighborhoods. But these facts alone do not prove racism, although the woke refers to such events to demonstrate rampant racism. The truth is that many times the drivers or the taxicab commissioner who restricts the drivers are black themselves. Many of the drivers who refuse to make home pizza deliveries live in the very neighborhoods where they refuse to make in-home deliveries. They do so not because of racism

---

[53] Many legal corrections have been passed such as the Civil Rights Act of 1964, Voting Rights Act of 1965, and the Fair Housing Act of 1968.

but because they fear for their safety. It is hard to make the case that black drivers and commissioners are racist against black people.[54]

This should remind us to consider other factors before joining the systemic racism frenzy of the woke and race-baiters. For the woke to seek to substantiate the presence of systemic racism by saying such things as we know racism is systemic, or if they were black, they would know does not prove systemic racism. Providing verifiable anecdotal evidence only proves racism exists (which no one denies), but it does not demonstrate systemic racism. It does not demonstrate that racism is in the DNA of America. There will always be various forms of ungodly discrimination in a fallen world (not just racial discrimination), all which Christians should denounce.

Additionally, the subjective and vague term *microaggressions* is not sufficient to prove ever-present racism or even that an individual is a racist or acting racist. Referring to the subjectivity of microaggressions, Nick Haslam, Professor of Psychology at the University of Melbourne, says, "It takes the subjective perception of the supposed target as sufficient evidence that a prejudiced act has occurred, even if that is sincerely denied by the supposed perpetrator."[55] If racism is deemed to be systemic, it is crucial to ask, what will it take to eliminate it, and how will we know it has been eliminated? Be specific. James Lindsay says critical race theory "*cannot* be satisfied, so it becomes a kind of activist black hole that threatens to destroy everything it is introduced into."[56] Many critical race theorists conclude that rather than making progress

---

54 Walter E. Williams, *Race & Economics: How Much Can Be Blamed on Discrimination?* (Stanford: Hoover Institution Press, 2011), 119–21. The same can be said of grocery stores that may charge more in black neighborhoods for groceries than they do in white neighborhoods. While on the surface this appears to be a clear-cut case of racism (and it may be), it may only be pure economics; if the store in the black neighborhood suffers more loss due to theft and vandalism, the higher prices are economically justified.

55 Nick Haslam "The Trouble with 'Microaggressions,'" *The Conversation*, January 16, 2017, accessed March 25, 2021, https://theconversation.com/the-trouble-with-microaggressions-71364, para. 9.

56 James Lindsay, "Eight Big Reasons Critical Race Theory Is Terrible for Dealing with Racism," *New Discourses*, June 12, 2020, accessed February 11, 2021,

in eliminating racism since the founding of America, the Civil War, and the civil rights act, it has just become better hidden.

Thomas Sowell demonstrates how, after slavery ended, blacks increased their income faster than whites even though they had to confront many agreements made by whites to keep them down. By 1900, their incomes were one-half again higher than they were in 1867. They increased their earnings faster than the nation as a whole.[57] The significance of this is that despite the egregious wrongs inflicted on them by whites, blacks still excelled. This is not to justify the ill-treatment of blacks by whites but rather to highlight that blacks can excel even under dire circumstances because they, like whites, are created in the image of God.

Since the victories of the civil rights movement of the sixties, many black militants, many of whom are Marxists, have used white guilt to make white people and their institutions responsible for the black people's well-being and success instead of promoting personal responsibility for how they prosper in life. Liberal progressive politicians and a host of business, community, and religious leaders have been willing to do anything out of white guilt to avoid the dreaded stigmatism of being called a racist. Using white guilt to advance black people is not the approach that all black people have adopted, but it is the method of many militants, along with leaders like Reverend Sharpton and Jesse Jackson.

This approach is as Marxian and demeaning to blacks today as it was in the riots of the sixties.[58] These social justice warriors will label injustices as the cause of problems in the black community countless times for each time they make even the slightest public reference to calling on black people to take personal responsibility. This is not a gross generalization of all blacks because many in the black community take responsibility for their lives and work hard at developing their family and their jobs. Candace

---

https://newdiscourses.com/2020/06/reasons-critical-race-theory-terrible-dealing-racism/, para. 3.

[57] Hoover Institution, "Discrimination and Disparities with Thomas Sowell," *YouTube*, May 3, 2018, accessed July 11, 2020, https://www.youtube.com/watch?v=U7hmTRT8tb4, 13:30–47.

[58] Steele, *White Guilt,* 30–33.

Owens and Brandon Tatum began the Blexit movement (Black exit from the Democratic Party) to set black people free from the oppression of the Democratic party and the social justice warriors.[59]

Walter E. Williams comments, "The experience of several ethnic minority groups in the United States and elsewhere seriously calls into question arguments that disadvantaged minorities in the United States *must* acquire political power and need measures to 'end racism' in order for socioeconomic growth to occur."[60] He further states, "There is little evidence that race-based discrimination is widespread in today's America."[61] This is in stark contrast to the continued paradigm presented by liberals, Black Lives Matter (BLM), and the woke that America is systemically racist. Unfortunately, this includes some leaders in the SBC.

Steele says,

> Wherever and whenever there is white guilt, a terrible illusion prevails: that social justice is not a condition but an agent. In this illusion, social justice procures an entirely better life for people apart from their own efforts. Therefore, it makes sense for minorities to make social justice a priority over their individual pursuit of education and wealth . . . The reason for this illusion is that white guilt *wants no obligation to minority developments.* It needs only the *display* of social justice to win moral authority. It gets no credit when blacks independently develop themselves.[62]

The truth is that neither the end of slavery nor the gains of the civil rights movement led by Martin Luther King guaranteed success for black people. They only provide the opportunity for it. The necessary agent is the

---

59 See https://blexitfoundation.org/, accessed July 9, 2020.

60 Williams, *Race & Economics*, 15.

61 Ibid., 133. He demonstrates how crime, the breakdown of the family, making poor moral choices, a lack of education, and a host of economic, non-racial considerations play a significant role in what is mischaracterized as racist issues.

62 Steele, *White Guilt*, 63.

person taking responsibility for his life and future; this requirement is the same for whites and blacks.

One need not look far for the presence of white guilt during the time of anarchy following the death of Floyd in the summer of 2020. For example, in reference to the riots following the death of George Floyd, Democrat Governor Gavin Newsom said, "The black community is not responsible for what is happening right now. We are — our institutions are — accountable to this moment."[63] Maura Healey, Democratic Attorney General of Massachusetts, described the rioting by saying, "Yes, America is burning, but that's how forests grow."[64] Two days after looters destroyed stores, Democrat Teresa Mosquera of the Seattle City Council said, "Colleagues, I hope we're all saying we understand why that destruction happened, and we understand why people are upset."[65] This is reminiscent of John Kerry's degrading white guilt comment many years ago. Walter Williams recalls, "In a campaign speech before a predominantly black audience, in reference to so many blacks in prison, presidential candidate John Kerry said, 'That's unacceptable, but it's not their fault.'"[66]

Operating out of white guilt is to benefit white people by doing whatever it takes to avoid being called a racist. It gives the appearance of caring and sympathy, but it is more about protecting oneself at the expense of others. It degrades black people by holding them to a lower standard of personal responsibility than the situation warrants and is inappropriate for

---

63 Maggie Angst, "On fourth day of protests, Newsom tells demonstrators: 'Your rage is real. Express it,'" SantaCruzSentinel.com, June 1, 2020, accessed June 22, 2020, https://www.santacruzsentinel.com/2020/06/01/trump-tells-governors-to-dominate-protesters-newsom-tells-them-you-matter-i-care/, para. 2.

64 Shira Schoenberg, "Healey: 'America is Burning. But That's 'How Forests Grow,'" CommonWealth Magazine, June 2, 2020, accessed June 22, 2020, https://commonwealthmagazine.org/criminal-justice/healey-america-is-burning-but-thats-how-forests-grow/, para. 1.

65 Deroy Murdock, "Looting and Rioting after George Floyd Killing Draw Shocking Support from Left," *Fox News*, June 9, 2020, accessed June 22, 2020, https://www.foxnews.com/opinion/george-floyd-democrats-police-deroy-murdock, para. 6.

66 Williams, *Liberty Versus the Tyranny of Socialism*, 341.

one created in the image of God. It is racist. Further, social justice is as racist as white guilt because it judges people by their skin color and how they are grouped to either be guilty or innocent.

The almost universal agreement on the apparent[67] injustice of the death of George Floyd is an example of associating such disparate groups as social justice advocates and non-social justice advocates. But the means for seeking justice by cultural Marxists and those who view Floyd's death as a heinous act but love America are categorically different.[68] The latter group sees Floyd's death and the wanton destruction of innocent lives and their property through rioting and looting as injustices. Social justice warriors view wanton destruction of innocents and their livelihood as a means to their goal. The social justice perspective vividly reminds us that social justice is better described as socialistic justice.

To oppose *either* the injustice against Floyd or the injustice perpetrated by the rioters against innocents is the very kind of partial and biased justice the rioters claim to protest. They employ the same sort of partial justice to make their case that they claim to be against. Christians must stand unequivocally against the injustice against Floyd and the injustice committed by the rioters against the innocents. We stand unashamedly for God's impartial justice. Second, to use cultural Marxism to describe an event, group, or person does not necessarily mean that everyone involved

---

67 I use the word "apparent" only because at the time of this writing, while every indication is that the officer did unjustifiably cause the death of George Floyd (something I agree with based on what we know at this time), there may still be facts of which I am unaware that will surface in the trials, which could alter or ameliorate the case. I am not ready to abandon the legal system of due process, as flawed as it may be, for a tragic system of trial by the internet.

68 Diana Chandler, "Pastors Urge Prayer, Gospel Outreach as Outrage Grows over George Floyd's Death," *Baptist Press*, May 27, 2020, accessed May 30, 2020, http://www.bpnews.net/54859/pastors-urge-prayer-gospel-outreach-as-outrage-grows-over-george-floyds-death, and Deroy Murdock, "Rioters Do Injustice to George Floyd, Tortured and Killed in a Case of Police Brutality," *Fox News*, May 29, 2020, accessed May 30, 2020, https://www.foxnews.com/opinion/deroy-murdock-rioters-do-injustice-to-george-floyd-killed-in-a-horrific-case-of-police-brutality.

is a card-carrying cultural Marxist or social justice warrior or even would describe themselves as such. Social justice warriors will welcome non-social justice warriors to join their fight, and they will join non-social justice warriors in their cause so long as it fits their overall plan.

Using these terms to speak about an event does not necessarily signify that some acts of violence, anarchy, or civil disobedience are driven exclusively by cultural Marxism. Nor do they preclude non-cultural Marxists from getting caught up in the emotion of the moment and rioting alongside the social justice warriors. But even the acts that are not solely driven by cultural Marxists are promoted and used by them to further their cause, which is the destruction of American society and culture to usher in their dream of a socialistic utopia. Such behavior by anyone facilitates their plan. We ignore these somewhat complex traits of how cultural Marxism and social justice work to our natural and spiritual peril.

BLM is the powerhouse behind many of these types of protests and riots.[69] BLM is a Marxist-run organization. Two of the three founders, Patrisse Cullors and Alicia Garza, claim to be "trained Marxists."[70] Here is the path to better understand the nature of Black Lives Matter. Herbert Marcuse and Antonio Gramsci laid the foundation of what is known as cultural Marxism. Mike Gonzalez, a policy expert at the Heritage Foundation, explains that Marcuse "taught the critical race theorist Angela Davis at Brandeis University."[71] Angela Davis "was the Communist Party's

---

69 Antifa is also involved with BLM in the rioting. Antifa is a loosely organized effort to fight what they see as fascism. They are, in fact, a very leftwing group of pro-socialists and communists who use the term fascism so broadly that it can encompass a vast array of ideas they oppose. They will often wrongly categorize love for America, patriotic acts, and words as fascism. We should not forget that America fought a costly world war against fascism and defeated it.

70 The Real News Network, "Short History of Black Lives Matter," *YouTube* July 23, 2015. https://www.youtube.com/watch?v=Zp-RswgpjD8, 7:10. See also Joseph R. John, "Black Lives Matter Co-Founder Confirms that Violent Mob Movement Is Run by 'Trained Marxists.'" *Citizens Journal*, July 22, 2020. https://www.citizensjournal.us/black-lives-matter-co-founder-confirms-that-violent-mob-movement-is-run-by-trained-marxists/.

71 Michael Cozzi, "Of Identity Politics, Angela Davis, and Herbert

candidate for Vice President in 1980 and 1984."[72] Gonzales further explains that "Angela Davis had a profound impact and was the inspiration behind the theory of Patrisse Cullors, who co-founded Black Lives Matter."[73] He also says Alicia Garza, another Black Lives Matter co-founder, "also admits on a video by Democracy Now! that she owed everything to Angela Davis."[74] Thus, we have the link from the Neo-Marxist Herbert Marcuse, who trained Angela Davis, who impacted and inspired the co-founders of Black Lives Matter, Patrisse Cullors and Alicia Garza. Black Lives Matter is neo-Marxist to its core.

Additionally, Davis is a founding member of the Committees of Correspondence for Democracy and Socialism. This organization began in 1992 and is a moderate group in the Communist Party of the USA. This organization works within the Democratic party toward socialism. They say, "We use an 'inside/outside' tactical approach, which means working inside the Democratic Party's arena where it makes sense to do so . . . We have no illusions about the two main parties of capitalism; we will need to move beyond them and replace them, not only for a 21st-century socialism, but even to win many structural reforms."[75]

Marcuse," *NewsMax.com*, January 26, 2021, accessed March 12, 2021, https://www.newsmax.com/books/books-mike-gonzalez-identity-politics/2021/01/26/id/1007205/, para. 12.

    72 Ibid., para. 13.

    73 Ibid., para. 14.

    74 Ibid., para. 15.

    75 A fuller quote says, "But we are first of all committed to both democracy and socialism. In fact, the path to socialism in our time is largely one of winning battles for democracy in the here and now. . . We are a unique group that is at once Marxist and pluralist . . . we try to build broad alliances of left and center forces, rather than just militant left blocs . . . We use an 'inside/outside' tactical approach, which means working inside the Democratic Party's arena where it makes sense to do so . . .We have no illusions about the two main parties of capitalism; we will need to move beyond them and replace them, not only for a 21st Century socialism, but even to win many structural reforms. Basic change never comes from elections alone, but it almost always proceeds through electoral battles. *Committees of Correspondence for Democracy and Socialism,* accessed February 16, 2021, https://www.cc-ds.org/about-2/, paras. 3, 6–8.

The call to defund police departments across the nation was initiated and promoted by BLM. It is a Marxist plan to deconstruct further American society to usher in a Marxist society. The BLM website says, "We call for a national defunding of police."[76] But may we ask, who will protect innocent people from criminals and rioters such as the BLM constituency? The criminals and rioters?[77] Some progressives have tried to soften this to mean merely diverting some of the law-enforcement budgets to other things, but that is not what BLM, who started the *defund* police movement, meant, and mean. They mean the total disbanding of all levels of law-enforcement because from a Marxist perspective, what we call law and order, they call violence, which must be stopped.

At times during the riots of 2020, rioters would justify their violence based on what they called the violence of law enforcement—police, Immigration and Customs Enforcement (ICE), National Guard, and other law enforcement agencies. Rioters find that justification for violence in Marcuse's own words. He said, "If they use violence, they do not start a new chain of violence but try to break an established one . . . no third person, and least of all the educator and intellectual, has the right to preach them abstention."[78]

The most prominent claim of systemic racism charges that the police disproportionately kill blacks or even hunt down blacks just to kill them. Therefore, the police are so corrupt and systemically racist, they must be destroyed. But while the media optics give credence to that claim, the facts do not.

Relying on data from the FBI, the Kaiser Foundation, and Statista Research Inc, Edward Ring says,

---

76 "#DefundThePolice," May 30, 2020, accessed June 20, 2020, https://blacklivesmatter.com/defundthepolice/, para. 8.

77 See Appendix I in my book *A Corruption of Consequence* for eight reasons "Why Defunding the Police is Destructive to Civil Society," or you may see my article by the same name: https://ronniewrogers.com/2020/08/17/why-defunding-the-police-is-destructive-to-civil-society/.

78 Herbert Marcuse, "Repressive Tolerance" from *A Critique of Pure Tolerance,* online para. 41, accessed March 26, 2021, https://www.marcuse.org/herbert/publications/1960s/1965-repressive-tolerance-fulltext.html.

In 2018 a total of 209 blacks were killed by police, the overwhelming majority of them armed. This compares to 399 whites killed by police in that year . . . The root of the claim of a police war on blacks comes down to this: If you're black, in 2018 you had a one in 190,000 chance of having a fatal encounter with police, and if you're white, your chances of the same were only one in 495,000. Hence you will hear that blacks are 2.5 times as likely to be killed by police as whites.

If that were all there was to it, perhaps there'd be a reason for more concern. But here are facts that cannot be ignored: blacks commit more crimes. In terms of arrests, blacks are twelve times as likely as whites to be arrested for murder, three times as likely for rape, eleven times as likely for robbery, and four times as likely for aggravated assault. This brings us back to the crux of the issue, which is whether police encounters with blacks result in a disproportionate number of fatalities. If you look at the death per arrest rate, they do not. In 2018 (these statistics are fairly consistent from year to year) the chances of dying while being arrested were exactly the same for whites and blacks, a nearly infinitesimal 1/100th of 1 percent.[79]

An Obama administration study in which the research team was mostly doctors so that the injuries could be medically assessed found the following. Out of 1,041,737 calls to the police for service, only 893 resulted in any level of use of force (UOF) by the police. That is a rate of 0.086% (eighty-six one-thousandths). Most of the force used was physical or conducted electrical weapons (CEWs, such as tasers). Firearms were used only six times. Out of these police and citizen encounters, only sixteen resulted in moderate to severe injury to a suspect, and there was only one fatality. Based on the facts of their research, they concluded, "Police UOF is

---

79 Edward Ring, "When Will a Prominent Black Athlete Stand Up to the Mob?" *American Greatness*, September 3, 2020, accessed September 4, 2020, https://amgreatness.com/2020/09/03/when-will-a-prominent-black-athlete-stand-up-to-the-mob/, paras. 9–11. The article provides a chart using data from the FBI, Kaiser Foundation, and Statista Research Inc.

rare. When force is used, officers most commonly rely on unarmed physical force and CEWs. Significant injuries are rare."[80]

Whether racism is a factor in the death rate of criminals on the part of the police requires considering many factors other than a raw statistic or skin color. For example, the sheer fact that police killed 983 men in 2020 compared to only 38 females does not prove or demonstrate police favor females;[81] it matters how many males and females commit crimes. Of course, women commit far fewer than men. When considering police interactions with whites and blacks, the nature of the encounter matters. Did they all include an equal amount of violent crimes? What is the crime rate of the area in which the arrests were made? Did the individual's clothing or behavior mimic others who attacked or killed a police officer in a previous arrest? Did the individual resist arrest or comply? Did the suspect have a criminal record or even a violent criminal record, which was known to the officer? Had the suspect acted violently against the police before? Did the suspect have a weapon or appear to reach for one? Such factors do not prove the officer made a righteous arrest and use of deadly force, although they may. But they can demonstrate the use of force did not stem from racism.

Ashli Babbitt (a white woman) was fatally shot when she joined in the riotous breach of the Capitol security on January 6, 2021. The Capitol police officer who shot her was a black man. I have searched repeatedly

---

[80] The abstract shows the percentage of various uses of force and injuries sustained. Many hospitalizations were not due to injuries associated with the arrest but rather were self-inflicted by the one arrested. William P. Bozeman, et al, "Injuries Associated with Police Use of Force," *Journal of Trauma and Acute Care Surgery* 84.3 (2018) 466–72, doi: 10.1097/TA.0000000000001783, accessed September 14, 202. See also Denise-Marie Ordway, "Police Use of Force: Most Suspects in Three Cities Studied Were Not Injured," *Journalist's Resource*, May 1, 2018, accessed September 14, 2020, https://journalistsresource.org/studies/government/criminal-justice/police-use-force-injuries-research/?utm_source=feedburner&utm_medium=feed&utm_campaign=Feed%3A+journalistsresource+%28Journalist%27s+Resource%29.

[81] "Number of People Shot to Death by the Police in the United States from 2017 to 2021, by Gender," *Statistica.com*, 2021, accessed March 26, 2021, https://www.statista.com/statistics/585149/people-shot-to-death-by-us-police-by-gender/.

for his name and race, and I found neither.[82] The only reason I know he was a black officer is because I watched the video of the shooting, which showed his hand, thereby revealing his skin color, the gun going off, and her dying.[83] The investigation concluded he made a legitimate call to shoot.

My point in bringing this up is not to debate whether the officer made a good call to fire his weapon but instead to call attention to this.[84] When a black person is shot by a white officer, as with George Floyd in the summer of 2020, riots, destruction of billions of dollars of private and public property, the ruin of countless livelihoods, murdering of police officers, and numerous deaths of innocent people is excused and even supported by some.[85] The media runs pictures ad-nauseam, using every opportunity to quickly claim racism as the cause. Yet, there is a virtual silence in this black on white killing, and white people did not riot claiming racism, nor should they have. All the white leaders I know condemned the riots at the Capitol. I did it that day. The truth is, a black killing by a white officer no

---

[82] I searched on several different days, ending on February 15, 2021. See also the only "major law enforcement website and media company owned and operated by current and former law enforcement professionals and supported by media scholars and professionals (who are also current and former law enforcement officers)" which says, "We have looked frantically for any media outlet, anywhere, that has discussed this police shooting. We have not found it." "Media Remains Silent after Death of Unarmed Trump Supporter," *Law Officer*, January 11, 2021, accessed February 15, 2021, https://www.lawofficer.com/babbitt/, paras. 9–10.

[83] Jon Swaine et al, "Video Shows Fatal Shooting of Ashli Babbitt in the Capitol," *Washington Post*, January 8, 2021, accessed February 15, 2021, https://www.washingtonpost.com/investigations/2021/01/08/ashli-babbitt-shooting-video-capitol/, 2:15.

[84] Based on what I know at this time, I agree that the officer seems to have made a justified shoot.

[85] See also Christina Carrega, "After Breonna Taylor's Death, a Look at Other Black Women Killed during Police Encounters," *ABC News*, June 6, 2020, accessed February 15, 2021, https://abcnews.go.com/US/breonna-taylors-death-black-women-killed-police-encounters/story?id=71057133.

more demonstrates ipso facto racism than a white killing by a black officer demonstrates racism.[86]

The fact that a white officer killed a black criminal is insufficient to show racism, and that is a fact. Jumping to conclusions is not right for anyone, but particularly for a Christian. Examine all the facts before making a judgement. We know all too well that when time is given for all the facts to surface, the apparent racial incident can actually be devoid of racism.[87] If the facts demonstrate discrimination, Christians should be the first to oppose it. If the facts do not show discrimination, Christians should say so. In either case, Christians should resist the BLM zeitgeist that a white on black arrest or a white officer's use of force can prove racism by that fact alone.

The confusion that arises from black rioters killing innocent blacks and destroying their property comes from believing the words *black lives matter* is *only or even primarily* about civil rights instead of understanding it is about promoting the goal of cultural Marxism, which is to demonstrate that America is a failed system. And as a failed system, it needs to be replaced by the far superior system of socialism. Walter Williams notes the way people compare capitalism and Marxism is, "Often when people evaluate capitalism, they evaluate a system that exists on Earth. When they evaluate communism, they are talking about a non-existent utopia. What exists on Earth with all its problems and shortcomings, is always going to fail miserably when compared to a utopia."[88]

Even if BLM was not so brazenly forthright about who they are and their agenda, anyone should be able to see that defunding police departments is insanity unless you are trying to destroy society as it is. That is precisely what the cultural Marxists are seeking to accomplish. The idea that racism is systemic (used to mean comprehensively infected—always present) means social structures must be destroyed and replaced. Thus, they employ anarchy to accomplish the destruction of America and capitalism, which (theoretically)

---

86 Given the historical abuse by some officers in arrests of black people may incline one towards assuming racism, but the past cannot judge the present; that must be done by the facts.

87 See Shelby Steele's video on how the media got it wrong on the death of Michael Brown, accessed February 15, 2021, https://whatkilledmichaelbrown.com/.

88 Williams, *Liberty Versus the Tyranny of Socialism,* 25.

will lead to the dream of a socialistic society of equal outcomes. The cultural Marxists first destroyed private and public property. Then they destroyed secular statues and monuments, which was soon followed by the destruction of churches and religious symbols, all as they declared Black Lives Matter.[89]

The destructive rewriting and degrading of American history, emphasizing only the failures, all while obscuring and banishing the heroism, sacrifice, and the good of American history, is an essential part of critical theory and the Marxist plan. Marxism cannot takeover a strong, knowledgeable, moral, spiritual, and patriotic country. Those churches who have forsaken "Thus says the Lord" for beliefs and rhetoric that are more suitable for a plasticware party, or they even trumpet the message of woke socialistic justice have contributed to American's vulnerability to Marxism.

Our public education system has failed at both the primary and secondary level, where objective Christian morality, American history, and patriotism have all but vanished, inadequately preparing our children for further education and life. Add to this that our liberal, socialistic, and Marxian-centered academia has promoted socialism, decried faith, belittled patriotism, and demeaned capitalism for decades.[90] This academic climate has provided the needed pro-socialist intellectuals to frame the necessary arguments for socialism and against capitalism. The rioters in the street generate the required fear in the hearts of conservatives who then cave to white guilt and seek refuge in selfish suburbanism, wokeness, and tawdry clichés. Resultantly, America is a weakened opponent against Marxism. Given what I have seen and heard, I am not sure whether even all that we now know about BLM will convince the woke white evangelicals to disabuse themselves of identifying with BLM chants, marches, and clothing, although I pray it will.

I understand there is a difference between the declaration Black Lives Matter and the organization of Black Lives Matter. To wit, some who sup-

---

89 All of this began to take place in 2020. See Christine Rousselle, "Churches in 6 States Damaged by Violent Protests," Catholic News Agency, June 1, 2020, accessed July 16, 2020, https://www.catholicnewsagency.com/news/cathedrals-in-6-states-damaged-by-violent-protests-91111.

90 See my book *The Death of Man as Man: The Rise and Decline of Liberty* (Bloomington, IN: WestBow Press, 2016).

port the declaration do not support the organization. However, it seems to be unwise and unnecessary to opt for even the declaration BLM. First, as Christians, we must communicate our message clearly so that the listener knows who we are and what we represent and do not represent. It is virtually impossible to make clear who supports the declaration BLM and the organization and who just supports the declaration, at least, on anything other than a direct or personal level of conversation. If a person is echoing BLM, carrying a BLM sign, wearing BLM clothing, or painting BLM on something, it is almost impossible for observers to know whether he supports the declaration only or the declaration and the organization. Second, as Christians, we have the privilege and stewardship of exalting God, Scripture, and the gospel by declaring an unambiguous message that all people are created by God and in His image, and, therefore, all lives are sacred—matter. BLM may say black lives matter, but it does not tell us why or how much, whereas the Christian message does both.

Third, the two most significant civil rights movements in American history were not based on a potentially confusing slogan that only elevates lives with a specific skin color without telling why they matter, to whom they matter, or how much they matter. These civil rights advances were based on declaring the truth of Scripture and The Declaration of Independence. In his famous Gettysburg Address, Abraham Lincoln said, "Four score and seven years ago our fathers brought forth on this continent, a new nation, conceived in Liberty, and dedicated to the proposition that all men are created equal."[91] His timeline leads not to the Constitution but to the Declaration of Independence, which says, "*We hold these truths to be self-evident, that all men are created equal, that they are endowed by their Creator with certain unalienable Rights.*"[92]

In like manner, the civil rights movement of the 1960s was based on a Christian worldview that all men are created equal. Why would we, as Christians, do less?

---

91 Abraham Lincoln, "The Gettysburg Address," accessed September 1, 2020, http://www.abrahamlincolnonline.org/lincoln/speeches/gettysburg.htm, para. 1.

92 See the American Declaration of Independence, accessed September 1, 2020, https://www.archives.gov/founding-docs/declaration-transcript.

Additionally, I am not advocating saying "all lives matter" in place of BLM. Because without the why of being created in the image of God, it is equally inadequate. We must declare all lives matter because all humans are created in the image of God. When we say that, we are saying God created one human race in his image, of which all have sinned, and for whom Christ died because God loves every person. That declaration leads to only one place, the gospel. Why would we unnecessarily encumber the gospel message? BLM and others are against focusing on the universal humanity of whites and blacks, which unites all people. Crenshaw rejects emphasizing our universal humanity, with statements like "I am a person who happens to be black." Instead, she is purposely divisive by using the statement "I am black" as a resistance statement.[93] Her recommendation is the opposite of Lincoln, King, and the signs carried by black men in the Civil Rights Marches, which said, "I <u>Am</u> a Man." The "I <u>Am</u> a Man" poster carried by Memphis sanitation workers in their 1968 strike, and at protests after Dr. King's death... were a comment [on] the first line of the second paragraph of Declaration of Independence: "We hold these truths to be self-evident, that all men are created equal."[94] Today, Crenshaw, critical race theorists, and BLM emphasize identity politics over our shared humanity.

---

93 Crenshaw says, "We all can recognize the distinction between the claims 'I am Black' and the claim 'I am a person who happens to be Black.' 'I am Black' becomes not simply a statement of resistance, but also a positive discourse of self-identification... 'I am a person who happens to be Black,' on the other hand, achieves self-identification... by straining for a certain universality (in effect, 'I am first a person')." Kimberlé Williams Crenshaw, "Mapping the Margins: Intersectionality, Identity Politics and Violence Against Women of Color," *Women, Gender & Research* 2 (2006), para. 18.

94 Rachel Walman, "Sanitation Workers, the Declaration of Independence, and an 18th-Century English Potter: Tracing the Roots of the Iconic "I Am a Man" Poster," New York Historical Society, April 4, 2018, paras. 1 & 5, accessed March 27, 2021, https://historydetectives.nyhistory.org/2018/04/sanitation-workers-the-declaration-of-independence-and-an-18th-century-english-potter-tracing-the-roots-of-the-iconic-i-am-a-man-poster/.

As Christians, we should speak out against all injustices, including unlawful death by police and the infliction of wrongful harm on innocent people's lives and their livelihood, especially when such crimes are instrumental in advocating one's position against crime. We must recognize that carrying the BLM banner while rejecting some of the immoralities of BLM does nothing to neutralize the phrase. The BLM promoters do not care if Christians dislike some of their agenda because they welcome anyone who will advertise their brand. And the undeniable truth is that BLM is hollow and deceptive. Their duplicity is evident considering their silence about the millions of black babies murdered annually by abortion, blacks wantonly killed by blacks, and black innocents killed by black rioters; apparently, those black lives do not matter. In a strong sense, BLM rejected Martin Luther King for Jessie Jackson and Al Sharpton.

Therefore, the banner really means only some black lives matter, which is not a banner any Christian should carry. Although Christians strongly advocate for the family, dedicated and knowledgeable parenting, we do not use the phrase "planned parenthood." The reason is simple. The term planned parenthood has become synonymous with the organization that promotes and profits from prenatal babies' execution. We do not want to be remotely associated with them or make them more well-known, and I think we should feel and act the same way toward BLM.

We should pray for the gospel to advance in this situation. We should pray for pastors and Christians in the cities of destruction as they minister Christ's truth and love to the people. We should pray for those who have positions of influence in such tragedies to practice God's impartial justice and to speak up for Christ. We should pray for all the victims of actual injustice. In this tragedy, we should grieve for every victim of injustice, as Scripture defines injustice. We should, in our sphere of influence, speak often, clearly, and Christianly.

CHAPTER 15

THE RELEVANCE OF THE BIBLE TO 21ST CENTURY AMERICA

Mel Winstead

INTRODUCTION

I first saw and heard Richard Land when he came to preach in chapel at Southeastern Baptist Theological Seminary. I was a student there at the time (as were two of his children). Dr. Land's preaching and his stance on ethics were an inspiration to many of the students who were beneficiaries of the conservative resurgence in the Southern Baptist Convention. Fast-forward some years and Dr. Land was the president of a seminary for which I was teaching. He still has a keen eye for biblical application to current events, and his knowledge of American history and its intersecting with Christianity is unparalleled by any other mortal, methinks. Land's basis of support for his arguments on ethical and political issues has always been the Bible. For him, the Word of God is our authority and our guide (and this is the case because God exists, and the Bible is a direct, specific, and sufficient revelation from Him).

* * *

Other authors, scholars, and culture critics have sufficiently covered the topics of human sexuality, abortion, and social justice,[1] but my area

---

1 See Nancy R. Pearcey, *Love Thy Body* (Grand Rapids, MI: Baker, 2018) for very thorough and highly technical research on abortion and homosexuality,

of expertise is specifically Biblical studies; this fact, coupled with my years of pastoring uniquely equip me to offer a biblical look at these key topics. Many perspectives on these and other issues abound, but I think the biblical perspective needs to be re-heard. Consequently, the point of this chapter is to demonstrate that the Bible is timeless enough and robust enough to be relevant to today's hot topics; God's Word sufficiently speaks to these issues.

The hot-button issues that this chapter will address are abortion, human sexuality, and "social justice" (the last is aka Critical Race Theory[2]). This chapter will first set the stage in each section by briefly explaining and giving examples of the topic at hand. Next, it will demonstrate what the Bible has to say on the issue (the primary contribution perhaps, will be to offer several Scripture selections that are relevant to these three key issues). Then, based on the understanding of Scripture's teaching on the issue, the chapter will consider an application of the Bible to our worldview in these matters. In this way, we propose to make a simple contribution to Christians' understanding of these cultural issues by informing them that the Bible is clear on these issues. It should also be understood that for sake of space and the scope of this chapter, it is impossible to approach every aspect of each of the topics covered herein. Instead, I will primarily focus on allowing the voices that support and those voices that disagree with abortion, homosexuality, and CRT to be heard and exegeting and applying the biblical text to these matters. Finally, I will explain the hope available and a way forward based on the biblical text.

Brian E. Fisher, *Abortion. The Ultimate Exploitation of Women* (Frisco, TX: Online for Life, 2013) for a discussion of abortion, and Voddie T. Baucham, Jr., *Fault Lines. The Social Justice Movement and Evangelicalism's Looming Catastrophe* (Washington, D.C.: Salem Books, 2021) and Owen Strachan *Christianity and Wokeness: How the Social Justice Movement Is Hijacking the Gospel - and the Way to Stop It* (Washington, D.C., Salem Books. Kindle Edition, 2021) for a Christian approach to Critical Race Theory.

2 Hereafter, "CRT." To be clear, general social justice can be differentiated from the current CRT movement.

ABORTION

We've seen the billboards and bumper stickers that read: "Abortion stops a beating heart." Interestingly, certain branches of science have caught up to the ancient words such as those in Psalm 139, where the Bible states that God intricately "wove" humans in their mother's womb (Ps 139:13).[3] A commentator from 500 years ago wrote these words: "He thus represents God as sitting king in the very reins of man, as the centre of his jurisdiction, and shows it ought to be no ground of wonder that all the windings and recesses of our hearts are known to him who, when we were inclosed [sic] in our mother's womb, saw us as clearly and perfectly as if we had stood before him in the light of mid-day."[4] Only in the last several decades has mankind possessed the technology to see inside the womb to view the "wonderful" intricacies of human beginnings during fetal development. God saw us all along and He can see further than modern technological instruments. A theologian wisely stated that, "Living becomes an awesome business when you realize that you spend every moment of your life in the sight and company of an omniscient, omnipresent Creator."[5] And this creator God provides the absolute criteria for determining the value of human beings.[6]

Science today agrees about "life beginning at conception."[7] However, this nod to reality no longer seems to be the issue. Now, some pro-choice advocates have moved on to something even more frightening and evil (if

---

[3] Unless noted otherwise, scripture citations in this chapter are from the NASB.

[4] John Calvin, J. and J. Anderson, (2010). *Commentary on the Book of Psalms* (Vol. 5, p. 214). Bellingham, WA: Logos Bible Software.

[5] J. I. Packer, *Knowing God* (Downers Grove, IL: InterVarsity Press, 1993), 86.

[6] See pro-life websites such as http://humancoalition.org; www.ncvalues.org, and http://concernedwomen.org. I also direct your attention to John S. Feinberg and Paul D. Feinberg, *Ethics for a Brave New World* (Wheaton, IL: Crossway, 2010) wherein they give direction for moral decision making (chapter 1), what one's ethical options are generally, and what the specific answers are for the freedom to choose argument and the "hard cases" in the abortion argument (chapter 2 and 3).

[7] See Chapter 2, "The Joy of Death" in Pearcey, *Love Thy Body*.

that's even possible). As thoroughly discussed in Nancy Pearcey's *Love Thy Body*,[8] there's a current worldview of *personhood* that does not align with reality nor with Scripture. This concept of "personhood" is that personhood is divorced from the human body. What this means is that one can now say "sure, that's a human fetus in the womb, but it's still not viable, because it's not yet a 'person'." Of course, with this premise, *when* a human becomes a person, is anyone's guess. Do you see the subjectivity here? An added problem is that since pro-choice proponents are following what Pearcey explains as the "two-story dualism,"[9] then the subjective assignment of "personhood" applies to those outside the womb as well. What this means is that personhood does not apply to embryos, fetuses, children up to several years of age, the disabled, mentally disabled, and the elderly. Therefore, if the powers-that-be don't consider these people to be "persons," these people can be easily euthanized.

Pearcey has astutely and correctly observed that,

---

8 Pearcey, *Love Thy Body*. See especially Pearcey's chapters 2 and 3. She goes on in the couple of chapters after that to explain that some bioethicists (and this will mean politicians pretty soon) are involved in pushing for transhumans and "embryo farms." And, for instance, Pearcey boldly states, "Voluntary euthanasia may not remain voluntary." (91). If you think our culture has not taken a ride on a crazy train, you have your head in the sand. However! There is a solution. We need God, we need to repent, and we need revival in our land. Probably only revival or a revolution will help us now (only the former will bring long-lasting healing). See also Feinberg and Feinberg, *Ethics*, Chapter 3, on "Abortion, part 2."

9 Pearcey explains, "Secular thought today assumes a body/person split, with the body defined in the "fact" realm by empirical science (lower story) and the person defined in the "values" realm as the basis for rights (upper story). This dualism has created a fractured, fragmented view of the human being, in which the body is treated as separate from the authentic self." (14). Pearcey goes on to explain how this applies to the abortion issue is that abortion rests on the "personhood" theory. Within this theory, that a human is a human is biology (a fact); but that a human might be a "person" is an ethical call (a value) (19). She states, "The implication of this two-story view is that simply being human is not enough to qualify for rights" (20). See Pearcey's explanation on her page 25 on why personhood theory does not rest on empirical data nor on science.

> A culture that practices abortion and infanticide is a culture that demeans women and disrespects their unique contribution to the task of reproduction. It does not treat women's ability to gestate and bear children as a wondrous and awesome capacity but as a liability, a disadvantage, a disability. It does not value and protect women in their childbearing capacity but seeks to suppress women's bodily functions, using toxic chemicals and deadly devices to violently destroy the life inside her.[10]

A pro-choice voice is that of Jill Filipovic. In *The Guardian* she began a journalistic piece with these words,

> Do "pro-life" advocates care about life or do they care about punishment? The latest abortion debate out of Texas gives a clear answer: the goal is to hurt women, not defend life. The Texas state legislature is debating a provision that wouldn't just outlaw abortion, but legally qualify it as homicide. For context of how extreme that is, even in the United States before Roe v Wade made abortion broadly legal, the procedure was outlawed in most states but was not considered murder – abortion was its own crime. Texas in 2019 wants to be even more barbaric than that, and turn women who end their pregnancies into felons, killers, and even death row inmates. That's right: Texas, supposedly so concerned with the right to life, continues to execute its own citizens. And some members of the state legislature want to execute women, too, if those women end their pregnancies.[11]

In Sharayah Colter's chapter in the present volume we read, "In the cases of fetal surgery, the fetus is considered a patient—a stark contrast to the fetus not even being considered a person with rights when presented

---

10 Pearcey, *Love Thy Body*, 69.
11 "Death sentence for abortion? The hypocrisy of US 'pro-lifers' is plain to see," accessed November 07, 2021, https://www.theguardian.com/commentisfree/2019/apr/11/death-sentence-abortion-hypocrisy-pro-life.

by a mother for an abortion procedure rather than for fetal surgery. This non-scientific double standard can also be seen in the legal realm in that the homicide of a pregnant mother warrants that the perpetrator be arrested and tried on murder charges for both the mother and baby, while in many situations a baby of the same gestation can be killed by a doctor at the mother's request with no legal repercussions for either party." (see her footnotes also). So, to argue as Filipovic has is to ignore the law as it applies to any other case of homicide or capital crime.[12] Finally, it must be clarified that neither Colter nor most pro-life supporters are advocating for a death penalty for those who elect for abortion. We are just trying to save the lives of innocent babies.

The Bible teaches unequivocally that God is pro-life! That is, the Bible opposes abortion. This can be seen from the prophets to Jesus to the apostles of Christ. The Bible views "child sacrifice," as an "abominable thing" (Dt 12:31) in God's eyes (see His views in the Scripture passages below). Therefore, biblical morality demands a pro-life stance. Other biblical principles are applicable as well: failure to "protect the weak and helpless"; "think of others more highly than you do yourself" (Phil 2:3-4); "love your neighbor as yourself," (Mark 12:31)[13] remember that "children are a gift from the Lord" (Ps 127:3), etc.

Often people wonder "How is "child sacrifice of the Old Testament era" synonymous with modern-day abortion?" A major difference is that ancient child sacrifice was an attempt to appease the capricious gods that people worshipped. No woman today who goes to the clinic for this procedure is doing so to offer anything to any god. But a major similarity is the taking of a human life, and one who was made in the image of God the same as were the adults involved. Another similarity is that the infant is helpless and cannot defend itself. But this is where the Bible also gives direction – "protect the weak and helpless."

We read in the Bible about the "detestable practices" (2 Kings 16:3 NLT) of some of the people groups of the land of Canaan. The issue of

---

12 And it is to set up a false analogy.

13 If a living human as close in proximity as being in the womb isn't one's neighbor, one wonders what the definition of one's "neighbor" might be!

aborting infants and offering them to the gods was an abomination to God and the reason God asked Israel to kick those people out of their land. In fact, God revealed the following in His Word: "Instead, he followed the example of the kings of Israel, even sacrificing his own son in the fire. In this way, he followed the detestable practices of the pagan nations the LORD had driven from the land ahead of the Israelites." (2 Kings 16:3 NLT), and "They even sacrificed their own sons and daughters in the fire. They consulted fortune-tellers and practiced sorcery and sold themselves to evil, arousing the LORD's anger." (2 Kings 17:17 NLT), and "You shall not give any of your children to devote them by fire to Molech, and so profane the name of your God." (Lev 18:21).

Additionally, we find God's attitude toward child sacrifice in the following selections (emphasis by the author denoting God's punishment for – or His attitude toward – these acts):

> 2 Kings 3:26: When the king of Moab saw that the battle was going against him, then he took his eldest son who was going to reign in his stead and offered him for a burnt offering upon the wall. <u>And there came great wrath upon Israel</u>, and they withdrew from him and returned to their own land.

> 1 Kings 16:34: Ahab did more <u>to provoke the Lord, the God of Israel, to anger</u> than all the kings of Israel who were before him. In his days Hiel of Bethel built Jericho; he laid its foundation at the cost of Abiram his first born and set up its gates at the cost of his youngest son Segub.

> Lev 20:1: The Lord said to Moses: "Say to the people of Israel, any man of the people of Israel…<u>who gives any of his children to Molech shall be put to death</u>; the people of the land shall stone him with stones. <u>I myself will set my face against that man, and will cut him off from among his people</u>, because he has given his children to Molech, defiling my sanctuary, and profaning my holy name."

Dt 12:31: When the Lord your God cuts off before you the nations whom you go in to dispossess, and you dispossess them and dwell in their land, take heed that you be not ensnared to follow them, after they have been destroyed before you, and that you do not inquire about their gods, saying: 'How did these nations serve their gods? That I also may do likewise.' You shall not do so to the Lord your God; for <u>every abominable thing which the Lord hates they have done</u> for their gods; for they even burn their sons and their daughters in the fire to their gods.

Ex 20:13: "<u>You shall not murder.</u>"[14]

Lev 20:3: <u>I will turn against that man and cut him off from his people</u>, because he gave his offspring to Molech, defiling My sanctuary and profaning My holy name. (CSB)

Mark 10:14: But when Jesus saw this, He was indignant and said to them, "<u>Permit the children to come to Me; do not hinder them</u>; for the kingdom of God belongs to such as these.

Matt 21:16: And Jesus said to them, "Yes; have you never read, 'out of the mouth of infants and nursing babies you have prepared praise for yourself?'"

Rom 13:9: For this, "You shall not commit adultery, <u>you shall not murder</u>, you shall not steal, you shall not covet," and if there is any other commandment, it is summed up in this saying, "<u>You shall love your neighbor as yourself.</u>"

Phil 2:3-4: <u>Do nothing from selfishness or empty conceit, but with humility of mind regard one another as more important than yourselves; do not merely look out for your own personal interests, but also for the interests of others.</u>

---

14   See section above on the pro-choice argument.

The Relevance of the Bible to 21st Century America

A few clear points can be made from the biblical text. The above-cited texts include the Old Testament passages about child sacrifices, Jesus' attitude toward children, and the ethical commands found in the letters of the apostles. God's fiercest judgment it seems was against those pagan nations who were practicing the killing of infants.[15] Abortion is clearly, scientifically, factually, killing an innocent human child. It is infanticide, and infanticide is an abomination to God and an atrocity that He will not allow without impunity. God punished those perpetrators whose hearts led them to strike out at God's image by killing the most vulnerable humans among them, the ones they should have been protecting the most.

My closing thoughts on the abortion topic are as follows. The Bible has spoken on this issue and God's ways are best, His design is preferred, and His demands still stand. We have left the natural function for which God designed us. We have abandoned God's notion of humans being created in His image. We do not respect that or else we would not kill babies in the womb, the most needy and helpless humans among us. I also feel that in our involvement in politics, voters – Christian and non-Christian alike – need to consider that if people, whether they be individuals or governments or political parties, do not care about pre-born human life, they probably do not care about your life![16]

---

15 The Bible is very clear that God commanded Israel to wipe out the Canaanites *because of* the "detestable things which they have done for their gods" (Dt 20:17-18) for the purpose of *warning the Israelites* to steer clear of being involved in the same idolatrous behavior ("so that they may not teach you to do according to all their detestable things which they have done for their gods" (Dt 20:18)). In fact, God did the same to His people because of *their* idolatry (the punisher and the punished were reversed): "They even sacrificed their sons and their daughters to the demons, and shed innocent blood, The blood of their sons and their daughters, whom they sacrificed to the idols of Canaan; And the land was polluted with the blood. Thus, they became unclean in their practices, and played the harlot in their deeds. (Ps 106:37-39). There is a lesson here: God is pro-life!

16 A few years ago, one writer had this to say about the abortion and pro-life issue: "Abortion in America is, in the judgment of my very wise father, the greatest evil in our history. The American holocaust dwarves the evil of Nazi Germany in both numbers of the dead, and the numbers of we who know what is happening. . ... To be silent is to be complicit. It is to tell our children and grandchildren that we are as guilty as those Germans who knew and were silent. . ..," accessed January 10, 2018,

There's hope and a way forward. Notice the words of encouragement and challenge from Nancy Pearcey as we Christians consider helping those who *did* choose abortion. In a section titled "Welcoming the Wounded," Pearcey urges the Christian church to "strive to be known as a sanctuary for those wounded by the callous cynicism of the abortion culture." She goes on to ask, "What message is the church sending women that many are afraid of reaching out to those most equipped to help them?"[17] We concur that Christians should be offering help and encouragement for those who suffer postabortion fallout.

Human Sexuality

In this section, we deal only with homosexuality specifically because it has been the strongest proponent of non-traditional, unbiblical sex ethics.[18] If one calls homosexuality a sin or calls it immoral, some gays and others tend to call that person "homophobic," "intolerant," "bigoted," etc. But the irony is that some of the name-callers are much more intolerant – seen when they push for legislation that forces people to operate against one's own religious beliefs. Some people simply will not tolerate Christian beliefs. Additionally, although only 5.6%[19] of the US population is homosexual, the outcry from their quarters is very loud.[20]

---

https://www.ligonier.org/blog/should-churches-observe-sanctity-life-sunday/.

17   Pearcey, *Love Thy Body*, 77. Another great resource on abortion is Fisher, *Abortion*. See his last chapter for practical pointers on helping with the pro-life movement.

18   Some of the same principles apply to other SOGI issues (SOGI = "sexual orientation and gender identity"). See Pearcey, *Love Thy Body* for applications of Christian ethics to SOGI issues, especially pp. 1944ff.

19   According to a Gallup poll from February 24, 2021, https://news.gallup.com/poll/329708/lgbt-identification-rises-latest-estimate.aspx, accessed November 21, 2021. The poll shows that the actual breakdown of the 5.6% is: "3.1% of Americans identifying as bisexual, 1.4% as gay, 0.7% as lesbian and 0.6% as transgender." See also https://www.statista.com/statistics/719674/american-adults-who-identify-as-homosexual-bisexual-or-transgender/, accessed November 21, 2021.

20   See the vast research by Michael Brown in chapter 8 of this book.

Same-sex marriage was legalized a few summers ago by the U.S. Supreme Court. But in addition to that legislation – because that is evidently not enough for the Anti-Christian Legal Union or for the Homosexual Agenda[21] – some are now persecuting, suing, defaming, bullying, and "canceling" anyone who does not celebrate and affirm the homosexual lifestyle. So much for tolerance![22] In fact, the effects of homosexual behavior on homosexuals are now being blamed on non-homosexuals (or those who view homosexuality as a sin).[23] Even some Christians are [unnecessarily] confused about what's right and wrong!

Confusion over Christians' attitude toward homosexuality abounds because of misuse of Scripture such as the following thought from Matthew Vines, author of *God and the Gay Christian* (here, we begin to let pro-gay voices be heard):

> Jesus indicates in the Sermon on the Mount that good teachings should bear good fruit. The consequences of the evangelical church's categorical rejection of same-sex relationships have been anything but good: higher likelihoods of depression, illegal drug use, relational brokenness, and suicide. Those are all red flags that opposing same-sex marriage isn't the best understanding of Scripture. That

---

21 Activists laid out 6 strategies: 1) talk about gayness loud and often, 2) portray gays as victims, 3) give homosexual protectors a 'just cause', 4) make gays look good, 5) make the victimizers look bad, and 6) solicit funds (see Michael Brown's chapter "A Stealth Agenda" in this volume and Craig Osten and Alan Sears, *The Homosexual Agenda* (Nashville: B&H Books, 2003), 18).

22 This same intolerance double standard applies to SOGI issues.

23 In fact, the CDC states, "Homophobia, stigma, and discrimination may place gay and bisexual men at risk for multiple physical and mental health problems and affect whether they seek and are able to obtain high-quality health services," accessed September 24, 2016, http://www.cdc.gov/hiv/group/msm/index.html. Might I say that people *feel* guilty because they *are* guilty (before God). But there is hope, and change is available. I commend the following book to anyone interested: David Longacre, ed. *Gay . . . Such Were Some of Us* (Boone, NC: L'Edge Press. Harvest USA, 2009) and Rosaria Butterfield, *The Secret Thoughts of an Unlikely Convert* (Pittsburgh, PA: Crown & Covenant Publications, 2014).

bad fruit was the main reason I felt I needed to take a closer look at the Bible on this subject.[24]

But as one evangelical leader has proclaimed, "As hard as it may be to come to terms with, the Bible is clear regarding its teaching that homosexual behavior is not God's plan (Genesis 19; Leviticus 18:22; Romans 1:26-27; 1 Corinthians 6:9-10). Yet, to satisfy their own desires or to appease the culture, many would-be interpreters seek to make the Bible say otherwise. This kind of eisegesis must be avoided. At all costs."[25] Further, Vines' argument above not only doesn't account for the many times Jesus teaches on obeying the moral commands of God in the Old Testament, but his argument also doesn't account for the fact that people who rebelled against God's moral law were suffering dire consequences long before the evangelical church was even invented. That is to say, people who chose to live contrary to God's design have always suffered consequences, regardless of whether people were even involved, and before the modern evangelical "categorical rejection." Therefore, Vines' argument is nonsensical.

Why are people unnecessarily confused? In his book *God and the Transgender Debate*, Andrew Walker gives some of the reasons we are where we are on this subject. He includes relativism, post-christendom, radical individualism, sexual revolution, and Gnosticism.[26] The confusion is unnecessary because the Bible is manifestly clear about what God thinks about all things homosexual. Below is a discussion of several selections from the Bible that are relevant to the issue of human sexuality and all the subtopics surrounding this topic.

---

24 Matthew Vines, *God and the Gay Christian* (New York: Convergent Books, 2014).

25 Bobby Conway, *Does God Exist? And 51 Other Compelling Questions About God and the Bible.* (Eugene, OR: Harvest House, 2016), 85.

26 Andrew Walker, *God and the Transgender Debate* (n.p. The Good Book Company, 2017), 21-27.

The Relevance of the Bible to 21st Century America

Genesis 1-2

The first truth to note about homosexuality (and any other perversion of human sexuality) is that it is against God's design and purpose. God created mankind as "male and female" (Gen 1:27). God stated in Gen 2:18 and 20 that it wasn't good for man to be alone and so He made a "helper" "suitable" for the male. There are two different genders, and only two genders.[27]

A pro-gay commentator has this to say,

> But the story is only the vehicle for conveying the religious point. The story of Adam and Eve as such is incidental to the point. Genesis is not a lesson on sexual orientation. Nothing in those two chapters suggests that heterosexuality, in contrast to homosexuality, was a concern in the author's mind. To read that modern concern into the text is simply to misuse the Bible. A similar analysis applies to all the other Bible texts about the love of woman and man for one another.[28]

In response, however, as one Christian apologist states,

> ... the Old Testament begins with the affirmation of the creation order (the goodness of sexual pleasure within the context of a husband-wife relationship), and this creational order – as opposed to homosexual relationships – is appealed to by Jesus and Paul. ... Both Jesus and Paul appeal to God's design at creation ("from the beginning") in support of lifelong marriage between husband and wife as God's ideal and thus the context for human sexual activity (Matt 19:3-12; Mark 10:2-12; Rom 1:18-32; 1 Tim 4:3-4). The redemp-

---

[27] Else how will we defend women's rights if we don't know what a woman is? Also, consider for how many decades secularists have decried Christians for being anti-science; that script has now flip-flopped.

[28] Daniel A. Helminiak, *What the Bible Really Says* (Tajique, NM: Alamo Square Press, 2000), 121-22.

tive movement of the biblical witness is uniform and unwavering: it offers no support for homosexual acts.[29]

God created. God designed. Think about that for a moment. If God designed two genders (one with male hardware and one with female hardware), then that design is the best. And those designs are complementary. This is a *teleological* and *biological argument*. To try to force the two distinct genders to operate otherwise is a denigration of God's character and is to struggle against nature itself. God designed male and female for each other. To try to live otherwise is to fall into a false view of reality that divides one's spiritual life from one's physical body.[30]

Genesis 19

The next major passage to consider is Genesis 19 and the wrath of God on Sodom. Many of our Baptist preachers over the last couple of decades like to say in response to the homosexual movement, "If God doesn't judge America, He owes Sodom and Gomorrah an apology." But consider this: the massive movement and litigation won by the homosexual agenda (in addition to those involving gender identity issues) *might be* God's judgment on America. What has gone on morally speaking in our nation in the last few years lines up with the notion of God removing His blessing from a nation. Americans, by-and-large (including the Church), have rebelled against God, have refused to repent, have neglected the authority of His

---

[29] Paul Copan, *When God Goes to Starbucks* (Grand Rapids, MI: Baker, 2008), 81.

[30] Pearcey, *Love Thy Body*, especially Chapter 5, "The Body Impolitic." Pearcey perceptively observes that, "Christianity is often accused of being anti-sex and anti-body. But in reality it is the secular ethic that is anti-body. Gay activists downplay the body – our biological identity as male or female – and define our true selves by our feelings and desires. They assume that the body gives no reference points for our gender identity or our moral choices. In essence, the secular worldview has revived the ancient Gnostic disdain for the body. It is Christianity that honors the body as male and female, instead of subordinating biological sex to psychological feelings." (162).

The Relevance of the Bible to 21st Century America

Word in so many arenas, we should not be shocked at the chaos, corruption, and mayhem in our nation.[31]

A pro-gay interpretation of Genesis 19 is, "... the sin of Sodom and Gomorrah was not homosexuality at all..."[32], but it was instead that of a lack of hospitality. It was, in fact, "a gross violation of the hospitality code"[33] But the Hebrew term "yada" does not simply mean to "get acquainted with." Moses does use the term at least five times in a sexual connotation. If the men only wanted to check on the credentials of the visitors (for safety of the city) then the offer of Lot's daughter would make no sense. If Lot and the hospitality code are the problem, then the judgment fell on the city, while Lot escaped.[34] Feinberg and Feinberg explain, "Is it possible that the real problem at Sodom was rape, not the fact that it involved same-sex participants.... If so, surely there were rapes in Sodom and Gomorrah involving opposite-sex partners, but God never rained down fire and brimstone for those rapes."[35] Additionally, the inspired canonical comment in Jude 7 supports the accurate interpretation that it was a sexual problem at hand, and not a hospitality issue.[36] This can be referred to as a *divine wrath argument*, as well as an *inner-biblical argument*.

Leviticus 18:22

Additionally, the Bible in Lev. 18:22 states, "You shall not lie with a male as one lies with a female; it is an abomination." Homosexuality is an abomination before the Lord. One pro-gay interpreter writes, "The point is that the Holiness Code of Leviticus prohibits male same-sex acts for religious

---

[31] Pastor John MacArthur has preached precisely this over the years, and it aligns with the claims of Paul in Romans 1. MacArthur has said something to the affect that the rise of homosexuality in our country *is itself* God's judgment.

[32] Feinberg and Feinberg, *Ethics*, 312.

[33] Ibid.

[34] Ibid., 13-14.

[35] Ibid., 317.

[36] Thanks to a pastor friend Jonathan Hamilton for bringing this to my attention.

reasons, not for sexual reasons. The concern is to keep Israel distinct from the Gentiles . . . The implication is that the only reason for forbidding male-male sex is concern about uncleanness and holiness."[37] But this command against homosexual sex is sandwiched in-between a command against child sacrifice and a command against bestiality. These injunctions are moral laws and not civil laws. This is a *moral law argument*, not a ceremonial or ritual issue.[38] And as Donald Wold states, "All action leads to some end, and all actions come with consequences, leading either closer to the goal of holiness (i.e., perfect virtue) or farther from it, and moral responsibility is inherent in the quest. In the biblical writer's perspective, the quality of one's conduct is not measured by the relative or subjective standards of the moment; the rule is rather the eternal, immutable will of Yahweh as expressed in the law."[39]

The Gospels

Jesus affirmed God's design and purpose by quoting from Genesis in Matthew 19:4. Jesus did teach on God's design – one male and one female. There is no place for homosexuality to fit in here (or else Jesus is in tension with the Lev. 18:22 passage quoted above). Note Michael Brown's comment about Jesus also not commenting on pedophilia or bestiality, but that does not make those things okay (see chapter 8).[40] Another Christian apologist argues, ". . . the Old Testament begins with the affirmation of the creation order (the goodness of sexual pleasure within the context of a

---

37 Helminiak, *What the Bible Really Says*, 54.

38 The moral laws of the Pentateuch are repeated in the New Testament; this is the case because they are based on the very character of Almighty God. The natural law arguments against homosexuality and same-sex marriage are covered quite well in Frank Turek, *Correct, Not Politically Correct. How Same-Sex Marriage Hurts Everyone* (Charlotte, NC: CrossExamined.org, 2008). Another moral law argument is found in Robert R. Reilly, *Making Gay Okay* (San Francisco: Ignatius Press, 2015), in his chapter titled "Sodomy and Science," especially p. 130.

39 Donald J. Wold, *Out of Order: Homosexuality in the Bible and the Ancient Near East* (Grand Rapids, MI: Baker, 1998), 99-100.

40 Michael Brown, "Answering the Tough Questions Asked by Homosexuals," accessed October 14, 2021, https://youtu.be/-3Mtgj5R2Qk.

husband-wife relationship), and this creational order – as opposed to homosexual relationships – is appealed to by Jesus and Paul. . ... The redemptive movement of the biblical witness is *uniform* and *unwavering*: it offers no support for homosexual acts."[41]

Romans 1:18-32

Some have argued that Paul did not realize there were those with same-sex orientation. Homosexual acts would be a violation of heterosexual sex for those who were constitutionally heterosexuals or were so-oriented. But Paul is not, they say, condemning homosexual acts by those who are so-oriented or homosexual acts between consenting adults. Paul is, instead, condemning perversion, not "inversion."[42] Another pro-gay commentator writes, ". . . far from condemning same-sex acts, Paul is actually teaching that they are ethically neutral. Like heterosexual acts, homosexual acts are neither right nor wrong in themselves. They can be used for good or for evil, but in themselves they are neither. There is nothing wrong with gay or lesbian sex simply because it is homogenital."[43] This idea, however, does not account for the fact that even heterosexual acts are not neutral – they have God-given boundaries.

In referring to the Romans 1 passage, Matthew Vines said, "The first thing I realized was simple but significant: The longest discussion of same-sex behavior in Scripture—in Paul's letter to the Romans—referred only to lustful behavior. The types of loving committed gay marriages we see on a regular basis today are never discussed in the Bible. . ."[44] This is a pro-gay perspective, but the perspective from actual Bible scholars and theologians is different. Romans 1:26 treats lesbianism, 1:27 treats male homosexuality,

---

41 Copan, *When God Goes to Starbucks*, 81. Emphasis mine.

42 Feinberg and Feinberg, *Ethics*, 335.

43 Helminiak, *What the Bible Really Says*, 75.

44 Matthew Vines, "God and the Gay Christian," interview with Amazon, accessed September 24, 2016, https://www.amazon.com/God-Gay-Christian-Biblical-Relationships-ebook/dp/B00F1W0RD2.

and the passage is a clear and graphic description of these behaviors.[45] Additionally, as seen in the contrast of the word "natural" in Rom 1:26 to that which is "against nature" in the same verse demonstrates the apostle's view that homosexuality is a departure from what is natural.[46] The wording is also general so that an argument that Paul only speaks against homosexuality activity in reference to pederasty, for instance, or that it refers to non-consensual homosexual sex, is unfounded.[47] This is a *grammatical and contextual argument*.

Hear the pastoral call from the pastor-theologian John Piper on Romans 1:

> The reason Paul focuses on homosexuality in these verses is because it is the most vivid dramatization in life of the profoundest connec-

---

[45] Further, as MacArthur and Mayhue discussed, "Homosexual unions cannot rightly be called "marriages," since they involve only one gender, possess no ability to procreate, and cannot provide the kind of sexual companionship God intended." (John MacArthur and Richard Mayhue, eds. *Biblical Doctrine. A Systematic Summary of Bible Truth* (Wheaton, IL: Crossway, 2017), 431. Additionally, "gay Christian" is an oxymoron; 1 Cor 6:11 is definitive. To claim that a Christian can be gay is to argue against the soteriology offered in this passage. See https://youtu.be/l-bTqIJP2JI (Michael Brown vs. Matthew Vines); https://youtu.be/1FLYoSmtIyI (James White); https://youtu.be/HyVvjAdbaaQ (Matthew Vines talk); https://youtu.be/-3Mtgj5R2Qk (Michael Brown); https://youtu.be/mTmPzE5CLlM (former homosexual). In the fourth video just listed, Brown says that Jesus also didn't talk about pedophilia, beating your wife, etc. Also, if Jesus abolished the Law, then I guess adultery and idolatry are okay. No, He actually took things to a higher standard, explains Brown.) Also, consider this thought, Homosexual behavior is "evidence of God's judgment on those who reject his revelation." (Feinberg and Feinberg, *Ethics*, 335).

[46] Thomas R. Schreiner, *Romans. Baker Exegetical Commentary on the New Testament* (Grand Rapids, MI: Baker Academic, 1998), 96.

[47] Ibid. The word for "natural" means "innate" or "produced by nature" (G. Abbott-Smith, *A Manual Greek Lexicon of the New Testament* (Edinburgh: T&T Clark, 1999),475)). The contrasting use of the word at the end of v. 26 in the original is the accusative case and is used with a preposition which, in this construction means "against, contrary to" (Daniel B. Wallace, *Greek Grammar Beyond the Basics* (Grand Rapids, MI: Zondervan, 1996), 378).

tion between the disordering of heart-worship and the disordering of our sexual lives. We learn from Paul in Ephesians 5:31-32 that, from the beginning, manhood and womanhood existed to represent or dramatize God's relation to his people and then Christ's relation to his bride, the church. In this drama, the man represents God or Christ and is to love his wife as Christ loved the church. The woman represents God's people or the church. And sexual union in the covenant of marriage represents pure, undefiled, intense heart-worship. That is, God means for the beauty of worship to be dramatized in the right ordering of our sexual lives. But instead, we have exchanged the glory of God for images, especially of ourselves. The beauty of heart-worship has been destroyed. Therefore, in judgment, God decrees that this disordering of our relation to him be dramatized in the disordering of our sexual relations with each other. . .. Which leads us to one last word: The healing of the homosexual soul, as with every other soul, will be the return of the glory of God to its rightful place in our affections.[48]

This is a *theological* argument.

1 Corinthians 6:9-11

The two terms translated "effeminate" and "homosexual" in a modern English Bible do not refer to 21st century consenting, committed adult homosexual couples, according to pro-gay activists; instead, pro-gay commentators say the terms are limited to male prostitution or pederasty (in fact as one pro-gay interpreter states, "these texts condemn wanton, lewd, irresponsible male homogenital acts but not homogenital acts in general.[49] The word 'effeminate' simply refers 'moral looseness' and undisciplined behavior").[50] But other scholars explain, "The reference is clearly to someone who prac-

---

48   https://www.desiringgod.org/messages/the-other-dark-exchange-homosexuality, accessed October 15, 2016.
49   Helminiak, *What the Bible Really Says*, 105.
50   Ibid., 109.

tices homosexuality,"[51] and "Paul's opposition to all homosexual behavior . . . seems to derive from Leviticus 18:22 and 20:13, which represent absolute bans."[52] The two terms taken together simply make a general reference to the homosexual act. Further, what is clear is that these terms are found in a vice list and are soundly condemned by God in Scripture.[53]

Consider the context and what the apostle is saying. In response to a gay interpretation, another writer has stated, "The list says these persons will not enter heaven. Can it be the case that one who is only "soft" will be kept from heaven because of his softness?[54] The apostle prefaces the list of those who will not enter the kingdom of God with the warning "Do not be

---

51 Silva references Lev 18:22 of the LXX where the word is used in this context (Moisés Silva, ed. *New International Dictionary of New Testament Theology and Exegesis vol 1 A - D* (Grand Rapids, MI: Zondervan, 2014), 408). Other scholars' comments include: "Paul embraces the unanimous Jewish tradition in renouncing homosexuality (e.g., Gen 19:1-28; Lev 18:22; 20:13; Wis. 14:26; T. Levi 17:11; T. Naph. 3:3-4; Sib. Or. 3:596-600; Josephus, Ag. Ap. 2.24, 37; Philo, Spec. Laws 3.7)" (Thomas R. Schreiner, *New Testament Theology. Magnifying God in Christ* (Grand Rapids, MI: Baker Academic, 2008), 661), and "Homosexuality is not another option for two consenting adults; it is an aberration of God's design for the procreation, pleasure, and preservation of the human race" (MacArthur and Mayhue, eds. *Biblical Doctrine,* 431).

52 Roy E. Ciampa and Brian S. Rosner, *The First Letter to the Corinthians* (Grand Rapids, MI: Eerdmans, 2010), 242. The scholars continue, "Paul opposed homosexual behavior on the basis of creation theology and because it is marked as a vice in the Torah and was stressed as a vice by Jews" (242).

53 See the very detailed discussion in Chapter 8 of Feinberg and Feinberg, *Ethics.*

54 James B. DeYoung, *Homosexuality. Contemporary Claims Examined in Light of the Bible and Other Ancient Literature and Law* (Grand Rapids, MI: Kregel, 2000), 109. Al Mohler commented, "As Romans 1 makes absolutely clear, homosexuality is fundamentally an act of unbelief. As Paul writes, the wrath of God is revealed against all those "who suppress the truth in unrighteousness." God the Creator has implanted in all humanity a knowledge of Himself, and all are without excuse. This is the context of Paul's explicit statements on homosexuality," ("The Compassion of Truth: Homosexuality in Biblical Perspective," accessed September 24, 2016, https://albertmohler.com/2009/07/16/the-compassion-of-truth-homosexuality-in-biblical-perspective-2).

deceived." Why would he say that? Well, probably because so many people are easily deceived – by the Devil, by false teaching, by emotions, by family ties, by pleasure, by what is popular, by their abusers, and even by what becomes legal.

Verse eleven of this same passage offers hope. It offers hope by reminding some of these Corinthian Christians who had been converted from this "Corinthian" lifestyle that they had been "washed," "sanctified," and "justified."[55] God had cleaned them up and delivered them and given them new life![56] The hope found here also informs us that it is possible to be wholly delivered from homosexuality if one so desires and to live a normal Christ-honoring life. It has been done and continues to be done![57] This is a *soteriological* and *societal* argument.

MacArthur has stated, "There's absolutely no mistaking. Homosexual perversion and behavior are defiling. It produces God's judgment. God hasn't changed His opinion."[58] The consequences of perversion (perversion of the thought patterns) that coincide with this behavior are found Rom 1:18ff. Some camps, especially those in reparative therapy agree with this fact, though they might not use the word "defiling." But the fact is, as Joseph Nicolosi's research, for example, has amply demonstrated in many cases, the emotional neglect of young boys in their families led to trauma which led to a self-preservation mechanism of mollifying the trauma through participation in homosexual behavior, in order to find the love, nourishing, and

---

55 These are soteriological terms which encapsulate the positional and practical sanctification involved in "salvation." The practical sanctification part of it is pursued by Paul in 1 Cor 5:9, 11; Eph 4; 1 Thess 4:4; Heb 12:14, and many other selections in the New Testament letters. These passages are found in the sections where the Holy Spirit grants behavioral instructions to Christians. There are many commands in these sections concerning sexual morality; so, do not "wait" for God to deliver you further – you must obey!

56 See the testimonials in Longacre, *Gay . . . Such Were Some of Us.*

57 See the work by harvestusa.org and the research of reparative therapists such as Joseph Nicolosi.

58 John MacArthur, "Thinking Biblically About Homosexuality," accessed September 24, 2016, https://www.gty.org/library/sermons-library/80-322/thinking-biblically-about-homosexuality.

acceptance that was missing in the home.[59] This can be called a *psychological argument*. The fact that this type of therapy exists demonstrates the truth of 1 Cor 6:11: "such *were* some of you." There's hope and help to be had.

Additionally, the church must reach out! After talking about inviting homosexuals into your home and world to establish a relationship and to demonstrate the gospel through your own family life, Rosaria Butterfield states, "The best way . . . to taste the sweetness of the promises of salvation's fruits here on earth is to take personal risks for his glory."[60] And so, may we remember two points: "but speaking the truth in love," (Eph 4:15); *and* "Let all that you do be done in love" (1 Cor 16:14). We must approach all people and all circumstances with a humble and loving heart. And it is not loving to say nothing to people who continue in this kind of behavior. It is not acceptable to harm, "bash," or otherwise castigate people because of their sin (whatever that sinful behavior might be).[61] It is also not acceptable to passively allow the behavior and influence to spread if indeed it is wrong and harmful. Christians should inform themselves on the issues and be loving enough, when given the opportunity, to share the biblical truth with people that homosexuality is not God's design for them and is therefore harmful. Only the truth will set them free (John 8:31-32). The truth of God's Word will do His work.

My closing thoughts on the human sexuality topic are as follows. The Bible has spoken on this issue and God's ways are best, His design is preferred, and His demands still stand. We have left the natural function for which God designed us. We have abandoned God's notion of humans be-

---

59 Joseph Nicolosi, *Shame and Attachment Loss. The Practical Work of Reparative Therapy* (Liberal Mind Publishers, 2016).

60 Butterfield, *The Secret Thoughts of an Unlikely Convert*, 177.

61 Many people try to shut down a Christian's viewpoint by saying "all sins are the same, and therefore, why are you picking on this one particular sin?" Indeed, all people are born with a sin nature and therefore have the same propensity to break God's law. However, all sins are obviously not the same in scope and consequence. I say this because God only called certain sins an "abomination," and only certain sins were given the death penalty as judgement. Further, liars and thieves, for instance, are not pushing for legislation for all other citizens to accept their behavior. Therefore, to say that "all sin is sin" in order to shut down an argument is baseless.

ing created in His image. We do not respect that or else we would not show disdain for ourselves in the ways we do when we abuse our bodies and think they are separate from the real us.[62]

Social Justice (CRT)

Introduction

Consider this: "Justice doesn't need an adjective," says Pastor-theologian John MacArthur.[63] That being said, it needs to be understood that when people place an adjective before "justice," there's probably something they are after that's more than only "justice." Beware of deceptive political schemes that on the face of it publicly cry for "justice," but in reality keep people "down", support abortion, destroy the family unit, cause divisions, perpetuate racism, and destroy creativity and motivation for people to do all to the glory of God. As Carol Swain has written, "Social justice is rooted

---

62 See especially chapters 1 and 5 of Pearcey's *Love Thy Body*. In juxtaposing the notion of a unified body/mind human and that of a person liberated from their body (while still alive; this is the two-story dualism she references), Pearcey explains, "By contrast, a biblical worldview leads to a positive view of the body. It says that the biological correspondence between male and female is part of the original creation. Sexual differentiation is part of what God pronounced "very good" – *morally* good – which means it provides a reference point for morality. There is a purpose in the physical structures of our bodies that we are called to respect. A teleological morality creates harmony between biological identity and gender identity. The body/person is an integrated psychosexual unity. Matter does matter." (32). Emphasis original. In her chapter 5, "The Body Impolitic," Pearcey states the same thing in a different way, "Biblical morality affirms the high value of creation. In a teleological view, nature is not undifferentiated raw material with no positive character of its own. It exhibits a plan, a design, an order, and a purpose. Because of that, it gives rational grounds for our moral decisions. Our sexual identity is meant to be in harmony with our psychological identity. The goal is to overcome self-alienation and recover a sense of inner coherence." (162).

63 https://www.youtube.com/watch?v=3MMU7f0Bdw4, accessed July 25, 2021. He goes on to state that "social justice is another term for socialism."

in Marxism. Marxism is a radical worldview that seeks to destroy the family & overthrow the American political system by creating chaos, division, & friction. Clever packing has allowed dangerous ideas to seep into our classrooms, churches, & businesses."[64] The current Critical Race Theory is guilty of these atrocities.

Next, consider these voices from CRT supporters, the first found in a piece in the *Des Moines Register*. The piece quotes from Richard Delgado and Jean Stefancic in "Critical Race Theory: An Introduction" that CRT's writings would "reject our founding liberal principles of rationality, legal equity, constitutional neutrality, and incremental civil rights. The substitute: a race conscious approach to social change targeting mainstays 'of liberal jurisprudence such as affirmative action, neutrality, color blindness, role modeling, or the merit principle.'"[65] The author of the *Register* article, a CRT opponent remarks,

> CRT's call for "equity" doesn't sound threatening because it sounds like "equality," but there is a huge difference. Equality of opportunity is very different from "equity." Equality of opportunity means that all have a chance to succeed. CRT "equity" means that everyone gets equal rewards. Note the Marxist tones. Equality to CRT theorists is "mere nondiscrimination" and provides cover for white supremacy, patriarchy and oppression. UCLA law professor and CRT theorist Cheryl Harris proposes suspending private property rights, seizing land and wealth and redistributing them along racial lines."[66]

These and many other scholars and writers see the actual racism and other damage in this Trojan horse of CRT.

---

64   Carol Swain, https://twitter.com/carolmswain/status/1388447955452108810, accessed November 13, 2021.

65   Greg Ganske, "Understanding Critical Race Theory Reveals How it's Harmful to Race Relations," accessed November 13, 2021, https://www.desmoinesregister.com/story/opinion/columnists/iowa-view/2021/05/22/critical-race-theory-harmful-race-relations/5076052001/

66   Ibid.

The Relevance of the Bible to 21st Century America

Elements of CRT

Some of the elements of CRT are 1) racism is normal, 2) there is no objective truth, 3) knowledge is socially constructed, 4) people should be categorized by "races," or "classes," 5) a thirst for power,[67] and 6) people in the "oppressor" group cannot change but people in the "oppressed" group do not need to change (and can't change their path to the future).[68] These are

---

67 "Voddie Baucham Explains the Looming Catastrophe of Critical Race Theory in the Church," accessed August 18, 2021, https://www.youtube.com/watch?v=M-MpeHcviHik. See also, Strachan, *Christianity and Wokeness*, 9, 69-70. Additionally, the thirst for power can be readily seen in the marketplace of ideas wherein students are taught "to be skeptical of science, reason, and evidence; to regard knowledge as tied to identity, to read oppressive dynamics into every interaction; to politicize every facet of life . . . ." (Helen Pluckrose and James Lindsay, *Cynical Theories. How Activist Scholarship Made Everything about Race, Gender, and Identity – and Why This Harms Everybody* (Durham, NC: Pitchstone Publishing, 202. The goal is nothing short of a "soft revolution," to borrow a term from Pluckrose and Lindsay (216), and the goal is to force all people into the same relativistic, postmodern viewpoint. To build on what I stated earlier in this chapter: the goal is not tolerance nor is it inclusion; the goal is a fundamental forcing of one person to another's viewpoint by means of one or a combination of the following: "inclusion" policies, bullying, or outright canceling.

68 See the multiple videos of Voddie Baucham listed in footnotes in this chapter, and other videos with LSU Law Prof. Trahan (https://www.youtube.com/watch?v=hqaCDXosfuU&t=111s), and many others. CRT is being exposed very quickly and many Americans are waking up to the racism, division, and anti-Christian nature of CRT which manifests itself under other labels such as "wokeism," "social justice," "intersectionality," "equity," "white fragility," "antiracism" (see Baucham's discussions in Chapter 4, "A New Religion" in *Fault Lines*), and the like. Assuming our readers know something of CRT, I am not going to go into much detail at all about the history of its ideals or goals. Voddie Baucham has done that quite well in *Fault Lines*, and Ronnie Rogers has ably dealt with the theory in chapter 14 of the current volume. Additionally, it should be understood that while some readers might have problems with race relations that are based on their own personal experience, many people of all races and ethnicities have been hurt through the years because of prejudices. A reader might also take issue with the explanations of CRT given in this chapter because they have bought into a watered down, mainstream media version of it. However, I am tackling actual Critical Race

the explanations given by the architects and current supporters of CRT, and these kinds of tenets can be further seen in a recent New York Times article by Jacey Fortin,[69] an article at the American Bar Association by Janel George,[70] an article in the New York Post by Christopher Rufo,[71] and in writings such as those by Derrick Bell.[72]

Theory, the CRT that is doing the most damage in our nation and is counter-productive to bringing unity and peace. It is my contention that a Biblical perspective and the gospel of Jesus Christ is the only power that can bring true peace. Without Jesus Christ and His forgiveness of sins, all else that we attempt is in vain, and only perpetuates the problem. This is why (as dealt with in the section on the letter to the Colossians), the apostle Paul cycles back to the Lord Jesus so many times.

[69] Jacey Fortin, accessed November 13, 2021, https://www.nytimes.com/article/what-is-critical-race-theory.html.

[70] Janel George, accessed November 13, 2021, https://www.americanbar.org/groups/crsj/publications/human_rights_magazine_home/civil-rights-reimagining-policing/a-lesson-on-critical-race-theory/.

[71] Christopher F. Rufo, "Lie of Credit — American Express Tells its Workers Capitalism is Racist," accessed November 13, 2021, https://nypost.com/2021/08/11/american-express-tells-its-workers-capitalism-is-racist/. The fuller quote is here: "American Express, which made a $2.3 *billion* profit last quarter, invited the great-grandson of the Nation of Islam's founder to tell its employees that capitalism is evil. It was part of the credit card giant's critical race theory training program, which asks workers to deconstruct their racial and sexual identities, then rank themselves on a hierarchy of "privilege." According to a trove of documents I've reviewed, AmEx executives created an internal "Anti-Racism Initiative" after George Floyd's death last year, subjecting employees to a training program based on the core CRT tenets, including intersectionality, which reduces individuals to a tangle of racial, gender and sexual identities that determine whether he is an "oppressor" or "oppressed" in a given situation. In a foundational session, the outside consulting firm Paradigm trained AmEx employees to deconstruct their own intersectional identities, mapping their "race, sexual orientation, body type, religion, disability status, age, gender identity [and] citizenship" onto an official company worksheet. Employees could then determine whether they have "privilege" or are members of a "marginalized group": White males presumably end up in the oppressor position, while racial and sexual minorities are considered oppressed." See also https://www.americanbar.org/groups/crsj/publications/human_rights_magazine_home/civil-rights-reimagining-policing/a-lesson-on-critical-race-theory/.

[72] See the review by Linda Greenhouse, https://archive.nytimes.com/www.nytimes.com/books/00/06/04/specials/bell-well.html.

The Relevance of the Bible to 21st Century America

Opponents of CRT emphasize the racism inherent in CRT. In a piece about Carol Swain, FoxNews recently reported, "The former professor explained that critical race theory not only takes away from the root of academia but creates a "hostile learning environment" for students and teachers. When standards are lowered for minority students, when messages are sent about White privilege and minorities being victims and racism being permanent, that's something that's very damaging," she said. "It's not good for America. . . ."[73] Elsewhere, Dr. Swain has stated, "The demonization of a group of people because of the color of their skin is something that is discriminatory."[74] Swain's is one among many, many black voices in America currently decrying and fighting the CRT movement for the racism that it is.[75] Racism in CRT is seen precisely through what Swain has here demonstrated.

The tenets and the consequences of CRT are being fought against by black and white, "right" and "left." For our purposes, it must be noted that these elements can be briefly answered from a Christian worldview in the following comments. Racism is not normal, but sin is. Each individual is born as a sinner (Rom 3:23) and is in need of forgiveness of sin. The teach-

---

73 Angelica Stabile, "Public School Students Being 'Abused' by Critical Race Theory Education: Carol Swain, accessed November 13, 2021, https://www.foxnews.com/media/public-school-students-abused-critical-race-theory-education-carol-swain.

74 https://nationworldnews.com/critical-race-theory-may-violate-civil-rights-act-constitution-dr-carol-swain/, accessed November 13, 2021.

75 See, for example, Carol Swain: https://www.wsj.com/articles/SB10001424052748704335904574496250622719022; https://twitter.com/carolmswain/status/1388447955452108810; Jason L. Riley: https://www.wsj.com/articles/waukesha-killings-make-the-media-colorblind-again-postracial-america-race-agenda-11638310613; Thomas Sowell: https://www.nationalreview.com/2021/10/thomas-sowell-vs-critical-race-theory/; https://www.carolinajournal.com/opinion-article/exposing-the-faulty-narrative-upon-which-critical-race-theory-is-built/; Monique Duson: https://www.biola.edu/blogs/think-biblically/2020/critical-race-theory; https://www.impact360institute.org/videos/should-christians-use-critical-race-theory-as-a-road-to-racial-reconciliation-monique-duson/; North Carolina Lieutenant Governor Mark Robinson: https://www.foxnews.com/media/mark-robinson-critical-race-theory-struggle-north-carolina; South Carolina Senator Tim Scott: https://apnews.com/article/tim-scott-joe-biden-business-race-and-ethnicity-health-789601bb6410b6756358893bea33d5a9.

ing that there is no objective truth (architects of CRT say this is the case because objectivity is a lie taught by the hegemonic rulers[76] to keep people down) is itself a self-defeating statement[77] (CRT is an endgame of relativism – this is where relativism leads!). The power any of us might have is Providentially derivative and should be used to spread the gospel, protect the helpless, and uphold biblical values in other arenas. Another CRT element is to claim that white people are the oppressors and therefore they cannot have the knowledge of the fact that they are in fact racist ("ethnic Gnosticism"[78]). The answer here is again, this neglects the biblical doctrines of repentance, forgiveness, and original sin – all people are guilty. Jesus Christ died to break down the racial barriers that divide people (see Ephesians 2).

To expand another of these points, we offer some thoughts from Voddie Baucham. He applies the term "Ethnic Gnosticism" to the CRT elements that single out the "oppressors" and tells them they can't know that they are racist and can't change (and in fact, the "oppressed" will not accept apology even if it's offered ten times over). He explains that Gnosticism is "the idea that truth can be accessed through special, mystical knowledge."[79] In *Fault Lines*, Baucham deals with this issue of "ethnic Gnosticism" in his chapter 5 on "A New Priesthood." He ends that chapter with these words, "But the Bible also admonishes us to do things that fly in the face of Ethnic Gnosticism and its assumptions. The very idea of dividing people up by ethnicity, then declaring some of them wicked oppressors and others the oppressed, is inconsistent with the biblical doctrine of universal guilt [here he cites Rom 3:9-18, which everyone ought to remind themselves of] . . . . This is not the state of white men; it is the state of *all* men. As such, the idea

---

76 Voddie Baucham, "Defining Cultural Marxism and Hegemony," accessed August 18, 2021, https://www.youtube.com/watch?v=xjQHWXqS5Eg.

77 To learn more about relativism and how it is a false worldview, see the teachings of Frank Turek at Cross-examined.org.

78 Baucham, *Fault Lines*, 91. "Ethnic Gnosticism / Dr. Voddie Baucham," accessed August 18, 2021, https://www.youtube.com/watch?v=Ip3nV6S_fYU.

79 Ibid. And see "Ethnic Gnosticism / Dr. Voddie Baucham," accessed August 18, 2021, https://www.youtube.com/watch?v=Ip3nV6S_fYU. See several other videos of Voddie Baucham on YouTube as well. Also see his *Fault Lines*, and Owen Strachan's *Christianity and Wokeness* (both are must-reads).

that there is special knowledge or revelation available to some and hidden from others by virtue of their race or position in the oppressor/oppressed scheme is unthinkable – and unbiblical."[80] Additionally, here is where CRT proponents think that "oppressed" minorities have a higher objectivity to their viewpoints for the simple fact that they have experienced things (whether real or perceived) that the "oppressors" haven't. Never mind rational thought processes and objective truth. In this system, Baucham explains, "narrative is an alternative, and ultimately superior, truth."[81] Baucham concludes, "Christians simply must reject this worldview."[82]

CRT and the New Testament; Colossians 2:8 as a Case Study

So, what about "Gnosticism" in the New Testament? In New Testament scholarship, we now understand that Gnosticism as a finalized and unified philosophy did not exist until the 2nd century.[83] But some of the main tenets of what later came to be known as Gnosticism did exist.[84] Some of these tenets clearly plagued the New Testament churches. These tenets included mysticism, legalism, a false view of the person and nature of Christ, a "secret knowledge,"[85] and asceticism. Therefore, it is quite evident that the here-

---

80 Baucham, *Fault Lines*, 111, emphasis original.
81 Ibid., 94. Experience does not equal objectivity.
82 Ibid.
83 See Doug Moo, *The Pillar New Testament Commentary. The Letters to the Colossians and to Philemon* (Grand Rapids, MI: Eerdmans, 2008); and Christopher Tuckett, "Gnosticism," in *Dictionary of Biblical Criticism and Interpretation*, ed. Stanley E. Porter (New York: Routledge, 2007), 127-29. Also, for a great treatment of the tenets of Gnosticism that were afoot in the 1st century, see Ronald H. Nash, *The Gospel and the Greeks. Did the New Testament Borrow from Pagan Thought?* (Phillipsburg, NJ: P&R Publishing, 2003).
84 There never really was an "unified" system.
85 A must-read on this issue of a secret knowledge is Baucham's *Fault Lines* and Strachan's *Christianity and Wokeness* (two must-reads for every Christian in America today). You can also see Baucham's further explanations and applications of ethnic Gnosticism to cultural Marxism (woke-ism, social justice, CRT)

sy – whatever one might name the heresy – was just that – a heresy. The apostle Paul and the apostle John both battled these false ideologies in their letters. Consider one of the primary New Testament passages (and in fact, the whole letter of Colossians) in which scholars see some tenets that were later used in Gnosticism but were already plaguing the church in the mid-first century. We will see that these tenets pushed false views of Christs' person and work, His sufficiency, and His followers' identity, and then we'll see the relevance to modern CRT.

"See to it that no one takes you captive through philosophy and empty deception, according to the tradition of men, according to the elementary principles of the world, rather than according to Christ." (Col 2:8 NASB)

<u>*"Don't let anyone capture you*</u> *with empty philosophies and high-sounding nonsense that come from human thinking and from the spiritual powers of this world, rather than from Christ."* (Col 2:8 NLT)

The command here is clear: these Christians were not to allow themselves to be captured, cheated, spoiled, deceived by any philosophy, any worldview, any thought pattern, any cultural mantra, or cultural mandate that is "empty deception." The deception of this first-century false teaching was not according to the teachings of Christ and the principles of His Word, and they were not based on the unchanging character of God (which is transcribed in many of the commands and principles in the Bible).

The empty deception, the hollowness, the inconsistent and anti-biblical worldview that belongs to the CRT movement includes racism within the movement's own goals and methodologies, and undermining of the gospel of Jesus Christ, a perpetuation of worldly racism, a denial of the biblical notion that all people are created in the image of God, roadblocks to the biblical notion of individual responsibility, unchristian ethics, and more.[86] For instance, CRT is clearly and unarguably against the biblical

---

in the following YouTube videos: https://www.youtube.com/watch?v=EaH4DL-R2i0I; https://www.youtube.com/watch?v=GRMFBdDDTkI.

86 Strachan (*Christianity and Wokeness*), warns, "It is past time for Christians to wake up—not to the so-called "truths" of CRT, but to the deception that is creeping into our churches." (55).

teachings of hard work and all human beings being made in the image of God. Notice this selection from the New York Times,

> Even common phrases are subjected to race-based regulation: White employees are told not to utter phrases such as "I don't see color," "We are all human beings" and "Everyone can succeed in this society if they work hard enough" — all categorized as "microaggressions." At one high-profile "anti-racism" event, AmEx execs invited Khalil Muhammad — great-grandson of Nation of Islam founder Elijah Muhammad — to lecture on "race in corporate America." He argued that the system of capitalism was founded on racism and that "racist logics and forms of domination" have shaped Western society from the Industrial Revolution to the present. "American Express has to do its own digging about how it sits in relationship to this history of racial capitalism," Muhammad said. "You are complicit in giving privileges in one community against the other, under the pretext that we live in a meritocratic system where the market judges everyone the same.[87]

Christians must be alert to the labels of CRT because it will label any part of the Christian message with which it does not agree as microaggressions, or racist in some way. The message of the Bible is that we are all humans, in this thing together, and we all need a Savior – and a spiritual one at that (not a political savior). The message of the Bible and therefore of Judeo-Christianity (and many other cultures around the world) is that a person is to work for their daily bread and be diligent as a citizen. A Christian's identity is that they are in union with Jesus Christ, in solidarity with Jesus Christ and other believers, and it does not matter their skin color. This is the point of Ephesians 2. Anyone who can't see this truth from Ephesians 2 doesn't understand the purpose of the death of Jesus Christ. These are Bib-

---

[87] Christopher F. Rufo, "Lie of Credit — American Express Tells its Workers Capitalism is Racist," accessed November 13, 2021, https://nypost.com/2021/08/11/american-express-tells-its-workers-capitalism-is-racist/.

lical notions and when they are attacked by political systems, they must be defended. CRT is an anti-biblical worldview.[88]

"Don't let anyone capture *you* with . . .." (Col 2:8 NLT)

Next, the apostle says in an emphatic way by the way he writes it – you! You, beware that you, *of all people*, do not allow yourselves to be carried off as spoil in an ideological war.[89] These Christians, of all people, had been taught the truths of God to a sufficient level or point that they should be able to recognize that any teaching or movement that denigrated the person of Christ or the work of Christ or the sufficiency of Christ to teach one how to live toward one's fellow man is an un-biblical notion. Confusion on these matters is unnecessary!

Today's CRT movement attempts to defang the gospel. As MacArthur has stated, "if we tell people they are not responsible for what they are, you just cut them off from the Savior . . . If I don't come to grips with my own wretchedness . . . this aids and abets the sinner's pride – that I am a victim, not a perpetrator."[90] Further, Christians, of all people, should be grounded in the truth-claims of Christianity. These truth-claims are brokered quite clearly in Colossians regarding who Christ is and the effects that should have on Christians' behavior. A letter like Colossians does double duty in explaining the person and work of Christ *and* presenting the ethical appeals based on those truths.

"Don't let anyone capture you with empty philosophies and high-sounding nonsense . . .." (Col 2:8 NLT)

The philosophy that plagued the early church was deceptive (Paul was not deriding philosophy proper, only the deceptive philosophies). This was

---

88 More can be done in our society to help with racial reconciliation, but CRT is not helpful.

89 We learn in 2 Corinthians 10 the weapons of our warfare are mighty through God, that is, we have the truths in Scripture that we need to deal with these and any other societal ills (see 2 Peter 1:3 and 2 Tim 3:16-17, as well).

90 "John MacArthur on C.R.T. and Social Justice Movement," accessed August 10, 2021, https://www.youtube.com/watch?v=3MMU7f0Bdw4. MacArthur goes on to say that the current social justice movement is "the most destructive thing I've ever seen happen to the Evangelical movement."

a false teaching that was undermining the spiritual health, faith, witness, and effectiveness of the Church at Colossae. Additionally, it was not that this was some single thought-pattern with certain rules. It was instead a hodge-podge of religious ideas. It was syncretistic, it included tenets of Judaism, notions of Greek thoughts which included aeons or emanations as a ladder to God (a false view of Christ) and a special rite or knowledge (a wrong view of God's methodology and vehicle for truth; hence, it was early relativism).

We can infer from the clear comments of the apostle that this bad philosophy took away from people's clear understanding of Jesus Christ, it lacked the capability to impart "spiritual wisdom and understanding" (Col 1:9) which results in good behavior, it undermined an understanding of the heart of Christianity – "Christ in you" (1:27), it undermined God's plan for ultimate reconciliation – "peace through the blood of His cross" (1:20), it threatened to tear people away from the hope they had in the gospel (1:23), it threatened to tear people away from their walk with the Lord (2:6-7), that is, it threatened to take people away from their Christian moorings and teachings, it wrongly acted as a judge and arbiter (2:16), though it was useless to actually bring about righteousness (see v. 23), and it caused Christians to forget their identity in Christ which leads to moral living, brother-love, and good citizenry (3:1-14).

This has definite relevance to the current social justice movement because this movement is deceptive; it cannot improve biblical unity; in fact, it undermines true unity by creating and perpetuating disunity. It accomplishes this by inciting riots, inciting feelings of oppression, creating distrust of government and neighbors, and continual use of an unbiblical concept of "race." The teachings of CRT can therefore be categorized as "bad philosophy and high-sounding nonsense."

"Don't let anyone capture you with empty philosophies and high-sounding nonsense that come from human thinking . . .." (Col 2:8 NLT)

The apostle is referring to a human tradition, regardless of the source, that was opposed to what had been divinely revealed.[91] Simpson and Bruce

---

91 See comments in W. Robertson Nicoll, *The Expositor's Greek New Testament, vol. III* (Grand Rapids, MI: Eerdmans, 1956), 522. Rogers and Rogers com-

comment that "If the Colossians embraced it [the heresy], they would be the losers and not the gainers thereby. For those who had 'received Christ Jesus the Lord' it would be unacceptable; it was a human tradition which ran counter to the essential truths of their Christian faith and life. It sounded well, it appealed to natural religious instincts, but there was nothing in it for Christians."[92]

The apostle contrasts this deceitful philosophy with the teaching that comes from Christ. The apostle goes on in verses 16 and following to delineate some very specific avenues by which the deceitful philosophy at Colossae was attempting to lead the church. But he winds up saying that those avenues were clouds without rain because they were of no value against fleshly indulgence (verse 23). Only the gospel of Jesus Christ can change hearts. Additionally, he goes on to note that if one's identity is inextricably linked up with Jesus Christ and one finds their salvation in Jesus Christ, they should set their mind on the things above and consider themselves as "dead to immorality, impurity, passion, evil desire, and greed, which amounts to idolatry" (3:5). These people should "put on a heart of compassion, kindness, humility, gentleness, and patience; bearing with one another, and forgiving each other . . .." (3:12-13) (i.e., Christian virtues need to be attended to). The heresy at Colossae endangered the direction of the Colossian Christians and it took people's focus away from the Head of the Church, Jesus Christ.

The gospel is not a social gospel, one which takes Christians' focus away from Christ. The gospel of Jesus Christ includes the following irrefutable and irreducible elements: the holiness of God, the reality of man's sin,

---

ment that this tradition is a "man-made tradition to be contrasted with the true, living, divine tradition just alluded to" (Cleon Rogers, Jr. and Cleon Rogers, III, *The New Linguistic and Exegetical Key to the Greek New Testament* (Grand Rapids, MI: Zondervan, 1998) 464). And what had been divinely revealed was that Christ can change people, whereas CRT teaches that certain people from certain people groups cannot change – this falls under the rubric of a gnostic false view of Christ. Critical Race Theory is far more insidious than most people think.

92 E.K. Simpson and F.F. Bruce, *Commentary on the Epistles to the Ephesians and the Colossians* (Grand Rapids, MI: Eerdmans, 1982), 231.

the person and work of Jesus Christ (which is the focus of the letter to the Colossians), God's demands of all sinners, responsibilities to new converts (love him or her, admonish him or her, be an example to him or her, teach him or her), etc.[93] The CRT seeks to cancel all these bedrock gospel truths. It takes the heart out of the gospel, leaving only the shell, which is what "social gospel" is – an empty shell.

"Don't let anyone capture you with empty philosophies and high-sounding nonsense that come from human thinking <u>and from the spiritual powers of this world</u>, ..." (Col 2:8 NLT)

To whom or to what does the phrase "the spiritual powers of this world" refer? The word rendered "spiritual powers" or in other versions, "rudiments of the world" (KJV), or "elementary principles of the world" (NASB), can refer to "a presumed standard or set of customs."[94] Paul's warning is to be careful about walking in step with humanistic teachings which, in accordance with Paul's lexical choice here are "base," are nonsense, in comparison to following the teachings that come from Christ.

Further, the phrase "spiritual powers of this world" can refer to angelic beings. It is the case that, as Nicoll explained, the word is used of beings, that is, personality, and these "false teachers put these angels in the place of Christ."[95] And evil angels, specifically are the ones from whom all false teaching originates. Jesus had warned about the lies that come from liars' father, the Devil; Paul warned about "doctrines of demons" in 1 Tim 4:1; and he warned that Satan "disguises himself as an angel of light" (2 Cor 11:14). Paul warned the Colossian Christians concerning the baseless, or hollow arguments of the false teachers, whose source was diabolical, and whose endgame is no good for humans and civil society.

As already mentioned, CRT is based on unbiblical racist ideology, and therefore is not on board with God's anthropology. It also opposes redemp-

---

93 John MacArthur, *Nothing but the Truth. Upholding the Gospel in a Doubting Age* (Wheaton, IL: Crossway, 1999), 156-64.

94 Johannes Louw and Eugene Nida, *Greek-English Lexicon of the New Testament Based on Sematic Domains*, 41.12. BibleWorks10.

95 Nicoll, *The Expositor's Greek New Testament*, 523.

tion and salvation, as we have already seen. Baucham adds, "I believe we are being duped by an ideology bent on our demise. This ideology has used our guilt and shame over America's past, our love for the brethren, and our good and godly desire for reconciliation and justice as a means through which to introduce destructive heresies. We cannot embrace, modify, baptize, or christianize these ideologies. We must identify, resist, and repudiate them."[96]

"Be careful that no one takes you captive through philosophy and empty deceit based on human tradition, based on the elemental forces of the world, and <u>not based on Christ</u>." (Col 2:8 CSB)

As Robertson states, "The Gnostics were measuring Christ by their philosophy as many men are doing today. They have it backwards. Christ is the measure for all human knowledge since he is the Creator and the Sustainer of the universe."[97] Christ's people were to follow Christian thought patterns. For instance, in Col 1:27, we learn that a believer's hope is Christ "in us." This is our identity. One has but to study Ephesians chapter two and three and the letter to the Colossians. A Christian's identity is being part of Christ's body. Being in a manmade cultural "group" assigned by some political party is a false identity, a false narrative, a false hope, a false religion.[98]

The relevance of this section of the Bible to our situation today as far as the CRT movement is that people need to turn to Jesus Christ for their salvation, for their true spiritual freedom, for their deliverance from sin, for their peace with God. And Christians need to turn to the Bible. Then, and

---

[96] Baucham, *Fault Lines*, 204.

[97] A.T. Robertson, *Word Pictures in the New Testament. Vol. 4 The Epistles of Paul* (Nashville: Broadman Press, 1931), 491. John Eadie, *A Commentary on the Greek Text of the Epistle of Paul to the Colossians* (Grand Rapids, MI: Baker, 1979), 139 commented, "Christ is held up as the grand centre and source of true philosophy, and the reason is that Godhead was incarnate in Him, and that therefore His claims are paramount, both in person and function. He is not only the Wonder of wonders in Himself, but creation and redemption – the two prime books of study – trace themselves to Him as their one author."

[98] See especially Baucham, *Fault Lines*, chapters 4, 5, and 6, on "A New Religion," "A New Priesthood," and "A New Canon," and Strachan's discussion on pp. 65-72 of *Christianity and Wokeness*.

only then, will people understand and clearly see that the teachings they follow in the CRT movement are wanting, dangerous, racist, and are also "not according to Christ" (that is, CRT doctrine is anti-gospel). The teachings of the current CRT movement which have been shown to be based in Marxism[99] yield an ungodly division among people with different skin colors, hold to the notion of certain sins being unforgivable, hold people accountable for sins they did not commit, take people's eyes off of their own need for forgiveness, are highly relativistic, attempt to defang the gospel, mask the truth of the murder of untold numbers of unborn babies each year (to defend the unborn would be *real* social justice), and show hostility toward institutions that God Himself created (especially the family and the church).

My closing thoughts on the social justice topic are as follows. Our country needs a better way forward for race relations, to be sure, but the Bible and the gospel of Jesus Christ, not CRT, has the answers. Christians are urged not to separate people by "race" or "ethnicity." The substitutionary, saving death of Jesus Christ has broken down racial barriers (Ephesians chapter 2), so when people continue to play the race card, they are masking the gospel of Jesus Christ. The Bible has spoken on this issue and God's ways are best. We have abandoned the gospel of human depravity and its cure – divine forgiveness – and have abandoned God's notion of humans being created in His image. We do not respect that or else we would not use and divide others into unbiblical classes that create strife and chaos (and cause people to think that they can't do any better for themselves) to get our way politically or financially. Therefore, CRT is not for Christians and therefore not good for society. Our country definitely needs help in the area of justice and the area of racial reconciliation, but there is absolutely nothing redemptive in the current CRT movement. The ideology is anti-gospel and should therefore be pushed back by all Christians.

---

99 Baucham, *Fault Lines*, 101. Also see "'What is Critical Race Theory?' A Former Critical Theorist Answers (CRT Series: Episode 2)," accessed August 10, 2021, https://www.youtube.com/watch?v=hqaCDXosfuU; "Critical Race Theory Says Everything is Racist," accessed August 10, 2021, https://www.youtube.com/watch?v=xuSMvIVtd0A&list=PLEydc28qEA-ABlsf7Xp9c5Em1dtX2_oMf.

Drawing Conclusions and Applications

Abortion is condemned by God and His hatred of it is made explicit in the Bible. Human sexuality was designed by God and His design was two complementary sexes which He made to procreate biologically and to complete each other emotionally and psychologically. Social justice should mean justice for all humans in a humane society. This includes justice for the unborn, and justice for all people regardless of "race." Every living soul should be treated with dignity and respect because we were all created in the image of God and created for His glory and are all undeserving of the least of His mercies.

The truth claims of the Bible can be applied to the ethical issues of abortion, the homosexual agenda, and CRT. The Bible is just that robust – robust enough to meet our every question, problem, concern, frustration, and doubt. But we must respond to the God of the universe who has spoken and view Him as our authority.

I submit that the church in America needs another Reformation, and that could possibly start with the Baptist crowd having a new Reformation within its ranks. By Reformation, I simply mean a return to biblical authority and a biblical perspective. Baptist leaders like Jimmy Draper,[100] preachers like Paige Patterson and Richard Land, and philosophers like Norman Geisler[101] have warned time and again about the traps inherent in turning from inerrancy and authority of the Bible. And so, to adapt an old movie line, ". . . you get what we have here . . . which is the way [we want it], well, [we get it]."[102] If you are a Christian, wake up! Christians follow biblical values, not secular, humanistic ones.

The Bible is relevant to 21st century American Christianity and speaks clearly on the topics of abortion, human sexuality, and social justice. The

---

100 Jimmy Draper, *Authority: The Critical Issue for Southern Baptists* (Old Tappan, NJ: Fleming H. Revell Company, 1984).

101 See Norman Geisler and William Roach, *Defending Inerrancy* (Grand Rapids, MI: Baker Books, 2011).

102 Adapted from the 1967 film "Cool Hand Luke," produced by Gordon Carroll and written by Donn Pearce.

perspectives presented and defended in this chapter are solidly biblical. A biblical perspective should once again be heard. The fountains of grace that flowed from the wounds of our Lord are available to heal the lepers in our heads.[103] The Bible has the answer, and *therefore*, confusion among Christians on the topics in this volume is unnecessary!

---

103 Yes, this is an allusion to U2's "One."